AULUS GELLIUS

II

LCL 200

AULUS GELLIUS

ATTIC NIGHTS
BOOKS VI–XIII

WITH AN ENGLISH TRANSLATION BY
JOHN C. ROLFE

HARVARD UNIVERSITY PRESS
CAMBRIDGE, MASSACHUSETTS
LONDON, ENGLAND

First published 1927
Reprinted 1948, 1960, 1968, 1982, 1998

LOEB CLASSICAL LIBRARY® is a registered trademark
of the President and Fellows of Harvard College

ISBN 0-674-99220-2

*Printed in Great Britain by St Edmundsbury Press Ltd,
Bury St Edmunds, Suffolk, on acid-free paper.
Bound by Hunter & Foulis Ltd, Edinburgh, Scotland.*

CONTENTS

ATTIC NIGHTS

  CHAPTER HEADINGS   vii

  BOOK VI   1

  BOOK VII   89

  BOOK VIII   141

  BOOK IX   151

  BOOK X   211

  BOOK XI   297

  BOOK XII   351

  BOOK XIII   413

INDEXES   519

CAPITULA

CAPITULA LIBRI SEXTI

PAGINA

I. Admiranda quaedam ex annalibus sumpta de P. Africano superiore 2

II. De Caeselli Vindicis pudendo errore, quem offendimus in libris eius quos inscripsit *Lectionum Antiquarum* 6

III. Quid Tiro Tullius, Ciceronis libertus, reprehenderit in M. Catonis oratione quam pro Rodiensibus in senatu dixit ; et quid ad ea, quae reprehenderat, responderimus 10

IV. Cuiusmodi servos et quam ob causam Caelius Sabinus, iuris civilis auctor, pilleatos venundari solitos scripserit ; et quae mancipia sub corona more maiorum venierint ; atque id ipsum "sub corona" quid sit 32

V. Historia de Polo histrione memoratu digna . . . 34

VI. Quid de quorundam sensuum naturali defectione Aristoteles scripserit 36

VII. An "affatim," quasi "admodum," prima acuta pronuntiandum sit ; et quaedam itidem non incuriose tractata super aliarum vocum accentibus 38

VIII. Res ultra fidem tradita super amatore delphino et puero amato 42

IX. "Peposci" et "memordi," "pepugi" et "spepondi" et "cecurri" plerosque veterum dixisse, non, uti postea receptum est dicere, per *o* aut per *u* litteram in prima syllaba positam, atque id eos Graecae rationis exemplo dixisse ; praeterea notatum quod viri non indocti neque ignobiles a verbo "descendo," non "descendi," sed "descendidi," dixerunt 44

CHAPTER HEADINGS

BOOK VI

PAGE

I. Some remarkable stories about the elder Publius
Africanus, drawn from the annals 3

II. Of a disgraceful blunder of Caesellius Vindex, which
we find in his work entitled *Archaic Terms*. . . . 7

III. What Tullius Tiro, Cicero's freedman, criticized in
the speech which Marcus Cato delivered in the
senate in defence of the Rhodians; and our answer
to his strictures. 11

IV. What sort of slaves Caelius Sabinus, the writer on
civil law, said were commonly sold with caps on
their heads, and why; and what chattels were sold
under a crown in the days of our forefathers; and the
meaning of that same expression "under a crown". 33

V. A noteworthy story about the actor Polus . . . 35

VI. What Aristotle wrote of the congenital absence of
some of the senses 37

VII. Whether *affatim*, like *admodum*, should be pronounced with the acute accent on the first syllable;
with some painstaking observations on the accents
of other words 39

VIII. An incredible story about a dolphin which
loved a boy 43

IX. That many early writers used *peposci*, *memordi*,
pepugi and *cecurri*, and not, as was afterwards
customary, forms with *o* or *u* in the first syllable,
and that in so doing said that they followed
Greek usage; that it has further been observed
that men who were neither unlearned nor obscure
made from the verb *descendo*, not *descendi*, but
descendidi 45

CAPITULA

PAGINA

X. Ut "ususcapio" copulate recto vocabuli casu dicitur, ita "pignoriscapio" coniuncte eadem vocabuli forma dictum esse 50

XI. Neque "levitatem" neque "nequitiam" ea significatione esse qua in volgi sermonibus dicuntur . 50

XII. De tunicis chiridotis; quod earum usum P. Africanus Sulpicio Gallo obiecit 56

XIII. Quem "classicum" dicat M. Cato, quem "infra classem.". 58

XIV. De tribus dicendi generibus; ac de tribus philosophis qui ab Atheniensibus ad senatum Romam legati missi sunt 60

XV. Quam severe moribus maiorum in fures vindicatum sit; et quid scripserit Mucius Scaevola super eo quod servandum datum commodatumve esset . 62

XVI. Locus exscriptus ex satura M. Varronis, quae Περὶ Ἐδεσμάτων inscripta est, de peregrinis ciborum generibus; et appositi versus Euripidi, quibus delicatorum hominum luxuriantem gulam confutavit 64

XVII. Sermo habitus cum grammatico insolentiarum et inperitiarum pleno de significatione vocabuli quod est "obnoxius"; deque eius vocis origine . 66

XVIII. De observata custoditaque apud Romanos iurisiurandi sanctimonia; atque inibi de decem captivis, quos Romam Hannibal deiurio ab his accepto legavit 74

XIX. Historia ex annalibus sumpta de Tiberio Graccho, Gracchorum patre, tribuno plebis; atque inibi tribunicia decreta cum ipsis verbis relata . . 76

viii

CHAPTER HEADINGS

PAGE

X. As *ususcapio* is treated as a compound noun in the nominative case, so *pignoris capio* is taken together as one word in the same case 51

XI. That neither *levitas* nor *nequitia* has the meaning which is given to those words in ordinary conversation 51

XII. Of the tunics called *chiridotae*; that Publius Africanus reproached Sulpicius Gallus for wearing them 57

XIII. Whom Marcus Cato calls *classici*, or "belonging to a class," and whom *infra classem*, or "below class." 59

XIV. Of the three literary styles; and of the three philosophers who were sent as envoys by the Athenians to the senate at Rome 61

XV. How severely thieves were punished by the laws of our forefathers; and what Marcus Scaevola wrote about that which is given or entrusted to anyone's care 63

XVI. A passage about foreign varieties of food, copied from the satire of Marcus Varro entitled Περὶ Ἐδεσμάτων, or *On Edibles*; and with it some verses of Euripides, in which he assails the extravagant gluttony of luxurious men 65

XVII. A conversation held with a grammarian, who was full of insolence and arrogance, as to the meaning of the word *obnoxius*; and of the origin of that word 67

XVIII. On the strict observance by the Romans of the sanctity of an oath; and also the story of the ten prisoners whom Hannibal sent to Rome under oath 75

XIX. A story, taken from the annals, about Tiberius Gracchus, tribune of the commons and father of the Gracchi; and also an exact quotation of the decrees of the tribunes 77

CAPITULA

XX. Quod Vergilius a Nolanis ob aquam sibi non permissam sustulit e versu suo "Nolam" et posuit "oram"; atque ibi quaedam alia de iucunda consonantia litterarum 80

XXI. "Quoad vivet" "quoad" que "morietur" cur id ipsum temporis significent, cum ex duobus sint facta contrariis 84

XXII. Quod censores equum adimere soliti sunt equitibus corpulentis et praepinguibus; quaesitumque utrum ea res cum ignominia an incolumi dignitate equitum facta sit 86

CAPITULA LIBRI SEPTIMI

I. Quem in modum responderit Chrysippus adversum eos qui providentiam consistere negaverunt . . 90

II. Quo itidem modo et vim necessitatemque fati constituerit et esse tamen in nobis consilii iudiciique nostri arbitrium confirmaverit 94

III. Historia sumpta ex libris Tuberonis de serpente invisitatae longitudinis 100

IV. Quid idem Tubero novae historiae de Atilio Regulo a Carthaginiensibus capta litteris mandaverit; quid etiam Tuditanus super eodem Regulo scripserit 100

V. Quod Alfenus iureconsultus in verbis veteribus interpretandis erravit 102

VI. Temere inepteque reprehensum esse a Iulio Hygino Vergilium, quod "praepetes" Daedali pennas dixit; atque inibi quid sint "aves praepetes" et quid illae sint aves quas Nigidius "inferas" appellavit . . 106

VII. De Acca Larentia et Gaia Taracia; deque origine sacerdotii Fratrum Arvalium 110

VIII. Notata quaedam de rege Alexandro et de P. Scipione memoratu digna 112

IX. Locus exemptus ex *Annalibus* L. Pisonis historiae et orationis lepidissimae 116

CHAPTER HEADINGS

PAGE

XX. That Virgil removed *Nola* from one of his lines and substituted *ora* because the inhabitants of Nola had refused him water; and also some additional notes on the agreeable euphony of vowels . . . 81

XXI. Why it is that the phrases *quoad vivet* and *quoad morietur* indicate the very same time, although based upon opposite things 85

XXII. On the custom of the censors of taking their horses from corpulent and excessively fat knights; and the question whether such action also involved degradation or left them their rank as knights . . 87

BOOK VII

I. How Chrysippus replied to those who denied the existence of Providence 91

II. How Chrysippus also maintained the power and inevitable nature of fate, but at the same time declared that we had control over our plans and decisions 95

III. An account, taken from the works of Tubero, of a serpent of unprecedented length 101

IV. A new account, written by the above mentioned Tubero, of the capture of Regulus by the Carthaginians; and also what Tuditanus wrote about that same Regulus 101

V. An error of the jurist Alfenus in the interpretation of early words 103

VI. That Julius Hyginus was hasty and foolish in his criticism of Virgil for calling the wings of Daedalus *praepetes*; also a note on the meaning of *aves praepetes* and of those birds which Nigidius called *inferae* . 107

VII. On Acca Larentia and Gaia Taracia; and on the origin of the priesthood of the Arval Brethren . . 111

VIII. Some noteworthy anecdotes of King Alexander and of Publius Scipio 113

IX. A passage taken from the *Annals* of Lucius Piso, highly diverting in content and graceful in style . 117

CAPITULA

PAGINA

X. Historia super Euclida Socratico, cuius exemplo Taurus philosophus hortari adulescentes suos solitus ad philosophiam naviter sectandam 118

XI. Verba ex oratione Q. Metelli Numidici, quae libuit meminisse, ad officium gravitatis dignitatisque vitae ducentia 120

XII. Quod neque "testamentum," sicuti Servius Sulpicius existimavit, neque "sacellum," sicuti C. Trebatius, duplicia verba sunt, sed a "testatione" productum alterum, alterum a "sacro" imminutum 122

XIII. De quaestiunculis apud Taurum philosophum in convivio agitatis, quae "sympoticae" vocantur . 124

XIV. Poeniendis peccatis tres esse rationes a philosophis attributas ; et quamobrem Plato duarum ex his meminerit, non trium 126

XV. De verbo "quiesco," an e littera corripi an produci debeat 130

XVI. Verbum "deprecor" a poeta Catullo inusitate quidem, sed apte positum et proprie ; deque ratione eius verbi exemplisque veterum scriptorum . . . 132

XVII. Quis omnium primus libros publice praebuerit legendos ; quantusque numerus fuerit Athenis ante clades Persicas librorum in bibliothecis publicis . 138

CAPITULA LIBRI OCTAVI

I. "Hesterna noctu" rectene an cum vitio dicatur et quaenam super istis verbis grammatica traditio sit ; item quod decemviri in *XII. Tabulis* "nox" pro "noctu" dixerunt 142

II. Quae mihi decem verba ediderit Favorinus, quae usurpentur quidem a Graecis, sed sint adulterina et barbara ; quae item a me totidem acceperit, quae

xii

CHAPTER HEADINGS

PAGE

X. A story about Euclides, the Socratic, by whose example Taurus used to urge his pupils to be diligent in the pursuit of philosophy 119

XI. A passage from a speech of Quintus Metellus Numidicus, which it was my pleasure to recall, since it draws attention to the obligation of self-respect and dignity in the conduct of life . . . 121

XII. That neither *testamentum*, as Servius Sulpicus thought, nor *sacellum*, as Gaius Trebatius believed, is a compound, but the former is an extended form of *testatio*, the latter a diminutive of *sacrum* . . 123

XIII. On the brief topics discussed at the table of the philosopher Taurus, and called *Sympoticae*, or *Table Talk* 125

XIV. The three reasons given by the philosophers for punishing crimes ; and why Plato mentions only two of these, and not three 127

XV. On the verb *quiesco*, whether it should be pronounced with a long or a short *e* 131

XVI. On a use by the poet Catullus of *deprecor* which is unusual, it is true, but appropriate and correct ; and on the origin of that word, with examples from the early writers 133

XVII. Who was the first of all to establish a public library ; and how many books there were in the public libraries at Athens before the Persian invasions 139

BOOK VIII

I. Whether the expression *hesterna nocte*, for "last night," is right or wrong, and what the grammarians have said about those words ; also that the decemvirs in the *Twelve Tables* used *nox* for *noctu*, meaning "by night." 143

II. Ten words pointed out to me by Favorinus which, although in use by the Greeks, are of foreign origin and barbarous ; also the same number given him by

CAPITULA

PAGINA

ex medio communique usu Latine loquentium minime Latina sint neque in veterum libris reperiantur 142

III. Quem in modum et quam severe increpuerit
audientibus nobis Peregrinus philosophus adulescentem Romanum ex equestri familia, stantem
segnem apud se et assidue oscitantem 142

IV. Quod Herodotus, scriptor historiae memoratissimus, parum vere dixerit unam solamque pinum
arborum omnium caesam numquam denuo ex isdem
radicibus pullulare ; et quod item de aqua pluviali
et nive rem non satis exploratam pro comperta
posuerit 144

V. Quid illud sit, quod Vergilius " caelum stare pulvere," et quod Lucilius " pectus sentibus stare"
dixit 144

VI. Cum post offensiunculas in gratiam redeatur, expostulationes fieri mutuas minime utile esse, superque
ea re et sermo Tauri expositus et verba ex Theophrasti libro sumpta ; et quid M. quoque Cicero de
amore amicitiae senserit, cum ipsius verbis additum 144

VII. Ex Aristotelis libro, qui Περὶ Μνήμης inscriptus
est, cognita acceptaque de natura memoriae et
habitu ; atque inibi alia quaedam de exuberantia
aut interitu eius lecta auditaque 144

VIII. Quid mihi usu venerit, interpretari et quasi
effingere volenti locos quosdam Platonicos Latina
oratione 146

IX. Quod Theophrastus, philosophus omnis suae
aetatis facundissimus, verba pauca ad populum
Atheniensem facturus, deturbatus verecundia
obticuerit ; quodque idem hoc Demostheni apud
Philippum regem verba facienti evenerit. . . . 146

CHAPTER HEADINGS

PAGE

me which, though of general and common use by those who speak Latin, are by no means Latin and are not to be found in the early literature . . . 143

III. In what terms and how severely the philosopher Peregrinus in my hearing rebuked a young Roman of equestrian rank, who stood before him inattentive and constantly yawning 143

IV. That Herodotus, that most famous writer of history, was wrong in saying that the pine alone of all trees never puts forth new shoots from the same roots, after being cut down; and that he stated as an established fact about rainwater and snow a thing which had not been sufficiently investigated . . 145

V. On the meaning of Virgil's expression *caelum stare pulvere* and of Lucilius' *pectus sentibus stare* . . . 145

VI. That when a reconciliation takes place after trifling offences, mutual complaints are useless; and Taurus' discourse on that subject, with a quotation from the treatise of Theophrastus; and what Marcus Cicero also thought about the love arising from friendship, added in his own words 145

VII. What we have learned and know of the nature and character of memory from Aristotle's work entitled Περὶ Μνήμης, or *On Memory*; and also some other examples, of which we have heard or read, about extraordinary powers of memory or its total loss . 145

VIII. My experience in trying to interpret and, as it were, to reproduce in Latin certain passages of Plato 147

IX. How Theophrastus, the most eloquent philosopher of his entire generation, when on the point of making a brief speech to the people of Athens, was overcome by bashfulness and kept silence; and how Demosthenes had a similar experience when speaking before king Philip 147

CAPITULA

PAGINA

X. Qualis mihi fuerit in oppido Eleusino disceptatio cum grammatico quodam praestigioso, tempora verborum et puerilia meditamenta ignorante, remotarum autem quaestionum nebulas et formidines capiendis imperitorum animis ostentante . . 146

XI. Quam festive responderit Xanthippae uxori Socrates, petenti ut per Dionysia largiore sumptu cenitarent 146

XII. Quid significet in veterum libris scriptum "plerique omnes"; et quod ea verba accepta a Graecis videntur 146

XIII. "Eupsones," quod homines Afri dicunt, non esse verbum Poenicum, sed Graecum 148

XIV. Lepidissima altercatio Favorini philosophi adversus quendam intempestivum de ambiguitate verborum disserentem; atque inibi verba quaedam ex Naevio poeta et Cn. Gellio non usitate collocata; atque ibidem a P. Nigidio origines vocabulorum exploratae. 148

XV. Quibus modis ignominiatus tractatusque sit a C. Caesare Laberius poeta; atque inibi appositi versus super eadem re eiusdem Laberii 148

CAPITULA LIBRI NONI

I. Quamobrem Quintus Claudius Quadrigarius, in undevicesimo *Annali*, scripserit rectiores certioresque ictus fieri, si sursum quid mittas quam si deorsum 152

II. Qualibus verbis notarit Herodes Atticus falso quempiam cultu amictuque nomen habitumque philosophi ementientem 154

III. Epistula Philippi regis ad Aristotelem philosophum super Alexandro recens nato 158

CHAPTER HEADINGS

PAGE

X. A discussion that I had in the town of Eleusis with a conceited grammarian who, although ignorant of the tenses of verbs and the exercises of schoolboys, yet ostentatiously proposed abstruse questions of a hazy and formidable character, to impress the minds of the unlearned   147

XI. The witty reply of Socrates to his wife Xanthippe, when she asked that they might spend more money for their dinners during the Dionysiac festival . .   147

XII. On the meaning of *plerique omnes*, or "almost all," in the early literature, and on the probable Greek origin of that expression   147

XIII. That *eupsones*, a word used by the people of Africa, is not Phoenician, but Greek   149

XIV. A highly entertaining discussion of the philosopher Favorinus with a tiresome person who held forth on the double meaning of certain words ; also some unusual expressions from the poet Naevius and from Gnaeus Gellius ; and further, some investigations of the derivation of words proposed by Publius Nigidius   149

XV. How the poet Laberius was ignominiously treated by Gaius Caesar, with a quotation of Laberius' own words on that subject   149

BOOK IX

I. Why Quintus Claudius Quadrigarius, in the nineteenth book of his *Annals*, wrote that missiles hit their mark more accurately and surely if they are hurled from below, than if they are hurled from above   153

II. In what terms Herodes Atticus reproved a man who in appearance and dress falsely laid claim to the title and character of philosopher   155

III. A letter of king Philip to the philosopher Aristotle, apropos of the recent birth of his son Alexander .   159

CAPITULA

PAGINA

IV. De barbararum gentium prodigiosis miraculis ;
deque diris et exitiosis effascinationibus ; atque
inibi de feminis repente versis in mares 160

V. Diversae nobilium philosophorum sententiae de
genere ac natura voluptatis ; verbaque Hieroclis
philosophi quibus decreta Epicuri insectatus est . 168

VI. Verbum quod est ab "ago" frequentativum, in
syllaba prima quonam sit modulo pronuntiandum . 170

VII. De conversione foliorum in arbore olea brumali et
solstitiali die ; deque fidibus id temporis ictu alieno
sonantibus. 172

VIII. Necessum esse qui multa habeat multis indigere ;
deque ea re Favorini philosophi cum brevitate
eleganti sententia 174

IX. Quis modus sit vertendi verba in Graecis sententiis ;
deque his Homeri versibus quos Vergilius vertisse
aut bene apteque aut inprospere existimatus est . 174

X. Quod Annaeus Cornutus versus Vergilii, quibus
Veneris et Vulcani concubitum pudice operteque
dixit, reprehensione spurca et odiosa inquinavit . 182

XI. De Valerio Corvino ; et unde Corvinus 184

XII. De verbis quae in utramque partem significatione
adversa et reciproca dicuntur 186

XIII. Verba ex historia Claudi Quadrigari, quibus
Manli Torquati, nobilis adulescentis, et hostis Galli
provocantis pugnam depinxit 194

XIV. Quod idem Quadrigarius "huius facies" patrio
casu probe et Latine dixit ; et quaedam alia adposita
de similium vocabulorum declinationibus . . . 198

xviii

CHAPTER HEADINGS

PAGE

IV. On some extraordinary marvels found among barbarian peoples; and on awful and deadly spells; and also on the sudden change of women into men 161

V. Diverse views of eminent philosophers as to the nature and character of pleasure; and the words in which the philosopher Hierocles attacked the principles of Epicurus 169

VI. With what quantity the first syllable of the frequentative verb from *ago* should be pronounced . . . 171

VII. That the leaves of the olive tree turn over at the summer and the winter solstice, and that the lyre at that same season produces sounds from other strings than those that are struck 173

VIII. That it is inevitable that one who has much should need much, with a brief and graceful aphorism of the philosopher Favorinus on that subject 175

IX. What method should be followed in translating Greek expressions; and on those verses of Homer which Virgil is thought to have translated either well and happily or unsuccessfully 175

X. The low and odious criticism with which Annaeus Cornutus befouled the lines of Virgil in which the poet with chaste reserve spoke of the intercourse of Venus and Vulcan 183

XI. Of Valerius Corvinus and the origin of his surname 185

XII. On words which are used with two opposite meanings, both active and passive 187

XIII. A passage from the history of Claudius Quadrigarius, in which he pictured the combat of Manlius Torquatus, a young noble, with a hostile Gaul, who challenged the whole Roman army 195

XIV. That Quadrigarius also, with correct Latinity, used *facies* as a genitive; and some other observations on the inflection of similar words 199

CAPITULA

PAGINA

XV. De genere controversiae quod Graece ἄπορον appellatur 204

XVI. Quod Plinium Secundum, non hominem indoctum, fugerit latueritque vitium argumenti quod ἀντί-στρεφον Graeci dicunt 208

CAPITULA LIBRI DECIMI

I. "Tertium" ne "consul" an "tertio" dici oporteat; et quonam modo Cn. Pompeius, cum in theatro, quod erat dedicaturus, honores suos scriberet, quaestionem ancipitem istius verbi de consilio Ciceronis vitaverit 212

II. Quid Aristoteles de numero puerperii memoriae mandaverit 216

III. Locorum quorundam inlustrium conlatio contentioque facta ex orationibus C. Gracchi et M. Ciceronis et M. Catonis. 218

IV. Quod P. Nigidius argutissime docuit nomina non positiva esse, sed naturalia. 228

V. "Avarus" simplexne vocabulum sit, an compositum et duplex, sicut P. Nigidio videtur 230

VI. Multam dictam esse ab aedilibus plebei Appi Caeci filiae, mulieri nobili, quod locuta esset petulantius 230

VII. Fluminum, quae ultra imperium Romanum fluunt, prima magnitudine esse Nilum, secunda Histrum, proxima Rodanum, sicuti M. Varronem memini scribere 232

VIII. Inter ignominias militares quibus milites exercebantur, fuisse sanguinis dimissionem ; et quaenam esse videatur causa huiuscemodi castigationis . . 234

IX. Quibus modis quoque habitu acies Romana instrui solita sit, quaeque earum instructionum sint vocabula 234

xx

CHAPTER HEADINGS

PAGE

XV. On the kind of debate which the Greeks call
ἄπορος 205

XVI. How Plinius Secundus, although not without
learning, failed to observe and detect the fallacy in
an argument of the kind which the Greeks call
ἀντίστρεφον 209

BOOK X

I. Whether one ought to say *tertium consul* or *tertio*;
and how Gnaeus Pompeius, when he would inscribe
his honours on the theatre which he was about to
dedicate, by Cicero's advice evaded the difficulty in
the use of that word 213

II. What Aristotle has recorded about the number of
children born at one time 217

III. A collection of famous passages from the speeches
of Gaius Gracchus, Marcus Cicero and Marcus
Cato, and a comparison of them 219

IV. How Publius Nigidius with great cleverness showed
that words are not arbitrary, but natural . . . 229

V. Whether *avarus* is a single word or, as it appears
to Publius Nigidius, a compound, made up of two
parts 231

VI. That a fine was imposed by the plebeian aediles on
the daughter of Appius Claudius, a woman of rank,
because she spoke too arrogantly 231

VII. Marcus Varro, I remember, writes that of the
rivers which flow outside the limits of the Roman
empire the Nile is first in size, the Danube second,
and next the Rhone 233

VIII. That among the ignominious punishments which
are inflicted upon soldiers was the letting of blood;
and what seems to be the reason for such a penalty 235

IX. In what way, and in what form, the Roman army
is commonly drawn up, and the names of the formations 235

CAPITULA

PAGINA

X. Quae eius rei causa sit, quod et Graeci veteres et Romani anulum hoc digito gestaverint qui est in manu sinistra minimo proximus 236

XI. Verbum "mature" quid significet quaeque vocis eius ratio sit ; et quod eo verbo volgus hominum inproprie utitur ; atque inibi, quod "praecox" declinatum "praecocis" faciat, non "praecoquis" 238

XII. De portentis fabularum quae Plinius Secundus indignissime in Democritum philosophum confert ; et ibidem de simulacro volucri columbae. . . . 240

XIII. "Cum partim hominum" qua ratione veteres dixerint 244

XIV. "Iniuria mihi factum itur" quali verborum ordine Cato dixerit 246

XV. De flaminis Dialis deque flaminicae caerimonis ; verbaque ex edicto praetoris apposita, quibus dicit non coacturum se ad iurandum neque virgines Vestae neque Dialem 248

XVI. Quos errores Iulius Hyginus in sexto Vergilii animadverterit in Romana historia erratos . . . 254

XVII. Quam ob causam et quali modo Democritus philosophus luminibus oculorum sese privaverit ; et super ea re versus Laberii pure admodum et venuste facti 258

XVIII. Historia de Artemisia ; deque eo certamine quod aput Mausoli sepulcrum a scriptoribus inclutis decertatum est 260

XIX. Non purgari neque levari peccatum, cum praetenditur peccatorum quae alii quoque peccaverunt similitudo ; atque inibi verba ex oratione super ea re Demosthenis 264

XX. Quid sit "rogatio," quid "lex," quid "plebisscitum," quid "privilegium" ; et quantum ista omnia differant 266

XXI. Quam ob causam M. Cicero his omnino verbis "novissime" et "novissimus" observantissime uti vitarit 270

xxii

CHAPTER HEADINGS

PAGE

X. The reason why the ancient Greeks and Romans wore a ring on the next to the last finger of the left hand 237

XI. The derivation and meaning of the word *mature*, and that it is generally used improperly ; and also that the genitive of *praecox* is *praecccis* and not *praecoquis* 239

XII. Of extravagant tales which Plinius Secundus most unjustly ascribes to the philosopher Democritus ; and also about the flying image of a dove . . . 241

XIII. On what principle the ancients said *cum partim hominum* 245

XIV. In what connection Cato said *iniuria mihi factum itur* 247

XV. Of the ceremonies of the priest and priestess of Jupiter ; and words quoted from the praetor's edict, in which he declares that he will not compel either the Vestal virgins or the priest of Jupiter to take oath 249

XVI. Errors in Roman history which Julius Hyginus noted in Virgil's sixth book 255

XVII. Why and how the philosopher Democritus deprived himself of his eyesight ; and the very fine and elegant verses of Laberius on that subject . . 259

XVIII. The story of Artemisia ; and of the contest at the tomb of Mausolus in which celebrated writers took part 261

XIX. That a sin is not removed or lessened by citing in excuse similar sins which others have committed ; with a passage from a speech of Demosthenes on that subject 265

XX. The meaning of *rogatio, lex, plebiscitum* and *privilegium*, and to what extent all these terms differ . 267

XXI. Why Marcus Cato very scrupulously avoided any use of the words *novissime* and *novissimus* . . 271

CAPITULA

PAGINA

XXII. Locus exemptus ex Platonis libro qui inscribitur *Gorgias*, de falsae philosophiae probris, quibus philosophos temere incessunt qui emolumenta verae philosophiae ignorant 272

XXIII. Verba ex oratione M. Catonis de mulierum veterum victu et moribus; atque inibi, quod fuerit ius marito in adulterio uxorem deprehensam necare 276

XXIV. "Die pristini," "die crastini" et "die quarti" et "die quinti" qui elegantius locuti sint dixisse, non ut ea nunc vulgo dicuntur. 280

XXV. Telorum et iaculorum gladiorumque, atque inibi navium quoque vocabula, quae scripta in veterum libris reperiuntur 284

XXVI. Inscite ab Asinio Pollione reprehensum Sallustium, quod transfretationem "transgressum" dixerit, et "transgressos" qui transfretassent . . 286

XXVII. Historia de populo Romano deque populo Poenico, quod pari propemodum vigore fuerint aemuli. 290

XXVIII. De aetatum finibus pueritiae, iuventae, senectae, ex Tuberonis historia sumptum 292

XXIX. Quod particula "atque" non complexiva tantum sit, sed vim habeat plusculam variamque . 292

CAPITULA LIBRI UNDECIMI.

I. De origine vocabuli "terrae Italiae"; deque ea multa quae suprema appellatur, deque eius nominis ratione ac de lege Aternia; et quibus verbis antiquitus multa minima dici solita sit . . 298

II. Quod "elegantia" apud antiquiores, non de amoeniore ingenio, sed de nitidiore cultu atque victu dicebatur, eaque in vitio ponebatur 302

III. Qualis quantaque sit "pro" particulae varietas; deque exemplis eius varietatis. 304

CHAPTER HEADINGS

PAGE

XXII. A passage taken from Plato's book entitled *Gorgias*, on the abuse of false philosophy, with which those who are ignorant of the rewards of true philosophy assail philosophers without reason ... 273

XXIII. A passage from a speech of Marcus Cato on the mode of life and manners of women of the olden time; and also that the husband had the right to kill his wife, if she were taken in adultery ... 277

XXIV. That the most elegant speakers used the expressions *die pristini, die crastini, die quarti,* and *die quinti,* not those which are current now ... 281

XXV. The names of certain weapons, darts and swords, and also of boats and ships, which are found in the books of the early writers ... 285

XXVI. That Asinius Pollio showed ignorance in criticizing Sallust for using *transgressus* (crossing) for *transfretatio* (crossing the sea) and *transgressi* (those who had crossed) for *qui transfretaverant* (those who had crossed the sea). ... 287

XXVII. A story of the Roman and the Carthaginian people, showing that they were rivals of nearly equal strength ... 291

XXVIII. About the limits of the periods of boyhood, manhood and old age, taken from the *History* of Tubero ... 293

XXIX. That the particle *atque* is not only conjunctive, but has many and varied meanings ... 293

BOOK XI

I. On the origin of the term "the land of Italy"; of that fine which is called "supreme"; concerning the reason for the name and on the Aeternian law; and in what words the "smallest" fine used to be pronounced in ancient days ... 299

II. That the word *elegantia* in earlier days was not used of a more refined nature, but of excessive fastidiousness in dress and mode of life, and was a term of reproach ... 303

III. The nature and degree of the variety in the particle *pro*; and some examples of its different uses ... 305

CAPITULA

PAGINA

IV. Quem in modum Q. Ennius versus Euripidi aemulatus sit 306

V. De Pyrronis philosophis quaedam deque Academicis strictim notata : deque inter eos differentia . . 308

VI. Quod mulieres Romae per Herculem non iuraverint neque viri per Castorem 312

VII. Verbis antiquissimis relictisque iam et desitis minime utendum. 314

VIII. Quid senserit dixeritque M. Cato de Albino, qui homo Romanus Graeca oratione res Romanas, venia sibi ante eius imperitiae petita, composuit . 318

IX. Historia de legatis Mileti ac Demosthene rhetore in libris Critolai reperta 318

X. Quod C. Gracchus in oratione sua historiam supra scriptam Demadi rhetori, non Demostheni, adtribuit ; verbaque ipsius C. Gracchi relata . . 320

XI. Verba P. Nigidii, quibus differre dicit "mentiri" et "mendacium dicere." 324

XII. Quod Chrysippus philosophus omne verbum ambiguum dubiumque esse dicit, Diodorus contra nullum verbum ambiguum esse putat 324

XIII. Quid Titus Castricius de verbis deque sententia quadam C. Gracchi existimarit ; quodque esse eam sine ullo sensus emolumento docuerit 326

XIV. Sobria et pulcherrima Romuli regis responsio circa vini usum 330

XV. De "ludibundo" et "errabundo" atque id genus verborum productionibus ; et quod Laberius sic "amorabundam" dixit, ut dicitur "ludibunda" et "errabunda" ; atque inibi quod Sisenna per huiuscemodi verbum nova figura usus est . . . 332

xxvi

CHAPTER HEADINGS

PAGE

IV. How Quintus Ennius rivalled certain verses of Euripides 307

V. Some brief notes about the Pyrronian philosophers and the Academics ; and of the difference between them 309

VI. That at Rome women did not swear by Hercules nor men by Castor 313

VII. That very old words which have become antiquated and obsolete ought not to be used 315

VIII. What Marcus Cato thought and said of Albinus, who, though a Roman, wrote a history of Rome in the Greek language, having first asked indulgence for his lack of skill in that tongue 319

IX. The story of the Milesian envoys and the orator Demosthenes, found in the works of Critolaus . . 319

X. That Gaius Gracchus in a speech of his applied the story related above to the orator Demades, and not to Demosthenes ; and a quotation of Gracchus' words. 321

XI. The words of Publius Nigidius, in which he says that there is a difference between "lying" and "telling a falsehood" 325

XII. That the philosopher Chrysippus says that every word is ambiguous and of doubtful meaning, while Diodorus on the contrary thinks that no word is ambiguous 325

XIII. What Titus Castricius thought about the wording of a sentence of Gaius Gracchus ; and that he showed that it contributed nothing to the effectiveness of the sentence 327

XIV. The discreet and admirable reply of King Romulus as to his use of wine 331

XV. On *ludibundus* and *errabundus* and the suffix in words of that kind ; that Laberius used *amorabunda* in the same way as *ludibunda* and *errabunda* ; also that Sisenna in the case of a word of that sort made a new form 333

CAPITULA

PAGINA

XVI. Quod Graecorum verborum quorundam difficillima est in Latinam linguam mutatio, velut quod Graece dicitur πολυπραγμοσύνη 336

XVII. Quid significet in veteribus praetorum edictis: "qui flumina retanda publice redempta habent." . 340

XVIII. Qua poena Draco Atheniensis, in legibus quas populo Athensiensi scripsit, fures adfecerit; et qua postea Solon; et qua item decemviri nostri qui *Duodecim Tabulas* scripserunt; atque inibi adscriptum quod aput Aegyptios furta licita et permissa sunt, aput Lacedaemonios autem cum studio quoque adfectata et pro exercitio utili celebrata; ac praeterea M. Catonis de poeniendis furtis digna memoria sententia 342

CAPITULA LIBRI DUODECIMI

I. Dissertatió Favorini philosophi, qua suasit nobili feminae uti liberos quos peperisset, non nutricum aliarum, sed sibi suo lacte aleret 352

II. Quod Annaeus Seneca, iudicans de Q. Ennio deque M. Tullio, levi futtilique iudicio fuit 360

III. Lictoris vocabulum qua ratione conceptum ortumque sit; et super eo diversae sententiae Valgi Rufi et Tulli Tironis 366

IV. Versus accepti ex Q. Enni septimo *Annalium*, quibus depingitur finiturque ingenium comitasque hominis minoris erga amicum superiorem . . . 368

V. Sermo Tauri philosophi de modo atque ratione tolerandi doloris secundum Stoicorum decreta . . 372

VI. De aenigmate 382

VII. Quam ob causam Cn. Dolabella proconsul ream mulierem veneficii confitentemque ad Ariopagitas reiecerit 384

xxviii

CHAPTER HEADINGS

PAGE

XVI. That the translation of certain Greek words into the Latin language is very difficult, for example, that which in Greek is called πολυπραγμοσύνη . . 337

XVII. The meaning of the expression found in the old praetorian edicts: "those who have undertaken public contracts for clearing the rivers of nets" . 341

XVIII. The punishment which Draco the Athenian, in the laws which he made for his fellow citizens, inflicted upon thieves; that of Solon later; and that of our own decemvirs, who compiled the *Twelve Tables*; to which it is added, that among the Egyptians thefts were permitted and lawful, while among the Lacedaemonians they were even strongly encouraged and commended as a useful exercise; also a memorable utterance of Marcus Cato's about the punishment of theft 343

BOOK XII

I. A discourse of the philosopher Favorinus, in which he urged a lady of rank to feed with her own milk, and not with that of other nurses, the children whom she had borne 353

II. That the judgment passed by Annaeus Seneca on Quintus Ennius and Marcus Cicero was trifling and foolish 361

III. The meaning and origin of the word *lictor*, and the varying opinions of Valgius Rufus and Tullius Tiro on that subject 367

IV. Lines taken from the seventh book of the *Annals* of Ennius, in which the courteous bearing of an inferior towards a friend of higher rank is described and defined 369

V. A discourse of the philosopher Taurus on the method and manner of enduring pain, according to the principles of the Stoics 373

VI. On the Enigma 383

VII. Why Gnaeus Dolabella, the proconsul, referred to the court of the Areopagus the case of a woman charged with poisoning and admitting the fact . 385

xxix

CAPITULA

PAGINA

VIII. Reditiones in gratiam nobilium virorum memoratu dignae 386

IX. Quae dicantur vocabula ancipitia ; et quod honoris quoque vocabulum ancipiti sententia fuerit . . . 388

X. Quod "aeditumus" verbum Latinum sit . . . 390

XI. Errare istos qui spe et fiducia latendi peccent, cum latebra peccati perpetua nulla sit ; et super ea re Peregrini philosophi sermo et Sophocli poetae sententia 392

XII. Faceta responsio M. Ciceronis, amolientis a se crimen manifesti mendacii 394

XIII. "Intra Kalendas" cum dicitur, quid significet, utrum "ante Kalendas" an "Kalendis" an utrumque ; atque inibi, quid sit in oratione M. Tulli "intra oceanum" et "intra montem Taurum" et in quadam epistula "intra modum." 396

XIV. "Saltem" particula quam vim habeat et quam originem 408

XV. Quod Sisenna in libris *Historiarum* adverbis huiuscemodi saepenumero usus est : "celatim," "vellicatim," "saltuatim" 410

CAPITULA LIBRI TERTII DECIMI

I. Inquisitio verborum istorum M. Tulli curiosior quae sunt in primo *Antonianarum* libro, "multa autem inpendere videntur praeter naturam etiam praeterque fatum" ; tractatumque an idem duo ista significent, "fatum" atque "natura," an diversum. . 414

II. Super poetarum Pacuvii et Accii conloquio familiari in oppido Tarentino 418

III. An vocabula haec, "necessitudo" et "necessitas," differenti significatione sint 420

IV. Descripta Alexandi ad matrem Olympiadem epistula ; et quid Olympias festive ei rescripserit . 422

XXX

CHAPTER HEADINGS

PAGE

VIII. Noteworthy reconciliations between famous men 387

IX. What is meant by "ambiguous" words ; and that
even *honos* was such a word 389

X. That *aeditumus* is a Latin word 391

XI. That those are deceived who sin in the confident
hope of being undetected, since there is no permanent concealment of wrong-doing ; and on that
subject a discourse of the philosopher Peregrinus
and a saying of the poet Sophocles 393

XII. A witty reply of Marcus Cicero in which he tried
to refute the charge of a direct falsehood . . . 395

XIII. What is meant by the expression "within
the Kalends," whether it signifies "before the
Kalends," or "on the Kalends," or both ; also
the meaning of "within the Ocean" and "within
Mount Taurus" in a speech of Marcus Tullius, and
of "within the limit" in one of his letters . . . 397

XIV. The meaning and origin of the particle *saltem* . 409

XV. That Sisenna in his *Histories* has frequently used
adverbs of the type of *celatim*, *vellicatim*, and
saltuatim 411

BOOK XIII

I. A somewhat careful inquiry into these words of Marcus
Tullius in his first *Oration against Antony* : "But
many things seem to threaten contrary even to
nature and to fate"; and a discussion of the
question whether the words "fate" and "nature"
mean the same thing or something different . . 415

II. About an intimate talk of the poets Pacuvius and
Accius in the town of Tarentum 419

III. Whether the words *necessitas* and *necessitudo* differ
from each other in meaning 421

IV. Copy of a letter of Alexander to his mother
Olympias ; and Olympias' witty reply . . . 423

xxxi

CAPITULA

PAGINA

V. De Aristotele et Theophrasto et Eudemo philosophis; deque eleganti verecundia Aristotelis successorem diatribae suae eligentis 424

VI. Quid veteres Latini dixerint quas Graeci προσῳδίας appellant; item quod vocabulum barbarismi non usurpaverint neque Romani antiquiores neque Attici 426

VII. Diversum de natura leonum dixisse Homerum in carminibus et Herodotum in historiis 426

VIII. Quod Afranius poeta prudenter et lepide Sapientiam filiam esse Usus et Memoriae dixit 430

IX. Quid Tullius Tiro in commentariis scripserit de "Suculis" et "Hyadibus," quae sunt stellarum vocabula 432

X. Quid "sororis" ἔτυμον esse dixerit Labeo Antistius, et quid "fratris" P. Nigidius 434

XI. Quem M. Varro aptum iustumque esse numerum convivarum existimarit; ac de mensis secundis et de bellariis 436

XII. Tribunos plebis prensionem habere, vocationem non habere 440

XIII. Quod in libris *Humanarum* M. Varronis scriptum est aediles et quaestores populi Romani in ius a privato ad praetorem vocari posse 444

XIV. Quid sit "pomerium" 448

XV. Verba ex libro Messalae auguris, quibus docet qui sint minores magistratus, et consulem praetoremque conlegas esse; et quaedam alia de auspiciis . 450

XVI. Item verba eiusdem Messalae, disserentis aliud esse ad populum loqui, aliud cum populo agere; et qui magistratus a quibus avocent comitiatum . . 454

CHAPTER HEADINGS

PAGE

V. On the philosophers Aristotle, Theophrastus and Eudemus; and of the graceful tact of Aristotle in selecting a successor as head of his school . . . 425

VI. The term which the early Latins used for the Greek word προσῳδίαι or "tones"; also that the term *barbarismus,* or "outlandishness" was used neither by the early Romans nor by the people of Attica 427

VII. That Homer in his poems and Herodotus in his *Histories* spoke differently of the nature of the lion 427

VIII. That the poet Afranius wisely and prettily called Wisdom the daughter of Experience and Memory 431

IX. What Tullius Tiro wrote in his commentaries about the *Suculae,* or "Little Pigs," and the *Hyades,* which are the names of constellations 433

X. The derivation of *soror,* according to Antistius Labeo, and that of *frater,* according to Publius Nigidius 435

XI. Marcus Varro's opinion of the just and proper number of banqueters; his views about the dessert and about sweetmeats 437

XII. That the tribunes of the commons have the right to arrest, but not to summon 441

XIII. That it is stated in Marcus Varro's books on *Human Antiquities* that the aediles and quaestors of the Roman people might be cited before a praetor by a private citizen 445

XIV. The meaning of *pomerium* 449

XV. A passage from a book of the augur Messala, in which he shows who the minor magistrates are and that the consul and the praetor are colleagues; and certain observations besides on the auspices . . 451

XVI. Another passage from the same Messala, in which he argues that to speak to the people and to treat with the people are two different things; and what magistrates may call away the people when in assembly, and from whom 455

CAPITULA

PAGINA

XVII. "Humanitatem" non significare id quod vulgus putat, sed eo vocabulo qui sinceriter locuti sunt magis proprie esse usos 456

XVIII. Quid aput M. Catonem significent verba haec "inter os atque offam". 458

XIX. Platonem tribuere Euripidi Sophocli versum ; et similia quaedam alia 460

XX. De genere atque nominibus familiae Porciae. . . 462

XXI. Quod a scriptoribus elegantissimis maior ratio habita sit sonitus vocum atque verborum iucundioris, quae a Graecis εὐφωνία dicitur, quam regulae disciplinaeque quae a grammaticis reperta est . . 466

XXII. Verba Titi Castricii rhetoris ad discipulos adulescentes de vestitu atque calciatu non decoro . . . 476

XXIII. De Neriene Martis in antiquis conprecationibus 478

XXIV. Verba M. Catonis, egere se multis rebus et nihil tamen cupere dicentis 484

XXV. Quaesitum tractatumque quid sint "manubiae"; atque inibi dicta quaedam de ratione utendi verbis pluribus idem significantibus 486

XXVI. Verba P. Nigidii quibus dicit in nomine Valeri in casu vocandi primam syllabam acuendam esse ; et item alia ex eiusdem verbis ad rectam scripturam pertinentia 500

XXVII. De versibus, quos Vergilius sectatus videtur, Homeri ac Partheni 502

XXVIII. De sententia Panaetii philosophi, quam scripsit in libro *De Officiis* secundo, qua hortatur ut homines ad cavendas iniurias in omni loco intenti paratique sint 504

xxxiv

CHAPTER HEADINGS

PAGE

XVII. That *humanitas* does not mean what the common people think, but those who have spoken pure Latin have given the word a more restricted meaning 457

XVIII. The meaning of Marcus Cato's phrase "betwixt mouth and morsel" 459

XIX. That Plato attributes a line of Sophocles to Euripides; and some other matters of the same kind 461

XX. Of the lineage and names of the Porcian family . 463

XXI. That the most elegant writers pay more attention to the pleasing sound of words and phrases (what the Greeks call εὐφωνία, or "euphony") than to the rules and precepts devised by the grammarians . 467

XXII. The words of Titus Castricius to his young pupils on unbecoming clothes and shoes . . 477

XXIII. Of the *Nerio* of Mars in ancient prayers . . 479

XXIV. Remarks of Marcus Cato, who declared that he lacked many things, yet desired nothing . . . 485

XXV. The meaning of *manubiae* is asked and discussed; with some observations as to the propriety of using several words of the same meaning 487

XXVI. A passage of Publius Nigidius, in which he says that in *Valeri*, the vocative case of the name *Valerius*, the first syllable should have an acute accent; with other remarks of the same writer on correct writing 501

XXVII. Of verses of Homer and Parthenius which Virgil seems to have followed 503

XXVIII. Of an opinion of the philosopher Panaetius, which he expressed in his second book *On Duties*, where he urges men to be alert and prepared to guard against injuries on all occasions 505

CAPITULA

PAGINA

XXIX. Quod Quadrigarius "cum multis mortalibus" dixit; an quid et quantum differret, si dixisset "cum multis hominibus" 506

XXX. Non hactenus esse faciem qua vulgo dicitur . 510

XXXI. Quid sit in satura M. Varronis "caninum prandium" 512

CHAPTER HEADINGS

PAGE

XXIX. That Quadrigarius used the expression "with many mortals"; whether it would have made any difference if he had said "with many men," and how great a difference 507

XXX. That *facies* has a wider application than is commonly supposed 511

XXXI. The meaning of *caninum prandium* in Marcus Varro's satire 513

THE ATTIC NIGHTS
OF AULUS GELLIUS

BOOK VI

A. GELLII
NOCTIUM ATTICARUM

LIBER SEXTUS

I

Admiranda quaedam ex annalibus sumpta de P. Africano
superiore.

1 Quod de Olympiade, Philippi regis uxore, Alexandri matre, in historia Graeca scriptum est, id de P.
quoque Scipionis matre qui prior Africanus appellatus
2 est memoriae datum est. Nam et C. Oppius et
Iulius Hyginus, aliique qui de vita et rebus Africani
scripserunt, matrem eius diu sterilem existimatam
tradunt, P. quoque Scipionem, cum quo nupta erat,
3 liberos desperavisse. Postea in cubiculo atque in
lecto mulieris, cum absente marito cubans sola
condormisset, visum repente esse iuxta eam cubare
ingentem anguem eumque, his qui viderant territis et
clamantibus, elapsum inveniri non quisse. Id ipsum
P. Scipionem ad haruspices retulisse; eos, sacrificio
4 facto, respondisse fore ut liberi gignerentur, neque
multis diebus postquam ille anguis in lecto visus est,

---

¹ Fr. 2, Peter². ² Fr. 4, Peter² ; p. 37, Bunte.

THE ATTIC NIGHTS
OF AULUS GELLIUS

BOOK VI

I

Some remarkable stories about the elder Publius Africanus,
drawn from the annals.

THE tale which in Grecian history is told of
Olympias, wife of king Philip and mother of Alexander, is also recorded of the mother of that
Publius Scipio who was the first to be called
Africanus. For both Gaius Oppius[1] and Julius
Hyginus,[2] as well as others who have written of the
life and deeds of Africanus, declare that his mother
was for a long time thought to be barren, and that
Publius Scipio, her husband, had also given up hope
of offspring; that afterwards, in her own room and
bed, when she was lying alone in the absence of
her husband and had fallen asleep, of a sudden a
huge serpent was seen lying by her side; and that
when those who had seen it were frightened and
cried out, the snake glided away and could not be
found. It is said that Publius Scipio himself consulted soothsayers about the occurrence; that they,
after offering sacrifice, declared that he would have
children, and not many days after that serpent had
been seen in her bed, the woman began to experi-

mulierem coepisse concepti fetus signa atque sensum pati; exinde mense decimo peperisse natumque esse hunc P. Africanum qui Hannibalem et Carthaginienses in Africa bello Poenico secundo vicit.

5 Sed et eum inpendio magis ex rebus gestis quam ex illo ostento virum esse virtutis divinae creditum est.

6 Id etiam dicere haut piget, quod idem illi quos supra nominavi litteris mandaverint, Scipionem hunc Africanum solitavisse noctis extremo, priusquam dilucularet, in Capitolium ventitare ac iubere aperiri cellam Iovis atque ibi solum diu demorari, quasi consultantem de republica cum Iove, aeditumosque eius templi saepe esse demiratos, quod solum id temporis in Capitolium ingredientem canes semper in alios saevientes neque latrarent eum neque incurrerent.

7 Has volgi de Scipione opiniones confirmare atque approbare videbantur dicta factaque eius pleraque admiranda. Ex quibus est unum huiuscemodi :

8 Assidebat oppugnabatque oppidum in Hispania, situ,[1] moenibus, defensoribus validum et munitum, re etiam cibaria copiosum, nullaque eius potiundi spes erat, et quodam die ius in castris sedens dicebat

9 atque ex eo loco id oppidum procul visebatur. Tum

---

[1] situm, ω, *corrected in* ς.

---

[1] A similar story is told of Augustus (Suet. *Aug*. xciv. 4) as well as of Alexander the Great (§ 1 and Livy, xxvi. 19. 7).
[2] At Zama, 202 B.C.
[3] As well as Alexander and Augustus; see note 1.
[4] The name *Capitolium* was applied to the southern summit of the Capitoline Hill, and also to the temple of *Juppiter Optimus Maximus*. The temple contained three shrines, to Jupiter, Juno, and Minerva.

ence the indications and sensation of conception.[1] Afterwards, in the tenth month, she gave birth to that Publius Scipio who conquered Hannibal and the Carthaginians in Africa in the second Punic war.[2] But it was far more because of his exploits than because of that prodigy that he too[3] was believed to be a man of godlike excellence.

This too I venture to relate, which the same writers that I mentioned before have put on record : This Scipio Africanus used often to go to the Capitolium in the latter part of the night, before the break of day, give orders that the shrine of Jupiter be opened,[4] and remain there a long time alone, apparently consulting Jupiter about matters of state ; and the guardians of the temple were often amazed that on his coming to the Capitolium alone at such an hour the dogs,[5] that flew at all other intruders, neither barked at him nor molested him.

These popular beliefs about Scipio seemed to be confirmed and attested by many remarkable actions and sayings of his. Of these the following is a single example : He was engaged in the siege of a town[6] in Spain, which was strongly fortified and defended, protected by its position, and also well provisioned ; and there was no prospect of taking it. One day he sat holding court in his camp, at a point from which there was a distant view of the town.

[5] The temple was guarded at night by dogs, as were doubtless other similar places, and as it is said that the ruins of Pompeii are to-day. Geese were also used for the purpose ; see Cic *pro Sex. Rosc.* 56, *anseribus cibaria publice locantur et canes aluntur in Capitolio, ut significent, si fures venerint.*

[6] According to Valerius Maximus, iii. 7. 1, the town was Badia.

e militibus, qui in iure apud eum stabant, interro-
gavit quispiam ex more in quem diem locumque
10 vadimonium promitti iuberet; et Scipio, manum ad
ipsam oppidi quod obsidebatur arcem protendens,
" Perendie," inquit, " sese sistant illo in loco."
11 Atque ita factum; die tertio, in quem vadari
iusserat, oppidum captum est eodemque eo[1] die in
arce eius oppidi ius dixit.

II

De Caeselli Vindicis pudendo errore, quem offendimus in
libris eius quos inscripsit *Lectionum Antiquarum.*

1   TURPE erratum offendimus in illis celebratissimis
commentariis *Lectionum Antiquarum* Caeselli Vindicis, hominis hercle pleraque haut indiligentis.
2 Quod erratum multos fugit, quamquam multa in
Caesellio reprehendendo etiam per calumnias rima-
3 rentur.   Scripsit autem Caesellius Q. Ennium in
XIII. *Annali* " cor " dixisse genere masculino.
4   Verba Caeselli subiecta sunt : " Masculino genere,
ut multa alia, enuntiavit Ennius.   Nam in XIII.
5 *Annali* 'quem cor' dixit."   Ascripsit deinde versus
Ennii duo :

Hannibal audaci dum pectore de me hortatur
Ne bellum faciam, quem credidit esse meum cor?

----

[1] eo *omitted by RV.*

Then one of the soldiers who were on trial before
him asked in the usual way on what day and in
what place he bade them give bail for their appearance. Then Scipio, stretching forth his hand towards
the very citadel of the town which he was besieging,
said : "Appear the day after to-morrow in yonder
place." And so it happened ; on the third day, the
day on which he had ordered them to appear, the
town was captured, and on that same day he held
court in the citadel of the place.

II

Of a disgraceful blunder of Caesellius Vindex, which we
find in his work entitled *Archaic Terms.*

In those highly celebrated notes of Caesellius
Vindex *On Archaic Terms* we find a shameful oversight, although in fact the man is seldom caught
napping. This error has escaped the notice of many,
in spite of their diligent search for opportunities to
find fault with Caesellius, even through misrepre-
sentation. Now, Caesellius wrote that Quintus
Ennius, in the thirteenth book of his *Annals,* used
cor in the masculine gender.

I add Caesellius' own words : "Ennius used *cor,*
like many other words, in the masculine gender ;
for in *Annals* xiii. he wrote *quem cor.*" He then
quoted two verses of Ennius [1] :

While Hannibal, of bold breast, did me exhort
Not to make war, what heart thought he was
    mine ?

[1] 381 ff., Vahlen[2].

6 Antiochus est qui hoc dixit, Asiae rex.   Is admiratur
et permovetur, quod Hannibal Carthaginiensis bellum
7 se facere populo Romano volentem dehortetur.   Hos
autem versus Caesellius sic accipit, tamquam si Antiochus sic dicat : " Hannibal me ne bellum geram
dehortatur ; quod cum facit, ecquale putat cor
habere me et quam stultum esse me credit, cum id
mihi persuadere vult ? "
8   Hoc Caesellius quidem, sed aliud longe Ennius.
9 Nam tres versus sunt, non duo, ad hance Ennii
sententiam pertinentes, ex quibus tertium versum
Caesellius non respexit :

> Hannibal audaci dum pectore de me hortatur
> Ne bellum faciam, quem credidit esse meum cor
> Suasorem summum et studiosum robore belli.

10 Horum versuum sensus atque ordo sic, opinor, est :
" Hannibal ille audentissimus atque fortissimus,
quem ego credidi "—hoc est enim : " cor meum
credidit," proinde atque diceret " quem ego stultus
homo credidi "—" summum fore suasorem ad bellan-
dum, is me dehortatur dissuadetque ne bellum
11 faciam." Caesellius autem forte ῥαθυμότερον iunctura
ista verborum captus " quem cor " dictum putavit et
" quem " accentu acuto legit, quasi ad " cor " refer-
12 retur, non ad "Hannibalem." Sed non fugit me, si
aliquis sit tam inconditus, sic posse defendi " cor "
Caeselli masculinum, ut videatur tertius versus
separatim atque divise legendus, proinde quasi prae-
cisis interruptisque verbis exclamet Antiochus :
" suasorem summum !" Sed non dignum est eis
qui hoc dixerint responderi.

---

¹ Antiochus did not follow Hannibal's advice and suffered
a crushing defeat at Thermopylae in 191 B.C.

The speaker is Antiochus, king of Asia. He is surprised and indignant that Hannibal, the Carthaginian, discourages his desire to make war on the people of Rome.[1] Now, Caesellius understands the lines to mean that Antiochus says: " Hannibal dissuades me from making war. In so doing, what kind of heart does he think I have, and how foolish does he believe me to be, when he gives me such advice ? "

So Caesellius; but Ennius' meaning was quite different. For there are three verses, not two, which belong to this utterance of the poet's, and Caesellius overlooked the third verse :

Through valour war's great advocate and friend.

The meaning and arrangement of these three verses I believe to be this: " Hannibal, that boldest and most valiant of men, who I believed (for that is the meaning of *cor meum credidit*, exactly as if he had said " who I, foolish man, believed ") would strongly advise war, discourages and dissuades me from making war." Caesellius, however, somewhat carelessly misled as to the connection of the words, assumed that Ennius said *quem cor*, reading *quem* with an acute accent,[2] as if it belonged with *cor* and not with *Hannibal*. But I am well aware that one might, if anyone should have so little understanding, defend Caesellius' masculine *cor* by maintaining that the third verse should be read apart from the others, as if Antiochus had exclaimed in broken and abrupt language " a mighty adviser ! " But those who would argue thus do not deserve a reply.

[2] The interrogative *quem* would be stressed (have "an acute accent"), while the relative *quem* would not (*i.e.*, would have a grave accent).

III

Quid Tiro Tullius, Ciceronis libertus, reprehenderit in
M. Catonis oratione quam pro Rodiensibus in senatu
dixit; et quid ad ea, quae reprehenderat, responderimus.

1 CIVITAS Rodiensis et insulae opportunitate et
operum nobilitatibus et navigandi sollertia navali-
2 busque victoriis celebrata est. Ea civitas, cum
amica atque socia populi Romani foret, Persa tamen,
Philippi filio, Macedonum rege, cum quo bellum
populo Romano fuit, amico usa est, conixique sunt
Rodienses legationibus Romam saepe missis id
3 bellum inter eos componere. Sed, ubi ista pacificatio
perpetrari nequivit, verba a plerisque Rodiensibus
in contionibus eorum ad populum facta sunt, ut, si
pax non fieret, Rodienses regem adversus populum
4 Romanum adiutarent. Sed nullum super ea re
5 publicum decretum factum est. At ubi Perses
victus captusque est, Rodienses pertimuere ob ea
quae conpluriens in coetibus populi acta dictaque
erant, legatosque Romam miserunt, qui temeritatem
quorundam popularium suorum deprecarentur et
6 fidem consiliumque publicum expurgarent. Legati
postquam Romam venerunt et in senatum intro-

---

¹ The second Macedonian war, 171–168 B.C. The Rhodians
sided with the Romans until 169 B.C., when they sent envoys
to the Roman head-quarters and to the senate, declaring that
they would no longer tolerate a war which injured their
traffic with Macedonia and diminished their revenues; that
they were disposed to declare war against the party which
should refuse to make peace, and that they had already
formed an alliance with Crete and with the Asiatic cities.
The Romans, who had in the past treated the Rhodians
with special favour, were indignant and glad of the opportunity to humble the presumptuous State. When it was

III

What Tullius Tiro, Cicero's freedman, criticized in the speech which Marcus Cato delivered in the senate in defence of the Rhodians; and our answer to his strictures.

THE State of Rhodes is famed for the happy situation of the island, its celebrated works of art, its skill in seamanship and its naval victories. Although a friend and ally of the Roman people, that State was on cordial terms with Perses, son of Philip and king of Macedon, with whom the Romans were at war;[1] accordingly, the Rhodians often sent envoys to Rome and tried to reconcile the contending parties. But when their attempts at peace-making failed, many of the Rhodians harangued the people in their assemblies, urging that if peace were not made, the Rhodians should aid the king in his contest with the people of Rome; but as to that question no official action was taken. When, however, Perses was defeated and taken prisoner, the Rhodians were in great fear because of what had been said and done on many occasions in the popular assemblies; and they sent envoys to Rome, to apologize for the hastiness of some of their fellow-citizens and vindicate their loyalty as a community. When the envoys reached Rome and were admitted to the

proposed in the senate to declare war upon Rhodes, the Rhodians resorted to every means of placating the Romans. Cato pleaded their cause, pointing out that they had committed no offence, unless the Romans wished to punish mere wishes and thoughts. His words, however, were in vain. The senate deprived the Rhodians of their possessions on the mainland and humiliated them in other ways. Alliance with Rhodes was not renewed until 164 B.C., and then only after many entreaties.

missi sunt, verbisque suppliciter pro causa sua factis
e curia excesserunt, sententiae rogari coeptae;
7 cumque partim senatorum de Rodiensibus quere-
rentur maleque animatos eos fuisse dicerent bellum-
que illis faciendum censerent, tum M. Cato exurgit
et optimos fidissimosque socios, quorum opibus
diripiendis possidendisque non pauci ex summatibus
viris intenti infensique erant, defensum conserva-
tumque pergit orationemque inclutam dicit, quae et
seorsum fertur inscriptaque est *Pro Rodiensibus* et
in quintae *Originis* libro scripta est.
8   Tiro autem Tullius, M. Ciceronis libertus, sane
quidem fuit ingenio homo eleganti hautquaquam
rerum litterarumque veterum indoctus, eoque ab
ineunte aetate liberaliter instituto adminiculatore
et quasi administro in studiis litterarum Cicero usus
9 est.   Sed profecto plus ausus est quam ut tolerari
10 ignoscique possit. Namque epistulam conscripsit
ad Q. Axium, familiarem patroni sui, confidenter
nimis et calide, in qua sibimet visus est orationem
istam *Pro Rodiensibus* acri subtilique iudicio per-
11 censuisse.   Ex ea epistula lubitum forte nobis est
reprehensiones eius quasdam attingere, maiore
scilicet venia reprehensuri Tironem, cum ille reprehenderit Catonem.
12   Culpavit autem primum hoc, quod Cato "ineru-
dite et ἀναγώγως," ut ipse ait, principio nimis
insolenti nimisque acri et obiurgatorio usus sit, cum
vereri sese ostendit ne patres, gaudio atque laetitia

---

[1] p. 9, Lion.

senate, after having humbly pleaded their cause they left the House, and the senators were called upon for their opinions. When some of the members complained of the Rhodians, declaring that they had been disloyal, and recommended that war be declared upon them, then Marcus Cato arose. He endeavoured to defend and save our very good and faithful allies, to whom many of the most distinguished senators were hostile through a desire to plunder and possess their wealth; and he delivered that famous speech entitled *For the Rhodians*, which is included in the fifth book of his *Origins* and is also in circulation as a separate publication.

Now Tullius Tiro, Marcus Cicero's freedman, was unquestionably a man of refined taste and by no means unacquainted with our early history and literature. He had been liberally educated from his earliest years, and Cicero found in him an assistant, and in a sense a partner, in his literary work. But surely Tiro showed more presumption than can be tolerated or excused. For he wrote a letter [1] to Quintus Axius, a friend of his patron, with excessive assurance and warmth, in which, as he imagined, he criticized that speech *For the Rhodians* with keen and fine judgment. It chanced to take my fancy to touch upon certain of the animadversions which he makes in that letter, and I shall doubtless be the more readily pardoned for finding fault with Tiro, because he took Cato to task.

His first charge was that Cato, "ignorantly and absurdly," to use Tiro's own language, made use of a preamble which was excessively arrogant and excessively severe and fault-finding, in which he declared that he feared lest the fathers, having their

rerum prospere gestarum de statu mentis suae
deturbati, non satis consiperent neque ad recte
13 intellegendum consulendumque essent idonei. "In
principiis autem," inquit, "patroni, qui pro reis
dicunt, conciliare sibi et complacare iudices debent
sensusque eorum expectatione causae suspensos
rigentesque honorificis verecundisque sententiis com-
mulcere, non iniuriis atque imperiosis minationibus
14 confutare." Ipsum deinde principium apposuit,
cuius verba haec sunt: "Scio solere plerisque
hominibus rebus[1] secundis atque prolixis atque
prosperis[2] animum excellere atque superbiam atque
ferociam augescere atque crescere. Quo mihi nunc
magnae curae est, quod haec res tam secunde
processit, ne quid in consulendo advorsi eveniat,
quod nostras secundas res confutet, neve haec
laetitia nimis luxuriose eveniat. Advorsae res edo-
mant et docent quid opus siet facto, secundae res
laetitia transvorsum trudere solent a recte consulendo atque intellegendo. Quo maiore opere dico
suadeoque uti haec res aliquot dies proferatur, dum
ex tanto gaudio in potestatem nostram redeamus."
15 "Quae deinde Cato iuxta dicit, ea," inquit,
"confessionem faciunt, non defensionem, neque
propulsationem translationemve criminis habent,
sed cum pluribus aliis communicationem, quod
scilicet nihili[3] ad purgandum est. Atque etiam,"
inquit, "insuper profitetur Rodienses, qui accusa-
bantur quod adversus populum Romanum regi magis

---

[1] in rebus, Gell. xiii. 25. 14.
[2] *Damsté regards* atque prosperis *as a gloss.*
[3] nihili, *suggested by Hosius*; nihil, ω.

---

[1] *Origines,* v. 1, Jordan.

minds upset by joy and exultation at their success, might act unwisely and be in no state of mind for understanding and deliberating aright. Tiro says: " Advocates who are pleading for clients ought in their opening remarks to win over and propitiate the jurors with complimentary and respectful language; they ought, while their minds, as they wait to hear the case, are still in suspense and cool, to render them complacent, and not to arouse contradiction by insults and arrogant threats." Then he has given us Cato's own preamble, which runs as follows:[1] " I am aware that in happy, successful and prosperous times the minds of most men are wont to be puffed up, and their arrogance and self-confidence to wax and swell. Therefore I am now gravely concerned, since this enterprise has gone on so successfully, lest something adverse may happen in our deliberations, to bring to naught our good fortune, and lest this joy of ours may become too extravagant. Adversity subdues and shows what ought to be done; prosperity, since it inspires joy, commonly turns men aside from wise counsel and right understanding. Therefore it is with the greater emphasis that I advise and urge that this matter be put off for a few days, until we regain our self-command after so great rejoicing."

" Then what Cato says next," continues Tiro, " amounts to a confession rather than a defence; for it does not contain a refutation or shifting of the charge, but the sharing of it with many others, which of course amounts to nothing in the way of excuse. Moreover," says Tiro, " he also acknowledges that the Rhodians, who were accused of favouring the king's cause against the Roman people

cupierint faverintque, id eos cupisse atque favisse
utilitatis suae gratia, ne Romani Perse quoque rege
victo ad superbiam ferociamque et inmodicum
16 modum insolescerent." Eaque ipsa verba ponit,
ita ut infra scriptum : "Atque ego quidem arbitror
Rodienses noluisse nos ita depugnare, uti depug-
natum est, neque regem Persen vinci. Sed non
Rodienses modo id noluere, sed multos populos
atque multas nationes idem noluisse arbitror atque
haut scio an partim eorum fuerint, qui non nostrae
contumeliae causa id noluerint evenire ; sed enim
id metuere,[1] ne[2] si nemo esset homo quem vere-
remur, quidquid luberet faceremus. Ne sub solo
imperio nostro in servitute nostra essent, libertatis
suae causa in ea sententia fuisse arbitror. Atque
Rodienses tamen Persen publice numquam adiuvere.
Cogitate quanto nos inter nos privatim cautius
facimus. Nam unusquisque nostrum, si quis advorsus rem suam quid fieri arbitrantur, summa vi
contra nititur, ne advorsus eam fiat ; quod illi tamen
perpessi."
17 Sed, quod ad principium reprehensum attinet,
scire oportuit Tironem, defensos esse Rodienses a
Catone, sed ut a senatore et consulari et censorio
viro, quidquid optimum esse publicum existimabat
suadente, non ut a patrono causam pro reis dicente.
18 Alia namque principia conducunt reos apud iudices
defendenti et clementiam misericordiamque undique

---

[1] metuentes, *Damsté*; metueres nemo, *P.*
[2] ne *added by A. Schaefer.*

---

[1] *Origines*, v. 2, Jordan.

and wishing him success, did so from motives of
self-interest, for fear that the Romans, already proud
and self-confident, with the addition of a victory
over king Perses might become immoderately insolent." And he gives Cato's own words, as
follows :[1] " And I really think that the Rhodians did
not wish us to end the war as we did, with a victory
over king Perses. But it was not the Rhodians
alone who had that feeling, but I believe that many
peoples and many nations agreed with them. And
I am inclined to think that some of them did not
wish us success, not in order that we might be
disgraced, but because they feared that if there
were no one of whom we stood in dread, we would
do whatsoever we chose. I think, then, that it was
with an eye to their own freedom that they held that
opinion, in order not to be under our sole dominion
and enslaved to us. But for all that, the Rhodians
never publicly aided Perses. Reflect how much more
cautiously we deal with one another as individuals.
For each one of us, if he thinks that anything is being
done contrary to his interests, strives with might
and main to prevent it ; but they in spite of all
permitted this very thing to happen."

Now as to his criticism of Cato's introduction,
Tiro ought to have known that although Cato
defended the Rhodians, he did so as a senator who
had been consul and censor and was recommending
what he thought was best for the public welfare, not
as an advocate pleading the cause of the accused.
For one kind of introduction is appropriate for a man
who is defending clients before jurors and striving in
every way to excite pity and compassion ; quite
another for a man of eminent authority, when the

indaganti, alia, cum senatus de republica consulitur,
viro auctoritate praestanti, sententiis quorundam
iniquissimis permoto et pro utilitatibus publicis ac
pro salute sociorum graviter ac libere indignanti

19 simul ac dolenti. Quippe recte et utiliter in disciplinis rhetorum praecipitur, iudices de capite alieno
deque causa ad sese non pertinenti cognituros, ex qua
praeter officium iudicandi nihil ad eos vel periculi
vel emolumenti redundaturum est, conciliandos esse
ac propitiandos placabiliter et leniter existimationi

20 salutique eius qui apud eos accusatus est. At cum
dignitas et fides et utilitas omnium communis
agitur, ob eamque rem aut suadendum quid ut
fiat, aut, fieri iam coepto, differendum est, tum
qui se in eiusmodi principiis occupat, ut benivolos
benignosque sibi auditores paret, otiosam operam

21 in non necessariis verbis sumit. Iamdudum enim
negotia, pericula ipsa rerum communia consiliis eos
capiendis conciliant et ipsi potius sibi exposcunt

22 consultoris benivolentiam. Sed quod ait confessum
Catonem noluisse Rodiensis ita depugnari, ut de-
pugnatum est, neque regem Persem a populo
Romano vinci, atque id eum dixisse non Rodienses
modo, sed multas quoque alias nationes noluisse,
sed id nihil ad purgandum extenuandumve crimen
valere, iam hoc primum Tiro inprobe mentitur.

23 Verba ponit Catonis et aliis tamen eum verbis

---

[1] That is, towards the welfare of the State. Tiro seems
to be making a word-play, using *benivolos* and *benivolentiam*
in the same sense, but with a different application.

senate is asked for its opinion on a matter of State, and when, indignant at the highly unjust opinions of some of the members, he gives plain and emphatic expression at once to his indignation and his sorrow, speaking in behalf of the public welfare and the safety of our allies. Indeed, it is a proper and salutary rule of the schools of rhetoric, that jurors who are to pass judgment on the person of a stranger and on a case which does not personally concern them (so that apart from the duty of acting as jurors no danger or emolument will come to them) ought to be conciliated and induced by mild and soothing language to have regard for the reputation and safety of the prisoner at the bar. But when the common prestige, honour and advantage of all are involved, and therefore one must advise what is to be done, or what must be put off that has already been begun, then one who busies oneself with an introduction designed to make his hearers friendly and kindly disposed towards himself wastes his efforts in needless talk. For the common interests and dangers have themselves already disposed the jurors to listen to advice, and it is rather they themselves that demand good-will[1] on the part of their counsellor. But when Tiro says that Cato admitted that the Rhodians did not wish the Romans to fight as successfully as they did, and king Perses to be conquered by the Roman people, and when he asserts that he declared that not the Rhodians alone, but many other nations too, had the same feeling, but that this availed nothing in excuse or extenuation of their fault—in this very first point Tiro is guilty of a shameless lie. He quotes Cato's words, yet misrepresents him by giving them a false interpretation.

24 calumniatur. Non enim Cato confitetur noluisse
Rodienses victoriam esse populi Romani, sed sese
arbitrari dixit id eos noluisse, quod erat procul
dubio opinionis suae professio, non Rodiensium
25 culpae confessio. In qua re, ut meum quidem
iudicium est, non culpa tantum vacat, sed dignus
quoque laude admirationeque est, cum et ingenue
ac religiose dicere visus est contra Rodienses quod
sentiebat et, parta sibi veritatis fide, ipsum illud
tamen, quod contrarium putabatur, flexit et trans-
tulit, ut eos idcirco vel maxime aequum esset
acceptiores carioresque fieri populo Romano, quod
cum et utile iis esset et vellent regi esse factum,
nihil tamen adiuvandi eius gratia fecerunt.
26   Postea verba haec ex eadem oratione ponit :
" Ea nunc derepente tanta beneficia ultro citroque,
tantam amicitiam relinquemus ? quod illos dicimus
voluisse facere, id nos priores facere occupabimus ? "
27 " Hoc," inquit, " enthymema nequam et vitiosum
est. Responderi enim potuit : ' Occupabimus certe ;
nam, si non occupaverimus, opprimemur inciden-
dumque erit in insidias a quibus ante non cave-
28 rimus.' Recteque," inquit, " hoc vitio dat Lucilius
poetae Euripidae, quod, cum Polyphontes rex propterea se interfecisse fratrem diceret, quod ipse ante

---

[1] Cf. i. 6. 6.
[2] v 3, Jordan.

For Cato does not admit that the Rhodians did not wish the Roman people to be victorious, but said that he thought they did not; and this was unquestionably an expression of his own opinion, not a concession of the guilt of the Rhodians. On this point, in my judgment at least, Cato is not only free from reproach, but is even deserving of praise and admiration. For he apparently expressed a frank and conscientious opinion adverse to the Rhodians; but then, having established confidence in his candour,[1] he so changed and shifted that very statement which seemed to militate against them, that on that account alone it seemed right that they should be more highly esteemed and beloved by the people of Rome; inasmuch as they took no steps to aid the king, although they wished him to succeed and although his success would have been to their advantage.

Later on, Tiro quotes the following words from the same speech:[2] "Shall we, then, of a sudden abandon these great services given and received and this strong friendship? Shall we be the first to do what we say they merely wished to do?" "This," says Tiro, "is a worthless and faulty argument.[3] For it might be replied: 'Certainly we shall anticipate them, for if we do not, we shall be caught unawares and must fall into the snares against which we failed to guard in advance.' Lucilius," he says, "justly criticizes[4] the poet Euripides for this reason, that when king Polyphontes declared that he had killed his brother, because his brother had

[3] An enthymeme in logic was an argument consisting of two propositions, the antecedent and its consequence.

[4] 1169, Marx.

de nece eius consilium cepisset, Meropa fratris uxor hisce adeo eum[1] verbis eluserit:

Εἰ γάρ σ᾽ ἔμελλεν, ὡς σὺ φῄς, κτείνειν πόσις,
Χρὴ καὶ σὲ μέλλειν, ὡς χρόνος παρήλυθεν.

29 At hoc enim," inquit, "plane stultitiae plenum est, eo consilio atque ea fini facere velle aliquid,
30 uti numquam id facias quod velis." Sed videlicet Tiro animum non advertit non esse in omnibus rebus cavendis eandem causam, neque humanae vitae negotia et actiones et officia vel occupandi vel differendi vel etiam ulciscendi vel cavendi similia
31 esse pugnae[2] gladiatoriae. Nam gladiatori composito ad pugnandum pugnae haec proposita sors est, aut occidere, si occupaverit, aut occumbere, si
32 cessaverit. Hominum autem vita non tam iniquis neque tam indomitis necessitatibus conscripta est, ut idcirco prior iniuriam facere debeas, quam nisi
33 feceris pati possis. Quod tantum aberat a populi Romani mansuetudine, ut saepe iam in sese factas iniurias ulcisci neglexerit.

34 Post deinde usum esse Catonem dicit in eadem oratione argumentis parum honestis et nimis audacibus ac non viri qui alioqui fuit,[3] sed vafris ac fallaciosis et quasi Graecorum sophistarum sollertiis.
35 "Nam cum obiceretur," inquit, "Rodiensibus quod bellum populo Romano facere voluissent, negavit poena esse dignos, quia id non fecissent, etsi maxime voluissent," induxisseque eum dicit quam dialectici

---

[1] adeo eum, *Hertz*; ad eum, ω.
[2] pugnae et gl., ω; et *omitted in* ς.
[3] qui alioqui fuit, *Hosius*; qui ante fuit, *Damsté*; alius, *Scioppius*; alio, ω.

---

[1] Fr. 451, Nauck[2].

previously planned to slay him, Meropa, his brother's
wife, confuted the king with these words [1]:

> If, as you say, my husband planned your death,
> You too should only plan, till that time came.

But that," says Tiro, "is altogether full of absurdity,
to wish to do something, and yet have the design
and purpose of never doing what you wish to do."
But, as a matter of fact, Tiro failed to observe that
the reason for taking precautions is not the same in
all cases, and that the occupations and actions of
human life, and the obligations of anticipation or
postponement or even of taking vengeance or precautions, are not like a combat of gladiators. For to
a gladiator ready to fight the fortune of battle
offers the alternative, either to kill, if he should
conquer, or to die, if he should yield. But the life
of men in general is not restricted by such unfair or
inevitable necessities that one must be first to
commit an injury in order to avoid suffering injury.
In fact, such conduct was so alien to the humanity
of the Roman people that they often forbore to
avenge the wrongs inflicted upon them.

Then Tiro says that later in that same speech
Cato used arguments that were disingenuous and
excessively audacious, not suited to the character
which Cato showed at other times, but cunning and
deceitful, resembling the subtleties of the Greek
sophists. "For although," says he, "he charged
the Rhodians with having wished to make war on
the Roman people, he declared that they did not
deserve punishment, because they had not made
war in spite of their strong desire to do so." He
says that Cato introduced what the logicians call an

23

ἐπαγωγήν appellant, rem admodum insidiosam et sophisticam neque ad veritates magis quam ad captiones repertam, cum conatus sit exemplis decipientibus conligere confirmareque, neminem qui male facere voluit plecti aequum esse, nisi quod

36 factum voluit etiam fecerit. Verba autem ex ea oratione M. Catonis haec sunt; "Qui acerrime adversus eos dicit, ita dicit 'hostes voluisse fieri.' Ecquis est tandem, qui vestrorum, quod ad sese attineat, aequum censeat poenas dare ob eam rem, quod arguatur male facere voluisse? Nemo, opinor;

37 nam ego, quod ad me attinet, nolim." Deinde paulo infra dicit: "Quid nunc? Ecqua tandem lex est tam acerba, quae dicat 'si quis illud facere voluerit, mille, minus dimidium familiae, multa esto; si quis plus quingenta iugera habere voluerit, tanta poena esto; si quis maiorem pecuum numerum habere voluerit, tantum damnas esto?' Atqui nos omnia plura habere volumus et id nobis impune

38 est." Postea ita dicit: "Sed si honorem non aequum est haberi ob eam rem, quod bene facere voluisse quis dicit neque fecit tamen, Rodiensibus oberit, quod non male fecerunt, sed quia voluisse

39 dicuntur facere?" His argumentis Tiro Tullius M. Catonem contendere et conficere dicit Rodiensibus quoque impune esse debere, quod hostes quidem esse populi Romani voluissent, ut qui maxime

---

[1] Defined by Cicero, *Topica*, 42 f., as *inductio*, or an inductive argument, with examples; see also §§ 45–47, below.

[2] v. 4, Jordan.   [3] v. 5, Jordan.

[4] The law provided that a man should not be fined in a sum greater than half his property.

[5] This was forbidden by a Licinian Law, passed in 367 B.C.; the *iuger* was really about two-thirds of an acre. Another Licinian Law provided that no one should pasture more than

ἐπαγωγή,[1] a most treacherous and sophistical device, designed not so much for the truth as for cavil, since by deceptive examples he tried to establish and prove that no one who wished to do wrong deserved to be punished, unless he actually accomplished his desire. Now Cato's words in that speech are as follows:[2] "He who uses the strongest language against them says that they wished to be our enemies. Pray is there any one of you who, so far as he is concerned, would think it fair to suffer punishment because he is accused of having wished to do wrong? No one, I think; for so far as I am concerned, I should not." Then a little farther on he says:[3] "What? Is there any law so severe as to provide that if anyone wish to do so and so, he be fined a thousand sesterces, provided that be less than half his property;[4] if anyone shall desire to have more than five hundred acres,[5] let the fine be so much; if anyone shall wish to have a greater number of cattle, let the fine be thus and so. In fact, we all wish to have more, and we do so with impunity." Later he continues:[6] "But if it is not right for honour to be conferred because anyone says that he wished to do well, but yet did not do so, shall the Rhodians suffer, not because they did wrong, but because they are said to have wished to do wrong?" With such arguments Tullius Tiro says that Marcus Cato strove to show that the Rhodians also ought not to be punished, because although they had wished to be enemies of the Roman people,

---

100 head of cattle, or 500 of smaller animals, on the public lands. The number, and the amount of the fine, are here expressed indefinitely.

[6] v. 6, Jordan.

40 non fuissent. Dissimulari autem non posse ait quin
paria et consimilia non sint, plus quingenta iugera
habere velle, quod plebiscito Stolonis prohibitum
fuit, et bellum iniustum atque impium populo
Romano facere velle, neque item infitiari [1] posse
41 quin alia causa in praemio sit, alia in poenis. "Nam
beneficia," inquit, "promissa opperiri oportet neque
ante remunerari quam facta sint, iniurias autem
imminentis praecavisse iustum est quam expecta-
42 visse. Summa enim professio stultitiae," inquit,
"est, non ire obviam sceleribus cogitatis, sed manere
opperirique ut, cum admissa et perpetrata fuerint,
tum denique, ubi quae facta sunt infecta fieri non
possunt, poeniantur."

43 Haec Tiro in Catonem non nimis frigide neque
44 sane inaniter; sed enim Cato non nudam nec soli-
tariam nec inprotectam hanc ἐπαγωγήν facit, sed
multis eam modis praefulcit multisque aliis argumentis convelat et, quia non Rodiensibus magis
quam reipublicae consultabat, nihil sibi dictu factu-
que in ea re turpe duxit, quin omni sententiarum
45 via servatum ire socios niteretur. Ac primum ea
non incallide conquisivit, quae non iure naturae
aut iure gentium fieri prohibentur, sed iure legum
rei alicuius medendae aut temporis causa iussarum;
sicut est de numero pecoris et de modo agri prae-
46 finito. In quibus rebus quod prohibitum est fieri

---

[1] infitiari, ω; infitias iri, *Hosius*.

---

[1] That is, the Licinian Law of C. Licinius Stolo.

they had actually not been such. Furthermore, he
says that it cannot be denied that to wish to have
more than five hundred acres, which was forbidden
by Stolo's[1] bill, is not exactly the same thing as to
wish to make an unjust and unrighteous war
upon the Roman people ; also that it could not be
denied that rewards and punishments belong to
different categories. " For services," he says, " that
are promised should be awaited, and not rewarded
until they are performed ; but in the case of threaten-
ing injuries, it is fair to guard against them rather
than wait for them. For it is an admission of the
greatest folly," he declares, " not to go to meet
wickedness that is planned, but to await and expect
it, and then, when it has been committed and
accomplished, at last to inflict punishment, when
what is done cannot be undone."

These are the criticisms which Tiro passed upon
Cato, not altogether pointless or wholly unreason-
able ; but as a matter of fact, Cato did not leave this
ἐπαγωγή bare, isolated and unsupported, but he
propped it up in various ways and clothed it with
many other arguments. Furthermore, since he had
an eye as much to the interests of the State as to
those of the Rhodians, he regarded nothing that he
said or did in that matter as discreditable, provided
he strove by every kind of argument to save our
allies. And first of all, he very cleverly sought to
find actions which are prohibited, not by natural or
by international law, but by statutes passed to
remedy some evil or meet an emergency ; such for
example as the one which limited the number of
cattle or the amount of land. In such cases that
which is forbidden cannot lawfully be done ; but to

quidem per leges non licet; velle id tamen facere,
47 si liceat, inhonestum non est. Atque eas res contulit sensim miscuitque cum eo, quod neque facere
neque velle per sese honestum est; tum deinde, ne
disparilitas conlationis evidens fieret, pluribus id
propugnaculis defensat, neque tenues istas et enu-
cleatas voluntatum in rebus illicitis reprehensiones,
qualia in philosophorum otio disputantur, magni
facit, sed id solum[1] summa ope nititur, ut causa
Rodiensium, quorum amicitiam retineri ex republica
fuit, aut aequa iudicaretur aut quidem certe igno-
scenda. Atque interim neque fecisse Rodienses
bellum neque facere voluisse dicit, interim autem
facta sola censenda dicit atque in iudicium vocanda,
sed voluntates nudas inanesque neque legibus neque
poenis fieri obnoxias; interdum tamen, quasi deli-
quisse eos concedat, ignosci postulat et ignoscentias
utiles esse rebus humanis docet ac, nisi ignoscant,
metus in republica rerum novarum movet; sed
enim contra, si ignoscatur, conservatum iri ostendit
populi Romani magnitudinem.
48 Superbiae quoque crimen, quod tunc praeter
cetera in senatu Rodiensibus obiectum erat, mirifica
et prope divina responsionis figura elusit et eluit.
49 Verba adeo ipsa ponemus Catonis, quoniam Tiro
50 ea praetermisit: "Rodiensis superbos esse aiunt,
id obiectantes quod mihi et liberis meis minime
dici velim. Sint sane superbi. Quid id ad nos

---

[1] solum ex, *MSS.* ; ex *omitted by Carrio.*

---

[1] v. 7, Jordan.

wish to do it, if it should be allowed, is not dishonourable. And then he gradually compared and
connected such actions as these with that which in
itself it is neither lawful to do nor to wish to do.
Then finally, in order that the impropriety of the
comparison may not become evident, he defends it
by numerous bulwarks, not laying great stress on
those trivial and ideal censures of unlawful desires,
such as form the arguments of philosophers in their
leisure moments, but striving with might and main
for one single end, namely, that the cause of the
Rhodians, whose friendship it was to the interests of
the commonwealth to retain, should be shown either
to be just, or in any event, at least pardonable.
Accordingly, he now affirms that the Rhodians did
not make war and did not desire to do so; but again
he declares that only acts should be considered and
judged, and that mere empty wishes are liable
neither to laws nor punishment; sometimes, however, as if admitting their guilt, he asks that they
be pardoned and shows that forgiveness is expedient
in human relations, arousing fear of popular out-
breaks, if pardon is not granted, and on the other
hand showing that if they forgive, the greatness of
the Roman people will be maintained.

The charge of arrogance too, which in particular
was brought against the Rhodians in the senate at
that time, he evaded and eluded by a brilliant and
all but inspired mode of reply. I shall give Cato's
very words,[1] since Tiro has passed them by: "They
say that the Rhodians are arrogant, bringing a
charge against them which I should on no account
wish to have brought against me and my children.
Suppose they are arrogant. What is that to us?

29

attinet? Idne irascimini, si quis superbior est quam
51 nos?" Nihil prorsus hac compellatione dici potest
neque gravius neque munitius adversus homines
superbissimos facta, qui superbiam in sese amarent,
in aliis reprehenderent.

52 Praeterea animadvertere est, in tota ista Catonis
oratione omnia disciplinarum rhetoricarum arma
atque subsidia mota esse; sed non proinde ut in
decursibus ludicris aut simulacris proeliorum volup-
tariis fieri videmus. Non enim, inquam, distincte
nimis atque compte atque modulate res acta est,
sed quasi in ancipiti certamine, cum sparsa acies
est, multis locis Marte vario pugnatur, sic in ista
tum causa Cato, cum superbia illa Rodiensium
famosissima multorum odio atque invidia flagraret,
omnibus promisce tuendi atque propugnandi modis
usus est, et nunc ut optime meritos commendat, nunc
tamquam si innocentes purgat, nunc [1] ne bona divi-
tiaeque eorum expetantur obiurgat, nunc [2] quasi sit
erratum deprecatur, nunc ut necessarios reipublicae
ostentat, nunc clementiae, nunc mansuetudinis
maiorum, nunc utilitatis publicae commonefacit.
53 Eaque omnia distinctius numerosiusque fortassean
dici potuerint, fortius atque vividius potuisse dici
54 non videntur. Inique igitur Tiro Tullius, quod ex
omnibus facultatibus tam opulentae orationis, aptis
inter sese et cohaerentibus, parvum quippiam nu-
dumque sumpsit, quod obtrectaret tamquam non

---

[1] nunc, *added by Hertz*; neve, *Damsté*; purget, ne,
Mommsen.
[2] nunc et, *MSS.*; et *omitted by Hertz.*

Are you to be angry merely because someone is more arrogant than we are ? " Absolutely nothing could be said with greater force or weight than this apostrophe against men proud of their deeds, loving pride in themselves, but condemning it in others.

It is further to be observed that throughout that speech of Cato's recourse is had to every weapon and device of the art rhetorical ; but we are not conscious of their use, as we are in mock combats or in battles feigned for the sake of entertainment. For the case was not pleaded, I say, with an excess of refinement, elegance and observance of rule, but just as in a doubtful battle, when the troops are scattered, the contest rages in many parts of the field with uncertain outcome, so in that case at that time, when the notorious arrogance of the Rhodians had aroused the hatred and hostility of many men, Cato used every method of protection and defence without discrimination, at one time commending the Rhodians as of the highest merit, again exculpating them and declaring them blameless, yet again demanding that their property and riches should not be coveted, now asking for their pardon as if they were in the wrong, now pointing out their friendship to the commonwealth, appealing now to clemency, now to the mercy shown by our fore-fathers, now to the public interest. All this might perhaps have been said in a more orderly and euphonic style, yet I do not believe that it could have been said with greater vigour and vividness. It was therefore unfair of Tullius Tiro to single out from all the qualities of so rich a speech, apt in their connection with one another, a small and bare part to criticize, by asserting that it was not worthy

dignum M. Catone fuerit, quod delictorum non
perpetratorum voluntates non censuerit poeniendas.
55   Commodius autem rectiusque de his meis verbis,
quibus Tullio Tironi respondimus, existimabit iudi-
ciumque faciet, qui et orationem ipsam totam Catonis acceperit in manus et epistulam Tironis ad
Axium scriptam requirere et legere curaverit. Ita
enim nos sincerius exploratiusque vel corrigere
poterit vel probare.

IV

Cuiusmodi servos et quam ob causam Caelius Sabinus, iuris
civilis auctor, pilleatos venundari solitos scripserit ; et
quae mancipia sub corona more maiorum venierint ; atque
id ipsum " sub corona" quid sit.

1   PILLEATOS servos venum solitos ire, quorum nomine
venditor nihil praestaret, Caelius Sabinus iurisperitus
2 scriptum reliquit. Cuius rei causam esse ait, quod
eiusmodi condicionis mancipia insignia esse in ven-
dundo deberent, ut emptores errare et capi non
possent, neque lex vendundi opperienda esset, sed
oculis iam praeciperent quodnam esset mancipiorum
3 genus ; " Sicuti," inquit, "antiquitus mancipia iure
belli capta coronis induta veniebant et idcirco dicebantur 'sub corona' venire. Namque ut ea corona
signum erat captivorum venalium, ita pilleus impo-
situs demonstrabat eiusmodi servos venundari, quorum nomine emptori venditor nihil praestaret."

---

[1] Fr. 2, Huschke ; *De Manc.* fr. 19, Bremer.

of Marcus Cato to maintain that the mere desire for delinquencies that were not actually committed did not merit punishment.

But one will form a juster and more candid opinion of these words of mine, spoken in reply to Tullius Tiro, and judge accordingly, if one will take in hand Cato's own speech in its entirety, and will also take the trouble to look up and read the letter of Tiro to Axius. For then he will be able either to correct or confirm what I have said more truthfully and after fuller examination.

IV

What sort of slaves Caelius Sabinus, the writer on civil law, said were commonly sold with caps on their heads, and why ; and what chattels were sold under a crown in the days of our forefathers ; and the meaning of that same expression " under a crown."

CAELIUS SABINUS, the jurist, has written[1] that it was usual, when selling slaves, to put caps on those for whom the seller assumed no responsibility. He says that the reason for that custom was, that the law required that slaves of that kind be marked when offered for sale, in order that buyers might not err and be deceived ; that it might not be necessary to wait for the bill of sale, but might be obvious at once what kind of slaves they were. " Just so," he says, " in ancient times slaves taken by right of conquest were sold wearing garlands, and hence were said to be sold 'under a crown.' For as the crown was a sign that those who were being sold were captives, so a cap upon the head indicated that slaves were being sold for whom the seller gave the buyer no guarantee."

4   Est autem alia rationis opinio cur dici solitum sit
captivos "sub corona" venundari, quod milites cu-
stodiae causa captivorum venalium greges circum-
starent eaque circumstatio militum "corona" appel-
5 lata sit.   Sed id magis verum esse quod supra dixi,
M. Cato in libro quem composuit *De Re Militari*
docet.

Verba sunt haec Catonis: "Ut populus sua opera
potius ob rem bene gestam coronatus supplicatum
eat quam re male gesta coronatus veniat."

V

Historia de Polo histrione memoratu digna.

1   Histrio in terra Graecia fuit fama celebri, qui
gestus et vocis claritudine et venustate ceteris anti-
2 stabat; nomen fuisse aiunt Polum, tragoedias poet-
3 arum nobilium scite atque asseverate actitavit.   Is
4 Polus unice amatum filium morte amisit.   Eum
luctum quoniam satis visus est eluxisse, rediit ad
quaestum artis.
5   In eo tempore Athenis *Electram* Sophoclis acturus,
gestare urnam quasi cum Oresti ossibus debebat.
6 Ita compositum fabulae argumentum est, ut veluti

---

[1] Fr. 2, Jordan, p. 80.
[2] On this famous tragic actor see O'Connor, *Chapters in the History of Actors and Acting in Ancient Greece* (Princeton

34

There is, however, another explanation of the reason for the common saying that captives were sold "under a crown"; namely, because a guard of soldiers stood around the bands of prisoners that were offered for sale, and such a ring of soldiers was called *corona*. But that the reason which I first gave is the more probable one is made clear by Marcus Cato in the book which he wrote *On Military Science*.

Cato's words are as follows:[1] "That the people may rather crown themselves and go to offer thanks for success gained through their own efforts than be crowned and sold because of ill-success."

V

A noteworthy story about the actor Polus.[2]

THERE was in the land of Greece an actor of wide reputation, who excelled all others in his clear delivery and graceful action. They say that his name was Polus, and he often acted the tragedies of famous poets with intelligence and dignity. This Polus lost by death a son whom he dearly loved. After he felt that he had indulged his grief sufficiently, he returned to the practice of his profession.

At that time he was to act the *Electra* of Sophocles at Athens, and it was his part to carry an urn which was supposed to contain the ashes of Orestes. The plot of the play requires that Electra, who is repre-

dissertation, 1908), pp. 128 ff. He flourished toward the end of the fourth century B.C.

fratris reliquias ferens Electra comploret commi-
7 sereaturque interitum eius existimatum. Igitur
Polus, lugubri habitu Electrae indutus, ossa atque
urnam e sepulcro tulit filii et, quasi Oresti amplexus,
opplevit omnia non simulacris neque imitamentis,
8 sed luctu atque lamentis veris et spirantibus. Itaque
cum agi fabula videretur, dolor actus est.

VI

Quid de quorundam sensuum naturali defectione Aristoteles
scripserit.

1   Ex quinque his sensibus quos animantibus natura
tribuit, visu, auditu, gustu, tactu, odoratu, quas
Graeci αἰσθήσεις appellant, quaedam animalium
alia alio carent et aut caeca natura gignuntur aut
2 inodora inauritave. Nullum autem ullum gigni animal Aristoteles dicit, quod aut gustus sensu careat,
aut tactus.
3   Verba ex libro eius, quem Περὶ Μνήμης composuit, haec sunt : Τὴν δὲ ἁφὴν καὶ τὴν γεῦσιν πάντα
ἔχει, πλὴν εἴ τι τῶν ζώων ἀτελές.

sented as carrying her brother's remains, should lament and bewail the fate that she believed had overtaken him. Accordingly Polus, clad in the mourning garb of Electra, took from the tomb the ashes and urn of his son, embraced them as if they were those of Orestes, and filled the whole place, not with the appearance and imitation of sorrow, but with genuine grief and unfeigned lamentation. Therefore, while it seemed that a play was being acted, it was in fact real grief that was enacted.

VI

What Aristotle wrote of the congenital absence of some of the senses.

NATURE has given five senses to living beings; sight, hearing, taste, touch and smell, called by the Greeks αἰσθήσεις. Of these some animals lack one and some another, being born into the world blind, or without the sense of smell or hearing. But Aristotle asserts that no animal is born without the sense of taste or of touch.

His own words, from the book which he wrote *On Memory*, are as follows:[1] "Except for some imperfect animals, all have taste or touch."

[1] Περὶ Ὕπνου or *On Sleep*, 2. Gellius is mistaken in his title.

VII

An "affatim," quasi "admodum," prima acuta pronuntiandum sit; et quaedam itidem non incuriose tractata super
aliarum vocum accentibus.

1 ANNIANUS poeta praeter ingenii amoenitates litterarum quoque veterum et rationum in litteris oppido
quam peritus fuit et sermocinabatur mira quadam et
2 scita suavitate. Is "affatim," ut "admodum," prima
acuta, non media, pronuntiabat atque ita veteres
3 locutos censebat. Itaque se audiente Probum grammaticum hos versus in Plauti *Cistellaria* legisse dicit:

Pótine tu homo fácinus facere strénuum?—Aliorum áffatim est.
Quí faciant; sane égo me nolo fórtem perhiberí
virum,

4 causamque esse huic accentui dicebat, quod "affatim" non essent duae partes orationis, sed utraque
pars in unam vocem coaluisset, sicuti in eo quoque
quod "exadversum" dicimus secundam syllabam
debere acui existimabat, quoniam una, non duae
essent partes orationis; atque ita oportere apud
Terentium legi dicebat in his versibus:

In quo haéc discebat lúdo, exadversúm loco [1]
Tostrína erat quaedam.

[1] ilico *and* ei loco, *codd. Ter.*

---

[1] One of the few poets of Hadrian's time. He wrote
Falisca, on rural life, and Fescennini. Like other poets of
his time, he was fond of unusual metres; see *Gr. Lat.* vi.
122, 12, K.
[2] This seems to mean no more than "accent"; see note 2,
p. 9, above.

VII

Whether *affatim*, like *admodum*, should be pronounced with an acute accent on the first syllable : with some pains-taking observations on the accents of other words.

THE poet Annianus,[1] in addition to his charming personality, was highly skilled in ancient literature and literary criticism, and conversed with remarkable grace and learning. He pronounced *affatim*, as he did *admodum*, with an acute accent [2] on the first, and not on the medial, syllable ; and he believed that the ancients so pronounced the word. He adds that in his hearing the grammarian Probus thus read the following lines of the *Cistellaria* of Plautus : [3]

Canst do a valiant deed ?—Enough (*áffatim*) there be
Who can. I've no desire to be called brave,

and he said that the reason for that accent was that *affatim* was not two parts of speech, but was made up of two parts that had united to form a single word ; just as also in the word which we call *exadversum* he thought that the second syllable should have the acute accent, because the word was one part of speech, and not two. Accordingly, he maintained that the two following verses of Terence [4] ought to be read thus :

Over against (*exádversum*) the school to which she went
A barber had his shop.

[3] 231.   [4] *Phormio*, 88.

5 Addebat etiam quod "ad" praeverbium tum ferme
acueretur, cum significaret ἐπίτασιν, quam "intentionem" nos dicimus, sicut "adfabre" et "admodum" et "adprobe" dicuntur.

6   Cetera quidem satis commode Annianus. Sed
si hanc particulam semper, cum intentionem signi-
7 ficaret, acui putavit, non id perpetuum videtur; nam
et "adpotus" cum dicimus et "adprimus" et "adprime," intentio in his omnibus demonstratur, neque
tamen "ad" particula satis commode accentu acuto
8 pronuntiatur.   "Adprobus" tamen, quod significat
"valde probus," non infitias eo quin prima syllaba
9 acui debeat. Caecilius in comoedia quae inscribitur
Triumphus vocabulo isto utitur :

Hiérocles hospes ést mi adulescens ádprobus.

10   Num igitur in istis vocibus quas non acui diximus,
ea causa est, quod syllaba insequitur natura longior,
quae non ferme patitur acui priorem in vocabulis
11 syllabarum plurium quam duarum?   "Adprimum"
autem "longe primum" L. Livius in *Odyssia* dicit in
hoc versu :

Ibidemque vir summus adprimus Patroclus.

12 Idem Livius in *Odyssia* "praemodum" dicit, quasi
"admodum"; "parcentes," inquit, "praemodum,"
quod significat "supra modum," dictumque est quasi
"praeter modum"; in quo scilicet prima syllaba
acui debebit.

---

[1] 228, Ribbeck.[3]

[2] Gellius is perhaps thinking of such exceptions as *éxinde*
and *súbinde*, in which however the penult is not long by
nature, but by position.

[3] Fr. 11, Bährens.   [4] Fr. 29, Bährens.

He added besides that the preposition *ad* was commonly accented when it indicated πίτασις, or as we say, "emphasis," as in *ádfabre, ádmodum,* and *ádprobe.*

In all else, indeed, Annianus spoke aptly enough. But if he supposed that this particle was always accented when it denoted emphasis, that rule is obviously not without exceptions; for when we say *adpotus, adprimus,* and *adprime,* emphasis is evident in all those words, yet it is not at all proper to pronounce the particle *ad* with the acute accent. I must admit, however, that *adprobus,* which means "highly approved," ought to be accented on the first syllable. Caecilius uses that word in his comedy entitled *The Triumph* :[1]

Hierocles, my friend, is a most worthy (*ádprobus*) youth.

In those words, then, which we say do not have the acute accent, is not this the reason—that the following syllable is longer by nature, and a long penult does not as a rule[2] permit the accenting of the preceding syllable in words of more than two syllables? But Lucius Livius in his *Odyssey* uses *ádprimus* in the sense of "by far the first" in the following line :[3]

And then the mighty hero, foremost of all (*ádprimus*), Patroclus.

Livius in his *Odyssey* too pronounces *praemodum* like *admodum ;* he says[4] *parcentes praemodum,* which means "beyond measure merciful," and *praemodum* is equivalent to *praeter modum.* And in this word, of course, the first syllable will have to have the acute accent.

VIII

Res ultra fidem tradita super amatore delphino et puero
amato.

1 DELPHINOS venerios esse et amasios non modo
historiae veteres, sed recentes quoque memoriae
2 declarant. Nam et sub Caesare Augusto[1] in Puteo-
lano mari, ut Apion scriptum reliquit, et aliquot
saeculis ante apud Naupactum, ut Theophrastus
tradidit, amatores flagrantissimi delphinorum cogniti
3 compertique sunt. Neque hi amaverunt quod sunt
ipsi genus, sed pueros forma liberali in naviculis
forte aut in vadis litorum conspectos miris et humanis modis arserunt.
4 Verba subscripsi 'Aπίωνos, eruditi viri, ex *Aegyp-
tiacorum* libro quinto, quibus delphini amantis et
pueri non abhorrentis consuetudines, lusus, gesta-
tiones, aurigationes refert eaque omnia sese ipsum
5 multosque alios vidisse dicit: Αὐτὸς δ' αὖ εἶδον περὶ
Δικαιαρχίας παιδός[2]—Ὑάκινθος ἐκαλεῖτο—πόθοις ἐπτοη-
μένον δελφῖνα. προσσαίνει τὴν φωνὴν αὐτοῦ τὴν ψυχὴν
πτερούμενος ἐντὸς τάς τε ἀκάνθας ὑποστέλλων, μή τι τοῦ
ποθουμένου χρωτὸς ἀμύξῃ φειδόμενος, ἱππηδόν τε[3] περι-
βεβηκότα μέχρι διακοσίων ἀνῆγε σταδίων. ἐξεχεῖτο ἡ
Ῥώμη καὶ πᾶσα Ἰταλία τῆς Ἀφροδίτης[4] ξυνορῶντες ἡνιο-
6 χούμενον ἰχθύν. Ad hoc adicit rem non[5] minus mi-
randam. " Postea," inquit, " idem ille puer δελφι-

---

[1] Caesare Augusto, *Hosius*; Cesaribus (Cesaris, P) ω;
Caesaris Augusti imperio, *Hertz*.
[2] παιδός *added by Scioppius*.   [3] τε *added by Hertz.*
[4] ὑπ' Ἀφροδίτης, *Damsté.*   [5] non *added in* ς.

---

[1] *F.H.G.* iii. 510.
[2] The early Greek name of Puteoli.

VIII

An incredible story about a dolphin which loved a boy.

THAT dolphins are affectionate and amorous is shown, not only by ancient history, but also by tales of recent date. For in the sea of Puteoli, during the reign of Augustus Caesar, as Apion has written, and some centuries before at Naupactus, as Theophrastus tells us, dolphins are positively known to have been ardently in love. And they did not love those of their own kind, but had an extraordinary passion, like that of human beings, for boys of handsome figure, whom they chanced to have seen in boats or in the shoal waters near the shore.

I have appended the words of that learned man Apion, from the fifth book of his *Egyptian History*, in which he tells of an amorous dolphin and a boy who did not reject its advances, of their intimacy and play with each other, the dolphin carrying the boy and the boy bestriding the fish; and Apion declares that of all this he himself and many others were eye-witnesses. "Now I myself," he writes,[1] "near Dicaearchia[2] saw a dolphin that fell in love with a boy called Hyacinthus. For the fish with passionate eagerness came at his call, and drawing in his fins, to avoid wounding the delicate skin of the object of his affection, carried him as if mounted upon a horse for a distance of two hundred stadia. Rome and all Italy turned out to see a fish that was under the sway of Aphrodite." To this he adds a detail that is no less wonderful. "Afterwards," he says, "that same boy who was beloved by the

νερώμενος morbo adfectus obit suum diem. At ille
7 amans, ubi saepe ad litus solitum adnavit et puer,
qui in primo vado adventum eius opperiri consue-
verat, nusquam fuit, desiderio tabuit exanimatusque
est et in litore iacens inventus ab his qui rem
cognoverant, in sui pueri sepulcro humatus est."

IX

"Peposci" et "memordi," "pepugi" et "spepondi" et
"cecurri" plerosque veterum dixisse, non, uti postea receptum est dicere, per *o* aut per *u* litteram in prima
syllaba positam, atque id eos Graecae rationis exemplo
dixisse ; praeterea notatum quod viri non indocti neque
ignobiles a verbo "descendo" non "descendi," sed "descendidi" dixerunt.

1   " Poposci," "momordi," "pupugi," "cucurri" probabiliter dici videtur atque ita nunc omnes ferme
2 doctiores hisce verbis utuntur. Sed Q. Ennius in
Saturis "memorderit" dixit per *e* litteram, non
"momorderit :"

Meum (inquit) nón est, ac si mé canis memórderit.

3 Item Laberius in *Gallis* :

De íntegro património meo céntum milia núm-
mum
Memórdi.

4 Item idem Laberius in *Coloratore* :

Itáque leni pruná percoctus símul sub dentes
múlieris
Vení, bis, ter memórdit.

---

[1] With this story cf. Pliny, *Epist.* ix. 33.

dolphin fell sick and died. But the lover, when he had often come to the familiar shore, and the boy, who used to await his coming at the edge of the shoal water, was nowhere to be seen, pined away from longing and died. He was found lying on the shore by those who knew the story and was buried in the same tomb with his favourite." [1]

IX

That many early writers used *peposci, memordi pepugi, spepondi* and *cecurri,* and not, as was afterwards customary, forms with *o* or *u* in the first syllable, and that in so doing said that they followed Greek usage; that it has further been observed that men who were neither unlearned nor obscure made from the verb *descendo,* not *descendi,* but *descendidi.*

Poposci, momordi, pupugi and *cucurri* seem to be the approved forms, and to-day they are used by almost all better-educated men. But Quintus Ennius in his *Satires* wrote *memorderit* with an *e,* and not *momorderit,* as follows : [2]

'Tis not my way, as if a dog had bit me
  (*memorderit*).

So too Laberius in the *Galli* : [3]

              Now from my whole estate
A hundred thousand have I bitten off (*memordi*).

The same Laberius too in his *Colorator* : [4]

And when, o'er slow fire cooked, I came beneath
  her teeth,
Twice, thrice she bit (*memordit*).

[2] 63, Vahlen[2].   [3] 49, Ribbeck[3].
[4] 27, Ribbeck[3].

45

5 Item P. Nigidius *De Animalibus* libro II.: "Ut serpens si memordit, gallina diligitur et opponitur."

6 Item Plautus in *Aulularia*:

> Ut ádmemordit hóminem.

7 Sed idem Plautus in *Trigeminis* neque "praememordisse" neque "praemomordisse" dicit, sed "praemorsisse":

> Nísi fugissem (inquit) in[1] médium, credo, praémorsisset.

8 Item Atta in *Conciliatrice*:

> Ursum sé memordisse aútumat.

9 "Peposci" quoque, non "poposci," Valerius Antias libro *Annalium* XLV. scriptum reliquit: "Denique Licinius tribunus plebi perduellionis ei diem dixit et comitiis diem a M. Marcio praetore peposcit."

10 "Pepugero" aeque Atta in *Aedilicia* dicit:

> Sed sí pepugero, métuet.

11 Aelium quoque Tuberonem libro *Ad C. Oppium* scripto "occecurrit" dixisse, Probus adnotavit et haec eius verba apposuit: "Si generalis species
12 occecurrerit." Idem Probus Valerium Antiatem libro *Historiarum* XXII. "speponderant" scripsisse annotavit verbaque eius haec posuit: "Tiberius

---

[1] inquit in, *Skutsch*; in, *Winter*; inquit, *MSS.*

---

[1] Fr. 112, Swoboda. [2] Fr. 2, p. 95, Götz.
[3] 120, Götz. [4] 6, Ribbeck[3].
[5] Fr. 60, Peter[2].
[6] The trial was held before the *comitia centuriata*.

Also Publius Nigidius in his second book *On Animals*:[1] "As when a serpent bites (*memordit*) one, a hen is split and placed upon the wound." Likewise Plautus in the *Aulularia*:[2]

> How he the man did fleece (*admemordit*).

But Plautus again, in the *Trigemini*, said neither *praememordisse* nor *praemomordisse*, but *praemorsisse*, in the following line:[3]

> Had I not fled into your midst,
> Methinks he'd bitten me (*praemorsisset*).

Atta too in the *Conciliatrix* says:[4]

> A bear, he says, bit him (*memordisse*).

Valerius Antias too, in the forty-fifth book of his *Annals*, has left on record *peposci*, not *poposci*[5] in this passage: "Finally Licinius, tribune of the commons, charged him with high treason and asked (*peposcit*) from the praetor Marcus Marcius a day for holding the comitia."[6]

In the same way Atta in the *Aedilicia* says:[7]

> But he will be afraid, if I do prick him (*pepugero*).

Probus has noted that Aelius Tubero also, in his work dedicated to Gaius Oppius, wrote *occecurrit*, and he has quoted him as follows:[8] "If the general form should present itself (*occecurrerit*)." Probus also observed that Valerius Antias in the twenty-second book of his *Histories* wrote *speponderant*, and he quotes his words as follows:[9] "Tiberius Gracchus,

---

[7] Fr. 2, Ribbeck³.
[8] Fr. 2, Huschke; I. p. 367, Bremer.
[9] Fr. 57, Peter².

Gracchus, qui quaestor C. Mancino in Hispania fuerat, et ceteri qui pacem spepouderant."

13   Ratio autem istarum dictionum haec esse videri potest: quoniam Graeci in quadam specie praeteriti temporis, quod παρακείμενον appellant, secundam verbi litteram in *e* plerumque vertunt, ut γράφω γέγραφα, ποιῶ πεποίηκα, λαλῶ λελάληκα, κρατῶ κεκράτηκα, λούω λέλουκα, sic igitur mordeo "memordi,"
14 posco "peposci," tendo "tetendi," tango "tetigi," pungo "pepugi," curro "cecurri," tollo "tetuli,"
15 spondeo "spepondi" facit. Sic M. Tullius et C. Caesar "mordeo memordi," "pungo pepugi," "spondeo spepondi" dixerunt.

    Praeterea inveni, a verbo "scindo" simili ratione
16 non "sciderat," sed "sciciderat," dictum esse. L. Accius in *Sotadicorum* libro I. "sciciderat" dicit. Verba haec sunt:

    Num érgo aquila ita, ut hí praedicánt, sciciderat péctus?

17 Ennius quoque in *Melanippa* :

        cum saxum scíciderit.[1]

*   *   *   *   *

Valerius Antias in libro *Historiarum* LXXV. verba haec scripsit: ' Deinde funere locato ad forum de-
18 scendidit." Laberius quoque in *Catulario* ita scripsit:

    égo mirabar, quómodo mammaé mihi
    Déscendiderant [2] * * *

---

[1] in . . . sciciderit *from Priscian, i. 517. 10 K. by J. F. Gronov.*
[2] descendiderant *added in* σ.

---

    [1] Fr. 14, p. 1060, Orelli[2].   [2] ii. p. 158, Dinter.
        [3] Fr. i. 2, Müller; 8, Bährens.

who had been quaestor to Gaius Mancinus in Spain, and the others who had guaranteed (*speponderant*) peace."

Now the explanation of these forms might seem to be this: since the Greeks in one form of the past tense, which they call παρακείμενον, or "perfect," commonly change the second letter of the verb to *e*, as γράφω γέγραφα, ποιῶ πεποίηκα, λαλῶ λελάληκα, κρατῶ κεκράτηκα, λούω λέλουκα, so accordingly *mordeo* makes *memordi, posco peposci, tendo tetendi, tango tetigi, pungo pepugi, curro cecurri, tollo tetuli,* and *spondeo spepondi.* Thus Marcus Tullius[1] and Gaius Caesar[2] used *mordeo memordi, pungo pepugi, spondeo spepondi.*

I find besides that from the verb *scindo* in the same way was made, not *sciderat,* but *sciciderat.* Lucius Accius in the first book of his *Sotadici* writes *sciciderat.* These are his words:[3]

And had the eagle then, as these declare,
His bosom rent (*sciciderat*)?

Ennius too in his *Melanippa* says:[4]

When the rock he shall split (*sciciderit*).

*   *   *   *   *5

Valerius Antias in the seventy-fifth book of his *Histories* wrote these words:[6] "Then, having arranged for the funeral, he went down (*descendidit*) to the Forum." Laberius too in the *Catularius* wrote thus:[7]

I wondered how my breasts had fallen low (*descendiderant*).

[4] 252, Ribbeck[3].   [5] There is evidently a lacuna here.
[6] Fr. 62, Peter[2].   [7] 19, Ribbeck[3].

X

Ut[1] "ususcapio" copulate recto vocabuli casu dicitur, ita "pignoriscapio" coniuncte eadem vocabuli forma dictum esse.

1 Ut haec "ususcapio" dicitur copulato vocabulo, *a* littera in eo tractim pronuntiata, ita "pignoriscapio"
2 iuncte et producte dicebatur. Verba Catonis sunt ex primo *Epistolicarum Quaestionum* : "Pignoriscapio ob aes militare, quod aes a tribuno aerario miles
3 accipere debebat, vocabulum seorsum fit." Per quod satis dilucet, hanc "capionem" posse dici, quasi hanc "captionem," et in "usu" et in "pignore."

XI

Neque "levitatem" neque "nequitiam" ea significatione esse qua in vulgi sermonibus dicuntur.

1 "Levitatem" plerumque nunc pro inconstantia et mutabilitate dici audio et "nequitiam" pro sollertia
2 astutiaque. Sed veterum hominum qui proprie atque integre locuti sunt "leves" dixerunt, quos vulgo nunc viles et nullo honore dignos dicimus, et "levitatem" appellaverunt proinde quasi "vilitatem" et

---

[1] Ut *added by J. F. Gronov.*

---

[1] p. cviii., Jordan. It should be Varro rather than Cato.
[2] That is, pay in arrears.

X

As *ususcapio* is treated as a compound noun in the nominative case, so *pignoriscapio* is taken together as one word in the same case.

As *ususcapio* is treated as a compound word, in which the letter *a* is pronounced long, just so *pignoriscapio* was pronounced as one word with a long *a*. These are the words of Cato in the first book of his *Epistolary Questions*:[1] "*Pignoriscapio*, resorted to because of military pay[2] which a soldier ought to receive from the public paymaster, is a word by itself."[3] From this it is perfectly clear that one may say *capio* as if it were *captio*, in connection with both *usus* and *pignus*.

XI

That neither *levitas* nor *nequitia* has the meaning that is given to those words in ordinary conversation.

I observe that *levitas* is now generally used to denote inconsistency and changeableness, and *nequitia*, in the sense of craftiness and cunning. But those of the men of early days who spoke properly and purely applied the term *leves* to those whom we now commonly call worthless and meriting no esteem. That is, they used *levitas* with precisely the force of *vilitas*, and applied the term *nequam* to a man of no

[3] *Ususcapio* or *usucapio* is a "taking," or claim to possession, by right of actual tenure (*usus*); *pignoriscapio* is a seizure of goods. On the latter see Mommsen, *Staatsrecht*, i.³, p. 160, and cf. Suet. *Jul.* xvii. 2. The *a* is not long in either word, but has the accent, which may be what Gellius means.

"nequam" hominem nihili rei neque frugis bonae,
quod genus Graeci fere ἄσωτον vel ἀκόλαστον dicunt.

3 Qui exempla horum verborum requirit, ne in l bris
nimium remotis quaerat, inveniet ea in M. Tullii

4 secunda *Antonianarum*. Nam cum genus quoddam
sordidissimum vitae atque victus M. Antoni demon-
straturus esset, quod in caupona delitisceret, quod ad
vesperum perpotaret, quod ore involuto iter faceret
ne cognosceretur, haec aliaque eiusdemmodi cum in
eum dicturus esset: " Videte," inquit, " hominis levitatem," tamquam prorsus ista dedecora hoc con-

5 vicio[1] in homine notarentur. At postea, cum in
eundem Antonium probra quaedam alia ludibriosa
et turpia ingessisset, ad extremum hoc addidit:
" O hominem nequam! nihil enim magis proprie
possum dicere."

6 Sed ex eo loco M. Tullii verba compluscula libuit
ponere: " At videte levitatem hominis! Cum hora
diei decima fere ad Saxa Rubra venisset, delituit
in quadam cauponula atque ibi se occultans perpo-
tavit ad vesperum; inde cisio celeriter ad urbem
advectus, domum venit ore[2] involuto. Ianitor
rogat:[3] ' Quis tu?' ' A Marco tabellarius.' Con-
festim ad eam cuius causa venerat deducitur eique
epistulam tradit. Quam illa cum legeret flens—
erat enim scripta amatorie, caput autem litterarum

---

[1] vicio, ω: *corr. by J. F. Gronov, retained by Petschenig.*
[2] cap te involuto, *Cic.*
[3] rogat *omitted by Cic.*

Phil. ii. 77.
About four o'clock in the afternoon.
[3] His wife, Fulvia.

importance nor worth, the sort of man that the Greeks usually call ἄσωτος (beyond recovery) or ἀκόλαστος (incorrigible).

One who desires examples of these words need not resort to books that are very inaccessible, but he will find them in Marcus Tullius' second *Oration against Antony*. For when Cicero wished to indicate a kind of extreme sordidness in the life and conduct of Marcus Antonius, that he lurked in a tavern, that he drank deep until evening, and that he travelled with his face covered, so as not to be recognized—when he wished to give expression to these and similar charges against him, he said :[1] "Just see the worthlessness (*levitatem*) of the man," as if by that reproach he branded him with all those various marks of infamy which I have mentioned. But afterwards, when he had heaped upon the same Antony sundry other scornful and opprobrious charges, he finally added "O man of no worth (*nequam*)! for there is no term that I can use more fittingly."

But from that passage of Marcus Tullius I should like to add a somewhat longer extract : "Just see the worthlessness of the man ! Having come to Saxa Rubra at about the tenth hour of the day,[2] he lurked in a certain low tavern, and shutting himself up there drank deep until evening. Then riding swiftly to the city in a cab, he came to his home with covered face. The doorkeeper asked : 'Who are you?' 'The bearer of a letter from Marcus,' was the reply. He was at once taken to the lady on whose account he had come,[3] and handed her the letter. While she read it with tears—for it was written in amorous terms and its

hoc erat : sibi cum illa mima posthac nihil futurum,
omnem se amorem abiecisse illim [1] atque in hanc
transfudisse— cum mulier fleret uberius, homo
misericors ferre non potuit : caput aperuit, in collum
invasit.   O hominem nequam !—nihil enim magis
proprie possum dicere ; ergo ut te catamitum nec
opinato cum ostendisses, praeter spem mulier aspice-
ret, idcirco urbem terrore nocturno, Italiam multorum dierum metu perturbasti ? "

7   Consimiliter Q. quoque Claudius in primo *Annalium*
"nequitiam " appellavit luxum vitae prodigum effu-
sumque in hisce verbis : "Persuadent i cuidam
adulescenti Lucano, qui adprime summo genere
gnatus erat, sed luxuria et nequitia pecuniam mag-
8 nam consumpserat."   M. Varro in libris *De Lingua
Latina*, " Ut ex ' non ' et ex ' volo,' " inquit, " ' nolo,'
sic ex ' ne ' et 'quicquam,' media syllaba extrita,
9 compositum est ' nequam.' "   P. Africanus *Pro se
contra Tiberium Asellum* de multa ad populum :
" Omnia mala, probra, flagitia, quae homines faciunt,
in duabus rebus sunt, malitia atque nequitia.   Utrum
defendis, malitiam an nequitiam an utrumque simul ?
Si nequitiam defendere vis, licet; si tu in uno
scorto maiorem pecuniam absumpsisti quam quanti
omne instrumentum fundi Sabini in censum dedica-

---

[1] illim, *Lambinus* ; illi, ω.

main point was this: that hereafter he would have
nothing to do with that actress, that he had cast
aside all his love for her and transferred it to the
reader—when the woman wept still more copiously,
the compassionate man could not endure it; he
uncovered his face and threw himself on her neck.
O man of no worth!—for I can use no more fitting
term; was it, then, that your wife might unex-
pectedly see you, when you had surprised her by
appearing as her lover, that you upset the city with
terror by night and Italy with dread for many
days?"

In a very similar way Quintus Claudius too, in
the first book of his *Annals*, called a prodigal and
wasteful life of luxury *nequitia*, using these words:[1]
"They persuade a young man from Lucania, who was
born in a most exalted station, but had squandered
great wealth in luxury and prodigality (*nequitia*)."
Marcus Varro in his work *On the Latin Language*
says:[2] "Just as from *non* and *volo* we have *nolo*, so
from *ne* and *quicquam* is formed *nequam*, with the
loss of the medial syllable." Publius Africanus,
speaking *In his own Defence against Tiberius Asellus*
in the matter of a fine, thus addressed the people:[3]
"All the evils, shameful deeds, and crimes that
men commit come from two things, malice and
profligacy (*nequitia*). Against which charge do you
defend yourself, that of malice or profligacy, or both
together? If you wish to defend yourself against
the charge of profligacy, well and good; if you have
squandered more money on one harlot than you re-
ported for the census as the value of all the equip-

[1] Fr. 15, Peter[2].   [2] x. 5. 81.
[3] *O. R. F.*, p. 183, Meyer[2].

visti; si hoc ita est, qui spondet mille nummum? si tu plus tertia parte pecuniae paternae perdidisti atque absumpsisti in flagitiis; si hoc ita est, qui spondet mille nummum? Non vis nequitiam. Age malitiam saltem defende. Si tu verbis conceptis coniuravisti [1] sciens sciente animo tuo; si hoc ita est, qui spondet mille nummum?"

XII

De tunicis chiridotis; quod earum usum [2] P. Africanus Sulpicio Gallo obiecit.

1 Tunicis uti virum prolixis ultra brachia et usque in primores manus ac prope in digitos, Romae atque
2 in omni Latio indecorum fuit. Eas tunicas Graeco vocabulo nostri "chiridotas" appellaverunt feminisque solis vestem longe lateque diffusam non indecere [3] existimaverunt ad ulnas cruraque adversus
3 oculos protegenda. Viri autem Romani primo quidem sine tunicis toga sola amicti fuerunt; postea substrictas et breves tunicas citra umerum desinentis
4 habebant, quod genus Graeci dicunt ἐξωμίδας. Hac antiquitate indutus P. Africanus, Pauli filius, vir omnibus bonis artibus atque omni virtute praeditus,

---

[1] periuravisti, *H. Meyer.*   [2] usum, *added in* σ.
[3] non indecere, *suggested by Hosius*; indecere (incedere R) ω

---

[1] The lexicons and commentators define the *sponsio* as a "legal wager," in which the two parties to a suit put up a sum of money, which was forfeited by the one who lost his case; and they cite Gaius, *Inst.* iv. 93. But in iv. 94 Gaius says that only *one* party pledged a sum of money (unde etiam is, cum quo agetur, non restipulabatur), that it was

ment of your Sabine estate; if this is so, who pledges
a thousand sesterces?[1] If you have wasted more
than a third of your patrimony and spent it on your
vices; if that is so, who pledges a thousand sesterces?
You do not care to defend yourself against the charge
of profligacy; at least refute the charge of malice.
If you have sworn falsely in set terms knowingly
and deliberately; if this is so, who pledges a thousand
sesterces?"

XII

Of the tunics called *chiridotae;* that Publius Africanus
reproved Sulpicius Gallus for wearing them.

For a man to wear tunics coming below the arms
and as far as the wrists, and almost to the fingers, was
considered unbecoming in Rome and in all Latium.
Such tunics our countrymen called by the Greek
name *chiridotae* (long-sleeved), and they thought
that a long and full-flowing garment was not unbecoming for women only, to hide their arms and
legs from sight. But Roman men at first wore the
toga alone without tunics; later, they had close, short
tunics ending below the shoulders, the kind which
the Greeks call ἐξωμίδες (sleeveless).[2] Habituated
to this older fashion, Publius Africanus, son of
Paulus, a man gifted with all worthy arts and every
virtue, among many other things with which he

merely a preliminary to legal action, and that the sum was
not forfeited (non tamen haec summa sponsionis exigitur;
nec enim poenalis sed praeiudicialis, et propter hoc solum fit,
ut per eam de re iudicetur). Wagers, however, were common;
see Plaut. *Pers.* 186 ff.; *Cas.* prol 75; Catull. 44. 4; Ovid,
Ars Amat. i. 168.
    [2] More literally, "leaving the shoulders bare."

P. Sulpicio Gallo, homini delicato, inter pleraque
alia, quae obiectabat, id quoque probro dedit, quod
tunicis uteretur manus totas operientibus.

5   Verba sunt haec Scipionis: "Nam qui cotidie
unguentatus adversum speculum ornetur, cuius
supercilia radantur, qui barba vulsa feminibusque
subvulsis ambulet, qui in conviviis adulescentulus
cum amatore, cum chiridota tunica interior[1] accu-
buerit, qui non modo vinosus, sed virosus quoque sit,
eumne quisquam dubitet, quin idem fecerit quod
cinaedi facere solent?"

6   Vergilius quoque tunicas huiuscemodi quasi femi-
neas, probrosas criminatur:

Et tunicae (inquit) manicas et habent redimicula
    mitrae.

7   Q. quoque Ennius Carthaginiensium "tunicatam
iuventutem" non videtur sine probro dixisse.

XIII

Quem " classicum " dicat M. Cato, quem " infra classem."

1   " CLASSICI " dicebantur non omnes qui in quinque[2]
classibus erant, sed primae tantum classis homines,
qui centum et viginti quinque milia aeris ampliusve
2 censi erant. "Infra classem" autem appellabantur
secundae classis ceterarumque omnium classium, qui

---

    [1] interior, *Lipsius*; inferior, *ω*; cf. Suet. *Jul.* xlix. 1.
    [2] in quinque, *Scioppius*; inqu(a)e, *ω*.

---

      [1] *O. R. F.*, p. 181, Meyer[2].   *Aen.* ix. 616.

reproached Publius Sulpicius Gallus, an effeminate man, included this also, that he wore tunics which covered his whole hands. Scipio's words are these :[1] "For one who daily perfumes himself and dresses before a mirror, whose eyebrows are trimmed, who walks abroad with beard plucked out and thighs made smooth, who at banquets, though a young man, has reclined in a long-sleeved tunic on the inner side of the couch with a lover, who is fond not only of wine but of men—does anyone doubt that he does what wantons commonly do?"

Virgil too attacks tunics of this kind as effeminate and shameful, saying :[2]

> Sleeves have their tunics, and their turbans, ribbons.

Quintus Ennius also seems to have spoken not without scorn of "the tunic-clad men" of the Carthaginians.[3]

XIII

Whom Marcus Cato calls *classici* or "belonging to a class," and whom *infra classem* or "below class."

Not all those men who were enrolled in the five classes[4] were called *classici*, but only the men of the first class, who were rated at a hundred and twenty-five thousand *asses* or more. But those of the second class and of all the other classes, who were rated at

---

[3] *Ann.* 325, Vahlen[2].

[4] The five classes into which the Roman citizens were divided by the constitution attributed to Servius Tullius. The division was for military purposes and was made on the basis of a property qualification.

minore summa aeris, quam quod [1] supra dixi, cense-
3 bantur. Hoc eo strictim notavi, quoniam in M.
Catonis oratione, *Qua Voconiam legem suasit*, quaeri
solet quid sit " classicus," quid " infra classem."

XIV

De tribus dicendi generibus ; ac de tribus philosophis qui ab
Atheniensibus ad senatum Romam legati missi sunt.[2]

1 Et in carmine et in soluta oratione genera dicendi
probabilia sunt tria, quae Graeci χαρακτῆρας vocant
2 nominaque eis fecerunt ἁδρόν, ἰσχνόν, μέσον. Nos
quoque quem primum posuimus " uberem " vocamus,
secundum " gracilem," tertium " mediocrem."
3 Uberi dignitas atque amplitudo est, gracili venustas et subtilitas, medius in confinio est utriusque
modi particeps.
4 His singulis orationis virtutibus vitia agnata sunt
pari numero, quae earum modum et habitum simula-
5 cris falsis ementiuntur. Sic plerumque sufflati atque
tumidi fallunt pro uberibus, squalentes et ieiunidici [3]
pro gracilibus, incerti et ambigui pro mediocribus.
6 Vera autem et propria huiuscemodi formarum exempla in Latina lingua M. Varro esse dicit ubertatis
Pacuvium, gracilitatis Lucilium, mediocritatis Te-
7 rentium. Sed ea ipsa genera dicendi iam antiquitus
tradita ab Homero sunt tria in tribus : magnificum

---

[1] quam quod, *Skutsch ;* quod, ω ; quam ς.
[2] Romae legati sunt, *MSS.*
[3] ieiunidici, *MSS.*; ieiunidici, *J. Gronov. Heraeus suggests
in place of this rare word,* eiuncidi, *Varro R.R.* i. 31. 3;
ii. 10. 8; *Plin. N.H.* xvii. 176, *defined by a gloss as* tenuis.

a smaller sum than that which I just mentioned, were called *infra classem*. I have briefly noted this, because in connection with the speech of Marcus Cato *In Support of the Voconian Law* the question is often raised, what is meant by *classicus* and what by *infra classem*.

XIV

Of the three literary styles; and of the three philosophers who were sent as envoys by the Athenians to the senate at Rome.

BOTH in verse and in prose there are three approved styles, which the Greeks call χαρακτῆρες and to which they have given the names of ἁδρός, ἰσχνός and μέσος. We also call the one which I put first " grand," the second " plain," and the third " middle."

The grand style possesses dignity and richness, the plain, grace and elegance; the middle lies on the border line and partakes of the qualities of both.

To each of these excellent styles there are related an equal number of faulty ones, arising from unsuccessful attempts to imitate their manner and character. Thus very often pompous and bombastic speakers lay claim to the grand style, the mean and bald to the plain, and the unclear and ambiguous to the middle. But true and genuine Latin examples of these styles are said by Marcus Varro[1] to be: Pacuvius of the grand style, Lucilius of the plain, and Terence of the middle. But in early days these same three styles of speaking were exemplified in three men by Homer: the grand and rich in

[1] Fr. 80, Wilmanns.

in Ulixe et ubertum, subtile in Menelao et cohibitum, mixtum moderatumque in Nestore.

8   Animadversa eadem tripertita varietas est in tribus philosophis quos Athenienses Romam ad senatum [1] legaverant, inpetratum uti multam remitteret, quam fecerat is propter Oropi vastationem. Ea multa
9 fuerat talentum fere quingentum. Erant isti philosophi Carneades ex Academia, Diogenes Stoicus, Critolaus Peripateticus. Et in senatum quidem introducti interprete usi sunt C. Acilio senatore; sed ante ipsi seorsum quisque ostentandi gratia magno
10 conventu hominum dissertaverunt. Tum admirationi fuisse aiunt Rutilius et Polybius philosophorum trium sui cuiusque generis facundiam. "Violenta," inquiunt, "et rapida Carneades dicebat, scita et teretia Critolaus, modesta Diogenes et sobria."
11   Unumquodque autem genus, ut diximus, cum caste pudiceque ornatur, fit illustrius, cum fucatur atque praelinitur, fit praestigiosum.

XV

Quam severe moribus maiorum in fures vindicatum sit; et quid scripserit Mucius Scaevola super eo quod servandum datum commodatumve esset.

1   LABEO in libro *De Duodecim Tabulis* secundo acria et severa iudicia de furtis habita esse apud veteres

---

[1] senatum populi, *ω*; senatum populi R., *Hosius*; senatum publice, *Damsté.*

---

[1] The embassy was sent in 155 B.C. Plutarch, *Cat. Mai.*

Ulysses, the elegant and restrained in Menelaus, the middle and moderate in Nestor.

This threefold variety is also to be observed in the three philosophers whom the Athenians sent as envoys to the senate at Rome, to persuade the senators to remit the fine which they had imposed upon the Athenians because of the sack of Oropos; [1] and the fine amounted to nearly five hundred talents. The philosophers in question were Carneades of the Academy, Diogenes the Stoic, and Critolaus the Peripatetic. When they were admitted to the House, they made use of Gaius Acilius, one of the senators, as interpreter; but beforehand each one of them separately, for the purpose of exhibiting his eloquence, lectured to a large company. Rutilius [2] and Polybius [3] declare that all three aroused admiration for their oratory, each in his own style. "Carneades," they say, " spoke with a vehemence that carried you away, Critolaus with art and polish, Diogenes with restraint and sobriety."

Each of these styles, as I have said, is more brilliant when it is chastely and moderately adorned; when it is rouged and bepowdered, it becomes mere jugglery.

XV

How severely thieves were punished by the laws of our forefathers; and what Mucius Scaevola wrote about that which is given or entrusted to anyone's care.

LABEO, in his second book *On the Twelve Tables*,[4] wrote that cruel and severe judgments were passed

---

xxii. (*L.C.L.* ii., p. 369) says that the fine was five hundred talents.

  [2] Fr. 3, Peter².   [3] xxxiii. 2, p. 1287, H.
  [4] Fr. 23, Huschke; 1, Bremer.

scripsit, idque Brutum solitum dicere, et furti
damnatum esse qui iumentum aliorsum duxerat quam
quo utendum acceperat, item qui longius produxerat
2 quam in quem locum petierat. Itaque Q. Scaevola,
in librorum quos *De Iure Civili* composuit XVI.,
verba haec posuit : " Quod cui servandum datum
est, si id usus est, sive quod utendum accepit, ad
aliam rem atque accepit usus est, furti se obligavit."

XVI

Locus exscriptus ex satura M. Varronis, quae Περὶ Ἐδεσμάτων
inscripta est, de peregrinis ciborum generibus ; et appositi
versus Euripidi, quibus delicatorum hominum luxuriantem
gulam confutavit.

1   M. VARRO, in satura quam Περὶ Ἐδεσμάτων inscripsit, lepide admodum et scite factis versibus cenarum,
2 ciborum exquisitas delicias comprehendit. Nam
pleraque id genus, quae helluones isti terra et mari
conquirunt, exposuit inclusitque in numeros senarios.
3   Et ipsos quidem versus, cui otium erit in libro quo
4 dixi positos legat ; genera autem nominaque edulium
et domicilia ciborum omnibus aliis praestantia, quae
profunda ingluvies vestigavit, quae[1] Varro obpro-
brans exsecutus est, haec sunt ferme, quantum nobis
5 memoriae est · pavus e Samo, Phrygia attagena,

---

[1] quaeque, *Hertz.*

---

[1] *Resp.* 6. Bremer.
[2] Fr. 2, Huschke ; *Iur. Civ.* xvi. 1, Bremer (i, p. 97).

upon theft in early times, and that Brutus used to
say[1] that a man was pronounced guilty of theft
who had merely led an animal to another place than
the one where he had been given the privilege of
using it, as well as one who had driven it farther
than he had bargained to do.   Accordingly, Quintus
Scaevola, in the sixteenth book of his work *On the
Civil Law*, wrote these words:[2] "If anyone has used
something that was entrusted to his care, or having
borrowed anything to use, has applied it to another
purpose than that for which he borrowed it, he is
liable for theft."

XVI

A passage about foreign varieties of food, copied from the
satire of Marcus Varro entitled Περὶ Ἐδεσμάτων, or *On
Edibles ;* and with it some verses of Euripides in which
he assails the extravagant gluttony of luxurious men.

MARCUS VARRO, in the satire which he entitled Περὶ
Ἐδεσμάτων, in verses written with great charm and
cleverness, treats of exquisite elegance in banquets
and viands.   For he has set forth and described in
senarii[3] the greater number of things of that kind
which such gluttons seek out on land and sea.[4]

As for the verses themselves, he who has leisure
may find and read them in the book which I have
mentioned.   So far as my memory goes, these
are the varieties and names of the foods surpassing
all others, which a bottomless gullet has hunted
out and which Varro has assailed in his satire, with
the places where they are found : a peacock from
Samos, a woodcock from Phrygia, cranes of Media,

[3] That is, iambic trimeters, consisting of six iambic feet.
[4] Fr. 403, Bücheler.

grues Melicae, haedus ex Ambracia, pelamys Chalce-
donia, muraena Tartesia, aselli Pessinuntii, ostrea
Tarenti, pectunculus Siculus,[1] helops Rodius, scari
Cilices, nuces Thasiae, palma Aegyptia, glans
Hiberica.

6   Hanc autem peragrantis gulae et in sucos inqui-
rentis industriam atque has undiquevorsum indagines
cuppediarum maiore detestatione dignas censebimus,
si versus Euripidi recordemur, quibus saepissime
Chrysippus philosophus usus, tamquam ἡδυπαθείας[2]
edendi repertas esse, non per usum vitae necessa-
rium, sed per luxum animi parata atque facilia
fastidientis per inprobam satietatis lasciviam.

7   Versus Euripidi adscribendos putavi :

> Ἐπεὶ τί δεῖ βροτοῖσι, πλὴν δυεῖν μόνον,
> Δήμητρος ἀκτῆς, πώματός θ᾽ ὑδρηχόου,
> Ἅπερ πάρεστι καὶ πέφυχ᾽ ἡμᾶς τρέφειν ;
> Ὧν οὐκ ἀπαρκεῖ πλησμονή. τρυφῇ δέ τοι
> Ἄλλων ἐδεστῶν μηχανὰς θηρώμεθα.

XVII

Sermo habitus cum grammatico insolentiarum et inperitiarum
pleno de significatione vocabuli quod est "obnoxius";
deque eius vocis origine.

1   PERCONTABAR Romae quempiam grammaticum
primae in docendo celebritatis, non hercle experi-

---

[1] Siculus *added by* Hertz.
[2] ἡδυπαθείας *suggested by* Hosius (*cf.* Clem. Alex. *Paed.* ii.
1. 3, p. 164).

a kid from Ambracia, a young tunny from Chalcedon, a lamprey from Tartessus, codfish from Pessinus, oysters from Tarentum, cockles from Sicily, a swordfish from Rhodes,[1] pike from Cilicia, nuts from Thasos, dates from Egypt, acorns from Spain.

But this tireless gluttony, which is ever wandering about and seeking for flavours, and this eager quest of dainties from all quarters, we shall consider deserving of the greater detestation, if we recall the verses of Euripides of which the philosopher Chrysippus made frequent use,[2] to the effect that gastronomic delicacies were contrived, not because of the necessary uses of life, but because of a spirit of luxury that disdains what is easily attainable because of the immoderate wantonness that springs from satiety.

I have thought that I ought to append the verses of Euripides : [3]

What things do mortals need, save two alone,
The fruits of Ceres and the cooling spring,
Which are at hand and made to nourish us ?
With this abundance we are not content,
But hunt out other foods through luxury.

XVII

A conversation held with a grammarian, who was full of insolence and ignorance, as to the meaning of the word *obnoxius;* and of the origin of that word.

I inquired at Rome of a certain grammarian who had the highest repute as a teacher, not indeed

---

[1] Or perhaps a sturgeon ; the identification of some of these beasts and fish is very uncertain.
[2] p. 344, Baguet.   [3] Fr. 884, Nauck.[2]

undi vel temptandi gratia, sed discendi magis studio
et cupidine, quid significaret "obnoxius" quaeque
2 eius vocabuli origo ac ratio esset. Atque ille aspicit
me, inludens levitatem quaestionis pravitatemque :
"Obscuram," inquit, "sane rem quaeris multaque
3 prorsus vigilia indagandam ! Quis adeo tam linguae
Latinae ignarus est, quin sciat eum dici ' obnoxium '
cui quid ab eo cui esse ' obnoxius ' dicitur incommo-
dari et noceri potest, ut qui[1] habeat aliquem noxae,
id est culpae suae, conscium? Quin potius," inquit,
"haec mittis nugalia et affers ea quae digna quaeri
tractarique sint?"
4   Tum vero ego permotus, agendum iam oblique, ut
cum homine stulto, existimavi et "Cetera," inquam,
"vir doctissime, remotiora gravioraque si discere et
scire debuero, quando mihi usus venerit, tum quae-
ram ex te atque discam ; sed enim quia dixi saepe
' obnoxius ' et quid dicerem nescivi, didici ex te et
scire nunc coepi quod non ego omnium solus, ut
tibi sum visus, ignoravi, sed, ut res est, Plautus
quoque, homo linguae atque elegantiae in verbis
Latinae princeps, quid esset ' obnoxius ' nescivit ;
versus enim est in *Sticho* illius ita scriptus :

Nunc ego hercle perii pláne, non obnóxie,[2]

quod minime congruit cum ista, quam me docuisti,

---

[1] ut qui, *suggested by Hosius* ; et, *Acidalius* ; ei, ω.
[2] periei hercle vero plane, nihil obnoxie, *codd. Plaut.*

---

[1] 497. Cf. Salmasius, *ad loc.*, obnoxie perire dicitur, qui
non plane nec funditus perit, sed aliquam spem salutis
habet. Cf. *Poen.* 787 ; *Amph.* 372.

for the sake of trying or testing him, but rather from an eager desire for knowledge, what *obnoxius* meant and what was the origin and history of the word. And he, looking at me and ridiculing what he considered the insignificance and unfitness of the query, said: "Truly a difficult question is this that you ask, one demanding very many sleepless nights of investigation! Who, pray, is so ignorant of the Latin tongue as not to know that one is called *obnoxius* who can be inconvenienced or injured by another, to whom he is said to be *obnoxius* because the other is conscious of his *noxa*, that is to say, of his guilt? Why not rather," said he, "drop these trifles and put questions worthy of study and discussion?"

Then indeed I was angry, but thinking that I ought to dissemble, since I was dealing with a fool, I said; "If, most learned sir, I need to learn and to know other things that are more abstruse and more important, when the occasion arises I shall inquire and learn them from you; but inasmuch as I have often used the word *obnoxius* without knowing what I was saying, I have learned from you and am now beginning to understand what not I alone, as you seem to think, was ignorant of; for as a matter of fact, Plautus too, though a man of the first rank in his use of the Latin language and in elegance of diction, did not know the meaning of *obnoxius*. For there is a passage of his in the *Stichus* which reads as follows:

> By Heaven! I now am utterly undone,
> Not only partly so (*non obnoxie*).[1]

This does not in the least agree with what you have

significatione ; composuit enim Plautus tamquam duo
inter se contraria ' plane' et ' obnoxie,' quod a tua
significatione longe abest."

5 Atque ille grammaticus satis ridicule, quasi " obnoxius " et " obnoxie " non declinatione sola, sed re
atque sententia differrent, " Ego," inquit, " dixi quid
6 esset ' obnoxius,' non quid ' obnoxie.' " At tunc ego
admirans insolentis hominis inscitiam, " Mittamus,"
inquam, " sicuti vis, quod Plautus ' obnoxie ' dixit, si
7 id nimis esse remotum putas, atque illud quoque
praetermittamus, quod Sallustius in *Catilina* scribit :
8 ' Minari etiam [1] ferro, ni sibi obnoxia foret,' et quod
videtur novius pervulgatiusque esse, id me doce.
Versus enim Vergilii sunt notissimi :

Nam neque tunc astris [2] acies obtunsa videri,[3]
Nec fratris radiis obnoxia surgere luna,

9 quod tu ais ' culpae suae conscium.' Alio quoque
loco Vergilius verbo isto utitur a tua sententia
diverse in his versibus :

iuvat arva videre
Non rastris hominum, non ulli obnoxia curae ;

cura enim prodesse arvis solet, non nocere, quod tu
10 de ' obnoxio ' dixisti. Iam vero illud etiam Q. Enni
quo pacto congruere tecum potest, quod scribit in
Phoenice in hisce versibus :

---

[1] interdum, *Sall.*   [2] stellis, *Virg.*
             [3] videtur, *Virg.*

---

[1] xxiii. 3.   [2] *Georg.* i. 395–6.
[3] *Georg.* ii. 438.   [4] 257 ff., Ribbeck.[3]

taught me; for Plautus contrasted *plane* and *obnoxie*
as two opposites, which is far removed from your
meaning."

But that grammarian retorted foolishly enough,
as if *obnoxius* and *obnoxie* differed, not merely in
form, but in their substance and meaning: " I gave
a definition of *obnoxius*, not *obnoxie*." But then
I, amazed at the ignorance of the presumptuous
fellow, answered: "Let us, as you wish, disregard
the fact that Plautus said *obnoxie*, if you think that
too far-fetched ; and let us also say nothing of the
passage in Sallust's *Catiline* :[1] 'Also to threaten her
with his sword, if she would not be submissive
(*obnoxia*) to him'; but explain to me this example,
which is certainly more recent and more familiar.
For the following verses of Virgil's are very well
known :[2]

> For now the stars' bright sheen is seen undimmed.
> The rising Moon owes naught (*nec . . . obnoxia*)
>   to brother's rays ;

but you say that it means 'conscious of her guilt.'
In another place too Virgil uses this word with a
meaning different from yours, in these lines :[3]

> What joy the fields to view
> That owe no debt (*non obnoxia*) to hoe or care of
> man.

For care is generally a benefit to fields, not an
injury, as it would be according to your definition
of *obnoxius*. Furthermore, how can what Quintus
Ennius writes in the following verses from the
Phoenix[4] agree with you :

> Séd virum verá virtute vívere animatum áddecet,
> Fórtiterque innóxium stare [1] ádversum adversários.
> Éa libertas ést, qui pectus púrum et firmum gésti-
>   tat,
> Áliae res obnóxiosae nócte in obscurá latent " ?

11   At ille oscitans et alucinanti similis : "Nunc," inquit, "mihi operae non est.   Cum otium erit, revises
ad me atque disces quid in verbo isto et Vergilius et
Sallustius et Plautus et Ennius senserint."

12   At nebulo quidem ille, ubi hoc dixit, digressus
est ; si quis autem volet non originem solam verbi
istius, sed significationem quoque eius varietatemque
recensere, ut hoc etiam Plautinum spectet, adscripsi
versus ex *Asinaria* :

> Máximas opímitates gaúdio effertíssimas
> Súis eris ille úna mecum páriet gnatoque ét patri ;
> Ádeo ut aetatem ámbo ambobus nóbis sint obnóxii
> Nóstro dévinctí beneficio.

13 Qua vero ille grammaticus finitione usus est, ea videtur in verbo tam multiplici unam tantummodo usur-
pationem eius notasse, quae quidem congruit cum
significatu quo Caecilius usus est in *Chrysio* in his
versibus :

> quamquam ego mercéde huc conductús tua
> Advénio, ne tibi me ésse ob eam rem obnóxium
> Reáre ; audibis mále, si maledicís mihi.

---

[1] stare, *Bentley* ; vocare, *RV* ; vacare, *P.*

---

[1] 282.   [2] 21, Ribbeck.[3]

'Tis meet a man should live inspired by courage
    true,
In conscious innocence should boldly challenge
    foes.
True freedom his who bears a pure and steadfast
    heart,
All else less import has (*obnoxiosae*) and lurks in
    gloomy night "?

But our grammarian, with open mouth as if in a
dream, said: "Just now I have no time to spare.
When I have leisure, come to see me and learn
what Virgil, Plautus, Sallust and Ennius meant by
that word."

So saying that fool made off; but in case anyone
should wish to investigate, not only the origin of this
word, but also its variety of meaning, in order that he
may take into consideration this Plautine use also, I
have quoted the following lines from the *Asinaria :* [1]

He'll join with me and hatch the biggest jubilee,
Stuff'd with most joy, for son and father too.
For life they both shall be in debt (*obnoxii*) to
    both of us,
By our services fast bound.

Now, in the definition which that grammarian
gave, he seems in a word of such manifold content
to have noted only one of its uses—a use, it is true,
which agrees with that of Caecilius in these verses
of the *Chrysium :* [2]

Although I come to you attracted by your pay,
Don't think that I for that am subject to your
    will (*tibi . . . obnoxium*) ;
If you speak ill of me, you'll hear a like reply.

XVIII

De observata custoditaque apud Romanos iurisiurandi
sanctimonia ; atque inibi de decem captivis, quos Romam
Hannibal deiurio ab his accepto legavit.

1 IUSIURANDUM apud Romanos inviolate sancteque
habitum servatumque est.   Id et moribus legibusque
multis ostenditur, et hoc, quod dicemus, ei rei non
2 tenue argumentum esse potest.   Post [1] proelium
Cannense Hannibal, Carthaginiensium imperator, ex
captivis nostris electos decem Romam misit manda-
vitque eis pactusque est, ut, si populo Romano
videretur, permutatio fieret captivorum et pro his
quos alteri plures acciperent, darent argenti pondo
3 libram et selibram.   Hoc, priusquam proficisceren-
tur, iusiurandum eos adegit, redituros esse in castra
Poenica, si Romani captivos non permutarent.
4. 5   Veniunt Romam decem captivi.   Mandatum Poeni
6 imperatoris in senatu exponunt.   Permutatio senatui
7 non placita.   Parentes, cognati adfinesque captivorum
amplexi eos postliminio in patriam redisse dicebant
statumque eorum integrum incolumemque esse, ac ne
8 ad hostes redire vellent orabant.   Tum octo ex his
postliminium iustum non esse sibi responderunt,
quoniam deiurio vincti forent, statimque, uti iurati
9 erant, ad Hannibalem profecti sunt.   Duo reliqui

Post *added by Hertz* ; est. Post, *Lambecius.*

---

[1] Recovery of civic rights by a person who has been
reduced to slavery by capture in war, Pomponius, *Dig.*
xlix. 15. 5, and 19.

XVIII

On the strict observance by the Romans of the sanctity of
an oath ; and also the story of the ten prisoners whom
Hannibal sent to Rome under oath.

An oath was regarded and kept by the Romans
as something inviolable and sacred. This is evident
from many of their customs and laws, and this tale
which I shall tell may be regarded as no slight
support of the truth of the statement. After the
battle of Cannae Hannibal, commander of the
Carthaginians, selected ten Roman prisoners and
sent them to the city, instructing them and agree-
ing that, if it seemed good to the Roman people,
there should be an exchange of prisoners, and that
for each captive that one side should receive in
excess of the other side, there should be paid a
pound and a half of silver. Before they left, he
compelled them to take oath that they would return
to the Punic camp, if the Romans would not agree
to an exchange.

The ten captives come to Rome. They deliver
the message of the Punic commander in the senate.
The senate refused an exchange. The parents,
kinsfolk and connexions of the prisoners amid
embraces declared that they had returned to their
native land in accordance with the law of *postliminium*,[1] and that their condition of independence
was complete and inviolate ; they therefore besought
them not to think of returning to the enemy. Then
eight of their number rejoined that they had no
just right of *postliminium*, since they were bound by
an oath, and they at once went back to Hannibal,
as they had sworn to do. The other two remained

75

Romae manserunt solutosque esse se ac liberatos
religione dicebant, quoniam, cum egressi castra
hostium fuissent, commenticio consilio regressi
eodem, tamquam si ob aliquam fortuitam causam,
issent atque ita iureiurando satisfacto rursum iniurati
10 abissent. Haec eorum fraudulenta calliditas tam
esse turpis existimata est, ut contempti vulgo dis-
cerptique sint censoresque eos postea omnium
notarum et damnis et ignominiis adfecerint, quoniam
quod facturos deieraverant non fecissent.
11   Cornelius autem Nepos in libro *Exemplorum*
quinto id quoque litteris mandavit, multis in senatu
placuisse ut hi qui redire nollent, datis custodibus,
ad Hannibalem deducerentur, sed eam sententiam
numero plurium quibus id non videretur superatam ;
eos tamen qui ad Hannibalem non redissent usque
adeo intestabiles invisosque fuisse, ut taedium vitae
ceperint necemque sibi consciverint.

XIX

Historia ex annalibus sumpta de Tiberio Graccho, Gracchorum patre, tribuno plebis ; atque inibi tribunicia
decreta cum ipsis verbis relata.

1   Pulcrum atque liberale atque magnanimum factum
Tiberii Sempronii Gracchi in *Exemplis* repositum est.
2 Id exemplum huiuscemodi est : L. Scipioni Asiatico,
P. Scipionis Africani superioris fratri, C. Minucius
Augurinus tribunus plebi multam irrogavit eumque

---

[1] Corn. Nepos, *Ex.* fr 2, Peter[2].
[2] Nepos, *Ex.*, fr. 3, Peter[2].

in Rome, declaring that they had been released and
freed from their obligation because, after leaving
the enemy's camp, they had returned to it as if
for some chance reason, but really with intent to
deceive, and having thus kept the letter of the
oath, they had come away again unsworn. This
dishonourable cleverness of theirs was considered so
shameful, that they were generally despised and
reprobated; and later the censors punished them with
all possible fines and marks of disgrace, on the ground
that they had not done what they had sworn to do.

Furthermore Cornelius Nepos, in the fifth book
of his *Examples*,[1] has recorded also that many of the
senators recommended that those who refused to
return should be sent to Hannibal under guard,
but that the motion was defeated by a majority of
dissentients. He adds that, in spite of this, those
who had not returned to Hannibal were so infamous
and hated that they became tired of life and
committed suicide.

XIX

A story, taken from the annals, about Tiberius Gracchus,
tribune of the commons and father of the Gracchi; and
also an exact quotation of the decrees of the tribunes.

A FINE, noble and generous action of Tiberius
Sempronius Gracchus is recorded in the *Examples*.[2]
It runs as follows: Gaius Minucius Augurinus,
tribune of the commons, imposed a fine on Lucius
Scipio Asiaticus, brother of Scipio Africanus the
elder,[3] and demanded that he should give security

[3] The famous conqueror of Hannibal at Zama in 202 B.C.
He served as *legatus* under his brother in the war against
Antiochus, in 190 B.C.

3 ob eam causam praedes poscebat. Scipio Africanus fratris nomine ad collegium tribunorum provocabat, petebatque ut virum consularem triumphalemque a
4 collegae vi defenderent. Octo tribuni cognita causa decreverunt.

5 Eius decreti verba, quae posui, ex annalium monumentis exscripta sunt : " Quod P. Scipio Africanus postulavit pro L. Scipione Asiatico fratre, cum contra leges contraque morem maiorum tribunus pl. hominibus accitis per vim inauspicato sententiam de eo tulerit multamque nullo exemplo irrogaverit praedesque eum ob eam rem dare cogat aut, si non det, in vincula duci iubeat, ut eum a collegae vi prohibeamus. Et quod contra collega postulavit ne sibi intercedamus quominus suapte potestate uti liceat, de ea re nostrum sententia omnium ea est : Si L. Cornelius Scipio Asiaticus collegae arbitratu praedes dabit, collegae ne eum in vincula ducat intercedemus ; si eius arbitratu praedes non dabit, quominus collega sua potestate utatur non intercedemus."

6 Post hoc decretum cum Augurinus tribunus L. Scipionem praedes non dantem prendi et in carcerem duci iussisset, tunc Tiberius Sempronius Gracchus tr. pl., pater Tiberi atque C. Gracchorum, cum P.

---

[1] At this period there were ten tribunes ; Augurinus and Gracchus were the other two.

for its payment. Scipio Africanus appealed to the college of tribunes on behalf of his brother, asking them to defend against the violent measures of their colleague a man who had been consul and had celebrated a triumph. Having heard the case, eight[1] of the tribunes rendered a decision.

The words of their decree, which I have quoted, are taken from the records of the annals : " Whereas Publius Scipio Africanus has asked us to protect his brother, Lucius Scipio Asiaticus, against the violent measures of one of our colleagues, in that, contrary to the laws and the customs of our forefathers, that tribune of the commons, having illegally convened an assembly without consulting the auspices, pronounced sentence upon him and imposed an unprecedented fine, and compels him to furnish security for its payment, or if he does not do so, orders that he be imprisoned ; and whereas, on the other hand, our colleague has demanded that we should not interfere with him in the exercise of his legal authority—our unanimous decision in this matter is as follows : If Lucius Cornelius Scipio Asiaticus will furnish security in accordance with the decision of our colleague, we will forbid our colleague to take him to prison ; but if he shall not furnish the securities in accordance with our colleague's decision, we will not interfere with our colleague in the exercise of his lawful authority."

After this decree, Lucius Scipio refused to give security and the tribune Augurinus ordered him to be arrested and taken to prison. Thereupon Tiberius Sempronius Gracchus, one of the tribunes of the commons and father of Tiberius and Gaius

Scipioni Africano inimicus gravis ob plerasque in
republica dissensiones esset, iuravit palam in amicitiam inque gratiam se cum P. Africano non redisse,
atque ita decretum ex tabula recitavit.

7   Eius decreti verba haec sunt : " Cum L. Cornelius
Scipio Asiaticus triumphans hostium duces in carcerem coniectarit, alienum videtur esse dignitate
reipublicae, in eum locum imperatorem populi
Romani duci, in quem locum ab eo coniecti sunt
duces hostium ; itaque L. Cornelium Scipionem
Asiaticum a collegae vi prohibeo."

8   Valerius autem Antias contra hanc decretorum
memoriam contraque auctoritates veterum annalium
post Africani mortem intercessionem istam pro
Scipione Asiatico factam esse a Tiberio Graccho
dixit, neque multam irrogatam Scipioni, sed damnatum eum peculatus ob Antiochinam pecuniam, quia
praedes non daret, in carcerem duci coeptum atque
ita intercedente Graccho exemptum.

XX

Quod Vergilius a Nolanis ob aquam sibi non permissam
sustulit e versu suo " Nolam " et posuit " oram " ; atque
ibi quaedam alia de iucunda consonantia litterarum.

1   SCRIPTUM in quodam commentario repperi, versus
istos a Vergilio ita primum esse recitatos atque
editos :

---

[1] Page 267 note, Peter[2].   [2] Georg. ii. 244 f.

Gracchus, although he was a bitter personal enemy of Publius Scipio Africanus because of numerous disagreements on political questions, publicly made oath that he had not been reconciled with Publius Africanus nor become his friend, and then read a decree which he had written out.

That decree ran as follows: "Whereas Lucius Cornelius Scipio Asiaticus, during the celebration of a triumph, cast the leaders of the enemy into prison, it seems contrary to the dignity of our country that the Roman people's commander should be consigned to the same place to which he had committed the leaders of the enemy; therefore I forbid my colleague to take violent measures towards Lucius Scipio Asiaticus."

But Valerius Antias, contradicting this record of the decrees and the testimony of the ancient annals, has said[1] that it was after the death of Africanus that Tiberius Gracchus interposed that veto in behalf of Scipio Asiaticus; also that Scipio was not fined, but that being convicted of embezzlement of the money taken from Antiochus and refusing to give bail, was just being taken to prison when he was saved by this veto of Gracchus.

XX

That Virgil removed *Nola* from one of his lines and substituted *ora* because the inhabitants of Nola had refused him water; and also some additional notes on the agreeable euphony of vowels.

I have found it noted in a certain commentary that the following lines were first read and published by Virgil in this form:[2]

> Talem dives arat Capua et vicina Vesevo
> Nola iugo ;

postea Vergilium petisse a Nolanis, aquam uti duceret[1] in propinquum rus, Nolanos beneficium
petitum non fecisse, poetam offensum nomen urbis
eorum, quasi ex hominum memoria, sic ex carmine
suo derasisse, " oram "que pro " Nola " mutasse
atque ita reliquisse ;

> et vicina Vesevo
> Ora iugo.

2 Ea res verane an falsa sit, non laboro ; quin tamen
melius suaviusque ad aures sit " ora " quam " Nola,"
3 dubium id non est. Nam vocalis in priore versu
extrema eademque in sequenti prima canoro simul
atque iucundo hiatu tractim sonat. Est adeo in-
4 venire apud nobiles poetas huiuscemodi suavitatis
multa, quae appareat navata esse, non fortuita ; sed
5 praeter ceteros omnis apud Homerum plurima. Uno
quippe in loco tales tamque hiantes sonitus in
assiduis vocibus pluribus facit :

> Ἡ δ' ἑτέρη θέρεϊ προρέει εἰκυῖα χαλάζῃ
> *Ἡ χιόνι ψυχρῇ ἢ ἐξ ὕδατος κρυστάλλῳ,

atque item alio loco :

> Λᾶαν ἄνω ὤθεσκε ποτὶ λόφον.

6 Catullus quoque elegantissimus poetarum in hisce
versibus :

---

[1] *Hosius suggests* ducerent *or* duci liceret ; *Heraeus (Berl.
Ph. Woch. 1904, 1163 ff.) defends* duceret.

---

[1] *Iliad* xxii. 151.
[2] The instances referred to are προρέει εἰκυῖα, χαλάζῃ ἢ, and
ψυχρῇ ἢ.
[3] *Odyss.* xi. 596.   [4] xxvii. 1.

Such is the soil that wealthy Capua ploughs
And Nola near Vesuvius' height.

That afterwards Virgil asked the people of Nola
to allow him to run their city water into his estate,
which was near by, but that they refused to grant
the favour which he asked; that thereupon the
offended poet erased the name of their city from
his poem, as if consigning it to oblivion, changing
Nola to *ora* (region) and leaving the phrase in this
form :

The region near Vesuvius' height.

With the truth or falsity of this note I am not
concerned ; but there is no doubt that *ora* has a
more agreeable and musical sound than *Nola*. For
the last vowel in the first line and the first vowel
in the following line being the same, the sound is
prolonged by an hiatus that is at the same time
melodious and pleasing. Indeed, it is possible to
find in famous poets many instances of such melody,
which appears to be the result of art rather than
accident ; but in Homer they are more frequent than
in all other poets. In fact, in one single passage
he introduces a number of sounds of such a nature,
and with such an hiatus, in a series of successive
words ; for example :[1]

The other fountain e'en in summer flows,
Like unto hail, chill snow, or crystal ice,[2]

and similarly in another place :[3]

Up to the top he pushed (ἄνω ὤθεσκε) the stone.

Catullus too, the most graceful of poets, in the
following verses,[4]

83

Minister vetuli puer Falerni,
Inger mi calices amariores,
Ut lex Postumiae iubet magistrae
Ebria acina ebriosioris,

cum dicere " ebrio " posset et, quod erat usitatius,
" acinum " in neutro genere appellare, amans tamen
hiatus illius Homerici suavitatem, " ebriam " dixit
propter insequentis a litterae concentum. Qui
" ebriosa " autem Catullum dixisse putant aut
" ebrioso," nam id quoque temere scriptum invenitur,
in libros scilicet de corruptis exemplaribus factos
inciderunt.

XXI

" Quoad vivet " " quoad "que " morietur " cur id ipsum
temporis significent, cum ex duobus sint facta contrariis.

1   " Quoad vivet " cum dicitur,[1] cum item dicitur
" quoad morietur," videntur quidem duae res dici
contrariae ; sed idem atque unum tempus utraque
2 verba demonstrant. Item cum dicitur " quoad
senatus habebitur " et " quoad senatus dimittetur,"
tametsi " haberi " atque " dimitti " contraria sunt,
unum atque id ipsum tamen utroque in verbo
3 ostenditur. Tempora enim duo cum inter sese
opposita sunt atque ita cohaerentia ut alterius finis
cum alterius initio misceatur, non refert utrum per
extremitatem prioris an per initium sequentis locus
ipse confinis demonstretur.

[1] cum dicitur *supplied by Hertz.*

---

[1] Postumia is the *magistra bibendi*, who regulated the pro-
portion of wine and water and the size of the cups, and imposed
penalties for breaking her rules.   Cf. Hor. *Odes*, i. 4. 18.

Boy, who servest old Falernian,
Pour out stronger cups for me,
Following queen [1] Postumia's mandate,
Tipsier she than tipsy grape,

although he might have said *ebrio,* and used *acinum*
in the neuter gender, as was more usual, nevertheless through love of the melody of that Homeric
hiatus he said *ebria,* because it blended with the following *a.* But those who think that Catullus wrote
ebriosa or *ebrioso*—for that incorrect reading is
also found—have unquestionably happened upon
editions copied from corrupt texts.

XXI

Why it is that the phrases *quoad vivet* and *quoad morietur*
indicate the very same time, although based upon opposite
things.

When the expressions *quoad vivet,* or "so long as
he shall live," and *quoad morietur,* or "until he shall
die," are used, two opposite things really seem to be
said, but the two expressions indicate one and the
same time. Also when we say "as long as the
senate shall be in session," and "until the senate
shall adjourn," although "be in session" and "adjourn" are opposites, yet one and the same idea is
expressed by both phrases. For when two periods
of time are opposed to each other and yet are so
connected that the end of one coincides with the
beginning of the other, it makes no difference
whether the exact point of their meeting is designated by the end of the first period or the beginning
of the second.

XXII

Quod censores equum adimere soliti sunt equitibus corpulentis et praepinguibus ; quaesitumque utrum ea res cum
ignominia an incolumi dignitate equitum facta sit.

1   Nimis pingui homini et corpulento censores equum
adimere solitos, scilicet minus idoneum ratos esse [1]
cum tanti corporis pondere ad faciendum equitis
2 munus.   Non enim poena id fuit, ut quidam existimant, sed munus sine ignominia remittebatur.
3 Tamen Cato, in oratione quam *De Sacrificio Commisso*
scripsit, obicit hanc rem criminosius, uti magis videri
4 possit cum ignominia fuisse.   Quod si ita accipias,
id profecto existimandum est, non omnino incul-
patum neque indesidem visum esse, cuius corpus in
tam inmodicum modum luxuriasset exuberassetque.

[1] esse *omitted by Skutsch.*

XXII

On the custom of the censors of taking their horse from corpulent and excessively fat knights; and the question whether such action also involved degradation or left them their rank as knights.

THE censors used to take his horse from a man who was too fat and corpulent, evidently because they thought that so heavy a person was unfit to perform the duties of a knight. For this was not a punishment, as some think, but the knight was relieved of duty without loss of rank. Yet Cato, in the speech which he wrote *On Neglecting Sacrifice*,[1] makes such an occurrence a somewhat serious charge, thus apparently indicating that it was attended with disgrace. If you understand that to have been the case, you must certainly assume that it was because a man was not looked upon as wholly free from the reproach of slothfulness, if his body had bulked and swollen to such unwieldy dimensions.

[1] xviii. 5, Jordan.

BOOK VII

LIBER SEPTIMUS

I

Quem in modum responderit Chrysippus adversum eos qui providentiam consistere negaverunt.

1 Quibus non videtur mundus dei et hominum causa institutus neque res humanae providentia gubernari, gravi se argumento uti putant cum ita dicunt : " Si esset providentia, nulla essent mala." Nihil enim minus aiunt providentiae congruere, quam in eo mundo quem propter homines fecisse dicatur tantam

2 vim esse aerumnarum et malorum. Adversus ea Chrysippus cum in libro Περὶ Προνοίας quarto dissereret, " Nihil est prorsus istis," inquit, "insubidius,

3 qui opinantur bona esse potuisse, si non essent ibidem mala. Nam cum bona malis contraria sint, utraque necessum est opposita inter sese et quasi mutuo adversoque fulta nisu consistere; nullum

4 adeo contrarium est sine contrario altero. Quo enim pacto iustitiae sensus esse posset, nisi essent iniuriae ? aut quid aliud iustitia est quam iniustitiae privatio ? Quid item fortitudo intellegi posset, nisi ex ignaviae adpositione ? Quid continentia, nisi ex intemperantiae ? Quo item modo prudentia esset,

5 nisi foret contra inprudentia ? Proinde," inquit,

---

[1] Fr. ii. 1169, Arn.

BOOK VII

I

How Chrysippus replied to those who denied the existence
of Providence.

THOSE who do not believe that the world was
created for God and mankind, or that human affairs
are ruled by Providence, think that they are using a
strong argument when they say : " If there were a
Providence, there would be no evils." For they
declare that nothing is less consistent with
Providence than the existence of such a quantity of
troubles and evils in a world which He is said to
have made for the sake of man. Chrysippus, arguing
against such views in the fourth book of his treatise
On Providence,[1] says : " There is absolutely nothing
more foolish than those men who think that good
could exist, if there were at the same time no evil.
For since good is the opposite of evil, it necessarily
follows that both must exist in opposition to each
other, supported as it were by mutual adverse forces ;
since as a matter of fact no opposite is conceivable
without something to oppose it. For how could
there be an idea of justice if there were no acts of
injustice ? or what else is justice than the absence
of injustice ? How too can courage be understood
except by contrast with cowardice ? Or temperance
except by contrast with intemperance ? How also
could there be wisdom, if folly did not exist as its
opposite ? Therefore," said he, " why do not the

91

"homines stulti cur non hoc etiam desiderant, ut veritas sit et non sit mendacium? Namque itidem sunt bona et mala, felicitas et infortunitas, dolor et
6 voluptas. Alterum enim ex altero, sicuti Plato ait, verticibus inter se contrariis deligatum est; si tuleris unum, abstuleris utrumque."

7 Idem Chrysippus in eodem libro tractat consideratque dignumque esse id quaeri putat, εἰ αἱ τῶν ἀνθρώπων νόσοι κατὰ φύσιν γίνονται, id est, si[1] natura ipsa rerum vel providentia, quae compagem hanc mundi et genus hominum fecit, morbos quoque et debilitates et aegritudines corporum, quas patiuntur
8 homines, fecerit. Existimat autem non fuisse hoc principale naturae consilium, ut faceret homines morbis obnoxios, numquam enim hoc convenisse naturae auctori parentique omnium rerum bonarum.
9 "Sed cum multa," inquit, "atque magna gigneret pareretque aptissima et utilissima, alia quoque simul adgnata sunt incommoda his ipsis quae faciebat cohaerentia"; eaque non[2] per naturam, sed per sequellas quasdam necessarias facta dicit, quod ipse
10 appellat κατὰ παρακολούθησιν. "Sicut," inquit, "cum corpora hominum natura fingeret, ratio subtilior et utilitas ipsa operis postulavit ut tenuissimis minu-
11 tisque ossiculis caput compingeret. Sed hanc utilitatem rei maiorem alia quaedam incommoditas extrinsecus consecuta est, ut fieret caput tenuiter munitum et ictibus offensionibusque parvis fragile.
12 Proinde morbi quoque et aegritudines partae sunt,

---

[1] si *added by J. Gronov, or by Otho.*
[2] neque, *J. Gronov.*

---

[1] *Phaedo*, 3, p. 60 B.   [2] Fr. ii, 1170, Arn.

fools also wish that there may be truth, but no false-hood ? For it is in the same way that good and evil exist, happiness and unhappiness, pain and pleasure. For, as Plato says,[1] they are bound one to the other by their opposing extremes; if you take away one, you will have removed both."

In the same book [2] Chrysippus also considers and discusses this question, which he thinks worth investigating : whether men's diseases come by nature ; that is, whether nature herself, or Providence, if you will, which created this structure of the universe and the human race, also created the diseases, weakness, and bodily infirmities from which mankind suffers. He, however, does not think that it was nature's original intention to make men subject to disease ; for that would never have been consistent with nature as the source and mother of all things good. " But," said he, " when she was creating and bringing forth many great things which were highly suitable and useful, there were also produced at the same time troubles closely connected with those good things that she was creating " ; and he declared that these were not due to nature, but to certain inevitable consequences, a process that he himself calls κατὰ παρακολούθησιν. " Exactly as," he says, " when nature fashioned men's bodies, a higher reason and the actual usefulness of what she was creating demanded that the head be made of very delicate and small bones. But this greater usefulness of one part was attended with an external disadvantage ; namely, that the head was but slightly protected and could be damaged by slight blows and shocks. In the same way diseases too and illness were created at the same time with

13 dum salus paritur. Sicut hercle," inquit, " dum virtus hominibus per consilium naturae gignitur, vitia ibidem per adfinitatem contraria[1] nata sunt."

II

Quo itidem modo et vim necessitatemque fati constituerit et esse tamen in nobis consilii iudiciique nostri arbitrium confirmaverit.

1 Fatum, quod εἱμαρμένην Graeci vocant, ad hanc ferme sententiam Chrysippus, Stoicae princeps philosophiae, definit : " Fatum est," inquit, " sempiterna quaedam et indeclinabilis series rerum et catena, volvens semetipsa sese et inplicans per aeternos 2 consequentiae ordines, ex quibus apta nexaque est." Ipsa autem verba Chrysippi, quantum valui memoria, ascripsi, ut, si cui meum istud interpretamentum videbitur esse obscurius, ad ipsius verba animad-3 vertat. In libro enim Περὶ Προνοίας quarto εἱμαρμένην esse dicit φυσικήν τινα σύνταξιν τῶν ὅλων ἐξ ἀϊδίου τῶν ἑτέρων τοῖς ἑτέροις ἐπακολουθούντων καὶ μεταπολουμένων ἀπαραβάτου οὔσης τῆς τοιαύτης ἐπιπλοκῆς.

4 Aliarum autem opinionum disciplinarumque aucto-5 res huic definitioni ita obstrepunt : " Si Chrysippus," inquiunt, " fato putat omnia moveri et regi nec declinari transcendique posse agmina fati et volumina, peccata quoque hominum et delicta non suscensenda neque inducenda sunt ipsis voluntati-

---

[1] contraria, *Skutsch ;* contrariam, *MSS.*

---

[1] Fr. ii. 1000, Arn.

health. Exactly, by Heaven!" said he, "as vices, through their relationship to the opposite quality, are produced at the same time that virtue is created for mankind by nature's design."

II

How Chrysippus also maintained the power and inevitable nature of fate, but at the same time declared that we had control over our plans and decisions.

CHRYSIPPUS, the leader of the Stoic philosophy, defined fate, which the Greeks call εἱμαρμένη, in about the following terms:[1] "Fate," he says, "is an eternal and unalterable series of circumstances, and a chain rolling and entangling itself through an unbroken series of consequences, from which it is fashioned and made up." But I have copied Chrysippus' very words, as exactly as I could recall them, in order that, if my interpretation should seem too obscure to anyone, he may turn his attention to the philosopher's own language. For in the fourth book of his work *On Providence*, he says that εἱμαρμένη is "an orderly series, established by nature, of all events, following one another and joined together from eternity, and their unalterable interdependence."

But the authors of other views and of other schools of philosophy openly criticize this definition as follows: "If Chrysippus," they say, "believes that all things are set in motion and directed by fate, and that the course of fate and its coils cannot be turned aside or evaded, then the sins and faults of men too ought not to cause anger or be attributed to

busque eorum, sed necessitati cuidam et instantiae,
quae oritur ex fato," omnium quae sit rerum domina
et arbitra, per quam necesse sit fieri quicquid
futurum est ; et propterea nocentium poenas legibus
inique constitutas, si homines ad maleficia non
sponte veniunt, sed fato trahuntur.

6   Contra ea Chrysippus tenuiter multa et argute
disserit ; sed omnium fere quae super ea re scripsit
7 huiuscemodi sententia est : " Quamquam ita sit,"
inquit, " ut ratione quadam necessaria et principali
coacta atque conexa sint fato omnia, ingenia tamen
ipsa mentium nostrarum proinde sunt fato obnoxia,
8 ut proprietas eorum est ipsa et qualitas. Nam si
sunt per naturam primitus salubriter utiliterque
ficta, omnem illam vim, quae de fato extrinsecus
ingruit, inoffensius tractabiliusque transmittunt. Sin
vero sunt aspera et inscita et rudia nullisque artium
bonarum adminiculis fulta, etiamsi parvo sive nullo
fatalis incommodi conflictu urgeantur, sua tamen
scaevitate et voluntario impetu in assidua delicta et
9 in errores se ruunt. Idque ipsum ut ea ratione fiat,
naturalis illa et necessaria rerum consequentia efficit,
10 quae ' fatum ' vocatur. Est enim genere ipso quasi
fatale et consequens, ut mala ingenia peccatis et
erroribus non vacent."

11   Huius deinde fere rei exemplo non hercle nimis
alieno neque inlepido utitur. " Sicut," inquit,
"lapidem cylindrum si per spatia terrae prona atque
derupta iacias, causam[1] quidem ei et initium prae-

---

[1] causam, *Hosius* (*cf.* ii. 17. 6) ; causa, ω.

---

[1] Fr. ii. 1000, Arn.   [2] Fr. ii. 1000, Arn.

themselves and their inclinations, but to a certain unavoidable impulse which arises from fate," which is the mistress and arbiter of all things, and through which everything that will happen must happen; and that therefore the establishing of penalties for the guilty by law is unjust, if men do not voluntarily commit crimes, but are led into them by fate.

Against these criticisms Chrysippus argues at length, subtilely and cleverly, but the purport of all that he has written on that subject is about this:[1] "Although it is a fact," he says, "that all things are subject to an inevitable and fundamental law and are closely linked to fate, yet the peculiar properties of our minds are subject to fate only according to their individuality and quality. For if in the beginning they are fashioned by nature for health and usefulness, they will avoid with little opposition and little difficulty all that force with which fate threatens them from without. But if they are rough, ignorant, crude, and without any support from education, through their own perversity and voluntary impulse they plunge into continual faults and sin, even though the assault of some inconvenience due to fate be slight or non-existent. And that this very thing should happen in this way is due to that natural and inevitable connection of events which is called 'fate.' For it is in the nature of things, so to speak, fated and inevitable that evil characters should not be free from sins and faults."

A little later he uses an illustration of this statement of his, which is in truth quite neat and appropriate:[2] "For instance," he says, "if you roll a cylindrical stone over a sloping, steep piece of ground, you do indeed furnish the beginning and

cipitantiae feceris,[1] mox tamen ille praeceps volvitur,
non quia tu id etiam[2] facis, sed quoniam ita sese
modus eius et formae volubilitas habet; sic ordo et
ratio et necessitas fati genera ipsa et principia
causarum movet, impetus vero consiliorum menti-
umque nostrarum actionesque ipsas voluntas cuiusque
12 propria et animorum ingenia moderantur." Infert
deinde verba haec, his quae dixi congruentia: Διὸ
καὶ ὑπὸ τῶν Πυθαγορείων εἴρηται·

Γνώσει δ᾽ ἀνθρώπους αὐθαίρετα πήματ᾽ ἔχοντας,

ὡς τῶν βλαβῶν ἑκάστοις παρ᾽ αὐτοῖς γινομένων καὶ
καθ᾽ ὁρμὴν αὐτῶν ἁμαρτανόντων τε καὶ βλαπτομένων
13 καὶ κατὰ τὴν αὐτῶν διάνοιαν καὶ θέσιν.   Propterea
negat oportere ferri audirique homines aut nequam
aut ignavos et nocentes et audaces, qui, cum in
culpa et in maleficio revicti sunt, perfugiunt ad fati
necessitatem, tamquam in aliquod fani asylum et,
quae pessime fecerunt, ea non suae temeritati, sed
fato esse attribuenda dicunt.

14   Primus autem hoc sapientissimus ille et antiquissi-
mus poetarum dixit hisce versibus:

*Ω πόποι, οἷον δή νυ θεοὺς βροτοὶ αἰτιόωνται.
᾽Εξ ἡμέων γάρ φασι κάκ᾽ ἔμμεναι· οἱ δὲ καὶ αὐτοί
Σφῆσιν ἀτασθαλίῃσιν ὑπὲρ μόρον ἄλγε᾽ ἔχουσιν.

15 Itaque M. Cicero, in libro quem De Fato conscripsit,
cum quaestionem istam diceret obscurissimam esse

----

[1] fueris, *Hertz.*   [2] etiam, *Hosius*; iam, ω.

----

[1] Fr. ii. 1000, Arn.   [2] Χρύσεα ῎Επη, 54.
[3] Homer, *Odyss.* i. 32.   [4] Fr. 1, p. 582, Orelli².

cause of its rapid descent, yet soon it speeds onward, not because you make it do so, but because of its peculiar form and natural tendency to roll; just so the order, the law, and the inevitable quality of fate set in motion the various classes of things and the beginnings of causes, but the carrying out of our designs and thoughts, and even our actions, are regulated by each individual's own will and the characteristics of his mind." Then he adds these words, in harmony with what I have said :[1] "Therefore it is said by the Pythagoreans also :[2]

You'll learn that men have ills which they them-
        selves
Bring on themselves,

for harm comes to each of them through themselves, and they go astray through their own impulse and are harmed by their own purpose and determination." Therefore he says that wicked, slothful, sinful and reckless men ought not to be endured or listened to, who, when they are caught fast in guilt and sin, take refuge in the inevitable nature of fate, as if in the asylum of some shrine, declaring that their outrageous actions must be charged, not to their own heedlessness, but to fate.

The first to express this thought was the oldest and wisest of the poets, in these verses :[3]

Alas! how wrongly mortals blame the gods!
From us, they say, comes evil; they themselves
By their own folly woes unfated bear.

Therefore Marcus Cicero, in the book which he wrote *On Fate*,[4] after first remarking that this question is highly obscure and involved, declares that

et inplicatissimam, Chrysippum quoque philosophum
non expedisse se in ea ait[1] his verbis : " Chrysippus
aestuans laboransque quonam hoc modo[2] explicet,
et fato omnia fieri et esse aliquid in nobis, intricatur."

III

Historia sumpta ex libris Tuberonis de serpente invisitatae
longitudinis.

1   TUBERO in *Historiis* scriptum reliquit, bello primo
Poenico Atilium Regulum consulem in Africa, castris
apud Bagradam flumen positis, proelium grande atque
acre fecisse adversus unum serpentem in illis locis
stabulantem invisitatae inmanitatis, eumque magna
totius exercitus conflictione balistis atque catapultis
diu oppugnatum, eiusque interfecti corium longum
pedes centum et viginti Romam missum esse.[3]

IV

Quid idem Tubero novae historiae de Atilio Regulo a
Carthaginiensibus capto litteris mandaverit ; quid etiam
Tuditanus super eodem Regulo scripserit.

1   QUOD satis celebre est de Atilio Regulo, id nuperrime legimus scriptum in Tuditani libris : Regu-

---

[1] ait, *added by Lion.*
[2] hoc modo *after* intricatur *in* ω ; *transposed by Hertz* ; hoc
nodo *after* intricatur, *Damsté.*

even the philosopher Chrysippus[1] was unable to extricate himself from its difficulties, using these words: "Chrysippus, in spite of all efforts and labour, is perplexed how to explain that everything is ruled by fate, but that we nevertheless have some control over our conduct."

III

An account, taken from the works of Tubero, of a serpent of unprecedented length.

TUBERO in his *Histories* has recorded[2] that in the first Punic war the consul Atilius Regulus, when encamped at the Bagradas river in Africa,[3] fought a stubborn and fierce battle with a single serpent of extraordinary size, which had its lair in that region; that in a mighty struggle with the entire army the reptile was attacked for a long time with hurling engines and catapults; and that when it was finally killed, its skin, a hundred and twenty feet long, was sent to Rome.

IV

A new account, written by the above-mentioned Tubero, of the capture of Regulus by the Carthaginians; and also what Tuditanus wrote about that same Regulus.

I RECENTLY read in the works of Tuditanus the well-known story about Atilius Regulus:[4] That

[1] Fr. ii, 977, Arn. [2] Fr. 8, Peter².
[3] In 256 B.C. [4] Fr. 5, Peter².

---

[3] missum esse, *Lion*; *Hosius suggested* cos. (= consulem) *before* corium; misisse, ω.

lum captum ad ea quae in senatu Romae dixit,
suadens ne captivi cum Carthaginiensibus permuta-
rentur, id quoque addidisse, venenum sibi Carthaginienses dedisse, non praesentarium, sed eiusmodi
quod mortem in diem proferret, eo consilio, ut
viveret quidem tantisper quoad fieret permutatio,
post autem grassante sensim veneno contabesceret.

2 Eundem Regulum Tubero in *Historiis* redisse
Carthaginem novisque exemplorum modis excruci-
3 atum a Poenis dicit: "In atras," inquit, "et pro-
fundas tenebras eum claudebant ac diu post, ubi erat
visus sol ardentissimus, repente educebant et adversus
ictus solis oppositum continebant atque intendere
in caelum oculos cogebant. Palpebras quoque eius,
ne conivere posset, sursum ac deorsum diductas
4 insuebant." Tuditanus autem somno diu prohibitum
atque ita vita privatum refert, idque ubi Romae
cognitum est, nobilissimos Poenorum captivos liberis
Reguli a senatu deditos et ab his in armario muri-
cibus praefixo destitutos eademque insomnia cruciatos
interisse.

V

Quod Alfenus iureconsultus in verbis veteribus interpretandis erravit.

1 ALFENUS iureconsultus, Servii Sulpicii discipulus
rerumque antiquarum non incuriosus, in libro *Di-*

---

[1] Fr. 9, Peter.

Regulus, when a prisoner, in addition to the advice which he gave in the senate at Rome against making an exchange of prisoners with the Carthaginians, also declared that the Carthaginians had given him a poison, not of immediate effect, but such as to delay his death for a season; that their design was that he should live for a time, until the exchange was accomplished, but afterwards should waste away as the drug gradually took effect.

Tubero in his *Histories* says[1] that this Regulus returned to Carthage and was put to death by the Carthaginians with tortures of a novel kind: "They confined him," he says, "in a dark and deep dungeon, and a long time afterwards suddenly brought him out, when the sun was shining most brightly, and exposed him to its direct rays, holding him and forcing him to fix his gaze upon the sky. They even drew his eyelids apart upward and downward and sewed them fast, so that he could not close his eyes." Tuditanus, however, reports that Regulus was for a long time deprived of sleep and so killed, and that when this became known at Rome, Carthaginian captives of the highest rank were handed over by the senate to his sons, who shut them in a chest studded within with spikes;[2] and that they too were tortured to death by lack of sleep.

V

An error of the jurist Alfenus in the interpretation of early words.

THE jurist Alfenus, a pupil of Servius Sulpicius and a man greatly interested in matters antiquarian,

[2] See McCartney, *The Figurative Use of Animal Names* (Univ. of Penna diss.), Lancaster, Pa., 1912.

gestorum tricesimo et quarto, *Coniectaneorum* autem
secundo : " In foedere," inquit, " quod inter populum
Romanum et Carthaginienses factum est, scriptum
invenitur ut Carthaginienses quotannis populo Romano
darent certum pondus 'argenti puri puti,' quaesitumque est quid esset 'purum putum.' Respondi,"
inquit, " ego 'putum' esse 'valde purum,' sicut
novum 'novicium' dicimus et proprium 'propicium,'
augere atque intendere volentes 'novi' et 'proprii'
significationem."

2 Hoc ubi legimus, mirabamur eandem adfinitatem
visam esse Alfeno "puri" et "puti," quae sit
3 "novicii" et "novi"; nam, si esset "puricium,"
4 tum sane videretur dici quasi "novicium." Id etiam
mirum fuit, quod "novicium" per augendi figuram
dictum existimavit, cum sit "novicium" non quod
magis novum sit, sed quod a "novo" dictum sit
5 inclinatumque. His igitur assentimus, qui "putum"
esse dicunt a "putando" dictum et ob eam causam
prima syllaba brevi pronuntiant, non longa, ut existimasse Alfenus videtur, qui a "puro" id esse factum
6 scripsit. "Putare" autem veteres dixerunt vacantia
ex quaque re ac non necessaria aut etiam obstantia
et aliena auferre et excidere, et quod esse utile ac
7 sine vitio videretur relinquere. Sic namque arbores
et vites et sic rationes etiam "putari" dictum.
8 Verbum quoque ipsum "puto," quod declarandae
sententiae nostrae causa dicimus, non significat profecto aliud quam id agere nos in re dubia obscuraque,
ut decisis amputatisque falsis opinionibus, quod vide-

---

[1] Fr. 1, Huschke ; Resp. 14, Dig. 99, Bremer (i, pp. 287,
322, 330).
[2] That is, to clear one's accounts.

in the thirty-fourth book of his *Digests* and the second of his *Miscellanies*, says:[1] "In a treaty which was made between the Roman people and the Carthaginians the provision is found, that the Carthaginians should pay each year to the Roman people a certain weight of *argenti puri puti*, and the meaning of *puri puti* was asked. I replied," he says, "that *putus* meant 'very pure,' just as we say *novicius* for *novus* (new) and *propicius* for *proprius* (proper), when we wish to augment and amplify the meaning of *novus* and *proprius*."

Upon reading this, I was surprised that Alfenus should think that the relation of *purus* and *putus* was the same as that of *novicius* and *novus*; for if the word were *puricius*, then it would indeed appear to be formed like *novicius*. It was also surprising that he thought that *novicius* was used to imply amplification, since in fact *novicius* does not mean "more new," but is merely a derivative and variant of *novus*. Accordingly, I agree with those who think that *putus* is derived from *puto* and therefore pronounce the word with the first syllable short, not long as Alfenus seems to have thought it, since he wrote that *putus* came from *purus*. Moreover, the earlier writers used *putare* of removing and pruning away from anything whatever was superfluous and unnecessary, or even injurious and foreign, leaving only what seemed useful and without blemish. For that was the meaning of *putare*, "to prune," as applied to trees and vines, and so too as used of accounts.[2] The verb *puto* itself also, which we use for the purpose of stating our opinion, certainly means nothing else than that in an obscure and difficult matter we do our best, by cutting away and lopping

atur esse verum et integrum et incorruptum retine-
9 amus. Argentum ergo in Carthaginiensi foedere
"putum" dictum est quasi exputatum excoctumque
omnique aliena materia carens omnibusque ex eo
vitiis detractis emaculatum et candefactum.
10 Scriptum est autem "purum putum," non in Carthaginiensi solum foedere, sed cum in multis aliis
veterum libris, tum in Q. quoque Ennii tragoedia
quae inscribitur *Alexander*, et in satira M. Varronis
quae inscripta est Δὶς Παῖδες οἱ Γέροντες.

VI

Temere inepteque reprehensum esse a Iulio Hygino Vergilium,
quod "praepetes" Daedali pennas dixit ; atque inibi quid
sint "aves praepetes" et quid illae sint aves quas Nigidius
"inferas" appellavit.

1   DAEDALUS, ut fama est, fugiens Minoia regna,
    Praepetibus pennis ausus se credere caelo.

2 In his Vergilii versibus reprehendit Iulius Hyginus
"pennis praepetibus" quasi inproprie et inscite
3 dictum. "Nam 'praepetes,'" inquit, "aves ab
auguribus appellantur, quae aut opportune prae-
4 volant aut idoneas sedes capiunt." Non apte igitur
usum verbo augurali existimavit in Daedali volatu,
nihil ad augurum disciplinam pertinente.
5 Sed Hyginus nimis hercle ineptus fuit, cum quid
"praepetes" essent se scire ratus est, Vergilium

---

¹ 62, Ribbeck³.   ² Fr. 91, Bücheler.
³ *Aen.* vi. 14 f.   ⁴ Fr. 6, Fun.

off false views, to retain what seems true and pure and sound. Therefore in the treaty with Carthage silver was called *putum*, as having been thoroughly purified and refined, as free from all foreign matter, and as spotless and whitened by the removal from it of all impurities.

But the expression *purum putum* occurs, not only in the treaty with Carthage, but also in many other early writings, including the tragedy of Quintus Ennius entitled *Alexander*,[1] and the satire of Marcus Varro called Δὶς Παῖδες οἱ Γέροντες,[2] or *Old Men are Children for a Second Time*.

VI

That Julius Hyginus was hasty and foolish in his criticism of Virgil for calling the wings of Daedalus *praepetes*; also a note on the meaning of *aves praepetes* and of those birds which Nigidius called *inferae*.

From Minos' realms in flight brave Daedalus
  On pinion swift (*praepetibus*), 'tis said, did dare the
    sky.

In these lines of Virgil[3] Julius Hyginus ‘criticizes the use of *pennis praepetibus* as an improper and ignorant expression. "For," says he, "those birds are called *praepetes* by the augurs which either fly onward auspiciously or alight in suitable places." Therefore he thought it inappropriate in Virgil to use an augural term in speaking of the flight of Daedalus, which had nothing to do with the science of the augurs.

But of a truth it was Hyginus who was altogether foolish in supposing that the meaning of *praepetes* was known to him, but unknown to Virgil and to

autem et Cn. Matium, doctum virum, ignorasse, qui
in secundo *Iliadis* Victoriam volucrem "praepetem"
appellavit in hoc versu:

Dum dat vincendi praepes Victoria palmam.

6 Cur autem non Q. quoque Ennium reprehendit, qui
in *Annalibus* non pennas Daedali, sed longe diversius:

Brundisium (inquit) pulcro praecinctum praepete
portu?

7 Set si vim potius naturamque verbi considerasset
neque id solum quod augures dicerent inspexisset,
veniam prorsus poetis daret similitudine ac translatione verborum, non significatione propria utenti-
8 bus. Nam quoniam non ipsae tantum aves quae
prosperius praevolant, sed etiam loci quos capiunt,
quod idonei felicesque sunt, "praepetes" appellantur,
idcirco Daedali pennas "praepetes" dixit, quoniam
ex locis in quibus periculum metuebat in loca tutiora
9 pervenerat. Locos porro "praepetes" et augures
appellant et Ennius in *Annalium* primo dixit:

praepetibus sese pulcrisque locis dant.

10 Avibus autem "praepetibus" contrarias aves "inferas" appellari, Nigidius Figulus in libro primo
Augurii Privati ita dicit: "Discrepat dextra sinistrae,
11 praepes inferae." Ex quo est coniectare "praepetes" appellatas quae altius sublimiusque volitent,

---

1 Fr. 3, Bährens (*F.P.R.*).
2 488, Vahlen². Cf. Gell. ix. 4. 1.
3 94, Vahlen².
4 That is, low-flying, as opposed to swift-, or high-, flying.
5 Fr. 80, Swoboda.

Gnaeus Matius, a learned man, who in the second book of his *Iliad* called winged Victory *praepes* in the following line:[1]

> While Victory swift (*praepes*) the victor's palm bestows.

Furthermore, why does he not find fault also with Quintus Ennius, who in his *Annals* uses *praepes*, not of the wings of Daedalus, but of something very different, in the line:[2]

> Brundisium girt with fair, propitious (*praepete*) port?

But if Hyginus had regarded the force and origin of the word rather than merely noting the meaning given to it by the augurs, he would certainly pardon the poets for using words in a figurative and metaphorical sense rather than literally. For since not only the birds themselves which fly auspiciously, but also the places which they take, since these are suitable and propitious, are called *praepetes*, therefore Virgil called the wings of Daedalus *praepetes*, since he had come from places in which he feared danger into safer regions. Furthermore, the augurs call places *praepetes*, and Ennius in the first book of his *Annals* said:[3]

> In fair, propitious (*praepetibus*) places they alight.

But birds that are the opposite of *praepetes* are called *inferae*, or "low,"[4] according to Nigidius Figulus, who says in the first book of his *Private Augury*:[5] "The right is opposed to the left, *praepes* to *infera*." From this we may infer that birds were called *praepetes* which have a higher and loftier

cum differre a "praepetibus" Nigidius "inferas" dixerit.

12 Adulescens ego Romae, cum etiamtum ad grammaticos itarem, audivi Apollinarem Sulpicium, quem inprimis sectabar, cum de iure augurio quaereretur et mentio "praepetum avium" facta esset, Erucio Claro praefecto urbi dicere, "praepetes" sibi videri esse alites, quas Homerus ταννπτέρυγας appellaverit, quoniam istas potissimum augures spectarent quae ingentibus alis patulae atque porrectae praevolarent. Atque ibi hos Homeri versus dixit:

Τύνη δ' οἰωνοῖσι τανυπτερύγεσσι κελεύεις
Πείθεσθαι, τῶν οὔ τι μετατρέπομ' οὐδ' ἀλεγίζω.

VII

De Acca Larentia et Gaia Taracia; deque origine sacerdotii
Fratrum Arvalium.

1 Accae Larentiae et Gaiae Taraciae, sive illa Fufetia est, nomina in antiquis annalibus celebria sunt. Earum alterae post mortem, Taraciae autem vivae, amplissimi honores a populo Romano habiti.

2 Et Taraciam quidem virginem Vestae fuisse lex Horatia testis est quae super ea ad populum lata. Qua lege ei plurimi honores fiunt, inter quos ius quoque testimonii dicendi tribuitur, "testabilis"que una omnium feminarum ut sit datur. Id verbum est

3 legis ipsius Horatiae; contrarium est in *Duodecim*

---

¹ *Iliad* xii. 237 f.
² viii. 22; the date of this *privilegium* (see x. 20. 4) is uncertain.

flight, since Nigidius said that the *praepetes* were contrasted with the *inferae*.

In my youth in Rome, when I was still in attendance on the grammarians, I gave special attention to Sulpicius Apollinaris. Once when there was a discussion about augural law and mention had been made of *praepetes aves*, I heard him say to Erucius Clarus, the city prefect, that in his opinion *praepetes* was equivalent to Homer's ταννπτέρυγες, or "wide-winged," since the augurs had special regard to those birds whose flight was broad and wide because of their great wings. And then he quoted these verses of Homer :[1]

You bid me trust the flight of wide-winged birds,
But I regard them not, nor think of them.

VII

On Acca Larentia and Gaia Taracia ; and on the origin of the priesthood of the Arval Brethren.

The names of Acca Larentia and Gaia Taracia, or Fufetia as she is sometimes called, are frequent in the early annals. To the former of these after her death, but to Taracia while she still lived, the Roman people paid distinguished honours. And that Taracia, at any rate, was a Vestal virgin is proved by the Horatian law which was laid before the people with regard to her. By this law very many honours are bestowed upon her and among them the right of giving testimony is granted her, and that privilege is given to no other woman in the State. The word *testabilis* is used in the Horatian law itself, and its opposite occurs in the *Twelve Tables* :[2] "Let him be

Tabulis scriptum: "Inprobus intestabilisque esto."
4 Praeterea si quadraginta annos nata sacerdotio abire
ac nubere voluisset, ius ei potestasque exaugurandi
atque nubendi facta est munificentiae et beneficii
gratia, quod campum Tiberinum sive Martium populo
condonasset.
5 Sed Acca Larentia corpus in vulgus dabat pecu-
6 niamque emeruerat ex eo quaestu uberem. Ea
testamento, ut in Antiatis *Historia* scriptum est,
Romulum regem, ut quidam autem alii tradiderunt,
7 populum Romanum bonis suis heredem fecit. Ob id
meritum a flamine Quirinali sacrificium ei publice fit
8 et dies e nomine eius in fastos additus. Sed Sabinus
Masurius in primo *Memorialium,* secutus quosdam
historiae scriptores, Accam Larentiam Romuli nutricem fuisse dicit. "Ea," inquit, "mulier ex duodecim filiis maribus unum morte amisit. In illius
locum Romulus Accae sese filium dedit seque et
ceteros eius filios 'fratres Arvales' appellavit. Ex eo
tempore collegium mansit fratrum Arvalium numero
duodecim, cuius sacerdotii insigne est spicea corona
et albae infulae."

VIII

Notata quaedam de rege Alexandro et de P. Scipione
memoratu digna.

1 Ἀπίων, Graecus homo, qui Πλειστονείκης appella-
2 tus est, facili atque alacri facundia fuit. Is cum de

---

[1] Fr. 1, Peter[2].
[2] Fr. 14, Huschke; 1, Bremer (ii, p. 368).

infamous and *intestabilis*, or ‘forbidden to testify.’ ”
Besides, if at the age of forty she should wish to
leave the priesthood and marry, the right and
privilege of withdrawing from the order and marry-
ing were allowed her, in gratitude for her generosity
and kindness in presenting to the people the *campus
Tiberinus* or *Martius*.

But Acca Larentia was a public prostitute and by
that trade had earned a great deal of money. In
her will she made king Romulus heir to her property,
according to Antias’ *History*;[1] according to some
others, the Roman people. Because of that favour
public sacrifice was offered to her by the priest of
Quirinus and a day was consecrated to her memory
in the Calendar. But Masurius Sabinus, in the first
book of his *Memorialia*, following certain historians,
asserts that Acca Larentia was Romulus’ nurse.
His words are:[2] “This woman, who had twelve
sons, lost one of them by death. In his place
Romulus gave himself to Acca as a son, and called
himself and her other sons ‘ Arval Brethren.’ Since
that time there has always been a college of Arval
Brethren, twelve in number, and the insignia of the
priesthood are a garland of wheat ears and white
fillets.”

VIII

Some noteworthy anecdotes of King Alexander and of
Publius Scipio.

Apion, a Greek, called Pleistoneices,[3] possessed a
fluent and lively style. Writing in praise of king

[3] “Of many quarrels,” a word coined in imitation of the
epithet applied to famous athletes: πλειστονίκης, “of many
victories.”

Alexandri regis laudibus scriberet : " Victi," inquit,
" hostis uxorem, facie incluta mulierem, vetuit in
conspectum suum deduci, ut eam ne oculis quidem
3 suis contingeret." Lepide igitur agitari potest,
utrum videri continentiorem par sit, Publiumne
Africanum superiorem, qui, Carthagine ampla civitate
in Hispania expugnata, virginem tempestivam, forma
egregia, nobilis viri Hispani filiam captam perductamque ad se patri inviolatam reddidit, an regem Alexandrum, qui Darii regis uxorem eandemque eiusdem
sororem, proelio magno captam, quam esse audiebat
exuperanti forma, videre noluit perducique ad sese
prohibuit.
4   Sed hanc utramque declamatiunculam super Alexandro et Scipione celebraverint, quibus abunde et
5 ingenii et otii et verborum est ; nos satis habebimus,
quod ex historia est, id dicere : Scipionem istum,
verone an falso incertum, fama tamen, cum esset
adulescens, haud sincera fuisse et propemodum constitisse, hosce versus a Cn. Naevio poeta in eum
scriptos esse :

> Etiám qui res magnás manu [1] saepe géssit glorióse,
> Cuius fácta viva núnc vigent, qui apud géntes
>   solus praéstat,
> Eum súus pater cum pállio uno domum [2] ab amíca
>   abduxit.

6   His ego versibus credo adductum Valerium Antiatem adversus ceteros omnis scriptores de Scipionis

---

[1] manu magnas, *Fleckeisen.*   [2] domum *added by Bährens.*

---

[1] *F.H.G.* iii. 515.
[2] Really New Carthage, captured in 210 B.C. ; the story is
told by Livy, xxvi. 50.

Alexander, he says : [1] "He forbade the wife of his vanquished foe, a woman of surpassing loveliness, to be brought into his presence, in order that he might not touch her even with his eyes." We have then the subject for a pleasant discussion—which of the two shall justly be considered the more continent : Publius Africanus the elder, who after he had stormed Carthage,[2] a powerful city in Spain, and a marriageable girl of wonderful beauty, the daughter of a noble Spaniard, had been taken prisoner and brought to him, restored her unharmed to her father ; or king Alexander, who refused even to see the wife of king Darius, who was also his sister, when he had taken her captive in a great battle and had heard that she was of extreme beauty, but forbade her to be brought before him.

But those who have an abundance of talent, leisure and eloquence may use this material for a pair of little declamations on Alexander and Scipio ; I shall be satisfied with relating this, which is a matter of historical record : Whether it be false or true is uncertain, but at any rate the story goes that your Scipio in his youth did not have an unblemished reputation, and that it was all but generally believed that it was at him that the following verses were aimed by the poet Gnaeus Naevius : [3]

E'en he who oft-times mighty deeds hath done,
Whose glory and exploits still live, to whom
The nations bow, his father once led home,
Clad in a single garment, from his love.

I think it was by these verses that Valerius Antias was led to hold an opinion opposed to that of all

[3] ii. 108, Ribbeck[3].

moribus sensisse et eam puellam captivam non reddi-
tam patri scripsisse, contra quam nos supra diximus,
sed retentam a Scipione atque in deliciis amoribusque
ab eo usurpatam.

IX

Locus exemptus ex *Annalibus* L. Pisonis historiae et orationis
lepidissimae.

1   Quod res videbatur memoratu digna, quam fecisse
Cn. Flavium, Anni filium, aedilem curulem, L. Piso
in tertio *Annali* scripsit, eaque res perquam pure et
venuste narrata a Pisone, locum istum totum huc ex
Pisonis *Annali* transposuimus.

2   "Cn.," inquit, "Flavius, patre libertino natus,
scriptum faciebat, isque in eo tempore aedili curuli
apparebat, quo tempore aediles subrogantur, eumque
3 pro tribu aedilem curulem renuntiaverunt. Aedilem
qui comitia habebat negat accipere, neque sibi
placere, qui scriptum faceret, eum aedilem fieri.

4 Cn. Flavius, Anni filius, dicitur tabulas posuisse,
scriptu sese abdicasse, isque aedilis curulis factus
est.

5   "Idem Cn Flavius, Anni filius, dicitur ad collegam
venisse visere aegrotum. Eo in conclave postquam
introivit, adulescentes ibi complures nobiles sede-
bant. Hi contemnentes eum, assurgere ei nemo

---

[1] Fr. 25, Peter[2].

[2] He was the secretary of the censor Appius Claudius
Caecus and became curule aedile in 303 B.C.

[3] Fr. 27, Peter[2].

[4] The expression *pro tribu* is difficult, but appears in Livy
ix, 46. 2 in the same connection, *cum fieri se pro tribu aedilem*

other writers about Scipio's character, and to write,[1]
contrary to what I said above, that the captured
maiden was not returned to her father, but was kept
by Scipio and possessed by him in amorous dalliance.

IX

A passage taken from the *Annals* of Lucius Piso, highly
diverting in content and graceful in style.

BECAUSE the action of Gnaeus Flavius,[2] the curule
aedile, son of Annius, which Lucius Piso described in
the third book of his *Annals,* seemed worthy of record,
and because the story is told by Piso in a very pure
and charming style, I have quoted the entire passage
from Piso's *Annals*:[3]

"Gnaeus Flavius, the son of a freedman," he says,
"was a scribe by profession and was in the service of
a curule aedile at the time of the election of the
succeeding aediles. The assembly of the tribes[4]
named Flavius curule aedile, but the magistrate who
presided at the election refused to accept him as an
aedile, not thinking it right that one who followed
the profession of scribe should be made an aedile.
Gnaeus Flavius, son of Annius, is said to have laid
aside his tablets and resigned his clerkship, and he
was then made a curule aedile.

"This same Gnaeus Flavius, son of Annius, is said
to have come to call upon a sick colleague. When
he arrived and entered the room, several young
nobles were seated there. They treated Flavius
with contempt and none of them was willing to

videret. Gronovius believed that it referred to the *tribus
praerogativa.* which voted first in order.

6 voluit. Cn. Flavius, Anni filius, aedilis, id arrisit,
sellam curulem iussit sibi afferri, eam in limine
apposuit, ne quis illorum exire posset utique hi
omnes inviti viderent sese in sella curuli sedentem."

X

Historia super Euclida Socratico, cuius exemplo Taurus philosophus hortari adulescentes suos solitus ad philosophiam
naviter sectandam.

1 PHILOSOPHUS TAURUS, vir memoria nostra in disciplina Platonica celebratus, cum aliis bonis multis sa-
lubribusque exemplis hortabatur ad philosophiam ca-
pessendam, tum vel maxime ista re iuvenum animos
expergebat, Euclidem quam dicebat Socraticum fac-
2 titavisse. "Decreto," inquit, "suo Athenienses
caverant, ut qui Megaris civis esset, si intulisse
Athenas pedem prensus esset, ut ea res ei homini
3 capitalis esset; tanto Athenienses," inquit, "odio
4 flagrabant finitimorum hominum Megarensium. Tum
Euclides, qui indidem Megaris erat quique ante id
decretum et esse Athenis et audire Socratem consue-
verat, postquam id decretum sanxerunt, sub noctem,
cum advesperasceret, tunica longa muliebri indutus
et pallio versicolore amictus et caput rica velatus, e
domo sua Megaris Athenas ad Socratem commeabat,
ut vel noctis aliquo tempore consiliorum sermonum-
que eius fieret particeps, rursusque sub lucem milia
passuum paulo amplius viginti eadem veste illa

rise in his presence. Gnaeus Flavius, son of Annius, the aedile, laughed at this rudeness; then he ordered his curule chair to be brought and placed it on the threshold, in order that none of them might be able to go out, and that all of them against their will might see him sitting on his chair of state."

X

A story about Euclides, the Socratic, by whose example the philosopher Taurus used to urge his pupils to be diligent in the pursuit of philosophy.

THE philosopher Taurus, a celebrated Platonist of my time, used to urge the study of philosophy by many other good and wholesome examples and in particular stimulated the minds of the young by what he said that Euclides the Socratic used to do. "The Athenians," said he, "had provided in one of their decrees that any citizen of Megara who should be found to have set foot in Athens should for that suffer death; so great," says he, "was the hatred of the neighbouring men of Megara with which the Athenians were inflamed. Then Euclides, who was from that very town of Megara and before the passage of that decree had been accustomed both to come to Athens and to listen to Socrates, after the enactment of that measure, at nightfall, as darkness was coming on, clad in a woman's long tunic, wrapped in a parti-coloured mantle, and with veiled head, used to walk from his home in Megara to Athens, to visit Socrates, in order that he might at least for some part of the night share in the master's teaching and discourse. And just before dawn he went back again, a distance of somewhat over twenty miles,

5 tectus redibat. At nunc," inquit, "videre est philosophos ultro currere, ut doceant, ad fores iuvenum divitum eosque ibi sedere atque opperiri prope ad meridiem, donec discipuli nocturnum omne vinum edormiant."

XI

Verba ex oratione Q. Metelli Numidici, quae libuit meminisse, ad officium gravitatis dignitatisque vitae ducentia.

1   Cum inquinatissimis hominibus non esse convicio decertandum neque in maledictis adversum inpudentes et inprobos velitandum, quia tantisper similis et compar eorum fias, dum paria et consimilia dicas atque audis,[1] non minus ex oratione Q. Metelli Numidici, sapientis viri, cognosci potest quam ex
2 libris et disciplinis philosophorum.   Verba haec sunt Metelli *Adversus C. Manlium, tribunum plebis,* a quo apud populum in contione lacessitus iactatusque
3 fuerat dictis petulantibus : "Nunc quod ad illum attinet, Quirites, quoniam se ampliorem putat esse, si se mihi inimicum dictitarit, quem ego mihi neque amicum recipio neque inimicum respicio, in eum ego non sum plura dicturus.   Nam cum indignissimum arbitror cui a viris bonis benedicatur, tum ne idoneum quidem cui a probis maledicatur.   Nam si in eo tempore huiusmodi homunculum nomines, in quo punire non possis, maiore honore quam contumelia adficias."

---

[1] audis, *Hosius* (*cf.* v. 11. 1, vi. 15. 2, *etc.*) ; audias, *ω.*

[1] *O.R.F.* p. 274, Meyer[2].

disguised in that same garb. But nowadays," said Taurus, "we may see the philosophers themselves running to the doors of rich young men, to give them instruction, and there they sit and wait until nearly noonday, for their pupils to sleep off all last night's wine."

XI

A passage from a speech of Quintus Metellus Numidicus, which it was my pleasure to recall, since it draws attention to the obligation of self-respect and dignity in the conduct of life.

ONE should not vie in abusive language with the basest of men or wrangle with foul words with the shameless and wicked, since you become like them and their exact mate so long as you say things which match and are exactly like what you hear. This truth may be learned no less from an address of Quintus Metellus Numidicus, a man of wisdom, than from the books and the teachings of the philosophers. These are the words of Metellus from his speech *Against Gaius Manlius, Tribune of the Commons*,[1] by whom he had been assailed and taunted in spiteful terms in a speech delivered before the people : " Now, fellow citizens, so far as Manlius is concerned, since he thinks that he will appear a greater man, if he keeps calling me his enemy, who neither count him as my friend nor take account of him as an enemy, I do not propose to say another word. For I consider him not only wholly unworthy to be well spoken of by good men, but unfit even to be reproached by the upright. For if you name an insignificant fellow of his kind at a time when you cannot punish him, you confer honour upon him rather than ignominy."

XII

Quod neque "testamentum," sicuti Servius Sulpicius existimavit, neque "sacellum." sicuti C. Trebatius, duplicia
verba sunt. sed a "testatione" productum alterum,[1] alterum a "sacro" imminutum.

1 SERVIUS SULPICIUS iureconsultus, vir aetatis suae
doctissimus, in libro *De Sacris Detestandis* secundo,
qua ratione adductus "testamentum" verbum esse
2 duplex scripserit, non reperio; nam compositum
3 esse dixit a "mentis contestatione." Quid igitur
"calciamentum," quid "paludamentum," quid
"pavimentum," quid "vestimentum," quid alia mille
per huiuscemodi formam producta, etiamne ista omnia
4 composita dicemus? Obrepsisse autem videtur Servio, vel si quis est qui id prior dixit, falsa quidem,
sed non abhorrens neque inconcinna quasi mentis
quaedam in hoc vocabulo significatio, sicut hercle C.
5 quoque Trebatio eadem concinnitas obrepsit. Nam
in libro *De Religionibus* secundo: "'Sacellum' est,"
inquit, "locus parvus deo sacratus cum ara." Deinde
addit verba haec: "'Sacellum' ex duobus verbis
arbitror compositum 'sacri' et 'cellae,' quasi 'sacra
6 cella.'" Hoc quidem scripsit Trebatius; set quis
ignorat, "sacellum" et simplex verbum esse et non
ex "sacro" et "cella" copulatum, sed ex "sacro"
deminutum?

---

[1] alterum *added by Hertz.*

---

[1] Fr. 3, Huschke; i, p. 225, Bremer.

XII

That neither *testamentum*, as Servius Sulpicius thought, nor *sacellum*, as Gaius Trebatus believed, is a compound, but the former is an extended form of *testatio*, the latter a diminutive of *sacrum*.

I DO not understand what reason led Servius Sulpicius the jurist, the most learned man of his time, to write in the second book of his work *On the Annulling of Sacred Rites* [1] that *testamentum* is a compound word; for he declared that it was made up of *mentis contestatio*, or "an attesting of the mind." What then are we to say about *calciamentum* (shoe), *paludamentum* (cloak), *pavimentum* (pavement), *vestimentum* (clothing), and thousands of other words that have been extended by a suffix of that kind? Are we to call all these also compounds? As a matter of fact, Servius, or whoever it was who first made the statement, was evidently misled by a notion of the presence of *mens* in *testamentum*, an idea that is to be sure false, but neither inappropriate nor unattractive, just as indeed Gaius Trebatius too was misled into a similar attractive combination. For he says in the second book of his work *On Religions* : [2] "A *sacellum*, or 'shrine,' is a small place consecrated to a god and containing an altar." Then he adds these words : "*Sacellum*, I think, is made up of the two words *sacer* and *cella*, as if it were *sacra cella*, or 'a sacred chamber.'" This indeed is what Trebatius wrote, but who does not know both that *sacellum* is not a compound, and that it is not made up of *sacer* and *cella*, but is the diminutive of *sacrum*?

XIII

De quaestiunculis apud Taurum philosophum in convivio
agitatis, quae "sympoticae" vocantur.

1 FACTITATUM observatumque hoc Athenis est ab
2 his qui erant philosopho Tauro iunctiores; cum
domum suam nos vocaret, ne omnino, ut dicitur,
immunes et asymboli veniremus, coniectabamus[1] ad
cenulam non cuppedias ciborum, sed argutias quae-
3 stionum. Unusquisque igitur nostrum commentus
paratusque ibat quod quaereret, eratque initium
4 loquendi edundi finis. Quaerebantur autem non
gravia nec reverenda, sed ἐνθυμημάτια quaedam lepida
et minuta et florentem vino animum lacessentia,
quale hoc ferme est subtilitatis ludicrae, quod dicam.
5 Quaesitum est quando moriens moreretur? cum
iam in morte esset, an cum etiamtum in vita foret;
et quando surgens surgeret? cum iam staret, an cum
etiamtum sederet; et qui artem disceret, quando
artifex fieret? cum iam esset, an cum etiamtum non
6 esset. Utrum enim horum dices, absurde atque ridicule dixeris, multoque absurdius videbitur, si aut
utrumque esse dicas aut neutrum.
7 Sed ea omnia cum captiones esse quidam futtiles
atque inanes dicerent, "Nolite," inquit Taurus,
"haec quasi nugarum aliquem ludum aspernari.

---

[1] convectabamus, *Petschenig.*

---

[1] Really, talk "over the wine," or after-dinner talk.

XIII

On the brief topics discussed at the table of the philosopher Taurus and called *Sympoticae*, or *Table Talk*.[1]

This custom was practised and observed at Athens by those who were on intimate terms with the philosopher Taurus; when he invited us to his home, in order that we might not come wholly tax-free,[2] as the saying is, and without a contribution, we brought to the simple meal, not dainty foods, but ingenious topics for discussion. Accordingly, each one of us came with a question which he had thought up and prepared, and when the eating ended, conversation began. The questions, however, were neither weighty nor serious, but certain neat but trifling ἐνθυμημάτια, or problems, which would pique a mind enlivened with wine; for instance, the examples of playful subtlety which I shall quote.

The question was asked, when a dying man died—when he was already in the grasp of death, or while he still lived? And when did a rising man rise—when he was already standing, or while he was still seated? And when did one who was learning an art become an artist—when he already was one, or when he was still learning? For whichever answer you make, your statement will be absurd and laughable, and it will seem much more absurd, if you say that it is in either case, or in neither.

But when some declared that all these questions were pointless and idle sophisms, Taurus said : "Do not despise such problems, as if they were mere trifling

[2] The reference is to a dinner to which each guest brought his contribution (*symbolum*); cf. Hor. *Odes*, iv. 12. 14 f., non ego te meis *immunem* meditor tinguere poculis ; Catull. xiii.

8 Gravissimi philosophorum super hac re serio quaesiverunt ; et alii moriendi verbum atque momentum manente adhuc vita dici atque fieri putaverunt, alii nihil in eo tempore vitae reliquerunt totumque illud,
9 quod mori dicitur, morti vindicaverunt ; item de ceteris similibus in diversa tempora et in contrarias
10 sententias discesserunt. Sed Plato," inquit, " noster neque vitae id tempus neque morti dedit, idemque in
11 omni consimilium rerum disceptatione fecit. Vidit quippe utrumque esse pugnans neque posse ex duobus contrariis, altero manente, alterum constitui quaestionemque fieri per diversorum inter se finium mortis et vitae cohaerentiam, et idcirco peperit ipse expressitque aliud quoddam novum in confinio tempus, quod verbis propriis atque integris τὴν ἐξαίφνης φύσιν appellavit idque ipsum ita, uti dico," inquit, " in libro, cui *Parmenides* titulus est, scriptum ab eo reperietis."
12 Tales aput Taurum symbolae taliaque erant mensarum secundarum, ut ipse dicere solitus erat, τραγημάτια.

XIV

Poeniendis peccatis tres esse rationes a philosophis attributas ; et quamobrem Plato duarum ex his meminerit, non trium.

1 POENIENDIS peccatis tres esse debere causas existi-
2 matum est. Una est causa, quae Graece vel κόλασις

---

[1] See Pease, "Things without Honor," *Class. Phil.* xxi. (1926), pp. 97 ff.
[2] *Parm.* 21, p. 156 D ; cf. vi. 21, above. [3] See note 2, p. 125.

amusements. The most earnest of the philosophers have seriously debated this question.[1] Some have thought that the term 'die' was properly used, and that the moment of death came, while life still remained; others have left no life in that moment, but have claimed for death all that period which is termed 'dying.' Also in regard to other similar problems they have argued for different times and maintained opposite opinions. But our master Plato," [2] said he, "assigned that time neither to life nor to death, and took the same position in every discussion of similar questions. For he saw that the alternatives were mutually contrary, that one of the two opposites could not be maintained while the other existed, and that the question arose from the juxtaposition of two opposing extremes, namely life and death. Therefore he himself devised, and gave a name to, a new period of time, lying on the boundary between the two, which he called in appropriate and exact language ἡ ἐξαίφνης φύσις, or 'the moment of sudden separation.' And this very term, as I have given it," said he, "you will find used by him in the dialogue entitled *Parmenides*."

Of such a kind were our "contributions" [3] at Taurus' house, and such were, as he himself used to put it, the τραγημάτια or "sweetmeats" of our desserts.

XIV

The three reasons given by the philosophers for punishing crimes; and why Plato mentions only two of these, and not three.

IT has been thought that there should be three reasons for punishing crimes. One of these, which

vel νουθεσία dicitur, cum poena adhibetur casti-
gandi atque emendandi gratia, ut is qui fortuito
3 delinquit attentior fiat correctiorque.   Altera est,
quam hi qui vocabula ista curiosius diviserunt τιμωρίαν appellant.   Ea causa animadvertendi est, cum
dignitas auctoritasque eius in quem est peccatum
tuenda est, ne praetermissa animadversio contemptum
eius pariat et honorem levet ; idcircoque id ei voca-
4 bulum a conservatione honoris factum putant.   Tertia
ratio vindicandi est quae παράδειγμα a Graecis nominatur cum poenitio propter exemplum necessaria
est, ut ceteri a similibus peccatis, quae prohiberi
publicitus interest, metu cognitae poenae deterrean-
tur.   Idcirco veteres quoque nostri " exempla " pro
maximis gravissimisque poenis dicebant.   Quando
igitur aut spes magna est ut is qui peccavit citra
poenam ipse sese ultro corrigat, aut spes contra nulla
est emendari eum posse et corrigi, aut iacturam
dignitatis, in quem peccatum est, metui non necessum est, aut non id peccatum est cuius exemplum
necessario metu sanciendum sit : tum, quicquid ita
delictum est non sane dignum esse imponendi poenae
studium visum est.
5   Has tris ulciscendi rationes et philosophi alii
plurifariam et noster Taurus in primo *Commen-*

the Greeks call either κόλασις or νουθεσία, is the
infliction of punishment for the purpose of correction
and reformation, in order that one who has done
wrong thoughtlessly may become more careful and
scrupulous. The second is called τιμωρία by those
who have made a more exact differentiation between
terms of this kind. That reason for punishment
exists when the dignity and the prestige of the one
who is sinned against must be maintained, lest the
omission of punishment bring him into contempt
and diminish the esteem in which he is held; and
therefore they think that it was given a name
derived from the preservation of honour (τιμή). A
third reason for punishment is that which is called
by the Greeks παράδειγμα, when punishment is
necessary for the sake of example, in order that
others through fear of a recognized penalty may be
kept from similar sins, which it is to the common
interest to prevent. Therefore our forefathers also
used the word *exempla*, or " examples," for the
severest and heaviest penalties. Accordingly, when
there is either strong hope that the culprit will
voluntarily correct himself without punishment, or
on the other hand when there is no hope that he
can be reformed and corrected; or when there is no
need to fear loss of prestige in the one who has
been sinned against; or if the sin is not of such a
sort that punishment must be inflicted in order
that it may inspire a necessary feeling of fear—then
in the case of all such sins the desire to inflict
punishment does not seem to be at all fitting.

Other philosophers have discussed these three
reasons for punishment in various places, and so too
had our countryman Taurus in the first book of the

tariorum, quos *in Gorgian Platonis* composuit, scriptas
6 reliquit. Plato autem ipse verbis apertis duas solas
esse poeniendi causas dicit : unam, quam primo in
loco propter corrigendum, alteram, quam in tertio
7 propter exempli metum posuimus. .Verba haec
sunt Platonis in *Gorgia* : Προσήκει δὲ παντὶ τῷ
ἐν τιμωρίᾳ ὄντι ὑπ' ἄλλου ὀρθῶς τιμωρουμένῳ ἢ βελτίονι
γίγνεσθαι καὶ ὀνίνασθαι, ἢ παραδείγματι ἄλλοις[1] γίγνεσθαι, ἵνα ἄλλοι οἱ[2] ὁρῶντες πάσχοντα φοβούμενοι βελτίους
8 γίγνωνται. In hisce verbis facile intellegas τιμωρίαν
Platonem dixisse, non ut supra scripsi quosdam
dicere, sed ita ut promisce dici solet pro omni
9 punitione. Anne autem quasi omnino parvam et
contemptu dignam praeterierit poenae sumendae
causam propter tuendam laesi hominis auctoritatem,
an magis quasi ei quam dicebat rei non necessariam
praetermiserit, cum de poenis, non in vita neque
inter homines, sed post vitae tempus capiendis
scriberet, ego in medium relinquo.

XV

De verbo " quiesco," an *e* littera corripi an produci debeat.

1 AMICUS noster, homo multi studii atque in bonarum disciplinarum opere frequens, verbum "quie-
2 scit" usitate *e* littera correpta dixit. Alter item
amicus, homo in doctrinis, quasi in praestigiis,

---

[1] τοῖς ἄλλοις, *Plato.*   [2] οἱ *omitted in MSS. of Plato.*

[1] 81, p. 525 A.

Commentaries which he wrote *On the Gorgias of Plato*. But Plato himself says in plain terms that there are only two reasons for punishment : one being that which I put first—for the sake of correction ; the second, that which I gave in the third place—as an example to inspire fear. These are Plato's own words in the *Gorgias* :[1] " It is fitting that everyone who suffers punishment, when justly punished by another, either be made better and profit thereby, or serve as an example to others, in order that they, seeing his punishment, may be reformed through fear." In these words you may readily understand that Plato used τιμωρία, not in the sense that I said above is given it by some, but with the general meaning of any punishment. But whether he omitted the maintenance of the prestige of an injured person as a reason for inflicting punishment, on the ground that it was altogether insignificant and worthy of contempt, or rather passed over it as something not germane to his subject, since he was writing about punishments to be inflicted after this life and not during life and among men, this question I leave undecided.

XV

On the verb *quiesco*, whether it should be pronounced with a long or a short *e*.

A FRIEND of mine, a man of much learning and devoted to the liberal arts, pronounced the verb *quiescit* (" be quiet ") in the usual manner, with a short *e*. Another man, also a friend of mine, marvellous in the use of grammatical rules as jugglers' tricks, so to say, and excessively fastidious

mirificus communiumque vocum respuens nimis et
fastidiens, barbare eum dixisse opinatus est, quoniam
3 producere debuisset, non corripere. Nam " quiescit"
ita oportere dici praedicavit, ut " calescit, nitescit,
4 stupescit " et alia huiuscemodi multa. Id etiam
addebat, quod "quies" *e* producto, non brevi dice-
5 retur. Noster autem, qua est rerum omnium verecunda mediocritate, ne si Aelii quidem, Cincii et
Santrae dicendum ita censuissent, obsecuturum se
fuisse ait contra perpetuam Latinae linguae consuetudinem, neque se tam insignite locuturum, ut
6 absona inauditaque diceret; litteras tamen super hac
re fecit inter exercitia quaedam ludicra et " quiesco "
non esse his simile quae supra posui, nec a " quiete "
dictum, sed ab eo "quietem," Graecaeque vocis et
modum et originem verbum istud habere demon-
stravit, rationibusque haut sane frigidis docuit
" quiesco " *e* littera longa dici non convenire.

XVI

Verbum "deprecor" a poeta Catullo inusitate quidem, sed
apte positum et proprie ; deque ratione eius verbi exemplisque veterum scriptorum.

1 EIUSMODI quispiam qui tumultuariis et inconditis

---

[1] Mentioned as typical grammarians   The *gens Aelia*
included several famous jurists and men of letters ; the
reference here is to Lucius Aelius Stilo, the teacher of Varro

in rejecting common words, thought that the first
man had been guilty of a barbarism, maintaining
that he ought to have lengthened the *e*, rather than
shortened it. For he asserted that *quiescit* ought
to be pronounced like *calescit, nitescit, stupescit* and
many other words of that kind. He also added the
statement that *quies* (quiet) is pronounced with the *e*
long, not short. But my first-named friend, with
the unassuming modesty which was characteristic
of him in all matters, said that not even if the Aelii,
the Cincii and the Santrae[1] had decided that the
word ought to be so pronounced, would he follow
their ruling against the universal usage of the Latin
language, nor would he speak in such an eccentric
fashion as to be discordant and strange in his diction.
Nevertheless he wrote a letter on the subject,
among some exercises for his own amusement, in
which he tried to prove that *quiesco* is not like those
words which I have quoted above; that it is not
derived from *quies* but rather *quies* from *quiesco*. He
also maintained that *quiesco* has the form and derivation of a Greek word,[2] and he tried to show, by
reasons that were by no means without force, that
the word should not be pronounced with a long *e*.[3]

XVI

On a use by the poet Catullus of the word *deprecor*, which is
unusual, it is true, but appropriate and correct ; and on
the origin of that word, with examples from early writers.

As we chanced to be strolling one evening in the

and Cicero. Santra was a grammarian of the first century
B.C.; the Cincii were less well known

[2] A fanciful derivation from Ionic ἔχω, ἔσχω.

[3] The *e* is however long ; *quiésco* occurs in *C.I.L.* vi, 6250
and 25521.

linguae exercitationibus ad famam sese facundiae
promiserat[1] neque orationis Latinae usurpationes
rationesve[2] ullas didicerat, cum in Lycio forte
2 vespera ambularemus, ludo ibi et voluptati fuit. Nam
cum esset verbum " deprecor " doctiuscule positum in
Catulli carmine, quia id ignorabat, frigidissimos
versus esse dicebat omnium quidem iudicio venustis-
simos, quos subscripsi :

> Lesbia mi dicit semper male nec tacet umquam
>   De me ; Lesbia me dispeream nisi amat.
> Quo signo ? quia sunt totidem mea ; deprecor
>   illam
> Assidue, verum dispeream nisi amo.

3 " Deprecor " hoc in loco vir bonus ita esse dictum putabat, ut plerumque a vulgo dicitur, quod significat
" valde precor " et " oro " et " supplico," in quo
" de " praepositio ad augendum et cumulandum
4 valet. Quod si ita esset, frigidi sane versus forent.
5 Nunc enim contra omnino est ; nam " de " praepositio, quoniam est anceps, in uno eodemque verbo
duplicem vim[3] capit. Sic enim " deprecor " a
Catullo dictum est, quasi " detestor " vel " exsecror "
6 vel " depello " vel " abominor "; contra autem
valet, cum Cicero *Pro P. Sulla* ita dicit : " Quam[4]
7 multorum hic vitamst[5] a Sulla deprecatus." Item
in dissuasione legis agrariae : " Si quid deliquero,

---

[1] promoverat, *suggested by Hosius* ; promiserat, *ω.*
[2] rationes *added by Hertz* ; u. veras, *Carrio* ; u. venustas, *Petschenig.*
[3] duplicem (or duum) vim, *Hosius* ; dum, *V* ; diversum, *Dziatzko.*
[4] quam, *omitted by Cic.*
[5] est, *Cic.* ; sit, *V.*

Lyceum,[1] we were furnished with sport and amusement by a certain man, of the kind that lays claim
to a reputation for eloquence by a superficial and
ill-regulated use of language, without having learned
any of the usages and principles of the Latin tongue.
For while Catullus in one of his poems had used the
word *deprecor* rather cleverly, that fellow, unable to
appreciate this, declared that the following verses
which I have quoted were very flat, although in the
judgment of all men they are most charming:[2]

My Lesbia constantly speaks ill of me
And ceases not. By Jove! she cares for me!
How do I know? 'Tis just the same with me;
I rail at, but by Jove! I worship, her.

Our good man thought that *deprecor* in this
passage was used in the sense that is commonly
given the word by the vulgar; that is, "I pray
earnestly," "I beseech," "I entreat," where the
preposition *de* is used intensively and emphatically.
And if that were so, the verses would indeed be
flat. But as a matter of fact the sense is exactly
the opposite; for the preposition *de*, since it has a
double force, contains two meanings in one and the
same word. For *deprecor* is used by Catullus in the
sense of "denounce, execrate, drive away," or "avert
by prayers"; but it also has the opposite meaning,
when Cicero *In Defence of Publius Sulla* speaks as
follows:[3] "How many men's lives did he beg off
(*est deprecatus*) from Sulla." Similarly in his speech
Against the Agrarian Law Cicero says:[4] "If I do any

---

[1] A gymnasium at Athens, the favourite resort of Aristotle
and his pupils.
[2] xcii.   [3] § 72.   [4] ii. 100.

nullae sunt imagines, quae me a vobis deprecentur."

8   Sed neque solus Catullus ita isto verbo usus est.
Pleni sunt adeo libri similis in hoc verbo significationis, ex quibus unum et alterum, quae subpetierant,
9 apposui. Q. Ennius in *Erectheo* non longe secus
dixit quam Cattullus :

Qui núnc (inquit) aerumna meá libertatém paro,
Quibus sérvitutem meá miseria déprecor ;

signat[1] "abigo" et "amolior," vel prece adhibita
10 vel quo alio modo. Item Ennius in *Cresphonte* :

Ego cum meae vítae parcam, létum inimico
déprecer.

11 Cicero in libro sexto *De Republica* ita scripsit : " Quod
quidem eo fuit maius, quia, cum causa pari collegae
essent, non modo invidia pari non erant, sed etiam
Claudi invidiam Gracchi caritas deprecabatur " ; hic
quoque item non est " valde precabatur," sed quasi
propulsabat invidiam[2] et defensabat invidiam, quod
Graeci propinqua significatione παραιτεῖσθαι dicunt.
12   Item *Pro Aulo Caecina* consimiliter Cicero verbo
isto utitur.   " Quid," inquit, " huic[3] homini facias ?
Nonne concedas interdum ut excusatione summae
stultitiae summae improbitatis odium deprecetur ? "

---

[1] ⟨in hoc versu "deprecor"⟩ signat, *Skutsch.*
[2] invidiam *omitted by ς*.   [3] huic tu, *Cic.*

---

[1] 128, Ribbeck³.   [2] 121, Ribbeck³.
[3] 2.2.   [4] § 30.

wrong, there are no masks of ancestors to intercede (*deprecentur,* " beg off ") for me with you by their prayers."

But Catullus was not alone in using this word with that meaning. Indeed, the books are full of cases of its occurrence in the same sense, and of these I have quoted one or two which had come to mind. Quintus Ennius in the *Erectheus,* not differing greatly from Catullus, says : [1]

Who now win freedom by my own distress
For those whose slavery I by woe avert (*deprecor*).

He means " I drive away " and " remove," either by resort to prayer or in some other way. Similarly in the *Chresphontes* Ennius writes : [2]

When I my own life spare, may I avert (*deprecer*)
Death from mine enemy.

Cicero, in the sixth book of his *Republic,* wrote : [3] " Which indeed was so much the more remarkable, because, while the colleagues were in the same case, they not only did not incur the same hatred, but the affection felt for Gracchus even averted (*deprecabatur*) the unpopularity of Claudius." Here too the meaning is not " earnestly entreated," but " warded off " unpopularity, so to speak, and defended him against it, a meaning which the Greeks express by the parallel word παραιτεῖσθαι.

Cicero also uses the word in the same way in his *Defence of Aulus Caecina,* saying : [4] " What can you do for a man like this ? Can you not sometimes permit one to avert (*deprecetur*) the odium of the greatest wickedness by the excuse of the most abysmal folly ? " Also in the first book of his second

13 Item *In Verrem* actionis secundae primo : " Nunc
vero quid faciat Hortensius ? Avaritiaene crimina
frugalitatis laudibus deprecetur ? At hominem
flagitiosissimum, libidinosissimum nequissimumque
defendit." Sic igitur Catullus eadem se facere dicit
quae Lesbiam, quod et malediceret ei palam respu-
eretque et recusaret detestareturque assidue et tamen
eam penitus deperiret.

XVII

Quis omnium primus libros publice praebuerit legendos ;
quantusque numerus fuerit Athenis ante clades Persicas
librorum in bibliothecis publicorum.[1]

1 Libros Athenis disciplinarum liberalium publice ad
legendum praebendos primus posuisse dicitur Pisistratus tyrannus. Deinceps studiosius accuratiusque ipsi
Athenienses auxerunt ; sed omnem illam postea
librorum copiam Xerxes, Athenarum potitus, urbe
ipsa praeter arcem incensa, abstulit asportavitque in
2 Persas. Eos porro libros universos multis post
tempestatibus Seleucus rex, qui Nicanor appellatus
est, referendos Athenas curavit.

3 Ingens postea numerus librorum in Aegypto ab
Ptolemaeis regibus vel conquisitus vel confectus est
ad milia ferme voluminum septingenta ;[2] sed ea
omnia bello priore Alexandrino, dum diripitur ea
civitas, non sponte neque opera consulta, sed a
militibus forte auxiliaris incensa sunt.

[1] publicorum, *MSS.*; publicis, *Hertz.*
[2] septuaginta, *s*, *Isid.* vi. 3. 5.

---

[1] ii. 2. 192. [2] In 480 B.C.
[3] *i.e.* copied from other manuscripts.
[4] In 48 B.C. By no means all of the Alexandrian Library
was destroyed at that time, and the losses were made good,

Arraignment of Verres :[1] " Now what can Hortensius do ? Will he try to avert (*deprecetur*) the charge of avarice by the praise of economy ? But he is defending a man who is utterly disgraced and sunk in lust and crime." So then Catullus means that he is doing the same as Lesbia, in publicly speaking ill of her, scorning and rejecting her, and constantly praying to be rid of her, and yet loving her to madness.

XVII

Who was the first of all to establish a public library ; and how many books there were in the public libraries at Athens before the Persian invasions.

THE tyrant Pisistratus is said to have been the first to establish at Athens a public library of books relating to the liberal arts. Then the Athenians themselves added to this collection with considerable diligence and care ; but later Xerxes, when he got possession of Athens and burned the entire city except the citadel,[2] removed that whole collection of books and carried them off to Persia. Finally, a long time afterwards, king Seleucus, who was surnamed Nicanor, had all those books taken back to Athens.

At a later time an enormous quantity of books, nearly seven hundred thousand volumes, was either acquired or written[3] in Egypt under the kings known as Ptolemies ; but these were all burned during the sack of the city in our first war with Alexandria,[4] not intentionally or by anyone's order, but accidentally by the auxiliary soldiers.

at least in part, by Antony in 41 B.C. A part of the library was burned under Aurelian, in A.D. 272, and the destruction seems to have been completed in 391.

BOOK VIII

LIBER OCTAVUS[1]

I

"Hesterna noctu" rectene an cum vitio dicatur
et quaenam super istis verbis grammatica traditio
sit; item quod decemviri in *XII. Tabulis* "nox"
pro "noctu" dixerunt.

II

Quae mihi decem verba ediderit Favorinus, quae
usurpentur quidem a Graecis, sed sint adulterina
et barbara; quae item a me totidem acceperit,
quae ex medio communique usu Latine loquentium
minime Latina sint neque in veterum libris reperiantur.

III

Quem in modum et quam severe increpuerit
audientibus nobis Peregrinus philosophus adulescentem Romanum ex equestri familia, stantem
segnem apud se et assidue oscitantem.

Et adsiduo oscitantem vidit, atque illius quidem
delicatissimas mentis et corporis halucinationes.

---

[1] Except for one or two brief and doubtful fragments
only the chapter headings of Book VIII are preserved, and
that only in the late and inferior manuscripts (ς).

BOOK VIII

I

WHETHER the expression *hesterna nocte,* for "last night," is right or wrong, and what the grammarians have said about those words; also that the decemvirs in the *Twelve Tables*[1] used *nox* for *noctu,* meaning "by night."[2]

II

TEN words pointed out to me by Favorinus which, although in use by the Greeks, are of foreign origin and barbarous; also the same number given him by me which, though of general and common use by those who speak Latin, are by no means Latin and are not to be found in the early literature.

III

IN what terms and how severely the philosopher Peregrinus in my hearing rebuked a young Roman of equestrian rank, who stood before him inattentive and constantly yawning.

. . . and saw him continually yawning and noticed the degenerate dreaminess expressed in his attitude of mind and body.[3]

[1] viii. 12.   [2] See Macr. *Sat.* i. 4.
[3] This fragment is preserved by Nonius, II, p. 121, 19, *s.v. halucinari.*

IV

Quod Herodotus, scriptor historiae memoratissimus, parum vere dixerit unam solamque pinum arborum omnium caesam numquam denuo ex isdem radicibus pullulare; et quod item de aqua pluviali et nive rem non satis exploratam pro comperta posuerit.

V

Quid illud sit, quod Vergilius "caelum stare pulvere," et quod Lucilius "pectus sentibus stare" dixit.

VI

Cum post offensiunculas in gratiam redeatur, expostulationes fieri mutuas minime utile esse, superque ea re et sermo Tauri expositus et verba ex Theophrasti libro sumpta; et quid M. quoque Cicero de amore amicitiae senserit, cum ipsius verbis additum.

VII

Ex Aristotelis libro, qui Περὶ Μνήμης inscriptus est, cognita acceptaque de natura memoriae et habitu; atque inibi alia quaedam de exuberantia aut interitu eius lecta auditaque.

---

[1] vi. 37. [2] ii. 22.
[3] "The sky on columns of dust upborne," *Aen.* xii 407, where the poet is describing the effect of an advancing troop of cavalry.
[4] "The breast with thorns is filled," Lucil. 213, Marx. According to Nonius, p. 392, 2, *stat* means "is full of."

IV

THAT Herodotus, that most famous writer of history, was wrong in saying[1] that the pine alone of all trees never puts forth new shoots from the same roots, after being cut down; and that he stated as an established fact[2] about rainwater and snow a thing which had not been sufficiently investigated.

V

ON the meaning of Virgil's expression *caelum stare pulvere*[3] and of Lucilius' *pectus sentibus stare*.[4]

VI

THAT when a reconciliation takes place after trifling offences, mutual complaints are useless; and Taurus' discourse on that subject, with a quotation from the treatise of Theophrastus; and what Marcus Cicero also thought about the love arising from friendship, added in his own words.[5]

VII

WHAT we have learned and know of the nature and character of memory from Aristotle's work entitled Περὶ Μνήμης or *On Memory*; and also some other examples, of which we have heard or read, about extraordinary powers of memory or its total loss.[6]

Donatus, *ad* Ter. *Andr.* iv. 2 16 (69), quotes Lucilius for *stat sentibus fundus*, *i.e.*, "the farm is full of thorns" (1301, Marx).

[5] Cf. i. 3. 10 f.

[6] See Nonius, *s.v. meminisse*, p. 441. 4, M.

VIII

Quid mihi usu venerit, interpretari et quasi effingere volenti locos quosdam Platonicos Latina oratione.

IX

Quod Theophrastus, philosophus omnis suae aetatis facundissimus, verba pauca ad populum Atheniensem facturus, deturbatus verecundia obticuerit; quodque idem hoc Demostheni apud Philippum regem verba facienti evenerit.

X

Qualis mihi fuerit in oppido Eleusino disceptatio cum grammatico quodam praestigioso, tempora verborum et puerilia meditamenta ignorante, remotarum autem quaestionum nebulas et formidines capiendis imperitorum animis ostentante.

halophantam mendacem velit.

XI

Quam festive responderit Xanthippae uxori Socrates, petenti ut per Dionysia largiore sumptu cenitarent.

XII

Quid significet in veterum libris scriptum " plerique omnes " ; et quod ea verba accepta a Graecis videntur.

VIII

My experience in trying to interpret and, as it were, to reproduce in Latin certain passages of Plato.

IX

How Theophrastus, the most eloquent philosopher of his entire generation, when on the point of making a brief speech to the people of Athens, was overcome by bashfulness and kept silence; and how Demosthenes had a similar experience when speaking before king Philip.

X

A discussion that I had in the town of Eleusis with a conceited grammarian who, although ignorant of the tenses of verbs and the exercises of schoolboys, ostentatiously proposed abstruse questions of a hazy and formidable character, to impress the minds of the unlearned.

Would wish a lying scoundrel.[1]

XI

The witty reply of Socrates to his wife Xanthippe, when she asked that they might spend more money for their dinners during the Dionysiac festival.

XII

On the meaning of *plerique omnes,* or "almost all," in the early literature; and on the probable Greek origin of that expression.

[1] Whether these words, from Nonius, II., p. 120, 12, M. belong here is uncertain.

XIII

"Eupsones," quod homines Afri dicunt, non esse verbum Poenicum, sed Graecum.

XIV

Lepidissima altercatio Favorini philosophi adversus quendam intempestivum de ambiguitate verborum disserentem; atque inibi verba quaedam ex Naevio poeta et Cn. Gellio non usitate collocata; atque ibidem a P. Nigidio origines vocabulorum exploratae.

XV

Quibus modis ignominiatus tractatusque sit a C. Caesare Laberius poeta; atque inibi appositi versus super eadem re eiusdem Laberii.

Historia ex libris Heraclidae Pontici iucunda memoratu et miranda.

---

[1] See Macr. *Sat.* ii. 7.
[2] This heading, of uncertain number, is quoted in *Gramma-*

XIII

THAT *eupsones*, a word used by the people of Africa, is not Phoenician, but Greek.

XIV

A HIGHLY entertaining discussion of the philosopher Favorinus with a tiresome person who held forth on the double meaning of certain words; also some unusual expressions from the poet Naevius and from Gnaeus Gellius; and further, some investigations of the derivation of words by Publius Nigidius.

XV

How the poet Laberius was ignominiously treated by Gaius Caesar, with a quotation of Laberius' own words on that subject.[1]

A pleasant and remarkable story from the books of Heracleides of Pontus.[2]

---

tici Latini ii. 246, 6, K., and attributed to Agellius, *Noctium Atticarum* viii., or according to the greater number of MSS., viiii.

BOOK IX

LIBER NONUS

I

Quamobrem Quintus Claudius Quadrigarius, in undevicesimo [1]
Annali, scripserit rectiores certioresque ictus fieri, si
sursum quid mittas quam si deorsum.

1 QUINTUS CLAUDIUS in undevicesimo *Annali*, cum
oppidum a Metello proconsule oppugnari, contra
ab oppidanis desuper e muris propugnari describeret,
ita scripsit: "Sagittarius cum funditore utrimque
summo studio spargunt fortissime. Sed sagittam
atque lapidem deorsum an sursum mittas, hoc
interest; nam neutrum potest deorsum versum
recte mitti, sed sursum utrumque optime. Quare
milites Metelli sauciabantur multo minus et, quod
maxime opus erat, a pinnis hostis defendebant
facillime funditore."

2 Percontabar ego Antonium Iulianum rhetorem,
cur hoc ita usu veniret quod Quadrigarius dixisset,
ut contigui magis directioresque ictus fiant, si vel
lapidem vel sagittam sursum versus iacias quam
deorsum, cum proclivior faciliorque iactus sit ex
supernis in infima quam ex infimis in superna.

---

[1] undevicesimo. *Q*; duodevicesimo, *ω*.

---

[1] Fr. 85, Peter[2].

BOOK IX

I

Why Quintus Claudius Quadrigarius, in the nineteenth book of his *Annals*, wrote that missiles hit their mark more accurately and surely if they are hurled from below, than if they are hurled from above.

WHEN Quintus Claudius, in the nineteenth book of his *Annals*, was describing an attack upon a town by the proconsul Metellus, and its defence against him by the townspeople from the top of the walls, he wrote these words:[1] "The archers and slingers on both sides showered their weapons with the utmost vigour and courage. But there is this difference between shooting an arrow or a stone downward or upward; for neither missile can be discharged accurately downward, but both upwards with excellent effect. Therefore the soldiers of Metellus suffered far fewer wounds, and, what was of the greatest importance, they very easily drove the enemy back from the battlements by means of their slingers."

I asked Antonius Julianus, the rhetorician, why what Quadrigarius had said was so; namely, that the shots of missiles are closer and more accurate if you discharge a stone or an arrow upwards rather than downwards, in spite of the fact that a throw from above downward is swifter and easier than one in the opposite direction. Then

3 Tum Iulianus, comprobato genere quaestionis,
"Quod de sagitta," inquit, "et lapide dixit, hoc
4 de omni fere missili telo dici potest. Facilior
autem iactus est, sicuti dixisti, si desuper iacias,
5 si quid iacere tantum velis, non ferire. Sed cum
modus et impetus iactus temperandus derigendus-
que est, tum, si in prona iacias, moderatio atque
ratio mittentisque praecipitantia qualicumque ipsa
6 et pondere cadentis teli corrumpitur. At si in
editiora mittas et ad percutiendum superne aliquid
manum et oculos conlinies, quo motus a te datus
7 tulerit, eo telum ibit quod ieceris." Ad hanc ferme
sententiam Iulianus super istis Q. Claudii verbis
nobiscum sermocinatus est.

8   Quod ait idem Q. Claudius: "a pinnis hostis
defendebant facillime," animadvertendum est usum
esse eum verbo "defendebant," non ex vulgari
consuetudine, sed admodum proprie et Latine.
9 Nam "defendere" et "offendere" inter sese adversa sunt, quorum alterum significat ἐμποδὼν ἔχειν,
id est incurrere in aliquid et incidere, alterum
ἐκποδὼν ποιεῖν, id est avertere atque depellere, quod
hoc in loco Claudio dicitur.

II

Qualibus verbis notarit Herodes Atticus falso quempiam cultu
amictuque nomen habitumque philosophi ementientem.

1   AD Herodem Atticum, consularem virum in-
genioque amoeno et Graeca facundia celebrem,

Julianus, after commending the character of the question, said : " His statement about an arrow and a stone may be made about almost any missile weapon. But, as you have said, throwing is easier if you throw downwards, provided you wish only to throw, and not to hit a mark. But when the direction and force of the throw must be regulated and guided, then, if you are throwing downwards, the control and command of the marksman are impaired by the downward impulse itself, such as it is, and by the weight of the falling missile. But if you throw your weapon upwards, and direct hand and eye to hitting something above you, the missile which you have hurled will go to the spot to which the impulse which you have given bears it." It was to this general effect that Julianus chatted with us about those words of Quintus Claudius.

With regard to the remark of the same Claudius, " they very easily drove the enemy from the battlements," it must be observed that he used the word *defendebant,* not in the sense which it commonly has, but yet quite properly and in accordance with good Latin usage. For *defendere* and *offendere* are opposed to each other, the latter meaning ἐμποδὼν ἔχειν, that is, " to run against something and fall upon it," the former, ἐκποδὼν ποιεῖν, that is, " to avert and drive away "; and the latter is Claudius' meaning in this passage.

II

In what terms Herodes Atticus reproved a man who in appearance and dress falsely laid claim to the title and character of philosopher.

To Herodes Atticus, the ex-consul, renowned for his personal charm and his Grecian eloquence, there

adiit nobis praesentibus palliatus quispiam et cri-
nitus barbaque prope ad pubem usque porrecta ac
2 petit aes sibi dari εἰς ἄρτους. Tum Herodes inter-
3 rogat quisnam esset. Atque ille, vultu sonituque
vocis obiurgatorio, philosophum sese esse dicit et
mirari quoque addit cur quaerendum putasset quod
4 videret. "Video," inquit Herodes, "barbam et
5 pallium, philosophum nondum video. Quaeso autem
te, cum bona venia dicas mihi quibus nos uti posse
argumentis existimas, ut esse te philosophum nosci-
6 temus?" Interim aliquot ex his qui cum Herode
erant erraticum esse hominem dicere et nulli[1] rei
incolamque esse sordentium ganearum, nisi accipiat
quod petat[2] convicio turpi solitum incessere; atque
ibi Herodes "Demus," inquit, "huic aliquid aeris,
7 cuicuimodi est, tamquam homines, non tamquam
homini," et iussit dari pretium panis triginta
dierum.
8   Tum nos aspiciens qui eum sectabamur, "Musonius," inquit, "aeruscanti cuipiam id genus et
philosophum sese ostentanti dari iussit mille nummum, et cum plerique dicerent nebulonem esse
hominem malum et malitiosum et nulla re bona
dignum, tum Musonium subridentem dixisse aiunt:
9 ἄξιος οὖν ἐστιν ἀργυρίου. Sed hoc potius," inquit,
"dolori mihi et aegritudini est, quod istiusmodi
animalia spurca atque probra nomen usurpant
10 sanctissimum et philosophi appellantur. Maiores
autem mei Athenienses nomina iuvenum fortissi-

---

[1] nullius, *BQ*².
[2] petat *or* petierit, *Skutsch*; petit, *MSS.*

---

[1] p. 132, Hense.

once came, when I was present, a man in a cloak, with long hair and a beard that reached almost to his waist, and asked that money be given him εἰς ἄρτους, that is, "for bread." Then Herodes asked him who on earth he was, and the man, with anger in his voice and expression, replied that he was a philosopher, adding that he wondered why Herodes thought it necessary to ask what was obvious. "I see," said Herodes, "a beard and a cloak; the philosopher I do not yet see. Now, I pray you, be so good as to tell me by what evidence you think we may recognize you as a philosopher." Meanwhile some of Herodes' companions told him that the fellow was a vagabond of worthless character, who frequented foul dives and was in the habit of being shamefully abusive if he did not get what he demanded. Thereupon Herodes said : "Let us give him some money, whatever his character may be, not because he is a man, but because we are men," and he ordered enough money to be given him to buy bread for thirty days.

Then, turning to those of us who were with him, he said : "Musonius[1] ordered a thousand sesterces to be given to a fakir of this sort who posed as a philosopher, and when several told him that the fellow was a rascal and knave and deserving of nothing good, Musonius, they say, replied with a smile : ἄξιος οὖν ἐστὶν ἀργυρίου, 'then he deserves money.' But," said Herodes, "it is rather this that causes me resentment and vexation, that foul and evil beasts of this sort usurp a most sacred name and call themselves philosophers. Now, my ancestors the Athenians by public decree made it unlawful for slaves ever to be given the names of those valiant youths Harmodius

morum Harmodii et Aristogitonis, qui libertatis
recuperandae gratia Hippiam tyrannum interficere
adorsi erant, ne umquam servis indere liceret decreto publico sanxerunt, quoniam nefas ducerent
nomina libertati patriae devota servili contagio
11 pollui. Cur ergo nos patimur nomen philosophiae
inlustrissimum in hominibus deterrimis exordescere?
Simili autem," inquit, " exemplo ex contraria specie
antiquos Romanorum audio praenomina patriciorum
quorundam male de republica meritorum et ob eam
causam capite damnatorum censuisse, ne cui eiusdem gentis patricio inderentur, ut vocabula quoque
eorum defamata atque demortua cum ipsis viderentur."

III

Epistula Philippi regis ad Aristotelem philosophum super
Alexandro recens nato.

1 Philippus, Amyntae filius, terrae Macedoniae rex,
cuius virtute industriaque Macetae locupletissimo
imperio aucti gentium nationumque multarum potiri
coeperant et cuius vim atque arma toti Graeciae
cavenda metuendaque inclitae illae Demosthenis
2 orationes contionesque vocificant—is Philippus, cum
in omni fere tempore negotiis belli victoriisque
adfectus exercitusque esset, a liberali tamen Musa
et a studiis humanitatis numquam afuit, quin lepide

---

[1] In 514 B.C. They slew Hipparchus, brother of Hippias
and son of Pisistratus. Hippias was afterwards driven from
the city and the tyrannicides, who had lost their lives in
their attempt, received almost divine honours.

and Aristogeiton, who to restore liberty tried to slay the tyrant Hippias;[1] for they thought it impious for the names of men who had sacrificed themselves for their country's freedom to be disgraced by contact with slavery. Why then do we allow the glorious title of philosopher to be defiled in the person of the basest of men? Moreover," said he, "I hear that the early Romans, setting a similar example in a case of the opposite nature, voted that the forenames of certain patricians who had deserved ill of their country and for that reason had been condemned to death should never be given to any patrician of the same clan, in order that their very names might seem to be dishonoured and done to death, as well as the malefactors themselves."[2]

III

A letter of king Philip to the philosopher Aristotle with regard to the recent birth of his son Alexander.

PHILIP, son of Amyntas, was king of the land of Macedonia. Through his valour and energy the Macedonians had greatly increased and enriched their kingdom, and had begun to extend their power over many nations and peoples, so that Demosthenes, in those famous orations and addresses,[3] insists that his power and arms are to be feared and dreaded by all Greece. This Philip, although almost constantly busied and distracted by the labours and triumphs of war, yet never was a stranger to the Muse of the liberal arts and the pursuit of culture, but his

---

[2] An example, the discarding of the forename Lucius by the Claudii, is given by Suetonius, *Tib.* i. 2.

[3] The *Philippics.*

3 comiterque pleraque et faceret et diceret. Feruntur
adeo libri epistularum eius, munditiae et venustatis
et prudentiae plenarum, velut sunt illae litterae
quibus Aristoteli philosopho natum esse sibi Alexandrum nuntiavit.

4 Ea epistula, quoniam curae diligentiaeque in
liberorum disciplinas hortamentum est, exscribenda
5 visa est ad commonendos parentum animos. Expo-
nenda est igitur ad hanc ferme sententiam :

" Philippus Aristoteli salutem dicit.

Filium mihi genitum scito. Quod equidem dis
habeo gratiam, non proinde quia natus est, quam
pro eo, quod nasci contigit temporibus vitae tuae.
Spero enim fore ut eductus eruditusque a te, dignus
existat et nobis et rerum nostrarum [1] susceptione."

6 Ipsius autem Philippi verba haec sunt :

Φίλιππος Ἀριστοτέλει χαίρειν.

Ἴσθι μοι γεγονότα υἱόν. πολλὴν οὖν τοῖς θεοῖς ἔχω
χάριν, οὐχ οὕτως ἐπὶ τῇ γενέσει τοῦ παιδός, ὡς ἐπὶ τῷ
κατὰ τὴν σὴν ἡλικίαν αὐτὸν γεγονέναι· ἐλπίζω γάρ αὐτὸν
ὑπὸ σοῦ τραφέντα καὶ παιδευθέντα ἄξιον ἔσεσθαι καὶ ἡμῶν
καὶ τῆς τῶν πραγμάτων διαδοχῆς.

IV

De barbararum gentium prodigiosis miraculis ; deque diris
et exitiosis effascinationibus ; atque inibi de feminis repente
versis in mares.

1 Cum e Graecia in Italiam rediremus et Brundisium
iremus egressique e navi in terram in portu illo

---

[1] nostrarum, *Skutsch ;* istarum, *MSS. ;* ipsarum, *suggested
by Hosius.*

acts and words never lacked charm and refinement. In fact collections of his letters are in circulation, which abound in elegance, grace, and wisdom, as for example, the one in which he announced to the philosopher Aristotle the birth of his son Alexander.[1]

Since this letter is an encouragement to care and attention in the education of children, I thought that it ought to be quoted in full, as an admonition to parents. It may be translated, then, about as follows:

" Philip to Aristotle, Greeting.

" Know that a son is born to me. For this indeed I thank the gods, not so much because he is born, as because it is his good fortune to be born during your lifetime. For I hope that as a result of your training and instruction he will prove worthy of us and of succeeding to our kingdom."

But Philip's own words are these:

Φίλιππος Ἀριστοτέλει χαίρειν.

Ἴσθι μοι γεγονότα υἱόν. πολλὴν οὖν τοῖς θεοῖς ἔχω χάριν, οὐχ οὕτως ἐπὶ τῇ γενέσει τοῦ παιδός, ὡς ἐπὶ τῷ κατὰ τὴν σὴν ἡλικίαν αὐτὸν γεγονέναι· ἐλπίζω γὰρ αὐτὸν ὑπὸ σοῦ τραφέντα καὶ παιδευθέντα ἄξιον ἔσεσθαι καὶ ἡμῶν καὶ τῆς τῶν πραγμάτων διαδοχῆς.

IV

On some extraordinary marvels found among barbarian peoples ; and on awful and deadly spells ; and also on the sudden change of women into men.

When I was returning from Greece to Italy and had come to Brundisium, after disembarking I was

---

[1] At Pella, in 356 B.C.

inclito spatiaremur, quem Q. Ennius remotiore
paulum, sed admodum scito vocabulo "praepetem"
appellavit, fasces librorum venalium expositos vi-
2 dimus. Atque ego avide statim pergo ad libros.
3 Erant autem isti omnes libri Graeci miraculorum
fabularumque pleni, res inauditae, incredulae, scriptores veteres non parvae auctoritatis: Aristeas
Proconnesius et Isigonus Nicaeensis et Ctesias et
4 Onesicritus et Philostephanus et Hegesias; ipsa
autem volumina ex diutino situ squalebant et habitu
5 aspectuque taetro erant. Accessi tamen perconta-
tusque pretium sum et, adductus mira atque in-
sperata vilitate, libros plurimos aere pauco emo
eosque omnis duabus proximis noctibus cursim·
transeo; atque in legendo carpsi exinde quaedam
et notavi mirabilia et scriptoribus fere nostris in-
temptata eaque his commentariis aspersi, ut qui eos
lectitarit ne rudis omnino et ἀνήκοος inter istiusmodi
rerum auditiones reperiatur.

6   Erant igitur in illis libris scripta huiuscemodi:
Scythas illos penitissimos, qui sub ipsis septentrio-
nibus aetatem agunt, corporibus hominum vesci
eiusque victus alimento vitam ducere et ἀνθρω-
ποφάγους nominari; item esse homines sub eadem
regione caeli unum oculum in frontis medio habentes, qui appellantur Arimaspi, qua fuisse facie
Cyclopas poetae ferunt; alios item esse homines

---

[1] *Ann.* 488, Vahlen[2]; cf. vii. **6. 6**, where Gellius quotes
the line and discusses the word.

[2] See the Index.

[3] The Arimaspi are mentioned as good riders by Aeschylus,
Prom. 805.   Since Herodotus (iv. 27 ; *L.C.L.* ii, p. 227) says
that in Scythian ἄριμα meant "one" and σποῦ, "eye," Strabo
(i, 2, 10 ; *L.C.L.* vol. i, pp. 77 f.) thought that Homer might

strolling about in that famous port, which Quintus
Ennius called *praepes*, or "propitious," [1] using an
epithet that is somewhat far-fetched, but altogether
apt. There I saw some bundles of books exposed
for sale, and I at once eagerly hurried to them.
Now, all those books were in Greek, filled with
marvellous tales, things unheard of, incredible ; but
the writers were ancient and of no mean authority :
Aristeas of Proconnesus, Isigonus of Nicaea, Ctesias
and Onesicritus, Philostephanus and Hegesias. [2] The
volumes themselves, however, were filthy from long
neglect, in bad condition and unsightly. Nevertheless, I drew near and asked their price ; then,
attracted by their extraordinary and unexpected
cheapness, I bought a large number of them for a
small sum, and ran through all of them hastily in
the course of the next two nights. As I read, I
culled from them, and noted down, some things that
were remarkable and for the most part unmentioned
by our native writers ; these I have inserted here and
there in these notes, so that whoever shall read them
may not be found to be wholly ignorant and ἀνήκοος,
or "uninstructed," when hearing tales of that kind.

Those books, then, contained matter of the following sort : that the most remote of the Scythians, who
pass their life in the far north, eat human flesh and
subsist on the nourishment of that food, and are
called ἀνθρωποφάγοι, or "cannibals." Also that
there are men in the same latitude having one eye
in the middle of the forehead and called Arimaspi,
who are of the appearance that the poets give the
Cyclopes. [3] That there are also in the same region

have derived his Cyclopes from the Scythian Arimaspi. See
Milton, *P. L.* 2, 945.

apud eandem caeli plagam singulariae velocitatis,
vestigia pedum habentes retro porrecta, non, ut
ceterorum hominum, prosum spectantia;[1] praeterea
traditum esse memoratumque in ultima quadam
terra, quae "Albania" dicitur, gigni homines, qui
in pueritia canescant et plus cernant oculis per
noctem quam interdiu; item esse compertum et
creditum, Sauromatas, qui ultra Borysthenen fluvium
longe colunt, cibum capere semper diebus tertiis,
medio abstinere.

7   Id etiam in isdem libris scriptum offendimus,
quod postea in libro quoque Plinii Secundi *Naturalis
Historiae* septimo legi, esse quasdam in terra Africa
hominum familias voce atque lingua effascinantium,
8 qui si impensius forte laudaverint pulchras arbores,
segetes laetiores, infantes amoeniores, egregios
equos, pecudes pastu atque cultu opimas, emoriantur
repente haec omnia, nulli aliae causae obnoxia.
Oculis quoque exitialem fascinationem fieri in isdem
libris scriptum est traditurque esse homines in
Illyriis qui interimant videndo quos diutius irati
viderint, eosque ipsos mares feminasque, qui visu
ita[2] nocenti sunt, pupillas in singulis oculis binas
9 habere.   Item esse in montibus terrae Indiae
homines caninis capitibus et latrantibus eosque
vesci avium et ferarum venatibus; atque esse item
alia aput ultimas orientis terras miracula homines,

---

[1] prosum spectantia, *Hagen;* prosprofium petet anti-
spectancia, δ; prospectantia, γ.
[2] ita, *Q;* tam, ω.

---

[1] Cf. Pliny, *N.H.* vii. 11; Augustine, *Civ. Dei*, xvi. 8.
[2] That is, every *third* day, according to the Roman method

other men, of marvellous swiftness, whose feet are
turned backwards and do not point forward, as in
the rest of mankind.[1] Further, that it was handed
down by tradition that in a distant land called
Albania men are born whose hair turns white in
childhood and who see better by night than in the
daytime. That it was also a matter of assured belief
that the Sauromatae, who dwell far away beyond
the river Borysthenes, take food only every other
day [2] and fast on the intervening day.

In those same books I ran upon this statement
too, which I later read also in the seventh book of
the *Natural History* of Plinius Secundus,[3] that in the
land of Africa there are families of persons who
work spells by voice and tongue ; for if they should
chance to have bestowed extravagant praise upon
beautiful trees, plentiful crops, charming children,
fine horses, flocks that are well fed and in good
condition, suddenly, for no other cause than this,
all these would die. That with the eyes too a
deadly spell is cast, is written in those same books,
and it is said that there are persons among the
Illyrians who by their gaze kill those at whom they
have looked for some time in anger ; and that those
persons themselves, both men and women, who
possess this power of harmful gaze, have two pupils
in each eye. Also that in the mountains of the
land of India there are men who have the heads
of dogs, and bark, and that they feed upon birds
and wild animals which they have taken in the chase.
That in the remotest lands of the east too there are

of reckoning ; cf. **xvii**. 12. 2, febrim *quartis* diebus recurren-
tem, and **xvii**. 12. 5, haec *biduo* medio intervallata febris, and
see *Class. Phil.* viii, pp. 1 ff.　　　　　　[3] vii. 16.

qui "monocoli" appellentur, singulis cruribus sal-
tatim currentes, vivacissimae pernicitatis ; quosdam
etiam esse nullis cervicibus, oculos in humeris
10 habentes. Iam vero hoc egreditur omnem modum
admirationis, quod idem illi scriptores gentem esse
aiunt aput extrema Indiae, corporibus hirtis et
avium ritu plumantibus, nullo cibatu vescentem,
sed spiritu florum naribus hausto victitantem ;
11 Pygmaeos quoque haut longe ab his nasci, quorum
qui longissimi sint, non longiores esse quam pedes
duo et quadrantem.
12 Haec atque alia istiusmodi plura legimus, sed cum
ea scriberemus, tenuit nos non idoneae scripturae
taedium, nihil ad ornandum iuvandumque usum vitae
13 pertinentis. Libitum tamen est in loco hoc miraculorum notare id etiam, quod Plinius Secundus, vir in
temporibus aetatis suae ingenii dignitatisque gratia
auctoritate magna praeditus, non audisse neque
legisse, sed scire sese atque vidisse in libro *Naturalis*
14 *Historiae* septimo scripsit. Verba igitur haec, quae
infra posui, ipsius sunt, ex eo libro sumpta, quae
profecto faciunt ut neque respuenda neque ridenda
sit notissima illa veterum poetarum de Caenide et
15 Caeneo cantilena. Ex feminis, inquit, mutari in
mares, non esse fabulosum. " Invenimus in annalibus, Q. Licinio Crasso, C. Cassio Longino consulibus, Casini puerum factum ex virgine sub parentibus
iussuque haruspicum deportatum in insulam deser-
tam. Licinius Mucianus prodidit visum esse a se

---

[1] Cf. Plin. *N.H.* vii. 23.
[2] vii. 36.
[3] Caenis was a girl whom her lover Poseidon changed into
a man and who was then called Caeneus ; see Ovid, *Met.* xii.
171 ff. ; Virg. *Aen.* vi. 448.

othermarvellous men called *monocoli*, or " one-legged,"
who run by hopping with their single leg and are of
a most lively swiftness.[1] And that there are also
some others who are without necks and have eyes
in their shoulders. But all bounds of wonder are
passed by the statement of those same writers, that
there is a tribe in farthest India with bodies that
are rough and covered with feathers like birds, who
eat no food but live by inhaling the perfume of
flowers. And that not far from these people is the
land of Pygmies, the tallest of whom are not more
than two feet and a quarter in height.

These and many other stories of the kind I read;
but when writing them down, I was seized with
disgust for such worthless writings, which contribute
nothing to the enrichment or profit of life. Nevertheless, the fancy took me to add to this collection
of marvels a thing which Plinius Secundus, a man of
high authority in his day and generation by reason
of his talent and his position, recorded in the seventh
book of his *Natural History*,[2] not as something that
he had heard or read, but that he knew to be true
and had himself seen. The words therefore which I
have quoted below are his own, taken from that
book, and they certainly make us hesitate to reject
or ridicule that familiar yarn of the poets of old about
Caenis and Caeneus.[3] He says that the change of
women into men is not a fiction. " We find," says
he, " in the annals that in the consulship of Quintus
Licinius Crassus and Gaius Cassius Longinus [4] a girl at
Casinum was changed into a boy in the house of her
parents and by direction of the diviners was deported
to a desert island. Licinius Mucianus has stated

[4] 171 B.C.

Argis Arescontem, cui nomen Arescusae fuisset,[1]
nupsisse etiam, mox barbam et virilitatem provenisse
uxoremque duxisse; eiusdem sortis et Zmyrnae
puerum a se visum. Ipse in Africa vidi mutatum in
marem die nuptiarum L. Cossitium civem Thysdri-
tanum, vivebatque cum proderem haec."

16   Idem Plinius in eodem libro verba haec scripsit :
" Gignuntur homines utriusque sexus, quos 'herm-
aphroditos' vocamus, olim 'androgynos' vocatos et
in prodigiis habitos, nunc vero in deliciis."

V

Diversae nobilium philosophorum sententiae de genere ac
natura voluptatis ; verbaque Hieroclis philosophi quibus
decreta Epicuri insectatus est.

1   DE voluptate veteres philosophi diversas senten-
2 tias dixerunt. Epicurus voluptatem summum bonum
esse ponit, eam tamen ita definit : σαρκὸς εὐσταθὲς
3 κατάστημα. Antisthenes Socraticus summum malum
dicit ; eius namque hoc verbum est : μανείην μᾶλλον
4 ἢ ἡσθείην. Speusippus vetusque omnis Academia
voluptatem et dolorem duo mala esse dicunt opposita
inter sese, bonum tamen esse quod utriusque medium
5 foret. Zeno censuit voluptatem esse indifferens, id
est neutrum, neque bonum neque malum, quod ipse

------

[1] fuisse, *Plin.*

------

[1] vii. 34.   [2] Fr. 28, Usener.

that he saw at Argos one Arescontes, whose name
had been Arescusa; that she had even been married,
but presently grew a beard, became a man, and had
taken a wife: and that at Smyrna also he had seen a
boy who had experienced the same change. I myself
in Africa saw Lucius Cossutius, a citizen of Thysdrus,
who had been changed into a man on his wedding
day and was still living when I wrote this."

Pliny also wrote this in the same book:[1] "There
are persons who from birth are bisexual, whom we
call 'hermaphrodites'; they were formerly termed
androgyni and regarded as prodigies, but now are
instruments of pleasure."

V

Diverse views of eminent philosophers as to the nature and
character of pleasure; and the words in which the
philosopher Hierocles attacked the principles of Epicurus.

As to pleasure the philosophers of old expressed
varying opinions. Epicurus makes pleasure the highest good, but defines it [2] as σαρκὸς εὐσταθὲς κατάστημα,
or "a well-balanced condition of body." Antisthenes
the Socratic calls it the greatest evil; for this is the
expression he uses:[3] μανείην μᾶλλον ἢ ἡσθείην; that
is to say, "may I go mad rather than feel pleasure."
Speusippus and all the old Academy declare[4] that
pleasure and pain are two evils opposed to each
other, but that what lay midway between the two
was the good. Zeno thought[5] that pleasure was
indifferent, that is neutral, neither good nor evil, that,

[3] *F.P.G.* ii. 286. 65.   [4] *F.P.G.* iii. 92. 169.
[5] p. 169, Pearson; i. 195, Arn.

6 Graeco vocabulo ἀδιάφορον appellavit. Critolaus
Peripateticus et malum esse voluptatem ait et
multa alia mala parere ex sese, iniurias,[1] desidias,
7 obliviones, ignavias. Plato ante hos omnis ita varie
et multiformiter de voluptate disseruit, ut cunctae
istae sententiae quas exposui videantur ex sermonum
eius fontibus profluxisse ; nam proinde unaquaque
utitur, ut et ipsius voluptatis natura fert, quae est
multiplex, et causarum quas tractat, rerumque quas
8 efficere vult ratio desiderat. Taurus autem noster,
quotiens facta mentio Epicuri erat, in ore atque in
lingua habebat verba haec Hieroclis Stoici, viri
sancti et gravis, ἡδονὴ τέλος, πόρνης δόγμα· οὐκ ἔστιν
πρόνοια, οὐδὲ πόρνης δόγμα.

VI

Verbum quod est ab "ago" frequentativum, in syllaba prima
quonam sit modulo pronuntiandum.

1　Ab eo quod est "ago" et "egi," verba sunt quae
appellant grammatici "frequentativa," "actito" et
2 "actitavi." Haec quosdam non sane indoctos viros
audio ita pronuntiare, ut primam in his ·litteram
corripiant, rationemque dicunt, quoniam in verbo
principali, quod est "ago," prima littera breviter
3 pronuntiatur. Cur igitur ab eo quod est "edo" et
"ungo," in quibus verbis prima littera breviter
dicitur, "esito" et "unctito," quae sunt eorum frequentativa, prima littera longa promimus et contra

---

[1] incurias, *Kronenberg.*

namely, which he himself called by the Greek term
ἀδιάφορον. Critolaus the Peripatetic declares that
pleasure is an evil and gives birth to many other
evils: injustice, sloth, forgetfulness, and cowardice.
Earlier than all these, Plato discoursed in so many
and varied ways about pleasure, that all those opinions
which I have set forth may seem to have flowed from
the founts of his discourses; for he makes use of each
one of them according to the suggestion offered by the
nature of pleasure itself, which is manifold, and
according to the demands made by the character of
the topics which he is treating and of the effect that
he wishes to produce. But our countryman Taurus,
whenever mention was made of Epicurus, always had
on his lips and tongue these words of Hierocles the
Stoic, a man of righteousness and dignity: "Pleasure
an end, a harlot's creed; there is no Providence, not
even a harlot's creed."

VI

*With what quantity the first syllable of the frequentative
verb from ago should be pronounced.*

From *ago* and *egi* are derived the verbs *actito* and
actitavi, which the grammarians call "frequentatives."[1]
These verbs I have heard some men, and those not
without learning, pronounce with a shortening of the
first syllable, and give as their reason that the first
letter of the primitive *ago* is pronounced short. Why
then do we make the first vowel long in the frequentative forms *esito* and *unctito*, which are derived
from *edo* and *ungo*, in which the first letter is short;

---

[1] Most modern grammarians prefer the more comprehensive
term "intensives."

"dictito," ab eo verbo quod est "dico," correpte dicimus? Num ergo potius "actito" et "actitavi" producenda sunt? quoniam frequentativa ferme omnia eodem modo in prima syllaba dicuntur, quo participia praeteriti temporis ex his verbis unde ea profecta sunt in eadem syllaba pronuntiantur, sicuti "lego lectus" facit "lectito"; "ungo unctus," "unctito"; "scribo scriptus," "scriptito"; "moveo motus," "motito"; "pendeo pensus," "pensito"; "edo esus," "esito"; "dico" autem "dictus" "dictito" facit; "gero gestus," "gestito"; "veho vectus," "vectito"; "rapio raptus," "raptito"; "capio captus," "captito"; "facio factus," "factito." Sic igitur "actito" producte in prima syllaba pronuntiandum, quoniam ex eo fit quod est "ago" et "actus."

VII

De conversione foliorum in arbore olea brumali et solstitiali die; deque fidibus id temporis ictu alieno sonantibus.

1   VULGO et scriptum et creditum est, folia olearum arborum brumali et solstitiali die converti et quae pars eorum fuerit inferior atque occultior, eam supra
2 fieri atque exponi ad oculos et ad solem. Quod nobis quoque semel atque iterum experiri volentibus ita esse propemodum visum est.
3   Sed de fidibus rarius dictu et mirabilius est; quam rem et alii docti viri et Suetonius etiam Tranquillus, in libro *Ludicrae Historiae* primo, satis compertam

---

[1] The title as given in full by Suidas is "*On the Festivals and Games of the Romans*, two books." See Fr. 181, Reiff.

and, on the contrary, pronounce the first vowel short in *dictito* from *dīco*? Accordingly, should not *actito* and *actitavi* rather be lengthened? For the first syllable of almost all frequentatives is pronounced in the same way as the same syllable of the past participle of the verbs from which they are formed: for example, *lego lēctus* makes *lēctito*; *ungo ūnctus, ūnctito*; *scrībo scrīptus, scrīptito*; *moveo mōtus, mōtito*; *pendeo pēnsus, pēnsito*; *edo ēsus, ēsito*; but *dīco dīctus* forms *dīctito*; *gĕro gĕstus, gĕstito*; *vĕho vĕctus, vĕctito*; *răpio răptus, răptito*; *căpio căptus, căptito*; *făcio făctus, făctito*. So then *āctito* should be pronounced with the first syllable long, since it is from *ago* and *āctus*.

VII

That the leaves of the olive tree turn over at the summer and the winter solstice, and that the lyre at that same season produces sounds from other strings than those that are struck.

It is commonly both written and believed that at the winter and the summer solstice the leaves of olive trees turn over, and that the side which had been underneath and hidden becomes uppermost and is exposed to sight and to the sun. And I myself was led to test this statement more than once, and found it to be almost exactly true.

But about the lyre there is an assertion that is less often made and is even more remarkable. And this both other learned men and also Suetonius Tranquillus, in the first book of his *History of the Games*,[1]

esse satisque super ea constare adfirmat: nervias in
fidibus brumali die alias digitis pelli, alias sonare.

VIII

Necessum esse qui multa habeat multis indigere; deque ea
re Favorini philosophi cum brevitate eleganti sententia.

1 VERUM est profecto quod observato rerum usu
sapientes viri dixere, multis egere qui multa habeat,
magnamque indigentiam nasci non ex inopia magna,
sed ex magna copia; multa enim desiderari ad
2 multa quae habeas tuenda. Quisquis igitur, multa
habens, cavere atque prospicere velit ne quid egeat
neve quid desit, iactura opus esse, non quaestu, et
minus habendum esse, ut minus desit.
3 Hanc sententiam memini a Favorino inter ingentes omnium clamores detornatam inclusamque
verbis his paucissimis: Τὸν γὰρ μυρίων καὶ πεντακισ-
χιλίων χλαμύδων δεόμενον οὐκ ἔστι μὴ πλειόνων δεῖσθαι·
οἷς γὰρ ἔχω προσδεόμενος, ἀφελὼν ὧν ἔχω, ἀρκοῦμαι
οἷς ἔχω.

IX

Quis modus sit vertendi verba in Graecis sententiis; deque
his Homeri versibus quos Vergilius vertisse aut bene
apteque aut inprospere existimatus est.

1 QUANDO ex poematis Graecis vertendae imitandae-
que sunt insignes sententiae, non semper aiunt

---

[1] Fr. 81, Marres. We may compare Hor. *Epist.* i. 6. 40 ff.
[2] *ad ea quae habet tuenda*; see § 1.

declare to have been fully investigated and to be generally accepted; namely, that when some strings of the lyre are struck with the fingers at the time of the winter solstice, other strings give out sound.

VIII

That it is inevitable that one who has much should need much, with a brief and graceful aphorism of the philosopher Favorinus on that subject.

THAT is certainly true which wise men have said as the result of observation and experience, that he who has much is in need of much, and that great want arises from great abundance and not from great lack; for many things are wanted to maintain the many things that you have. Whoever then, having much, desires to provide and take precaution that nothing may fail or be lacking, needs to lose, not gain, and must have less in order to want less.

I recall that Favorinus once, amid loud and general applause, rounded off this thought, putting it into the fewest possible words:[1] "It is not possible for one who wants fifteen thousand cloaks not to want more things;[2] for if I want more than I possess, by taking away from what I have I shall be contented with what remains."

IX

What method should be followed in translating Greek expressions; and on those verses of Homer which Virgil is thought to have translated either well and happily or unsuccessfully.

WHENEVER striking expressions from the Greek poets are to be translated and imitated, they say that

enitendum ut omnia omnino verba in eum in quem
2 dicta sunt modum vertamus. Perdunt enim gratiam pleraque, si quasi invita et recusantia violentius
3 transferantur. Scite ergo et considerate Vergilius,
cum aut Homeri aut Hesiodi aut Apollonii aut Parthenii aut Callimachi aut Theocriti aut quorundam
aliorum locos effingeret, partim reliquit, alia expressit.

4 Sicuti nuperrime, aput mensam cum legerentur
utraque simul *Bucolica* Theocriti et Vergilii, animadvertimus reliquisse Vergilium quod Graecum
quidem mire quam suave est, verti autem neque
5 debuit neque potuit. Sed enim quod substituit pro
eo, quod omiserat, non abest quin iucundius lepidiusque sit :

Βάλλει καὶ μάλοισι τὸν αἰπόλον ἁ Κλεαρίστα
Τὰς αἶγας παρελᾶντα καὶ ἁδύ τι ποππυλιάζει.

6 Malo me Galatea petit, lasciva puella,
Et fugit ad salices et se cupit ante videri.

7 Illud quoque alio in loco animadvertimus caute
omissum, quod est in Graeco versu dulcissimum

Τίτυρ', ἐμὶν τὸ καλὸν πεφιλημένε, βόσκε τὰς αἶγας
Καὶ ποτὶ τὰν κράναν ἄγε, Τίτυρε· καὶ τὸν ἐνόρχαν
Τὸν Λιβυκὸν κνάκωνα φυλάσσεο, μή τυ κορύξῃ.

---

[1] Cf. Hor. *Ars Poet.* 149–150.
[2] *Idyls* v. 88 f ; the translation is that of Edmonds, *L.C.L.*
[3] *Ecl.* iii. 64 ff., translation by Dryden.
[4] *Idyls* iii. 3 ff.

we should not always strive to render every single word with exact literalness. For many things lose their charm if they are transplanted too forcibly— unwillingly, as it were, and reluctantly.[1] Virgil therefore showed skill and good judgment in omitting some things and rendering others, when he was dealing with passages of Homer or Hesiod or Apollonius or Parthenius or Callimachus or Theocritus, or some other poet.

For example, when very recently the *Bucolics* of Theocritus and Virgil were being read together at table, we perceived that Virgil had omitted something that in the Greek is, to be sure, wonderfully pleasing, but neither could nor ought to have been translated. But what he has substituted for that omission is almost more charming and graceful. Theocritus writes:[2]

> But when her goatherd boy goes by you should see my Cleärist
> Fling apples, and her pretty lips call pouting to be kissed.

Virgil has:[3]

> My Phyllis me with pelted apples plies,
> Then tripping to the woods the wanton hies,
> And wishes to be seen before she flies.

Also in another place I notice that what was very sweet in the Greek was prudently omitted. Theocritus writes:[4]

> O Tityrus, well-belovéd, feed my goats,
> And lead them to the fount, good Tityrus;
> But 'ware yon buck-goat yellow, lest he butt.

ATTIC NIGHTS OF AULUS GELLIUS

8 Quo enim pacto diceret : τὸ καλὸν πεφιλημένε, verba
hercle non translaticia, sed cuiusdam nativae dulce-
9 dinis? Hoc igitur reliquit et cetera vertit non
infestiviter, nisi quod " caprum" dixit, quem Theo-
10 critus ἐνόρχαν appellavit—auctore enim M. Varrone
is demum Latine " caper" dicitur, qui excastratus
est :—

11 Tityre, dum redeo, brevis est via, pasce capellas
Et potum pastas age, Tityre, et inter agendum
Occursare capro, cornu ferit ille, caveto.

12 Et quoniam de transferendis sententiis loquor,
memini audisse me ex Valerii Probi discipulis, docti
hominis et in legendis pensitandisque veteribus
scriptis bene callidi, solitum eum dicere, nihil quicquam tam inprospere Vergilium ex Homero vertisse
quam versus hos amoenissimos, quos de Nausicaa
Homerus fecit :

Οἵη δ᾽ Ἄρτεμις εἶσι κατ᾽ οὔρεος ἰοχέαιρα,
Ἢ κατὰ Τηΰγετον περιμήκετον ἢ Ἐρύμανθον
Τερπομένη κάπροισι καὶ ὠκείῃς ἐλάφοισιν·
Τῇ δέ θ᾽ ἅμα νύμφαι, κοῦραι Διὸς αἰγιόχοιο,
Ἀγρονόμοι παίζουσι· γέγηθε δέ τε φρένα Λητώ·
Πασάων δ᾽ ὑπὲρ ἥ γε κάρη ἔχει ἠδὲ μέτωπα,
Ῥεῖα δ᾽ ἀριγνώτη πέλεται, καλαὶ δέ τε πᾶσαι,—

---

1 Fr. 104, G. & S.
2 Ecl. ix. 23.
3 Odyss. vi. 102 ff., translation by Dryden.
4 Aen. i. 498. ff.

But how could Virgil reproduce τὸ καλὸν πεφιλημένε ("well-beloved"), words that, by Heaven! defy translation, but have a certain native charm? He therefore omitted that expression and translated the rest very cleverly, except in using *caper* for Theocritus' ἐνόρχας; for, according to Marcus Varro,[1] a goat is called *caper* in Latin only after he has been castrated. Virgil's version is:[2]

> Till I return—not long— feed thou my goats;
> Then, Tityrus, give them drink, but as you go,
> Avoid the buck-goat's horn—the fellow butts!

And since I am speaking on the subject of translation, I recall hearing from pupils of Valerius Probus, a learned man and well trained in reading and estimating the ancient writings, that he used to say that Virgil had never translated Homer less successfully than in these delightful lines which Homer wrote about Nausicaa:[3]

> As when o'er Erymanth Diana roves,
> Or wide Taÿgetus' resounding groves,
> A silver train the huntress queen surrounds,
> Her rattling quiver from her shoulder sounds;
> Fierce in the sport, along the mountain's brow
> They bay the boar or chase the bounding roe;
> High o'er the lawn, with more majestic pace,
> Above the nymphs she treads with stately grace;
> Distinguished excellence the goddess proves,
> Exults Latona as the virgin moves:
> With equal grace Nausicaa trod the plain,
> And shone transcendent o'er the beauteous train.

This passage Virgil renders thus:[4]

13 Qualis in Eurotae ripis aut per iuga Cynthi
  Exercet Diana choros, quam mille secutae
  Hinc atque hinc glomerantur Oriades. Illa
       pharetram
  Fert humero gradiensque deas supereminet omnis.
  Latonae tacitum pertemptant gaudia pectus.

14 Primum omnium id visum esse dicebant Probo, quod
aput Homerum quidem virgo Nausicaa, ludibunda
inter familiares puellas in locis solis, recte atque commode confertur cum Diana venante in iugis montium
inter agrestes deas, nequaquam autem conveniens
Vergilium fecisse, quoniam Dido in urbe media ingrediens inter Tyrios principes cultu atque incessu
serio, "instans operi," sicut ipse ait, "regnisque
futuris," nihil eius similitudinis capere possit, quae
15 lusibus atque venatibus Dianae congruat; tum
postea, quod Homerus studia atque oblectamenta in
venando Dianae honeste aperteque dicit, Vergilius
autem, cum de venatu deae nihil dixisset, pharetram
tantum facit eam ferre in humero, tamquam sit onus
et sarcina ; atque illud impense Probum esse demira-
tum in Vergilio dicebant, quod Homerica quidem
Λητώ gaudium gaudeat genuinum et intimum atque
in ipso penetrali cordis et animae vigens, siquidem
non aliud est : γέγηθε δέ τε φρένα Λητώ, ipse autem,
imitari ea volens, gaudia fecerit pigra et levia et
cunctantia et quasi in summo pectore supernantia :
16 nescire enim sese, quid significaret aliud " pertemp-

---

  [1] *Aen.* i. 504.
  [2] *Pertempto* means "try thoroughly," hence "affect
deeply." Probus must have taken *per* in the sense of
"over," "on the surface," thus giving *pertempto* a meaning
of which no example exists.

As on Eurotas' banks or Cynthus' heights
Diana guides her dancing bands, whose train
A thousand Oreads follow, right and left;
A quiver bears she on her shoulder fair,
And as she treads, the goddesses o'ertops;
Joys thrill Latona's silent breast.

First of all, they said that Probus thought that in
Homer the maiden Nausicaa, playing among her girl
companions in solitary places, was consistently and
properly compared with Diana hunting on the
mountain heights among the rural goddesses; but
that Virgil had made a comparison that was by no
means suitable, since Dido, walking with dignified
dress and gait in the midst of a city, and surrounded
by the Tyrian chiefs, " pressing on the work of her
rising kingdom," as he himself says,[1] can have no
points of similarity corresponding with the sports
and hunts of Diana. Then secondly, that Homer
mentions plainly and directly Diana's interest and
pleasure in the chase, while Virgil, not having said
a word about the goddess' hunting, merely pictures
her as carrying a quiver on her shoulder, as if it
were a burden or a pack. And they said that Probus
was particularly surprised at this feature of Virgil's
version, that while Homer's Leto rejoices with a joy
that is unaffected, deep, and springing from the very
depths of her heart and soul—for the words γέγηθε
δέ τε φρένα Λητώ, or " Leto rejoiced in heart," mean
nothing else—Virgil, on the other hand, in his
attempt to imitate this, has depicted a joy that is
passive, mild, slow, and as it were floating on the
surface of the heart; for Probus said that he did not
know what else the word *pertemptant* could mean[2]

tant"; praeter ista omnia florem ipsius totius loci
Vergilium videri omisisse, quod hunc Homeri versum
exigue secutus sit:

Ῥεῖα δ᾽ ἀριγνώτη πέλεται, καλαὶ δέ τε πᾶσαι,[1]

17 quando nulla maior cumulatiorque pulcritudinis laus
dici potuerit, quam quod una inter omnis pulcras ex-
celleret, una facile et ex omnibus nosceretur.

X

Quod Annaeus Cornutus versus Vergilii, quibus Veneris et
Vulcani concubitum pudice operteque dixit, reprehensione
spurca et odiosa inquinavit.

1 ANNIANUS poeta, et plerique cum eo eiusdem
Musae viri, summis adsiduisque laudibus hos Vergilii
versus ferebat, quibus Vulcanum et Venerem iunctos
mixtosque iure coniugii, rem lege naturae operien-
dam, verecunda quadam translatione verborum, cum
2 ostenderet demonstraretque, protexit. Sic enim
scripsit:

Ea verba locutus
Optatos dedit amplexus placidumque petivit
Coniugis infusus gremio per membra soporem.

3 Minus autem difficile esse arbitrabantur, in istiusmodi re dicenda, verbis uti uno atque altero brevi
tenuique eam signo demonstrantibus, sicut Homerus
dixerit: παρθενίην ζώνην et λέκτροιο θεσμόν et ἔργα
4 φιλοτήσια, tot vero et tam evidentibus ac tamen non
praetextatis, sed puris honestisque verbis venerandum

---

[1] Literally, "And is readily recognized, though all are fair.'
[2] A name of Celtic origin, according to Schulze, *Eigenn.* 426.

Besides all this, Virgil seemed to have left out the flower of the whole passage, by giving only a faint shadow of this verse of Homer's:

And shone transcendent o'er the beauteous train.[1]

For no greater or more complete praise of beauty can be expressed than that she alone excelled where all were beautiful, that she alone was easily distinguished from all the rest.

X

The low and odious criticism with which Annaeus Cornutus befouled the lines of Virgil in which the poet with chaste reserve spoke of the intercourse of Venus and Vulcan.

THE poet Annianus,[2] and with him many other devotees of the same Muse, extolled with high and constant praise the verses of Virgil in which, while depicting and describing the conjugal union of Vulcan and Venus, an act that nature's law bids us conceal, he veiled it with a modest paraphrase. For thus he wrote:[3]

So speaking, the desired embrace he gave,
And sinking on the bosom of his spouse,
Calm slumber then he wooed in every limb.

But they thought it less difficult, in speaking of such a subject, to use one or two words that suggest it by a slight and delicate hint, such as Homer's παρθενίη ζώνη, or "maiden girdle";[4] λέκτροιο θεσμόν, "the right of the couch";[5] and ἔργα φιλοτήσια, "love's labours";[6] that no other than Virgil has ever spoken of those sacred mysteries of chaste intercourse in so

---

[3] *Aen.* viii. 404 ff.   [4] *Odyss.* xi. 245.
[5] *Odyss.* xxiii. 296.   [6] *Odyss.* xi. 246.

illud concubii pudici secretum neminem quemquam
alium dixisse.

5 Sed Annaeus Cornutus, homo sane pleraque alia
non indoctus neque inprudens, in secundo tamen
librorum, quos *De Figuris Sententiarum* conposuit,
egregiam totius istius verecundiae laudem insulsa
6 nimis et odiosa scrutatione violavit. Nam cum genus
hoc figurae probasset et satis circumspecte factos
esse versus dixisset, " ' Membra ' tamen," inquit,
" paulo incautius nominavit."

XI

De Valerio Corvino ; et unde Corvinus.

1 DE MAXIMO VALERIO, qui Corvinus appellatus est
ob auxilium propugnationemque corvi alitis, haut
quisquam est nobilium scriptorum qui secus dixerit.
2 Ea res prorsus miranda sic profecto est in libris
3 annalibus memorata : " Adulescens tali genere
4 editus, L. Furio, Claudio Appio consulibus fit tribunus militaris. Atque in eo tempore copiae
Gallorum ingentes agrum Pomptinum insederant
instruebaturque[1] acies a consulibus, de vi ac
5 multitudine hostium satis agentibus. Dux interea
Gallorum, vasta et ardua proceritate armisque auro
praefulgentibus, grandia ingrediens et manu telum
reciprocans incedebat perque contemptum et super-

---

[1] instruebatur, *Skutsch ;* instruebanturque, *codd.*

---

[1] Having in mind a special meaning of *membrum.*
[2] *e.g.* Claud. Quad. Fr. 12, Peter[2].   [3] **349 B.C.**

many and such plain words, which yet were not licentious, but pure and honourable.

But Annaeus Cornutus, a man in many other respects, to be sure, lacking neither in learning nor taste, nevertheless, in the second book of the work which he compiled *On Figurative Language*, defamed the high praise of all that modesty by an utterly silly and odious criticism. For after expressing approval of that kind of figurative language, and observing that the lines were composed with due circumspection, he added: "Virgil nevertheless was somewhat indiscreet in using the word *membra*." [1]

XI

Of Valerius Corvinus and the origin of his surname.

THERE is not one of the well-known historians who has varied in telling the story of Valerius Maximus, who was called Corvinus because of the help and defence rendered him by a raven. That truly remarkable event is in fact thus related in the annals: [2] In the consulship of Lucius Furius and Appius Claudius,[3] a young man of such a family[4] was appointed tribune of the soldiers. And at that time vast forces of Gauls had encamped in the Pomptine district, and the Roman army was being drawn up in order of battle by the consuls, who were not a little disquieted by the strength and number of the enemy. Meanwhile the leader of the Gauls, a man of enormous size and stature, his armour gleaming with gold, advanced with long strides and flourishing his spear, at the same time casting haughty and contemptuous glances

---

[4] That is, as had been described in what preceded.

biam circumspiciens despiciensque omnia, venire
iubet et congredi, si quis pugnare secum ex omni
6 Romano exercitu auderet. Tum Valerius tribunus,
ceteris inter metum pudoremque ambiguis, impetrato
prius a consulibus ut in Gallum tam inaniter adro-
gantem pugnare sese permitterent, progreditur
intrepide modesteque obviam ; et congrediuntur et
consistunt et conserebantur iam manus. Atque ibi
7 vis quaedam divina fit : corvus repente inprovisus
advolat et super galeam tribuni insistit atque inde
in adversari os atque oculos pugnare incipit ; in-
silibat, obturbabat et unguibus manum laniabat et
prospectum alis arcebat atque, ubi satis saevierat,
8 revolabat in galeam tribuni. Sic tribunus, spectante
utroque exercitu, et sua virtute nixus et opera alitis
propugnatus, ducem hostium ferocissimum vicit
interfecitque atque ob hanc causam cognomen habuit
9 Corvinus. Id factum est annis quadringentis quinque
post Romam conditam.
10 Statuam Corvino isti divus Augustus in foro suo
statuendam curavit. In eius statuae capite corvi
simulacrum est, rei pugnaeque quam diximus moni-
mentum.

XII

De verbis quae in utramque partem significatione adversa et
reciproca dicuntur.

1 Ut "formidulosus" dici potest et qui formidat et
qui formidatur, ut "invidiosus" et qui invidet et

---

[1] In the colonnades of his Forum Augustus placed statues
of "the leaders who had raised the estate of the Roman

in all directions. Filled with scorn for all that he saw, he challenged anyone from the entire Roman army to come out and meet him, if he dared. Thereupon, while all were wavering between fear and shame, the tribune Valerius, first obtaining the consuls' permission to fight with the Gaul who was boasting so vainly, advanced to meet him, boldly yet modestly. They meet, they halt, they were already engaging in combat. And at that moment a divine power is manifest: a raven, hitherto unseen, suddenly flies to the spot, perches on the tribune's helmet, and from there begins an attack on the face and the eyes of his adversary. It flew at the Gaul, harassed him, tore his hand with its claws, obstructed his sight with its wings, and after venting its rage flew back to the tribune's helmet. Thus the tribune, before the eyes of both armies, relying on his own valour and defended by the help of the bird, conquered and killed the arrogant leader of the enemy, and thus won the surname Corvinus. This happened four hundred and five years after the founding of Rome.

To that Corvinus the deified Augustus caused a statue to be erected in his Forum.[1] On the head of this statue is the figure of a raven, a reminder of the event and of the combat which I have described.

XII

On words which are used with two opposite meanings, both active and passive.

As the adjective *formidulosus* may be used both of one who fears and of one who is feared, *invidiosus* of

people from obscurity to greatness": see Suetonius, *Aug.* xxxi. 5.

cui invidetur, ut "suspiciosus" et qui suspicatur
et qui suspectus est, ut "ambitiosus" et qui ambit
et qui ambitur, ut item "gratiosus" et qui adhibet
gratias et qui admittit, ut "laboriosus" et qui
laborat et qui labori est, ut pleraque alia huiuscemodi in utramque partem dicuntur, ita "infestus"
2 quoque ancipiti significatione est. Nam et is "infestus" appellatur, qui malum infert cuipiam, et
contra, cui aliunde impendet malum, is quoque
"infestus" dicitur.

3 Sed quod prius posui profecto exemplis non
indiget; sic adeo multi locuntur, ut "infestum" dicant inimicum atque adversum; alterum autem illud
4 ignorabilius obscuriusque est. Quis enim e medio
facile dixerit "infestum" esse, cui alter infestus
est? Sed et veteres plerique ita dixerunt et M.
Tullius, in oratione quam *Pro Cn. Plancio* scripsit,
5 vocabulo hoc sic usus est: "Dolebam," inquit,
"iudices, et acerbe ferebam, si huius salus ob eam
ipsam causam esset infestior, quod is meam salutem
atque vitam sua benivolentia, praesidio custodiaque
6 texisset." Nos igitur de origine et ratione verbi
quaerebamus, atque ita in Nigidianis scriptum invenimus: "'Infestum' est a 'festinando' dictum;
nam qui instat," inquit, "alicui eumque properans
urget opprimereque eum studet festinatque, aut
contra de cuius periculo et exitio festinatur, is
uterque 'infestus' dicitur ab instantia atque im-
minentia fraudis, quam vel facturus cuipiam vel
passurus est."

---

[1] § 1.   [2] Fr. 47, Swoboda.
[3] The usual derivation is from *in* + *fendo* (cf. *offendo*), but
this is rejected by Walde, who compares Gk. θάρσος.

one who envies and of one who is envied, *suspiciosus* of one who suspects and of one who is suspected, *ambitiosus* of one who courts favour and of one who is courted, *gratiosus* also of one who gives, and of one who receives, thanks, *laboriosus* of one who toils and of one who causes toil—as many other words of this kind are used in both ways, so *infestus* too has a double meaning. For he is called *infestus* who inflicts injury on anyone, and on the other hand he who is threatened with injury from another source is also said to be *infestus*.

But the meaning which I gave first surely needs no illustration, so many are there who use *infestus* in the sense of hostile and adverse; but that second meaning is less familiar and more obscure. For who of the common run would readily call a man *infestus* to whom another is hostile? However, not only did many of the earlier writers speak in that way, but Marcus Tullius also gave the word that meaning in the speech which he wrote *In Defence of Gnaeus Plancius*, saying:[1] "I were grieved, gentlemen of the jury, and keenly distressed, if this man's safety should be more endangered (*infestior*) for the very reason that he had protected my life and safety by his own kindliness, protection and watchfulness." Accordingly, I inquired into the origin and meaning of the word and found this statement in the writings of Nigidius:[2] "*Infestus* is derived from *festinare*," says he, "for one who threatens anyone, and is in haste to attack him, and hurries eagerly to crush him; or on the other hand one whose peril and ruin are being hastened— both of these are called *infestus* from the urgent imminence of the injury which one is either about to inflict on someone, or to suffer."[3]

7 Ne quis autem de "suspicioso," quod supra posuimus, et de "formiduloso" in eam partem quae minus usitata est, exemplum requirat, de "suspicioso" aput M. Catonem *De Re Floria* ita scriptum : "Sed nisi qui palam corpore pecuniam quaereret aut se lenoni locavisset, etsi famosus et suspiciosus fuisset, vim in corpus liberum non aecum

8 censuere adferri." "Suspiciosum" enim Cato hoc in loco suspectum significat, non suspicantem :

9 "formidulosum" autem, qui formidetur, Sallustius in *Catilina* ita dicit : "Igitur talibus viris non labor insolitus, non locus ullus asper aut arduus erat, non armatus hostis formidulosus."

10 Item C. Calvus in poematis "laboriosus" dicit, non, ut vulgo dicitur, qui laborat, sed in quo laboratur :

Durum (inquit) rus fugit et laboriosum.

11 Eadem ratione Laberius quoque in *Sororibus :*

Ecastor (inquit) mustum somniculosum,

12 et Cinna in poematis :

Somnículosam ut Poénus aspidém Psyllus.

13 "Metus" quoque et "iniuria" atque alia quaedam id genus sic utroqueversum dici possunt ; nam "metus hostium" recte dicitur et cum timent

---

[1] lvii. 1, Jordan. [2] vii. 5. [3] Fr. 2, Bährens, *F. P. R.*

[4] 86, Ribbeck[3]. [5] Fr. 2, Bährens.

[6] Some such word as "handle" is to be supplied.

[7] The Psylli, according to Pliny, *Nat. Hist.* vii. 14, were an African people whose bodies contained a poison deadly to serpents, and gave out an odour which put snakes to flight ; see also *Nat. Hist.* viii. 93 ; Dio Cassius, li. 14. *Psyllus* came

Now, that no one may have to search for an example of *suspiciosus*, which I mentioned above, and of *formidulosus* in its less usual sense, Marcus Cato, *On the property of Florius*, used *suspiciosus* as follows :[1] " But except in the case of one who practised public prostitution, or had hired himself out to a procurer, even though he had been ill-famed and suspected (*suspiciosus*), they decided that it was unlawful to use force against the person of a freeman." For in this passage Cato uses *suspiciosus* in the sense of "suspected," not that of "suspecting." Sallust too in the *Catiline* uses *formidulosus* of one who is feared, in this passage :[2] "To such men consequently no labour was unfamiliar, no region too rough or too steep, no armed foeman to be dreaded (*formidulosus*)."

Gaius Calvus also in his poems uses *laboriosus*, not in the ordinary sense of "one who toils," but of that on which labour is spent, saying :[3]

The hard and toilsome (*laboriosum*) country he will shun.

In the same way Laberius also in the *Sisters* says :[4]

By Castor ! sleepy (*somniculosum*) wine !

and Cinna in his poems :[5]

As Punic Psyllus doth [6] the sleepy (*somniculosam*) asp.[7]

Metus also and *iniuria*, and some other words of the kind, may be used in this double sense ; for *metus hostium*, "fear of the enemy," is a correct expression

to be a general term for snake-charmers and healers of snake-bites, as in Suetonius, *Aug.* xvii. 4.

14 hostes et cum timentur. Itaque Sallustius in
Historia prima "metum Pompei" dixit, non quo
Pompeius metueret, quod est usitatius, sed quo
metueretur. Verba haec Sallusti sunt : "Id bellum
excitabat metus Pompei victoris, Hiempsalem in
15 regnum restituentis." Item alio in loco : "Postquam remoto metu Punico simultates exercere
16 vacuum fuit." "Iniurias" itidem dicimus tam
illorum qui patiuntur, quam qui faciunt, quarum
dictionum exempla sunt facilia inventu.
17   Illud etiam dictum a Vergilio eandem habet
formam communicatae ultro et citro significationis :

et vulnere (inquit) tardis Ulixi,

cum diceret "vulnus," non quod accepisset Ulixes,
18 sed quod dedisset. "Nescius" quoque dicitur tam
19 is qui nescitur, quam qui nescit. Sed super eo
qui nescit, frequens huius vocabuli usus est, in-
20 frequens autem est de eo quod nescitur. "Ignarus"
aeque utroqueversum dicitur, non tantum qui
21 ignorat, set et qui ignoratur. Plautus in *Rudente* :

Quae ín locis nésciis néscia spé sumus.

22 Sallustius : More humanae cupidinis ignara visendi.
Vergilius :

ignarum Laurens habet ora Mimanta.

---

[1] i. 53, Maur.   [2] i. 12, Maur.
[3] *Aen.* ii. 436.   [4] v. 275.
[5] That is, not knowing what to expect
[6] *Hist.* i. 103, Maur.   [7] *Aen.* x. 706.

both when the enemy fear and when they are feared.
Thus Sallust in the first book of his *History*[1] speaks
of "the fear of Pompey," not implying that Pompey
was afraid, which is the more common meaning, but
that he was feared. These are Sallust's words: "That
war was aroused by the fear of the victorious Pompey,
who was restoring Hiempsal to his kingdom." Also
in another passage:[2] "After the fear of the Carthaginians had been dispelled and there was leisure to
engage in dissensions." In the same way we speak
of the "injuries," as well of those who inflict them
as of those who suffer them, and illustrations of that
usage are readily found.

The following passage from Virgil affords a similar
instance of this kind of double meaning; he says:[3]

> Slow from Ulysses' wound,

using *vulnus*, not of a wound that Ulysses had suffered,
but of one that he had inflicted. *Nescius* also is used
as well of one who is unknown as of one who
does not know; but its use in the sense of one who
does not know is common, while it is rarely used of
that which is unknown. *Ignarus* has the same double
application, not only to one who is ignorant, but also
to one who is not known. Thus Plautus in the
Rudens says:[4]

> In unknown (*nesciis*) realms are we where hope
> knows naught (*nescia*).[5]

And Sallust:[6] "With the natural desire of mankind to visit unknown (*ignara*) places."
And Virgil:[7]

> Unknown (*ignarum*) the Laurentine shore doth
> Mimas hold.

XIII

Verba ex historia Claudi Quadrigari, quibus Manli Torquati,
nobilis adulescentis, et hostis Galli provocantis pugnam
depinxit.

1 TITUS MANLIUS summo loco natus adprimeque
2 nobilis fuit. Ei Manlio cognomentum factum est
3 Torquatus. Causam cognomenti fuisse accepimus
torquis ex auro induvies, quam ex hoste quem
4 occiderat detractam induit. Sed quis hostis et quid
genus, quam formidandae vastitatis et quantum in-
solens provocator et cuimodi fuerit pugna decertatum, Q. Claudius primo *Annalium* purissime atque
inlustrissime simplicique et incompta orationis anti-
5 quae suavitate descripsit. Quem locum ex eo libro
philosophus Favorinus cum legeret, non minoribus
quati adficique animum suum motibus pulsibusque
dicebat, quam si ipse coram depugnantes eos
spectaret.

6 Verba Q. Claudi, quibus pugna ista depicta est,
7 adscripsi: "Cum interim Gallus quidam nudus
praeter scutum et gladios duos torque atque armil-
lis decoratus processit, qui et viribus et magnitudine
et adulescentia simulque virtute ceteris antistabat.
8 Is maxime proelio commoto atque utrisque summo
studio pugnantibus, manu significare coepit utris-
9 que, quiescerent. Pugnae facta pausa est. Ex-
10 templo silentio facto cum voce maxima conclamat,

XIII

A passage from the history of Claudius Quadrigarius, in which he pictured the combat of Manlius Torquatus, a young noble, with a hostile Gaul, who challenged the whole Roman army.

TITUS MANLIUS was a man of the highest birth and of exalted rank. This Manlius was given the surname Torquatus. The reason for the surname, we are told, was that he wore as a decoration a golden neck-chain, a trophy taken from an enemy whom he had slain. But who the enemy was, and what his nationality, how formidable his huge size, how insolent his challenge, and how the battle was fought— all this Quintus Claudius has described in the first book of his *Annals* with words of the utmost purity and clearness, and with the simple and unaffected charm of the old-time style. When the philosopher Favorinus read this passage from that work, he used to say that his mind was stirred and affected by no less emotion and excitement than if he were himself an eye-witness of their contest.

I have added the words of Quintus Claudius in which that battle is pictured: "In the meantime a Gaul came forward, who was naked except for a shield and two swords and the ornament of a neck-chain and bracelets; in strength and size, in youthful vigour and in courage as well, he excelled all the rest. In the very height of the battle, when the two armies were fighting with the utmost ardour, he began to make signs with his hand to both sides, to cease fighting. The combat ceased. As soon as silence was secured, he called out in a mighty voice that if anyone wished to engage him in single combat,

11 si quis secum depugnare vellet, uti prodiret.   Nemo
audebat propter magnitudinem atque inmanitatem
12 faciei.[1]   Deinde Gallus inridere coepit atque lin-
13 guam exertare.   Id subito perdolitum est cuidam
Tito Manlio, summo genere gnato, tantum flagitium
civitati adcidere, e tanto exercitu neminem prodire.
14 Is, ut dico,[2] processit neque passus est virtutem
Romanam ab Gallo turpiter spoliari.[3]   Scuto pedestri
et gladio Hispanico cinctus contra Gallum con-
15 stitit.   Metu magno ea congressio in ipso ponti,
16 utroque exercitu inspectante, facta est.   Ita, ut
ante dixi, constiterunt : Gallus sua disciplina scuto
proiecto cunctabundus;[4] Manlius, animo magis
quam arte confisus, scuto scutum percussit atque
17 statum Galli conturbavit.   Dum se Gallus iterum
eodem pacto constituere studet, Manlius iterum
scuto scutum percutit atque de loco hominem
iterum deiecit ; eo pacto ei sub Gallicum gladium
successit atque Hispanico pectus hausit ; deinde
continuo umerum dextrum eodem successu[5] incidit
neque recessit usquam, donec subvertit, ne Gallus
18 impetum in ictu haberet.   Ubi eum evertit, caput
praecidit, torquem detraxit eamque sanguinulentam
19 sibi in collum inponit.   Quo ex facto ipse posteri-
que eius Torquati sunt cognominati."
20   Ab hoc Tito Manlio, cuius hanc pugnam Quadrigarius descripsit, imperia et aspera et immitia

---

[1] On this form of the genitive see ix. 14.

[2] ilico, *Mommsen* ; iudico, X^1.

[3] spurcari, *Damsté*.

[4] cunctabundus, π ; cantabundus, ς ; cautabundus, *reliqui codd.*

[5] successu, *Damsté* ; *cf.* successit *above* ; conisu, *Mommsen* ; concessu, ω ; concussu, ς.

196

he should come forward. This no one dared do, because of his great size and savage aspect. Then the Gaul began to laugh at them and to stick out his tongue. This at once roused the great indignation of one Titus Manlius, a youth of the highest birth, that such an insult should be offered his country, and that no one from so great an army should accept the challenge. He, as I say, stepped forth, and would not suffer Roman valour to be shamefully tarnished by a Gaul. Armed with a foot soldier's shield and a Spanish sword, he confronted the Gaul. Their meeting took place on the very bridge, in the presence of both armies, amid great apprehension. Thus they confronted each other, as I said before: the Gaul, according to his method of fighting, with shield advanced and awaiting an attack ; Manlius, relying on courage rather than skill, struck shield against shield, and threw the Gaul off his balance. While the Gaul was trying to regain the same position, Manlius again struck shield against shield, and again forced the man to change his ground. In this fashion he slipped in under the Gaul's sword and stabbed him in the breast with his Spanish blade. Then at once with the same mode of attack he struck his adversary's right shoulder, and he did not give ground at all until he overthrew him, without giving the Gaul a chance to strike a blow. After he had overthrown him, he cut off his head, tore off his neck-chain, and put it, covered with blood as it was, around his own neck. Because of this act, he himself and his descendants had the surname Torquatus." [1]

From this Titus Manlius, whose battle Quadrigarius described above, all harsh and cruel commands are

---

[1] Fr. 10[b], Peter[2].

"Manlia" dicta sunt, quoniam postea bello adversum Latinos cum esset consul, filium suum securi percussit, qui speculatum ab eo missus, . . . interdicto, hostem, a quo provocatus fuerat, occiderat.

XIV

Quod idem Quadrigarius "huius facies" patrio casu probe et Latine dixit; et quaedam alia adposita de similium vocabulorum declinationibus.

1 Quod autem supra scriptum est in Q. Claudi verbis: "Propter magnitudinem atque inmanitatem facies," id nos aliquot veteribus libris inspectis exploravimus atque ita esse, ut scriptum est, com-
2 perimus. Sic enim pleraque aetas veterum declinavit: "haec facies, huius facies," quod nunc propter rationem grammaticam "faciei" dicitur. Corruptos autem quosdam libros repperi, in quibus "faciei" scriptum est, illo quod ante scriptum erat oblitterato.
3 Meminimus etiam in Tiburti bibliotheca invenire nos in eodem Claudii libro scriptum utrumque "facies" et "facii." Sed "facies" in ordinem scriptum fuit et contra per *i* geminum "facii,"
4 neque id abesse a quadam consuetudine prisca existimavimus; nam et ab eo quod est "hic dies," tam "huius dies," quam "huius dii," et ab eo quod est "haec fames," tam "huius famis," quam "huius fami" dixerunt.

198

called "Manlian;" for at a later time, when he was
consul in a war against the Latins, Manlius caused
his own son to be beheaded, because he had been
sent by his father on a scouting expedition with
orders not to fight,[1] and disregarding the command,
had killed one of the enemy who had challenged
him.

XIV

That Quadrigarius also, with correct Latinity, used *facies*
as a genitive; and some other observations on the inflection of similar words.

THE expression that I quoted above from Quintus
Claudius,[2] "On account of his great size and savage
aspect (*facies*)," I have inquired into by examining
several old manuscripts, and have found it to be as
I wrote it. For it was in that way, as a rule, that
the early writers declined the word—*facies facies*—
whereas the rule of grammar now requires *faciei* as
the genitive. But I did find some corrupt manuscripts in which *faciei* was written, with erasure of
the former reading.

I remember too having found both *facies* and *facii*
written in the same manuscript of Claudius[3] in the
library at Tibur. But *facies* was written in the text
and *facii*, with double *i*, in the margin opposite; nor
did I regard that as inconsistent with a certain early
usage; for from the nominative *dies* they used both
dies and *dii* as the genitive, and from *fames*, both
famis and *fami*.

---

[1] There is a lacuna in the text, but this seems to express
the general sense.
[2] ix. 13. 11.   [3] Frag. 30, Peter².

5 Q. Ennius in XVI. *Annali* "dies" scripsit pro "diei" in hoc versu:

> Postremae longinqua dies quod fecerit aetas.

6 Ciceronem quoque adfirmat Caesellius in oratione, quam *Pro P. Sestio* fecit, "dies" scripsisse pro "diei," quod ego inpensa opera conquisitis veteribus libris plusculis ita, ut Caesellius ait, scriptum
7 inveni. Verba sunt haec M. Tullii: "Equites vero daturos illius dies poenas"; quocirca factum hercle est, ut facile his credam, qui scripserunt, idiographum librum Vergilii se inspexisse, in quo ita scriptum est:

> Libra dies somnique pares ubi fecerit horas,

id est "Libra diei somnique."
8 Sed sicut hoc in loco "dies" a Vergilio scriptum videtur, ita in illo versu non dubium est, quin "dii" scripserit pro "diei":

> Munera laetitiamque dii,

quod inperitiores "dei" legunt, ab insolentia
9 scilicet vocis istius abhorrentes. Sic autem "dies, dii" a veteribus declinatum est, ut "fames fami," "pernicies pernicii," "progenies progenii," "luxuries
10 luxurii," "acies acii." M. enim Cato in oratione, quam *De Bello Carthaginiensi* composuit, ita scripsit: "Pueri atque mulieres extrudebantur fami causa."
11 Lucilius in XII.:

> Rugosum atque fami plenum.

---

[1] Ann. 413, Vahlen [2]; Vahlen reads *postremo* and omits *quod*.
[2] *Ses'.* 28; our texts commonly read *diei*.
[3] *Georg.* i 208.   [4] The constellation of the Balance.
[5] *Aen.* i. 636.
[6] Making *munera dei* = "the gifts of the god (Bacchus)."

Quintus Ennius, in the sixteeth book of his *Annals*, wrote *dies* for *diei* in the following verse : [1]

Caused by the distant time of the last day (*dies*).

Caesellius asserts that Cicero also wrote *dies* for *diei* in his oration *For Publius Sestius*, and after sparing no pains and inspecting several old manuscripts, I found Caesellius to be right. These are the words of Marcus Tullius : [2] "But the knights shall pay the penalty for that day (*dies*)." As a result, I readily believe those who have stated that they saw a manuscript from Virgil's own hand, in which it was written : [3]

When Libra [4] shall make like the hours of day
        (*dies*) and sleep,

where *dies* is used for *diei*.

But just as in this place Virgil evidently wrote *dies,* so there is no doubt that he wrote *dii* for *diei* in the following line : [5]

As gifts for that day's (*dii*) merriment,

where the less learned read *dei*,[6] doubtless shrinking from the use of so uncommon a form. But the older writers declined *dies dii,* as they did *fames fami, pernicies pernicii, progenies progenii, luxuries luxurii, acies acii.* For Marcus Cato in his oration *On the Punic War* wrote as follows : [7] "The women and children were driven out because of the famine (*fami causa*)." Lucilius in his twelfth book has : [8]

Wrinkled and full of hunger (*fami*).

[7] xxxvii. 1, Jordan.
[8] 430, Marx, who completes the line with *distendere ventrem*, "to fill a belly."

12 Sisenna in *Historiarum* libro VI.: Romanos infe-
13 rendae pernicii causa venisse. Pacuvius in *Paulo*:

> Patér supreme nóstrae progeníí patris.

14 Cn. Matius in *Iliadis* XXI.:

> Altera pars acii vitassent fluminis undas.

15 Idem Matius in XXIII.:

> An maneat specii simulacrum in morte silentum.

16 C. Gracchus *De Legibus Promulgatis*: "Ea luxurii
17 causa aiunt institui"; et ibidem infra ita scriptum
est: "Non est ea luxuries, quae necessario parentur
18 vitae causa," per quod apparet eum ab eo quod
19 est "luxuries" "luxurii" patrio casu dixisse. M.
quoque Tullius, in oratione qua Sextum Roscium
defendit, "pernicii" scriptum reliquit. Verba haec
sunt: "Quorum nihil pernicii causa divino consilio,
sed vi ipsa et magnitudine rerum factum putamus."
20 Aut "facies" ergo in casu patrio aut "facii"
Quadrigarium scripsisse existimandum est; "facie"
autem in nullo veteri libro scriptum repperi.
21 In casu autem dandi qui purissime locuti sunt
non "faciei," uti nunc dicitur, sed "facie" dixerunt.
22 Lucilius in *Saturis*:

> primum (inquit) facie quod honestae et
>
> Aetati [1] accedit.

---

[1] et aetati, *L. Müller*; et annis, *Bährens;* tantis, *ω.*

---

[1] Fr. 128, Peter[2].   [2] i, p. 325, Ribbeck[3].
[3] Fr. 7, Bährens; *Iliad* xxi. 3 f.
[4] Fr. 8, Bährens; *Iliad* xxiii. 103 f.
[5] *O. R. F.*, p. 235, Meyer[2].   [6] *Pro Rosc. Amer.* 131.
[7] 1257, Marx, who fills out the second line with *naturae dotibus aetas;* tantis, *ω.*

Sisenna in the sixth book of his *History* writes:[1]
"That the Romans came for the purpose of dealing
destruction (*pernicii*)." Pacuvius in the *Paulus*
says:[2]

O sire supreme of our own race's (*progenii*) sire.

Gnaeus Matius in the twenty-first book of his *Iliad*:[3]

The army's (*acii*) other part the river's wave had
shunned.

Again Matius in Book xxiii writes:[4]

Or bides in death some semblance of a form (*specii*)
Of those who speak no more.

Gaius Gracchus, *On the Publishing of the Laws* has:[5]
"They say that those measures were taken because
of luxury (*luxurii causa*)," and farther on in the same
speech we find: "What is necessarily provided to
sustain life is not luxury (*luxuries*)," which shows
that he used *luxurii* as the genitive of *luxuries*.
Marcus Tullius also has left *pernicii* on record, in the
speech in which he defended Sextus Roscius. These
are his words:[6] "We think that none of these things
was produced by divine will for the purpose of
dealing destruction (*pernicii*), but by the very force
and greatness of Nature." We must therefore
suppose that Quadrigarius wrote either *facies* or
facii as the genitive; but I have not found the reading *facie* in any ancient manuscript.

But in the dative case those who spoke the best
Latin did not use the form *faciei*, which is now
current, but *facie*. For example, Lucilius in his
Satires:[7]

Which first is joined to a fair face
And youth.

23 Lucilius in libro septimo :

> Qui te diligat, aetati facieque tuae se
> Fautorem ostendat, fore amicum polliceatur ;

24 sunt tamen non pauci qui utrobique " facii " legant.
25 Sed C. Caesar in libro *De Analogia* secundo " huius
die " et " huius specie " dicendum putat.
26   Ego quoque in *Iugurtha* Sallustii summae fidei et
reverendae vetustatis libro " die " casu patrio scriptum
inveni.   Verba haec ita erant : " Vix decima parte
die reliqua."   Non enim puto argutiolam istam re-
cipiendam, ut die dictum quasi " **ex die** " existi-
memus.

XV

De genere controversiae quod Graece ἄπορον appellatur.

1   CUM Antonio Iuliano rhetore, per feriarum tempus
aestivarum decedere ex urbis aestu volentes, Nea-
2 polim concesseramus.   Atque ibi erat adulescens
tunc quispiam ex ditioribus cum utriusque linguae
magistris meditans et exercens ad causas Romae
orandas eloquentiae Latinae facultatem ; atque is
3 rogat Iulianum, uti sese audiat declamantem.   It
auditum Iulianus imusque nos cum eo simul.
4 Introit adulescens et praefatur arrogantius et elatius
quam aetatem eius decebat, ac deinde iubet exponi
controversias.

---

[1] 269, Marx.   [2] ii, p. 129, Dinter.
[3] *Jug.* xcvii. 3.

And in his seventh book:[1]

Who loves you, and who to your youth and charms
    (*facie*),
Plays courtier, promising to be your friend.

However, there are not a few who read *facii* in both these passages of Lucilius. But Gaius Caesar, in the second book of his treatise *On Analogy*,[2] thinks that we should use *die* and *specie* as genitive forms.

I have also found *die* in the genitive case in a manuscript of Sallust's *Jugurtha* of the utmost trustworthiness and of venerable age. These were the words:[3] "when scarcely a tenth part of the day (*die*) was left." For I do not think we ought to accept such a quibble as the assertion that *die* is used for *ex die*.

XV

On the kind of debate which the Greeks call ἄπορος.

With the rhetorician Antonius Julianus I had withdrawn to Naples during the season of the summer holidays, wishing to escape the heat of Rome. And there was there at the time a young man of the richer class studying with tutors in both languages, and trying to gain a command of Latin eloquence in order to plead at the bar in Rome; and he begged Julianus to hear one of his declamations. Julianus went to hear him and I went along with him. The young fellow entered the room, made some preliminary remarks in a more arrogant and presumptuous style than became his years, and then asked that subjects for debate be given him.

5 Aderat ibi nobiscum Iuliani sectator, iuvenis promptus et proficiens et offendens iam in eo, quod ille aput Iuliani aures in praecipiti stare et subitaria
6 dictione periculum sui facere audebat. Exponit igitur temptamenti gratia controversiam parum consistentem, quod genus Graeci ἄπορον vocant, Latine autem id non nimis incommode "inexplicabile" dici
7 potest. Ea controversia fuit huiusmodi : "De reo septem iudices cognoscant eaque sententia sit rata, quam plures ex eo numero dixerint. Cum septem iudices cognovissent, duo censuerunt reum exilio multandum, duo alii pecunia, tres reliqui capite
8 puniendum. Petitur ad supplicium ex sententia trium iudicum et contradicit."
9 Hac ille audita nec considerata neque aliis, ut proponerentur, expectatis, incipit statim mira celeritate in eandem hanc controversiam principia nescio quae dicere et involucra sensuum verborumque volumina vocumque turbas fundere, ceteris omnibus ex cohorte eius, qui audire eum soliti erant, clamore magno exultantibus, Iuliano autem male ac misere rubente
10 et sudante. Sed ubi deblateratis versuum multis milibus finem aliquando fecit egressique inde sumus, amici familiaresque eius Iulianum prosecuti, quidnam
11 existimaret, percontati sunt. Atque ibi Iulianus festivissime "Nolite quaerere," inquit, "quid sentiam ; adulescens hic sine controversia disertus est."

---

1 *Sine controversia* is of course used in a double sense : "without question," and "without an opponent" (*i.e.*, when there is no one to argue against him).

There was present there with us a pupil of Julianus, a man of ready speech and good ability, who was already offended that in the hearing of a man like Julianus the fellow should show such rashness and should dare to test himself in extempore speaking. Therefore, to try him, he proposed a topic for debate that was not logically constructed, of the kind which the Greeks call ἄπορος, and in Latin might with some propriety be termed *inexplicabile*, that is, "unsolvable." The subject was of this kind : "Seven judges are to hear the case of a defendant, and judgment is to be passed in accordance with the decision of a majority of their number. When the seven judges had heard the case, two decided that the defendant ought to be punished with exile ; two, that he ought to be fined ; the remaining three, that he should be put to death. The execution of the accused is demanded according to the decision of the three judges, but he appeals."

As soon as the young man had heard this, without any reflection and without waiting for other subjects to be proposed, he began at once with incredible speed to reel off all sorts of principles and apply them to that same question, pouring out floods of confused and meaningless words and a torrent of verbiage. All the other members of his company, who were in the habit of listening to him, showed their delight by loud applause, but Julianus blushed and sweat from shame and embarrassment. But when after many thousand lines of drivel the fellow at last came to an end and we went out, his friends and comrades followed Julianus and asked him for his opinion. Whereupon Julianus very wittily replied "Don't ask me what I think ; without controversy[1] this young man is eloquent."

XVI

Quod Plinium Secundum, non hominem indoctum, fugerit
latueritque vitium argumenti quod ἀντιστρέφον Graeci
dicunt.

1 PLINIUS SECUNDUS existimatus est esse aetatis suae
2 doctissimus. Is libros reliquit quos *Studiosorum* inscripsit, non medius fidius usquequaque aspernandos.
3 In his libris multa varie ad oblectandas eruditorum
4 hominum aures ponit. Refert etiam plerasque sententias quas in declamandis controversiis lepide
5 arguteque dictas putat. Sicuti hanc quoque sententiam ponit ex huiuscemodi controversia: "'Vir fortis
praemio quod optaverit donetur. Qui fortiter fecerat,
petit alterius uxorem in matrimonium et accepit. Is
deinde cuia uxor fuit fortiter fecit. Repetit eandem;
6 contradicitur.' Eleganter," inquit, "et probabiliter
ex parte posterioris viri fortis, uxorem sibi reddi
postulantis, hoc dictum est: 'Si placet lex, redde;
7 si non placet, redde.'" Fugit autem Plinium, sen-
tentiolam istam, quam putavit esse argutissimam,
vitio non carere quod Graece ἀντιστρέφον dicitur.
Et est vitium insidiosum et sub falsa laudis specie
latens; nihil enim minus converti ex contrario id
ipsum adversus eundem potest, atque ita a priore
illo viro forte dici: "Si placet lex, non reddo; si
non placet, non reddo."

---

[1] If the law was valid, the second man ought to be granted
what he desired; that is, the return of his wife. If the law
was not valid, the first man's desire should not have been
granted, and the second man's wife should not have been
taken from him. Cf. v. 10 for a similar argument.

XVI

How Plinius Secundus, although not without learning, failed
to observe and detect the fallacy in an argument of the kind
that the Greeks call ἀντιστρέφον.

PLINIUS SECUNDUS was considered the most learned
man of his time. He left a work, entitled *For Students of Oratory*, which is by no manner of means to be
lightly regarded. In that work he introduces much
varied material that will delight the ears of the
learned. He also quotes a number of arguments
that he regards as cleverly and skilfully urged in the
course of debates. For instance, he cites this argument from such a debate : " ' A brave man shall be
given the reward which he desires. A man who had
done a brave deed asked for the wife of another
in marriage, and received her. Then the man whose
wife she had been did a brave deed. He demands
the return of his wife, but is refused.' On the part
of the second brave man, who demanded the return
of his wife," says Pliny, " this elegant and plausible
argument was presented : ' If the law is valid, return
her to me ; if it is not valid, return her.' " [1] But it
escaped Pliny's notice that this bit of reasoning,
which he thought very acute, was not without the
fallacy which the Greeks call ἀντιστρέφον, or " a con-
vertible proposition." And that is a deceptive fallacy, which lies concealed under a false appearance of
truth ; for that very argument may just as easily be
turned about and used against the same man, and
might, for example, be put thus by that former
husband : " If the law is valid, I do not return her ;
if it is not valid, I do not return her."

BOOK X

LIBER DECIMUS

I

"Tertium"ne consul an "tertio" dici oporteat ; et quonam
modo Cn. Pompeius, cum in theatro, quod erat dedicaturus, honores suos scriberet,[1] quaestionem ancipitem
istius verbi de consilio Ciceronis vitaverit.

1 FAMILIARI meo cuipiam litteras Athenis Romam
2 misi. In his scriptum fuit me illi iam "tertium"
3 scripsisse. Is ad me rescripsit petivitque ut rationem
dicerem cur "tertium" ac non "tertio" scripsissem.
Id etiam adscripsit, ut eadem, quid super illo quoque
mihi videretur, facerem se certiorem, "tertium" ne
"consul" et "quartum" an "tertio" et "quarto"
dicendum esset, quoniam Romae doctum virum dicere
audisset "tertio" et "quarto consul," non "tertium
quartum" que ; idque in principio libri III.[2] Coelium
scripsisse et Quintum Claudium in libro undevicesimo
C. Marium creatum "septimo" consulem dixisse.
4 Ad haec ego rescripsi nihil amplius quam verba
M. Varronis, hominis, opinor, quam fuit Claudius
cum Coelio doctioris, quibus verbis utrumque de quo
5 ad me scripserat decideretur ; nam et Varro satis
aperte quid dici oporteret edocuit et ego adversus
eum qui doctus esse dicebatur litem meam facere
absens nolui.

---

[1] inscriberet, NOΠ.
[2] III. *added by Meltzer* ; libri, ω.

BOOK X

I

Whether one ought to say *tertium consul* or *tertio ;* and how Gnaeus Pompeius, when he would inscribe his honours on the theatre which he was about to dedicate, by Cicero's advice evaded the difficulty as to the form of that word.

I SENT a letter from Athens to a friend of mine in Rome. In it I said that I had now written him for the third time (*tertium*). In his reply he asked me to give my reason for having written *tertium* and not *tertio*. He added that he hoped I would at the same time inform him what I thought about the question whether one should say *tertium consul,* meaning " consul for the third time," and *quartum,* or *tertio* and *quarto ;* since he had heard a learned man at Rome say *tertio* and *quarto consul,* not *tertium* and *quartum ;* also, that Coelius had so written [1] at the beginning of his third book and that Quintus Claudius in his eleventh book said [2] that Marius was chosen consul for the seventh time, using *septimo.*

In reply to these questions, to decide both matters about which he had written to me, I contented myself with quoting Marcus Varro, a more learned man in my opinion than Coelius and Claudius together. For Varro has made it quite plain what ought to be said, and I did not wish, when at a distance, to enter into a dispute with a man who had the name of being learned.

[1] Fr. 59, Peter[2].   [2] Fr. 82, Peter[2].

6 Verba M. Varronis ex libro *Disciplinarum* quinto haec sunt: "Aliud est 'quarto' praetorem fieri et 'quartum'; quod 'quarto' locum adsignificat ac tres ante factos, 'quartum' tempus adsignificat et ter ante factum. Igitur Ennius recte, quod scripsit:

Quintus pater quartum fit consul,

et Pompeius timide, quod in theatro, ne adscriberet 'consul tertium' aut 'tertio,' extremas litteras non scripsit."

7 Quod de Pompeio Varro breviter et subobscure dixit, Tiro Tullius, Ciceronis libertus, in epistula quadam enarratius scripsit ad hunc ferme modum: "Cum Pompeius," inquit, "aedem Victoriae dedicaturus foret, cuius gradus vicem theatri essent, nomenque eius et honores scriberentur,[1] quaeri coeptum est, utrum 'consul tertio' inscribendum esset an 'tertium.' Eam rem Pompeius exquisitissime rettulit ad doctissimos civitatis, cumque dissentiretur et pars 'tertio,' alii 'tertium' scribendum contenderent, rogavit," inquit, "Ciceronem Pompeius, ut quod ei rectius videretur scribi iuberet." Tum Ciceronem iudicare de viris doctis veritum esse, ne, quorum opinionem inprobasset, ipsos videretur inprobasse. "Persuasit igitur Pompeio, ut neque 'tertium' neque 'tertio' scriberetur, sed ad secundum usque *t* fierent

[1] inscriberentur, NO²ΠX.

---

[1] p. 202, Bipont.
[2] That is, that he was fourth in order of election.
[3] *Ann.* 295, Vahlen².
[4] He wrote *tert.*; see § 7. *Tertium* is correct; the inscription on the Pantheon reads *M. Agrippa, L. f., cos. tertium fecit.*
[5] p. 12, Lion.

Marcus Varro's words, in the fifth book of his *Disciplinae*, are as follows:[1] "It is one thing to be made praetor *quarto,* and another *quartum*; for *quarto* refers to order and indicates that three were elected before him;[2] *quartum* refers to time and indicates that he had been made praetor three times before. Accordingly Ennius was right when he wrote:[3]

Quintus, his sire, a fourth time (*quartum*) consul is,

and Pompeius was timid when, in order to avoid writing *consul tertium* or *tertio* on his theatre, he did not write the final letters."[4]

What Varro briefly and somewhat obscurely hinted at concerning Pompey, Tullius Tiro, Cicero's freedman, wrote at greater length in one of his letters, substantially as follows:[5] "When Pompey was preparing to consecrate the temple of Victory, the steps of which formed his theatre,[6] and to inscribe upon it his name and honours, the question arose whether *consul tertium* should be written, or *tertio.* Pompey took great pains to refer this question to the most learned men of Rome, and when there was difference of opinion, some maintaining that *tertio* ought to be written, others *tertium,* Pompey asked Cicero," says Varro, "to decide upon what seemed to him the more correct form." Then Cicero was reluctant to pass judgment upon learned men, lest he might seem to have censured the men themselves in criticizing their opinion. "He accordingly advised Pompey to write neither *tertium* nor *tertio,* but to inscribe the first

[6] Because of the sentiment against a permanent theatre at Rome, Pompey placed a temple of Venus Victrix at the top of his theatre, so that the seats of the auditorium formed an approach to it. It was built in 55 B.C.

litterae, ut verbo non perscripto res quidem demon-
straretur, sed dictio tamen ambigua verbi lateret."

8 Id autem, quod et Varro et Tiro dixerunt, in
9 eodem nunc theatro non est ita scriptum. Nam
cum multis annis postea scaena, quae prociderat,
refecta esset, numerus tertii consulatus non uti initio
primoribus litteris, sed tribus tantum liniolis incisis
significatus est.

10 In M. autem Catonis quarta *Origine* ita per-
scriptum est: "Carthaginienses sextum de foedere
decessere." Id verbum significat quinquiens ante
11 eos fecisse contra foedus et tum sextum. Graeci
quoque in significandis huiuscemodi rerum numeris
τρίτον καὶ τέταρτον dicunt, quod congruit cum eo
quod Latine dicitur: "tertium quartumque."

II

Quid Aristoteles de numero puerperii memoriae mandaverit.

1 ARISTOTELES philosophus memoriae tradidit, mulierem in Aegypto uno partu quinque pueros enixam,
eumque esse finem dixit multiiugae hominum par-
tionis neque plures umquam simul genitos compertum,
2 hunc autem numerum ait esse rarissimum. Sed et
divo Augusto imperante qui temporum eius historiam
scripserunt ancillam Caesaris Augusti in agro Laurente
peperisse quinque pueros dicunt eosque pauculos dies
vixisse; matrem quoque eorum, non multo postquam
peperit, mortuam monumentumque ei factum iussu

---

[1] That is, by the Roman numeral III.
[2] Fr. 84, Peter[2].   [3] Cf. *Hist. Anim.* vii. 4, p. 584, 29.

four letters only, so that the meaning was shown without writing the whole word, but yet the doubt as to the form of the word was concealed."

But that of which Varro and Tiro spoke is not now written in that way on this same theatre. For when, many years later, the back wall of the stage had fallen and was restored, the number of the third consulship was indicated, not as before, by the first four letters, but merely by three incised lines.[1]

However, in the fourth book of Marcus Cato's *Origines* we find:[2] "The Carthaginians broke the treaty for the sixth time (*sextum*)." This word indicates that they had violated the treaty five times before, and that this was the sixth time. The Greeks too in distinguishing numbers of this kind use τρίτον καὶ τέταρτον, which corresponds to the Latin words *tertium quartumque*.

II

What Aristotle has recorded about the number of children born at one time.

THE philosopher Aristotle has recorded[3] that a woman in Egypt bore five children at one birth; this, he said, was the limit of human multiple parturition; more children than that had never been known to be born at one time, and even that number was very rare. But in the reign of the deified Augustus the historians of the time say that a maid servant of Caesar Augustus in the region of Laurentum brought forth five children, and that they lived for a few days; that their mother died not long after she had been delivered, whereupon a monument was erected to her by order of Augustus

Augusti in via Laurentina inque eo scriptum esse
numerum puerperii eius, de quo diximus.

III

Locorum quorundam inlustrium conlatio contentioque facta
ex orationibus C. Gracchi et M. Ciceronis et M. Catonis.

1 Fortis ac vehemens orator existimatur esse C.
Gracchus. Nemo id negat. Sed quod nonnullis
videtur severior, acrior ampliorque esse M. Tullio,
2 ferri id qui potest? Legebamus adeo nuper orationem
Gracchi *De Legibus Promulgatis*, in qua M. Marium
et quosdam ex municipiis Italicis honestos viros virgis
per iniuriam caesos a magistratibus populi Romani
quanta maxima invidia potest conqueritur.

3 Verba haec sunt quae super ea re fecit: "Nuper
Teanum Sidicinum consul venit. Uxor eius dixit
se in balneis virilibus lavari velle. Quaestori Sidicino
M. Mario datum est negotium, uti balneis exigerentur
qui lavabantur. Uxor renuntiat viro parum cito sibi
balneas traditas esse et parum lautas fuisse. Idcirco
palus destitutus est in foro eoque adductus suae
civitatis nobilissimus homo M. Marius. Vestimenta
detracta sunt, virgis caesus est. Caleni, ubi id
audierunt, edixerunt ne quis in balneis lavisse vellet,
cum magistratus Romanus ibi esset. Ferentini ob

---

[1] *O.R.F.*, p. 236, Meyer [2].

on the via Laurentina, and on it was inscribed the number of her children, as I have given it.

III

A collection of famous passages from the speeches of Gaius Gracchus, Marcus Cicero and Marcus Cato, and a comparison of them.

GAIUS GRACCHUS is regarded as a powerful and vigorous speaker. No one disputes this. But how can one tolerate the opinion of some, that he was more impressive, more spirited and more fluent than Marcus Tullius? Indeed, I lately read the speech of Gaius Gracchus *On the Promulgation of Laws,* in which, with all the indignation of which he is master, he complains that Marcus Marius and other distinguished men of the Italian free-towns were unlawfully beaten with rods by magistrates of the Roman people.

His words on the subject are as follows :[1] "The consul lately came to Teanum Sidicinum. His wife said that she wished to bathe in the men's baths. Marcus Marius, the quaestor of Sidicinum, was instructed to send away the bathers from the baths. The wife tells her husband that the baths were not given up to her soon enough and that they were not sufficiently clean. Therefore a stake was planted in the forum and Marcus Marius, the most illustrious man of his city, was led to it. His clothing was stripped off, he was whipped with rods. The people of Cales, when they heard of this, passed a decree that no one should think of using the public baths when a Roman magistrate was in town. At Ferentinum, for the

eandem causam praetor noster quaestores arripi
iussit; alter se de muro deiecit, alter prensus et
virgis caesus est."

4 In tam atroci re ac tam misera atque maesta
iniuriae publicae contestatione, ecquid est quod aut
ampliter insigniterque aut lacrimose atque miseranter
aut multa copiosaque invidia gravique et penetrabili
querimonia dixerit? Brevitas sane et venustas et
mundities orationis est, qualis haberi ferme in
comoediarum festivitatibus solet.

5 Item Gracchus alio in loco ita dicit: "Quanta
libido quantaque intemperantia sit hominum adulescentium, unum exemplum vobis ostendam. His
annis paucis ex Asia missus est qui per id tempus
magistratum non ceperat, homo adulescens pro legato.
Is in lectica ferebatur. Ei obviam bubulcus de plebe
Venusina advenit et per iocum, cum ignoraret qui
ferretur, rogavit num mortuum ferrent. Ubi id
audivit, lecticam iussit deponi, struppis, quibus lectica
deligata erat, usque adeo verberari iussit, dum animam
efflavit."

6 Haec quidem oratio super tam violento atque
crudeli facinore nihil profecto abest a cotidianis
7 sermonibus. At cum in simili causa aput M. Tullium
cives Romani, innocentes viri, contra ius contraque
leges virgis caeduntur aut supplicio extremo necantur,
quae ibi tunc miseratio! quae comploratio! quae
totius rei sub oculos subiectio! quod et quale invidiae
8 atque acerbitatis fretum effervescit! Animum hercle

---

[1] *O.R.F.*, p. 236, Meyer [2]

same reason, our praetor ordered the quaestors to be arrested; one threw himself from the wall, the other was caught and beaten with rods."

In speaking of such an atrocious action, in so lamentable and distressing a manifestation of public injustice, has he said anything either fluent or brilliant, or in such a way as to arouse tears and pity; is there anything that shows an outpouring of indignation and solemn and impressive remonstrance? Brevity there is, to be sure, grace, and a simple purity of expression, such as we sometimes have in the more refined of the comedies.

Gracchus also in another place speaks as follows:[1] "I will give you a single example of the lawlessness of our young men, and of their entire lack of self-control. Within the last few years a young man who had not yet held a magisterial office was sent as an envoy from Asia. He was carried in a litter. A herdsman, one of the peasants of Venusia, met him, and not knowing whom they were bearing, asked in jest if they were carrying a corpse. Upon hearing this, the young man ordered that the litter be set down and that the peasant be beaten to death with the thongs by which it was fastened."

Now these words about so lawless and cruel an outrage do not differ in the least from those of ordinary conversation. But in Marcus Tullius, when in a similar case Roman citizens, innocent men, are beaten with rods contrary to justice and contrary to the laws, or tortured to death, what pity is then aroused! What complaints does he utter! How he brings the whole scene before our eyes! What a mighty surge of indignation and bitterness comes seething forth! By Heaven! when I read those

meum, cum illa M. Ciceronis lego, imago quaedam
et sonus verberum et vocum et eiulationum circum-
9 plectitur; velut sunt ista quae de C. Verre dicit,
quae nos, ut in praesens potuimus, quantum memoria
subpeditabat, adscripsimus: "Ipse inflammatus scelere
et furore in forum venit. Ardebant oculi, toto ex
ore crudelitas eminebat. Expectabant omnes quo
tandem progressurus aut quidnam acturus esset, cum
repente hominem proripi atque in foro medio nudari
10 ac deligari et virgas expediri iubet." Iam haec
medius fidius sola verba: "nudari ac deligari et
virgas expediri iubet." tanti motus horrorisque sunt,
ut non narrari quae gesta sunt, sed rem geri prosus
videas.
11   Gracchus autem non querentis neque implorantis,
sed nuntiantis vicem: "Palus," inquit, "in foro
destitutus est, vestimenta detracta sunt, virgis caesus
12 est." Sed enim M. Cicero praeclare cum diutina
repraesentatione, non "caesus est," sed "caede-
batur," inquit, "virgis in medio foro Messanae civis
Romanus, cum interea nullus gemitus, nulla vox
illius miseri inter dolorem‧strepitumque[1] plagarum
audiebatur, nisi haec: 'civis Romanus sum!' Hac[2]
commemoratione civitatis omnia verbera depulsurum
cruciatumque a corpore deiecturum arbitrabatur."
13 Complorationem deinde tam acerbae rei et odium
in Verrem detestationemque aput civis Romanos
inpense atque acriter atque inflammanter facit, cum
haec dicit: "O nomen dulce libertatis! O ius

---

[1] crepitumque, γ, *Cic.*   [2] hac se, *Cic.*

---

[1] *In Verr.* ii. 5. 161.   [2] *In Verr.* ii. 5. 162.
[3] *Id.* ii. 5. 163.

words of Cicero's, my mind is possessed with the
sight and sound of blows, cries and lamentation.
For example, the words which he speaks about Gaius
Verres, which I have quoted so far as my memory
went, which was all that I could do at present:[1]
"The man himself came into the forum, blazing with
wickedness and frenzy. His eyes burned, every
feature of his face displayed cruelty. All were
waiting to see to what ends he would go, or what he
would do, when on a sudden he gave orders that the
man be dragged forth, that he be stripped in the
middle of the forum and bound, and that rods be
brought." Now, so help me! the mere words "he
ordered that he be stripped and bound, and rods
brought" arouse such emotion and horror that you
do not seem to hear the act described, but to see it
acted before your face.

But Gracchus plays the part, not of one who
complains or implores, but of a mere narrator: "A
stake," he says, "was planted in the forum, his
clothing was stripped off, he was beaten with rods."
But Marcus Cicero, finely representing the idea of
continued action, says,[2] not "he was beaten," but "a
citizen of Rome was being beaten with rods in the
middle of the forum at Messana, while in the meantime no groan, no sound was heard from that wretched
man amid his torture and the resounding blows
except these words, 'I am a Roman citizen.' By
thus calling to mind his citizenship he hoped to
avert all their stripes and free his body from torture."
Then Cicero with vigour, spirit and fiery indignation
complains of so cruel an outrage and inspires the
Romans with hatred and detestation of Verres by
these words:[3] "O beloved name of liberty! O

eximium nostrae civitatis! O lex Porcia legesque
Semproniae! O graviter desiderata et aliquando
reddita plebi Romanae tribunicia potestas! Hucine
tandem haec[1] omnia reciderunt, ut civis Romanus
in provincia populi Romani, in oppido foederatorum,
ab eo qui beneficio populi Romani fasces ac secures
haberet, deligatus in foro virgis caederetur? Quid?
cum ignes ardentesque laminae ceterique cruciatus
admovebantur, si te illius acerba imploratio et vox
miserabilis non leniebat,[2] ne civium quidem Romanorum, qui tum aderant, fletu gemituque maximo
commovebare?"

14 Haec M. Tullius atrociter, graviter, apte copiose-
15 que miseratus est. Sed si quis est tam agresti aure
ac tam hispida, quem lux ista et amoenitas orationis
verborumque modificatio parum delectat, amat autem
priora idcirco, quod incompta et brevia et non
operosa, sed nativa quadam suavitate sunt quodque
in his umbra et color quasi opacae vetustatis est, is,
si quid iudicii habet, consideret in causa pari M.
Catonis, antiquioris hominis, orationem, ad cuius vim
16 et copiam Gracchus nec adspiravit. Intelleget,
opinor, Catonem contentum eloquentia aetatis suae
non fuisse et id iam tum facere voluisse quod Cicero
17 postea perfecit. In eo namque libro qui *De Falsis
Pugnis* inscriptus est ita de Q. Thermo conquestus
est: "Dixit a decemviris parum bene sibi cibaria
curata esse. Iussit vestimenta detrahi atque flagro

---

[1] *Omitted by MSS. of Cic.* [2] inhibebat, *Cic.*

---

[1] ix, Jordan. [2] The local magistrates.

eminent justice of our country! O Porcian and
Sempronian laws! O authority of the tribunes,
earnestly desired and finally restored to the Roman
commons! Pray, have all these blessings fallen to
this estate, that a Roman citizen, in a province of the
Roman people, in a town of our allies, should be
bound and flogged in the forum by one who derived
the emblems of his power from the favour of the
Roman people? What! when fire and hot irons and
other tortures were applied, although your victim's
bitter lamentation and piteous outcries did not affect
you, were you not moved by the tears and loud
groans even of the Roman citizens who were then
present?''

These outrages Marcus Tullius bewailed bitterly
and solemnly, in appropriate and eloquent terms.
But if anyone has so rustic and so dull an ear that
this brilliant and delightful speech and the harmoni-
ous arrangement of Cicero's words do not give him
pleasure; if he prefers the earlier oration because it
is unadorned, concise and unstudied, yet has a certain
native charm, and because it has, so to say, a shade
and colour of misty antiquity—let such a one, if he has
any judgment at all, study the address in a similar
case of Marcus Cato, a man of a still earlier time, to
whose vigour and flow of language Gracchus could
never hope to attain. He will realize, I think, that
Cato was not content with the eloquence of his own
time, but aspired to do even then what Cicero later
accomplished. For in the speech which is entitled
On Sham Battles he thus made complaint of Quintus
Thermus:[1] "He said that his provisions had not
been satisfactorily attended to by the decemvirs.[2]
He ordered them to be stripped and scourged. The

caedi. Decemviros Bruttiani verberavere, videre multi mortales. Quis hanc contumeliam, quis hoc imperium, quis hanc servitutem ferre potest? Nemo hoc rex ausus est facere; eane fieri bonis, bono genere gnatis, boni consultis? Ubi societas? ubi fides maiorum? Insignitas iniurias, plagas, verbera, vibices, eos dolores atque carnificinas per dedecus atque maximam contumeliam, inspectantibus popularibus suis atque multis mortalibus, te facere ausum esse? Set quantum luctum, quantum gemitum, quid lacrimarum, quantum fletum factum audivi! Servi iniurias nimis[1] aegre ferunt; quid illos, bono genere natos, magna virtute praeditos, opinamini animi habuisse atque habituros, dum vivent?"

18 Quod Cato dixit: "Bruttiani verberavere," ne
19 qui fortasse de "Bruttianis" requirat, id significat: Cum Hannibal Poenus cum exercitu in Italia esset et aliquot pugnas populus Romanus adversas pugnavisset, primi totius Italiae Bruttii ad Hannibalem desciverunt. Id Romani aegre passi, postquam Hannibal Italia decessit superatique Poeni sunt, Bruttios ignominiae causa non milites scribebant nec pro sociis habebant, sed magistratibus in provincias euntibus parere et praeministrare servorum vicem iusserunt. Itaque hi sequebantur magistratus, tamquam in scaenicis fabulis qui dicebantur "lorarii," et quos erant iussi vinciebant aut verberabant; quod autem ex Bruttiis erant, appellati sunt "Bruttiani."

> [1] nimias, *Mommsen.*

---

[1] See § 18, below.
[2] The name *Bruttium* is of late origin

Bruttiani[1] scourged the decemvirs, many men saw it done. Who could endure such an insult, such tyranny, such slavery? No king has ever dared to act thus; shall such outrages be inflicted upon good men, born of a good family, and of good intentions? Where is the protection of our allies? Where is the honour of our forefathers? To think that you have dared to inflict signal wrongs, blows, lashes, stripes, these pains and tortures, accompanied with disgrace and extreme ignominy, since their fellow citizens and many other men looked on! But amid how great grief, what groans, what tears, what lamentations have I heard that this was done! Even slaves bitterly resent injustice; what feeling do you think that such men, sprung from good families, endowed with high character, had and will have so long as they live?"

When Cato said "the Bruttiani scourged them," lest haply anyone should inquire the meaning of *Bruttiani*, it is this: When Hannibal the Carthaginian was in Italy with his army, and the Romans had suffered several defeats, the Bruttii were the first people of all Italy to revolt to Hannibal. Angered at this, the Romans, after Hannibal left Italy and the Carthaginians were defeated, by way of ignominious punishment refused to enrol the Bruttii as soldiers or treat them as allies, but commanded them to serve the magistrates when they went to their provinces, and to perform the duties of slaves. Accordingly, they accompanied the magistrates in the capacity of those who are called "floggers" in the plays, and bound or scourged those whom they were ordered. And because they came from the land of the Bruttii,[2] they were called *Bruttiani*.

IV

Quod P. Nigidius argutissime docuit nomina non positiva
esse, sed naturalia.

1 NOMINA verbaque non positu fortuito, sed quadam
vi et ratione naturae facta esse, P. Nigidius in *Grammaticis Commentariis* docet, rem sane in philosophiae
2 disceptationibus celebrem. Quaeri enim solitum
aput philosophos, φύσει τὰ ὀνόματα sint ἢ θέσει. In
3 eam rem multa argumenta dicit, cur videri possint
verba esse naturalia magis quam arbitraria. Ex
4 quibus hoc visum est lepidum et festivum : " ' Vos,' "
inquit, " cum dicimus, motu quodam oris conveniente
cum ipsius verbi demonstratione utimur et labeas
sensim primores emovemus ac spiritum atque animam
porro versum et ad eos quibuscum sermocinamur
intendimus. At contra cum dicimus ' nos,' neque
profuso intentoque flatu vocis neque proiectis labris
pronuntiamus, sed et spiritum et labeas quasi intra
nosmet ipsos coercemus. Hoc idem fit et in eo,
quod dicimus ' tu,' ' ego ' et ' tibi ' et ' mihi.' Nam
sicuti, cum adnuimus et abnuimus, motus quidam
ille vel capitis vel oculorum a natura rei quam significat non abhorret, ita in his vocibus quasi gestus
quidam oris et spiritus naturalis est. Eadem ratio
est in Graecis quoque vocibus, quam esse in nostris
animadvertimus."

228

IV

How Publius Nigidius with great cleverness showed that
words are not arbitrary, but natural.

PUBLIUS NIGIDIUS in his *Grammatical Notes* shows
that nouns and verbs were formed, not by a chance
use, but by a certain power and design of nature, a
subject very popular in the discussions of the philosophers; for they used to inquire whether words
originate by " nature " or are man-made.[1]   Nigidius
employs many arguments to this end, to show that
words appear to be natural rather than arbitrary.
Among these the following seems particularly neat
and ingenious[2] : " When we say *vos*, or ' you,' " says
Nigidius, " we make a movement of the mouth suitable to the meaning of the word; for we gradually
protrude the tips of our lips and direct the impulse of
the breath towards those with whom we are speaking.
But on the other hand, when we say *nos*, or ' us,' we
do not pronounce the word with a powerful forward
impulse of the voice, nor with the lips protruded,
but we restrain our breath and our lips, so to speak,
within ourselves.   The same thing happens in the
words *tu* or ' thou,' *ego* or ' I,' *tibi* ' to thee,' and *mihi*
' to me.'   For just as when we assent or dissent, a
movement of the head or eyes corresponds with the
nature of the expression, so too in the pronunciation
of these words there is a kind of natural gesture made
with the mouth and breath.   The same principle
that we have noted in our own speech applies also to
Greek words."

[1] That is, whether language is a natural growth or a
conscious product.
[2] Fr. 41, Swoboda.

V

"Avarus" simplexne vocabulum sit, an compositum et
duplex, sicut P. Nigidio videtur.

1   "AVARUS" non simplex vocabulum, sed iunctum
copulatumque esse P. Nigidius dicit in *Commenta-*
riorum undetricesimo. "'Avarus' enim," inquit,
"appellatur, qui 'avidus aeris' est. Sed in ea
2 copula e littera," inquit, "detrita est." Item
"locupletem" dictum ait ex conpositis vocibus, qui
"pleraque loca," hoc est qui multas possessiones
teneret.
3   Sed probabilius id firmiusque est, quod de "locu-
plete" dixit. Nam de "avaro" ambigitur; cur
enim non videri possit ab uno solum verbo inclina-
tum, quod est "aveo," eademque esse fictura qua
est "amarus," de quo nihil dici potest quin duplex
non sit?

VI

Multam dictam esse ab aedilibus plebei Appi Caeci filiae,
mulieri nobili, quod locuta esset petulantius.

1   NON in facta modo, sed in voces etiam petulan-
tiores publice vindicatum est; ita enim debere esse
2 visa est Romanae disciplinae dignitas inviolabilis.
Appi namque illius Caeci filia, a ludis quos specta-

---

[1] Fr. 42, Swoboda.
[2] *Id.* fr. 44.
[3] The derivation from *locus* and the root *ple-* (of *pleo,*
plenus, etc.) seems to be correct.

V

Whether *avarus* is a simple word or, as it appears to Publius Nigidius, a compound, made up of two parts.

PUBLIUS NIGIDIUS, in the twenty-ninth book of his *Commentaries*,[1] declares that *avarus* is not a simple word, but is compounded of two parts: "For that man," he says, "is called *avarus*, or 'covetous,' who is *avidus aeris*, or 'eager for money;' but in the compound the letter *e* is lost." He also says [2] that a man is called by the compound term *locuples*, or "rich," when he holds *pleraque loca*, that is to say, "many possessions." [3]

But his statement about *locuples* is the stronger and more probable. As to *avarus* there is doubt; for why may it not seem to be derived from one single word, namely *aveo*,[4] and formed in the same way as *amarus*, about which there is general agreement that it is not a compound?

VI

That a fine was imposed by the plebeian aediles on the daughter of Appius Caecus, a woman of rank, because she spoke too arrogantly.

PUBLIC punishment was formerly inflicted, not only upon crimes, but even upon arrogant language; so necessary did men think it to maintain the dignity of Roman conduct inviolable. For the daughter of the celebrated Appius Caecus, when leaving the plays of

---

[4] This is, of course, the accepted etymology. The derivation of *amarus* is uncertain; it is perhaps connected with Greek ὠμός, "raw" (cf. *crudus* and *crudelis*). Sanscrit âma-s.

verat exiens, turba undique confluentis fluctuantis-
que populi iactata est. Atque inde egressa, cum se
male habitam doleret:[1] "Quid me nunc factum
esset," inquit, "quantoque artius pressiusque con-
flictata essem, si P. Claudius, frater meus, navali
proelio classem navium cum ingenti civium numero
non perdidisset? Certe quidem maiore nunc copia
populi oppressa intercidissem. Sed utinam," inquit,
"reviviscat frater aliámque classem in Siciliam
ducat atque istam multitudinem perditum eat, quae
3 me nunc male miseram convexavit!" Ob haec
mulieris verba tam inproba ac tam incivilia C.
Fundanius et Tiberius Sempronius, aediles plebei,
multam dixerunt ei aeris gravis viginti quinque
4 milia. Id factum esse dicit Capito Ateius in commentario *De Iudiciis Publicis* bello Poenico primo,
Fabio Licino et Otacilio Crasso consulibus.

VII

Fluminum, quae ultra imperium Romanum fluunt, prima
magnitudine esse Nilum, secunda Histrum, proxima
Rodanum, sicuti M. Varronem memini scribere.

1   OMNIUM fluminum quae in maria qua imperium
Romanum est fluunt, quam Graeci τὴν εἴσω θάλασσαν

---

[1] doleret *suggested by Hosius*; diceret, *MSS.*

---

[1] In 249 B.C. He was warned not to fight by the refusal of
the sacred chickens to eat; but he threw them overboard,
saying that they might drink, since they would not eat. See
Suet. *Tib.* ii. 2.

[2] The two plebeian aediles were first appointed with the
tribunes of the commons in 494 B.C. (see xvii. 21. 11), and the
designation *plebei* or *plebi* was perhaps not added until the

which she had been a spectator, was jostled by the
crowd of people that surrounded her, flocking together
from all sides. When she had extricated herself,
complaining that she had been roughly handled, she
added : "What, pray, would have become of me,
and how much more should I have been crowded and
pressed upon, had not my brother Publius Claudius
lost his fleet in the sea-fight and with it a vast number of citizens ?[1] Surely I should have lost my life,
overwhelmed by a still greater mass of people. How
I wish," said she, "that my brother might come to
life again, take another fleet to Sicily, and destroy
that crowd which has just knocked poor me about."
Because of such wicked and arrogant words, Gaius
Fundanius and Tiberius Sempronius, the plebeian
aediles,[2] imposed a fine upon the woman of twenty-
five thousand pounds of full-weight bronze.[3] Ateius
Capito, in his commentary *On Public Trials*, says[4] that
this happened in the first Punic war, in the consulship of Fabius Licinus and Otacilius Crassus.[5]

VII

Marcus Varro, I remember, writes that of the rivers which
flow outside[6] the limits of the Roman empire the Nile is
first in size, the Danube second, and next the Rhone.

Of all the rivers which flow into the seas included
within the Roman empire, which the Greeks call

appointment of two curule aediles in 388 B.C. They were
assistants to the tribunes, but also had the right of independ-
ent action, as here. Julius Caesar added two *aediles ceriales* ;
Suet. *Jul.* xli. 1.

[3] *Aes gravis* or *aes libralis* refers to the old coinage, when
the *as* was equal to a pound of copper or bronze.

[4] Fr. 2, Huschke ; 2 Bremer (ii, p. 284).

[5] 246 B.C.   [6] This was true in Varro's time.

appellant, maximum esse Nilum consentitur. Proxima magnitudine esse Histrum scripsit Sallustius.
2 Varro autem cum de parte orbis quae Europa dicitur dissereret, in tribus primis eius terrae fluminibus Rodanum esse ponit, per quod videtur eum facere Histro aemulum. Histros enim quoque in Europa fluit.

VIII

Inter ignominias militares quibus milites exercebantur, fuisse sanguinis dimissionem ; et quaenam esse videatur causa huiuscemodi castigationis.

1 FUIT haec quoque antiquitus militaris animadversio, iubere ignominiae causa militi venam solvi et
2 sanguinem dimitti. Cuius rei ratio in litteris veteribus, quas equidem invenire potui, non extat ; sed opinor factum hoc primitus in militibus stupentis animi et a naturali habitu declinatis, ut non tam
3 poena quam medicina videretur. Postea tamen ob pleraque alia delicta idem factitatum esse credo per consuetudinem, quasi minus sani viderentur omnes qui delinquerent.

IX

Quibus modis quoque habitu acies Romana instrui solita sit, quaeque earum instructionum sint vocabula.

1 VOCABULA sunt militaria, quibus instructa certo modo acies appellari solet : " frons," " subsidia,"

---

[1] *Hist.* iii. 80, Maur.   [2] *Ant. Hum.* xiii, fr. 6, Mirsch.
[3] Muretus, *Var. Lect.* xiii, p. 199, thought it was in order

"the inner sea," it is agreed that the Nile is the greatest. Sallust wrote[1] that the Danube is next in size; but Varro, when he discussed the part of the earth which is called Europe, placed[2] the Rhone among the first three rivers of that quarter of the earth, by which he seems to make it a rival of the Danube; for the Danube also is in Europe.

VIII

That among the ignominious punishments which were inflicted upon soldiers was the letting of blood ; and what seems to be the reason for such a penalty.

THIS also was a military punishment in old times, to disgrace a soldier by ordering a vein to be opened, and letting blood. There is no reason assigned for this in the old records, so far as I could find; but I infer that it was first done to soldiers whose minds were affected and who were not in a normal condition, so that it appears to have been not so much a punishment as a medical treatment. But afterwards I suppose that the same penalty was customarily inflicted for many other offences, on the ground that all who sinned were not of sound mind.[3]

IX

In what way and in what form the Roman army is commonly drawn up, and the names of the formations.

THERE are military terms which are applied to an army drawn up in a certain manner: "the front,"

that they might lose with ignominy the blood which they had been unwilling to shed for their country.

"cuneus," "orbis," "globus," "forfices," "serra,"
2 "alae," "turres." Haec et quaedam item alia invenire est in libris eorum qui de militari disciplina
3 scripserunt. Tralata autem sunt ab ipsis rebus quae
ita proprie nominantur, earumque rerum in acie
instruenda sui cuiusque vocabuli imagines osten-
duntur.

X

Quae eius rei causa sit, quod et Graeci veteres et Romani
anulum hoc digito gestaverint qui est in manu sinistra
minimo proximus.

1 VETERES GRAECOS anulum habuisse in digito accepimus sinistrae manus qui minimo est proximus.
Romanos quoque homines aiunt sic plerumque anulis
2 usitatos. Causam esse huius rei Apion in libris
Aegyptiacis hanc dicit, quod insectis apertisque
humanis corporibus, ut mos in Aegypto fuit, quas
Graeci ἀνατομάς appellant, repertum est nervum
quendam tenuissimum ab eo uno digito de quo diximus, ad cor hominis pergere ac pervenire ; propterea
non inscitum visum esse eum potissimum digitum
tali honore decorandum, qui continens et quasi
conexus esse cum principatu cordis videretur.

"reserves," "wedge," "ring," "mass," "shears,"
"saw," "wings," "towers."[1] These and some other
terms you may find in the books of those who have
written about military affairs. However, they are
taken from the things themselves to which the
names are strictly applied, and in drawing up an army
the forms of the objects designated by each of these
words is represented.

X

The reason why the ancient Greeks and Romans wore a ring
on the next to the little finger of the left hand.

I HAVE heard that the ancient Greeks wore a ring
on the finger of the left hand which is next to the
little finger. They say, too, that the Roman men
commonly wore their rings in that way. Apion in
his *Egyptian History* says[2] that the reason for this
practice is, that upon cutting into and opening
human bodies, a custom in Egypt which the Greeks
call ἀνατομαί, or "dissection," it was found that a
very fine nérve proceeded from that finger alone of
which we have spoken, and made its way to the human
heart; that it therefore seemed quite reasonable
that this finger in particular should be honoured with
such an ornament, since it seems to be joined, and as
it were united, with that supreme organ, the heart.

---

[1] The *globus* was a detached body of troops, *qui a sua acie
separatus incursat*. The *forfex* or *forceps* was arranged in the
form of a letter V, to take in the enemy's wedge (*cuneus*) and
attack it on both sides (Veget. iii. 19). The *serra* was a
constant advance and retreat, corresponding to the motion of
a saw (Paul.-Fest. p. 467, Linds.). The *turris* was probably
a kind of square formation for attack.

[2] *F.H.G.* iii. 511.

XI

Verbum "mature" quid significet quaeque vocis eius ratio
sit; et quod eo verbo volgus hominum inproprie utitur;
atque inibi, quod "praecox" declinatum "praecocis"
facit, non "praecoquis."

1 "MATURE" nunc significat "propere" et "cito"
contra ipsius verbi sententiam; aliud enim est
2 "mature" quam dicitur. Propterea P. Nigidius,
homo in omnium bonarum artium disciplinis egregius : "'Mature,'" inquit, "est, quod neque citius
est neque serius, sed medium quiddam et tem-
peratum est."
3 Bene atque proprie P. Nigidius. Nam et in
frugibus et in pomis "matura" dicuntur, quae neque
cruda et inmitia sunt neque caduca et decocta, sed
4 tempore suo adulta maturataque. Quoniam autem
id quod non segniter fiebat, "mature" fieri dicebatur, progressa plurimum verbi significatione, non
iam, quod non segnius, sed quod festinantius fit, id
fieri "mature" dicitur, quando ea quae praeter sui
temporis modum properata sunt "inmatura" verius
dicantur.
5 Illud vero Nigidianum rei atque verbi tempera-
mentum divos Augustus duobus Graecis verbis elegantissime exprimebat. Nam et dicere in sermonibus et scribere in epistulis solitum esse aiunt σπεῦδε
βραδέως, per quod monebat ut ad rem agendam
simul adhiberetur et industriae celeritas et dili-
gentiae tarditas, ex quibus duobus contrariis fit
6 "maturitas." Vergilius quoque, si quis animum

---

[1] Fr. 48, Swoboda.
[2] See Suetonius, *Aug.* xxv. 4. Hence the common *festina
lente* and German *Eile mit Weile*.

XI

The derivation and meaning of the word *mature*, and that it is generally used improperly ; and also that the genitive of *praecox* is *praecocis* and not *praecoquis*.

MATURE in present usage signifies "hastily" and "quickly," contrary to the true force of the word ; for *mature* means quite a different thing. Therefore Publius Nigidius, a man eminent in the pursuit of all the liberal arts, says :[1] " *Mature* means neither 'too soon' nor 'too late,' but something between the two and intermediate."

Publius Nigidius has spoken well and properly. For of grain and fruits those are called *matura*, or "mature," which are neither unripe and hard, nor falling and decayed, but full-grown and ripened in their proper time. But since that which was not done negligently was said to be done *mature*, the force of the word has been greatly extended, and an act is now said to be done *mature* which is done with some haste, and not one which is done without negligence ; whereas such things as are immoderately hastened are more properly called *inmatura*, or "untimely."

That limitation of the word, and of the action itself, which was made by Nigidius was very elegantly expressed by the deified Augustus with two Greek words ; for we are told that he used to say in conversation, and write in his letters, σπεῦδε βραδέως, that is, "make haste slowly,"[2] by which he recommended that to accomplish a result we should use at once the promptness of energy and the delay of carefulness, and it is from these two opposite qualities that *maturitas* springs. Virgil also, to one

239

adtendat, duo ista verba "properare" et "maturare" tamquam plane contraria scitissime separavit
in hisce versibus:

Frigidus agricolam si quando continet imber,
Multa, forent quae mox caelo properanda sereno,
Maturare datur.

7 Elegantissime duo verba ista divisit; namque in
praeparatu rei rusticae per tempestates pluvias,
quoniam otium est, " maturari" potest; per serenas,
quoniam tempus instat, " properari" necessum est.

8 Cum significandum autem est coactius quid factum
et festinantius, tum rectius " praemature" factum
id dicitur quam " mature," sicuti Afranius dixit in
togata, cui *Titulus* nomen est:

Adpetis dominátum demens praémature praé-
cocem,

9 in quo versu animadvertendum est quod " praecocem" inquit, non " praecoquem" ; est enim casus
eius rectus non " praecoquis," sed " praecox."

XII

De portentis fabularum quae Plinius Secundus indignissime
in Democritum philosophum confert; et ibidem de simulacro volucri columbae.

1 LIBRUM esse Democriti, nobilissimi philosophorum, *De Vi et Natura Chamaeleontis* eumque se legisse

---

who is observant, has skilfully distinguished the two words *properare* and *maturare* as clearly opposite, in these verses : [1]

> Whenever winter's rains the hind confine,
> Much is there that at leisure may be done
>   (*maturare*),
> Which in fair weather he must hurry on
>   (*properanda*).

Most elegantly has he distinguished between those two words ; for in rural life the preparations during rainy weather may be made at leisure, since one has time for them ; but in fine weather, since time presses, one must hasten.

But when we wish to indicate that anything has been done under too great pressure and too hurriedly, then it is more properly said to have been done *praemature,* or "prematurely," than *mature.* Thus Afranius in his Italian play called *The Title* says : [2]

> With madness premature (*praemature*) you seek
>   a hasty power.

In this verse it is to be observed that he says *praecocem* and not *praecoquem* ; for the nominative case is not *praecoquis,* but *praecox.*

XII

Of extravagant tales which Plinius Secundus most unjustly ascribes to the philosopher Democritus ; and also about the flying image of a dove.

PLINY THE ELDER, in the twenty-eighth book of his *Natural History* asserts [3] that there is a book of that

---

[2] ii, 335 Ribbeck. [3] •   [3] xxviii. 112.

Plinius Secundus in *Naturalis Historiae* vicesimo
octavo refert, multaque vana atque intoleranda
auribus deinde quasi a Democrito scripta tradit, ex
quibus pauca haec inviti meminimus, quia pertaesum
2 est : accipitrem avium rapidissimum a chamaeleonte
humi reptante, si eum forte supervolet, detrahi et
cadere vi quadam in terram ceterisque avibus[1]
3 laniandum sponte sua obiicere sese et dedere. Item
aliud ultra humanam fidem : caput et collum[2] chamaeleontis si uratur ligno quod appellatur " robur,"
imbres et tonitrus fieri derepente, idque ipsum usu
venire, si iecur eiusdem animalis in summis tegulis
4 uratur. Item aliud, quod hercle an ponerem dubi-
tavi, ita est deridiculae vanitatis, nisi idcirco plane
posui quod oportuit nos dicere quid de istiusmodi
admirationum fallaci inlecebra sentiremus, qua
plerumque capiuntur et ad perniciem elabuntur
ingenia maxime sollertia, eaque potissimum quae
discendi cupidiora sunt. Sed redeo ad Plinium.
5 Sinistrum pedem ait chamaeleontis ferro ex igni
calefacto torreri[3] cum herba, quae appellatur eodem
nomine chamaeleontis, et utrumque macerari un-
guento conligique in modum pastilli atque in vas
mitti ligneum et eum qui id vas ferat, etiamsi is in
medio palam versetur, a nullo videri posse.
6   His portentis atque praestigiis a Plinio Secundo
scriptis non dignum esse cognomen Democriti puto ;
7 vel illud quale est quod idem Plinius in decimo

---

[1] animalibus, *Plin.*   [2] guttur, *Plin.*
[3] torreri in furno, *Plin.*

---

[1] xxviii. 115.   [2] x. 137.

most famous philosopher Democritus *On the Power and Nature of the Chameleon*, and that he had read it ; and then he transmits to us many foolish and intolerable absurdities, alleging that they were written by Democritus. Of these unwillingly, since they disgust me, I recall a few, as follows : that the hawk, the swiftest of all birds, if it chance to fly over a chameleon which is crawling on the ground, is dragged down and falls through some force to the earth, and offers and gives itself up of its own accord to be torn to pieces by the other birds. Another statement too is past human belief, namely, that if the head and neck of the chameleon be burned by means of the wood which is called oak, rain and thunder are suddenly produced, and that this same thing is experienced if the liver of that animal is burned upon the roof of a house. There is also another story, which by heaven ! I hesitated about putting down, so preposterous is it ; but I have made it a rule that we ought to speak our mind about the fallacious seduction of marvels of that kind, by which the keenest minds are often deceived and led to their ruin, and in particular those which are especially eager for knowledge. But I return to Pliny. He says[1] that the left foot of the chameleon is roasted with an iron heated in the fire, along with an herb called by the same name, "chameleon" ; both are mixed in an ointment, formed into a paste, and put in a wooden vessel. He who carries the vessel, even if he go openly amid a throng, can be seen by no one.

I think that these marvellous and false stories written by Plinius Secundus are not worthy of the name of Democritus ; the same is true of what the same Pliny, in his tenth book, asserts[2] that Demo-

libro Democritum scripsisse adseverat, aves quasdam esse certis vocabulis et earum avium confuso sanguine gigni serpentem ; eum qui [1] ederit linguas avium et conloquia interpretaturum.

8 Multa autem videntur ab hominibus istis male sollertibus huiuscemodi commenta in Democriti nomen data, nobilitatis auctoritatisque eius perfugio 9 utentibus. Sed id quod Archytam Pythagoricum commentum esse atque fecisse traditur, neque minus admirabile neque tamen vanum aeque videri debet. Nam et plerique nobilium Graecorum et Favorinus philosophus, memoriarum veterum exequentissimus, affirmatissime scripserunt simulacrum columbae e. ligno ab Archyta ratione quadam disciplinaque mechanica factum volasse ; ita erat scilicet libramentis suspensum et aura spiritus inclusa atque 10 occulta concitum. Libet hercle super re tam abhorrenti a fide ipsius Favorini verba ponere : Ἀρχύτας Ταραντῖνος, τὰ ἄλλα καὶ μηχανικὸς ὤν, ἐποίησεν περιστερὰν ξυλίνην πετομένην· ὁπότε καθίσειεν, οὐκέτι ἀνίστατο. μέχρι γὰρ τούτου ***

XIII

"Cum partim hominum " qua ratione veteres dixerint.

1 " PARTIM hominum venerunt " plerumque dicitur, quod significat "pars hominum venit," id est "quidam homines." Nam "partim" hoc in loco adverbium est neque in casus inclinatur, sicuti " cum partim hominum " dici potest, id est cum quibusdam homi-

[1] quisquis, *Plin.*

critus wrote; namely, that there were certain birds
with a language of their own, and that by mixing the
blood of those birds a serpent was produced; that
whoso ate it would understand the language of
birds and their conversation.

Many fictions of this kind seem to have been
attached to the name of Democritus by ignorant men,
who sheltered themselves under his reputation and
authority. But that which Archytas the Pythagorean
is said to have devised and accomplished ought to
seem no less marvellous, but yet not wholly absurd.
For not only many eminent Greeks, but also the
philosopher Favorinus, a most diligent searcher of
ancient records, have stated most positively that
Archytas made a wooden model of a dove with such
mechanical ingenuity and art that it flew; so nicely
balanced was it, you see, with weights and moved by
a current of air enclosed and hidden within it. About
so improbable a story I prefer to give Favorinus' own
words: "Archytas the Tarentine, being in other
lines also a mechanician, made a flying dove out of
wood. Whenever it lit, it did not rise again. For
until this . . . ."[1]

XIII

On what principle the ancients said *cum partim hominum*.

PARTIM hominum venerunt is a common expression,
meaning "a part of the men came," that is, "some
men." For *partim* is here an adverb and is not
declined by cases. Hence we may say *cum partim
hominum*, that is, "with some men" or "with a certain

---

[1] There is a lacuna and the sense is uncertain.

2 nibus et quasi cum quadam parte hominum. M.
Cato in oratione *De Re Floria* ita scripsit : " Ibi pro
scorto fuit, in cubiculum subrectitavit[1] e convivio,
cum partim illorum iam saepe ad eundem modum
3 erat." Imperitiores autem " cum parti " legunt,
tamquam declinatum sit quasi vocabulum, non
dictum quasi adverbium.

4 Sed Q. Claudius in vicesimo primo *Annali* inso-
lentius paulo hac figura est ita usus : " Enim cum
partim copiis hominum adulescentium placentem[2]
sibi." Itemque Claudi in vicesimo tertio *Annali*
verba haec sunt : " Sed idcirco me fecisse, quod
utrum neglegentia partim magistratum[3] an avaritia
an calamitate populi Romani evenisse dicam, nescio."

XIV

"Iniuria mihi factum itur" quali verborum ordine Cato
dixerit.

1 Audio " illi iniuriam factum iri," audio " contumeliam dictum iri " vulgo quoque ita dici, vulgo
et istam esse verborum figuram iam in medio lo-
2 quendi usu, idcircoque exemplis supersedeo. Sed
" contumelia illi " vel " iniuria factum itur " paulo
3 est remotius, exemplum igitur ponemus. M. Cato

---

[1] subreptitavit, *early editors.*
[2] placent(i)um, *Lion.*
[3] *For* magistratuum, *which is read by* Q.

---

[1] p. 64. 8, Jordan.

part of the men." Marcus Cato, in his speech *On the property of Florius* has written as follows:[1] "There she acted like a harlot, she went from the banquet straight to the couch and with a part of them (*cum partim illorum*) she often conducted herself in the same manner." The less educated, however, read *cum parti*, as if *partim* were declined as a noun, not used as an adverb.

But Quintus Claudius, in the twenty-first book of his *Annals*, has used this figure in a somewhat less usual manner; he says: "For with the part of the forces (*cum partim copiis*) of young men that was pleasing to him."[2] Also in the twenty-third book of the *Annals* of Claudius are these words:[3] "But that I therefore acted thus, but whether to say that it happened from the negligence of a part of the magistrates (*neglegentia partim magistratum*), from avarice, or from the calamity of the Roman people, I know not."

XIV

In what connection Cato said *iniuria mihi factum itur.*

I hear the phrase *illi iniuriam factum iri,* or "injury will be done to him," I hear *contumeliam dictum iri,* or "insult will be offered," commonly so used everywhere, and I notice that this form of expression is a general one; I therefore refrain from citing examples. But *contumelia illi* or *iniuria factum itur,* "injury or insult is going to be offered him," is somewhat less common, and therefore I shall give an example of that. Marcus Cato, speaking *For Himself against*

[2] Fr. 87, Peter. The passage is corrupt and unintelligible.
[3] Fr. 89, Peter.

Pro Se contra C. Cassium : " Atque evenit ita, Quirites,
uti in hac contumelia quae mihi per huiusce petu-
lantiam factum itur, rei quoque publicae medius
4 fidius miserear, Quirites." Sicut autem " contumeliam factum iri " significat iri ad contumeliam facien-
dam, id est operam dari quo fiat, ita " contumelia
mihi factum itur " casu tantum inmutato idem dicit.

XV

De flaminis Dialis deque flaminicae caerimonis; **v**erbaque ex
edicto praetoris apposita, quibus dicit non coacturum se ad
iurandum neque virgines Vestae neque Dialem.

1   CAERIMONIAE impositae flamini Diali multae, item
castus multiplices, quos in libris qui *De Sacerdotibus
Publicis* compositi sunt, item in Fabii Pictoris libro-
2 rum primo scriptos legimus.   Unde haec ferme sunt,
3 quae commeminimus: Equo Dialem flaminem vehi
4 religio est ; item religio est[1] " classem procinctam "
extra pomerium, id est exercitum armatum, videre ;
idcirco rarenter flamen Dialis creatus consul est, cum
5 bella consulibus mandabantur ? item iurare Dialem
6 fas numquam est ; item anulo uti nisi pervio cassoque
7 fas non est.   Ignem e " flaminia," id est flaminis

---

[1] item . . . est, *added by Hertz.*

---

[1] p. 63. 6, Jordan.
[2] The *flamen* was the special priest of an individual deity.
There were three *flamines maiores*—of Jupiter (*Dialis*), Mars
and Quirinus—and twelve *flamines minores*. For " taboos "
imposed on priests see Frazer, *Golden Bough*, ch. 2.
[3] Fr. 19, 24, 35, 46, R. Peter ; fr. 3, Huschke ; *id.* Bremer
(i, p. 10).
[4] *Classis* originally meant one of the classes into which the

Gaius Cassius, says:[1] "And so it happened, fellow citizens, that in this insult which is going to be put upon me *(quae mihi factum itur)* by the insolence of this man I also, fellow citizens (so help me!), pity our country." But just as *contumeliam factum iri* means "to go to inflict an injury," that is, to take pains that it be inflicted, just so *contumelia mihi factum itur* expresses the same idea, merely with a change of case.

XV

Of the ceremonies of the priest and priestess of Jupiter; and words quoted from the praetor's edict, in which he declares that he will not compel either the Vestal virgins or the priest of Jupiter to take oath.

Ceremonies in great number are imposed upon the priest of Jupiter[2] and also many abstentions, of which we read in the books written *On the Public Priests*; and they are also recorded in the first book of Fabius Pictor.[3] Of these the following are in general what I remember: It is unlawful for the priest of Jupiter to ride upon a horse; it is also unlawful for him to see the "classes[4] arrayed" outside the pomerium,[5] that is, the army in battle array; hence the priest of Jupiter is rarely made consul, since wars were entrusted to the consuls; also it is always unlawful for the priest to take an oath; likewise to wear a ring, unless it be perforated and without a gem. It is against the law for fire to be taken from the *flaminia,* that is, from the home of the flamen

citizens were divided by the Servian constitution, then, collectively, the army composed of the classes.

[5] The pomerium was the religious boundary of the city; see xiii. 14.

8 Dialis domo, nisi[1] sacrum efferri ius non est ; vinc-
tum, si aedes eius introierit, solvi necessum est et
vincula per impluvium in tegulas subduci atque inde
9 foras in viam demitti. Nodum in apice neque in
10 cinctu neque in alia parte ullum habet ; si quis ad
verberandum ducatur, si ad pedes eius supplex pro-
11 cubuerit, eo die verberari piaculum est. Capillum
12 Dialis, nisi qui liber homo est, non detonset. Capram
et carnem incoctam et hederam et fabam neque tan-
13 gere Diali mos est neque nominare. Propagines e
14 vitibus altius praetentas non succedit. Pedes lecti,
in quo cubat, luto tenui circumlitos esse oportet et
de eo lecto trinoctium continuum non decubat neque
in eo lecto cubare alium fas est. Apud eius lecti
fulcrum capsulam esse cum strue atque ferto oportet.
15 Unguium Dialis et capilli segmina subter arborem
16 felicem terra operiuntur. Dialis cotidie feriatus est.
17 Sine apice sub divo esse licitum non est ; sub tecto
uti liceret, non pridem a pontificibus constitutum,
18 Masurius Sabinus scripsit et alia quaedam remissa
gratiaque aliquot caerimoniarum facta dicitur.
19   Farinam fermento inbutam adtingere ei fas non
20 est. Tunica intima, nisi in locis tectis, non exuit se,
ne sub caelo, tamquam sub oculis Iovis, nudus sit.
21 Super flaminem Dialem in convivio, nisi rex sacri-
22 ficulus, haut quisquam alius accumbit. Uxorem si

[1] nisi in, *Lipsius*.

---

[1] The opening in the roof of the *atrium* or main room of a
Roman house.

[2] Fr. 28, Huschke ; *Memor.* 16, Bremer (ii, p. 372).

[3] The priest who succeeded the kings, after their expulsion,
in presiding over the sacrifices. Although he nominally out-

Dialis, except for a sacred rite; if a person in fetters enter his house, he must be loosed, the bonds must be drawn up through the *impluvium*[1] to the roof and from there let down into the street. He has no knot in his head-dress, girdle, or any other part of his dress; if anyone is being taken to be flogged and falls at his feet as a suppliant, it is unlawful for the man to be flogged on that day. Only a free man may cut the hair of the Dialis. It is not customary for the Dialis to touch, or even name, a she-goat, raw flesh, ivy, and beans.

The priest of Jupiter must not pass under an arbour of vines. The feet of the couch on which he sleeps must be smeared with a thin coating of clay, and he must not sleep away from this bed for three nights in succession, and no other person must sleep in that bed. At the foot of his bed there should be a box with sacrificial cakes. The cuttings of the nails and hair of the Dialis must be buried in the earth under a fruitful tree. Every day is a holy day for the Dialis. He must not be in the open air without his cap; that he might go without it in the house has only recently been decided by the pontiffs, so Masurius Sabinus wrote,[2] and it is said that some other ceremonies have been remitted and he has been excused from observing them.

"The priest of Jupiter" must not touch any bread fermented with yeast. He does not lay off his inner tunic except under cover, in order that he may not be naked in the open air, as it were under the eye of Jupiter. No other has a place at table above the flamen Dialis, except the *rex sacrificulus*.[3] If the

ranked the flamens and the pontifex maximus, the office was unimportant.

23 amisit, flamonio decedit.   Matrimonium flaminis nisi
24 morte dirimi ius non est.   Locum in quo bustum est
   numquam ingreditur, mortuum numquam attingit ;
25 funus tamen exequi non est religio.

26   Eaedem ferme caerimoniae sunt flaminicae Dialis ;
27 alias seorsum aiunt observitare, veluti est quod vene-
28 nato operitur et quod in rica surculum de arbore
29 felici habet et quod scalas, nisi [1] quae Graecae appellantur, escendere ei plus tribus gradibus religiosum
30 est atque etiam, cum it ad Argeos, quod neque
   comit caput neque capillum depectit.

31   Verba praetoris ex edicto perpetuo de flamine
   Diali et de sacerdote Vestae adscripsi : " Sacer-
   dotem Vestalem et flaminem Dialem in omni mea
32 iurisdictione iurare non cogam."   Verba M. Varronis
   ex secundo *Rerum Divinarum* super flamine Diali haec
   sunt : " Is solum album habet galerum, vel quod
   maximus, vel quod Iovi immolata hostia alba id fieri
   oporteat."

[1] nisi, *added by Scaliger.*

---

[1] What these were is uncertain.   Probably they offered
less exposure of the person than an ordinary ladder.

[2] The term *Argei* was applied to twenty-four chapels dis-
tributed among the four regions of early Rome, and also
called *Sacella Argeiorum* and *Argea*.   It also designated the
same number of puppets, or bundles of straw in the shape
of men, which were thrown from the *Pons Sublicius* into the
Tiber by the Vestal virgins on the Ides of May.   See Fowler,
Roman Festivals, pp. 111 ff. and *Thes. Ling. Lat. s.v. Argei.*

Dialis has lost his wife he abdicates his office. The marriage of the priest cannot be dissolved except by death. He never enters a place of burial, he never touches a dead body; but he is not forbidden to attend a funeral.

The ceremonies of the priestess of Jupiter are about the same; they say that she observes other separate ones: for example, that she wears a dyed robe, that she has a twig from a fruitful tree in her head-dress, that it is forbidden for her to go up more than three rounds of a ladder, except the so-called Greek ladders;[1] also, when she goes to the Argei,[2] that she neither combs her head nor dresses her hair.

I have added the words of the praetor in his standing edict concerning the flamen Dialis and the priestess of Vesta:[3] " In the whole of my jurisdiction I will not compel the flamen of Jupiter or a priestess of Vesta to take an oath." The words of Marcus Varro about the flamen Dialis, in the second book of his *Divine Antiquities,* are as follows:[4] " He alone has a white cap, either because he is the greatest of priests, or because a white victim should be sacrificed to Jupiter."[5]

[3] *Fontes Jur. Rom.*, p. 197.
[4] Fr. 4, p. cxiii, Merkel.
[5] White was emblematic of royalty. Cf. Suetonius *Jul.* lxxix, 2.

XVI

Quos errores Iulius Hyginus in sexto Vergilii animadverterit,
in Romana historia erratos.

1   REPREHENDIT Hyginus Vergilium correcturumque
eum fuisse existimat quod in libro sexto scriptum
2 est.   Palinurus est aput inferos, petens ab Aenea ut
suum corpus requirendum et sepeliendum curet.   Is
hoc dicit :

> Eripe me his, invicte, malis, aut tu mihi terram
> Iniice, namque potes, portusque require Velinos.

3   " Quo," inquit, " modo aut Palinurus novisse et nominare potuit ' portus Velinos ' aut Aeneas ex eo
nomine locum invenire, cum Velia oppidum, a quo
portum qui in eo loco est ' Velinum ' dixit, Servio
Tullio Romae regnante, post annum amplius sescente-
simum quam Aeneas in Italiam venit conditum in
4 agro Lucano et eo nomine appellatum est?   Nam
qui ab Harpalo," inquit, "regis Cyri praefecto, ex
terra Phocide fugati sunt, alii Veliam, partim
5 Massiliam condiderunt.   Inscitissime igitur petit ut
Aeneas portum Velinum requirat, cum id nomen eo
6 tempore fuerit [1] nusquam gentium.   Neque simile,"
inquit, "illud videri debet, quod est in primo
carmine :

> Italiam fato profugus Lavinaque venit
> Litora,

[1] fuerit, Π ; fuit, ω.

---

[1] Fr. 7, Fun.   [2] *Aen.* vi. 365 ff.
[3] 578–534 B.C., traditional chronology.

XVI

Errors in Roman History which Julius Hyginus noted in
Virgil's sixth book.

Hyginus criticizes [1] a passage in Virgil's sixth book
and thinks that he would have corrected it.   Palinurus is in the Lower World, begging Aeneas to take care
that his body be found and buried.   His words are : [2]

> O save me from these ills, unconquered one ;
> Or throw thou earth upon me, for you can,
> And to the port of Velia return.

" How," said he, " could either Palinurus know and
name 'the port of Velia,' or Aeneas find the place
from that name, when the town of Velia, from which
he has called the harbour in that place ' Veline' was
founded in the Lucanian district and called by that
name when Servius Tullius was reigning in Rome, [3]
more than six hundred years after Aeneas came to
Italy ?   For of those," he adds, " who were driven
from the land of Phocis [4] by Harpalus, [5] prefect of
king Cyrus, some founded Velia, and others Massilia.
Most absurdly, then, does Palinurus ask Aeneas to
seek out the Veline port, when at that time no such
name existed anywhere.   Nor ought that to be considered a similar error," said he, " which occurs in
the first book : [6]

> Exiled by fate, to Italy fared and to Lavinian
> strand,

[4] Phocis, a district of Greece west of Boeotia, was confused by Hyginus with Phocaea, a city on the western coast
of Asia Minor.

[5] Probably an error for Harpagus.

[6] *Aen.* i. 2.

7 et aeque in sexto libro :

Chalcidicaque levis tandem superastitit arce,

8 quoniam poetae ipsi quaedam κατὰ πρόληψιν historiae
dicere ex sua persona concedi solet, quae facta ipse
postea scire potuit, sicut Vergilius scivit de Lavinio
9 oppido et de colonia Chalcidicensi. Sed Palinuros
qui potuit," inquit, "scire ea quae post annos
sescentos facta sunt, nisi quis eum divinasse aput
inferos putat, proinde ut animae defunctorum solent ?
10 Sed et si ita accipias, quamquam non ita dicitur,
Aeneas tamen, qui non divinabat, quo pacto potuit
requirere portum Velinum, cui nomen tunc, sicut
diximus, nullum usquam fuit ? "
11 Item hoc quoque in eodem libro reprehendit et
correcturum fuisse Vergilium putat, nisi mors occu-
12 passet. "Nam cum Thesea," inquit, "inter eos
nominasset, qui ad inferos adissent ac redissent,
dixissetque :

quid Thesea, magnum
Quid memorem Alciden ? et mi genus ab Iove
summo est,

postea tamen infert :

sedet aeternumque sedebit
Infelix Theseus.

13 Qui autem," inquit, "fieri potest, ut aeternum aput
inferos sedeat, quem supra cum is nominat qui
descenderit illuc atque inde rursum evaserint,
praesertim cum ita sit fabula de Theseo, atque si

---

[1] *Aen.* vi. 17.   [2] *Aen.* vi. 122.   [3] *Aen.* vi. 617.

and similarly in the sixth book : [1]

> At last stood lightly poised on the Chalcidian
> height,

since it is usually allowed the poet himself to mention, κατὰ πρόληψιν, 'by anticipation,' in his own person some historical facts which took place later and of which he himself could know; just as Virgil knew the town of Lavinium and the colony from Calchis. But how could Palinurus," he said, "know of events that occurred six hundred years later, unless anyone believes that in the Lower World he had the power of divination, as in fact the souls of the deceased commonly do ? But even if you understand it in that way, although nothing of the kind is said, yet how could Aeneas, who did not have the power of divination, seek out the Veline port, the name of which at that time, as we have said before, was not in existence anywhere ? "

He also censures the following passage in the same book, and thinks that Virgil would have corrected it, had not death prevented : " For," says he, " when he had named Theseus among those who had visited the Lower World and returned, and had said : [2]

> But why name Theseus? why Alcides great ?
> And my race too is from almighty Jove,

he nevertheless adds afterwards : [3]

> Unhappy Theseus sits, will sit for aye.

But how," says he, " could it happen that one should sit for ever in the Lower World whom the poet mentions before among those who went down there and returned again, especially when the story of

Hercules eum evellerit e petra et in lucem ad superos eduxerit?"

14 Item in his versibus errasse Vergilium dicit:

Eruet ille Argos Agamemnoniasque Mycenas
Ipsumque Aeaciden, genus armipotentis Achilli,
Ultus avos Troiae, templa intemerata [1] Minervae.

15 "Confudit," inquit, "et personas diversas et tempora. Nam neque eodem tempore neque per eosdem homines cum Achaeis et cum Pyrro bellatum est.
16 Pyrrus enim, quem dicit Aeaciden, de Epiro in Italiam transgressus cum Romanis depugnavit adver-
17 sus Manium Curium, in eo bello ducem. Argivum autem bellum, id est Achaicum, multis post annis a
18 L. Mummio imperatore gestum est. Potest igitur," inquit, "medius eximi versus, qui de Pyrro inportune inmissus est, quem Vergilius procul dubio exempturus," inquit, "fuit."

XVII

Quam ob causam et quali modo Democritus philosophus luminibus oculorum sese privaverit; et super ea re versus Laberii pure admodum et venuste facti.

1 DEMOCRITUM philosophum in monumentis historiae Graecae scriptum est, virum praeter alios vene-

[1] et temerata, *Virg.*

---

[1] *Aen.* vi. 838. The rendering is by Rhoades, except for "spotless" in the last line.
[2] Neoptolemus, also called Pyrrus (or Pyrrhus), the son of Achilles and Deidameia.

Theseus says that Hercules tore him from the rock and led him to the light of the Upper World?"

He also says that Virgil erred in these lines:[1]

> He Argos and Mycenae shall uproot,
> City of Agamemnon, and the heir
> Of Aeacus himself, from war-renowned
> Achilles sprung,[2] his ancestors of Troy
> Avenging and Minerva's spotless shrine.[3]

"He has confounded," says Hyginus, "different persons and times. For the wars with the Achaeans and with Pyrrus were not waged at the same time nor by the same men. For Pyrrus, whom he calls a descendant of Aeacus, having crossed over from Epirus into Italy, waged war with the Romans against Manius Curius, who was their leader in that war.[4] But the Argive, that is, the Achaean war, was carried on many years after under the lead of Lucius Mummius.[5] The middle verse, therefore, about Pyrrus," says he, "may be omitted, since it was inserted inopportunely; and Virgil," he said, "undoubtedly would have struck it out."

XVII

Why and how the philosopher Democritus deprived himself of his eye-sight; and the very fine and elegant verses of Laberius on that subject.

It is written in the records of Grecian story that the philosopher Democritus, a man worthy of

---

[3] Probably either Gellius or Hyginus misquotes Virgil. With their version we have a transfer of the epithet *intemerata* from Minerva to her shrine.

[4] 280–275 B.C.   [5] 146 B.C.

randum auctoritateque antiqua praeditum, luminibus
oculorum sua sponte se privasse, quia existimaret
cogitationes commentationesque animi sui in contem-
plandis naturae rationibus vegetiores et exactiores
fore, si eas videndi inlecebris et oculorum impedi-
2 mentis liberasset. Id factum eius modumque ipsum
quo caecitatem facile sollertia subtilissima conscivit,
Laberius poeta in mimo quem scripsit *Restionem*,
versibus quidem satis munde atque graphice factis
descripsit, sed causam voluntariae caecitatis finxit
aliam vertitque in eam rem quam tum agebat, non
3 inconcinniter. Est enim persona, quae hoc aput
Laberium dicit, divitis avari et parci, sumptum
plurimum asotiamque adulescentis vivide plorantis.[1]
4 Versus Laberiani sunt :

> Demócritus Abderítes physicus phílosophus
> Clipeúm constituit cóntra exortum Hyperíonis,
> Oculós effodere ut pósset splendore aéreo.
> Ita rádiis solis áciem effodit lúminis,
> Malís bene esse né videret cívibus.
> Sic égo fulgentis spléndorem pecúniae
> Volo élucificare éxitum aetatí meae,
> Ne in ré bona esse vídeam nequam fílium.

XVIII

Historia de Artemisia ; deque eo certamine quod aput Mausoli sepulcrum a scriptoribus inclutis decertatum est.

1 ARTEMISIA Mausolum virum amasse fertur supra
omnis amorum fabulas ultraque affectionis humanae

---

[1] vivide plorantis, *Bothe* ; viri deplorantis, ∞.

reverence beyond all others and of the highest authority, of his own accord deprived himself of eyesight, because he believed that the thoughts and meditations of his mind in examining nature's laws would be more vivid and exact, if he should free them from the allurements of sight and the distractions offered by the eyes. This act of his, and the manner too in which he easily blinded himself by a most ingenious device, the poet Laberius has described, in a farce called *The Ropemaker*, in very elegant and finished verses; but he has imagined another reason for voluntary blindness and applied it with no little neatness to his own subject. For the character who speaks these lines in Laberius is a rich and stingy miser, lamenting in vigorous terms the excessive extravagance and dissipation of his young son. These are the verses of Laberius :[1]

Democritus, Abdera's scientist,
Set up a shield to face Hyperion's rise,
That sight he might destroy by blaze of brass,
Thus by the sun's rays he destroyed his eyes,
Lest he should see bad citizens' good luck ;
So I with blaze and splendour of my gold,
Would render sightless my concluding years,
Lest I should see my spendthrift son's good luck.

XVIII

The story of Artemisia ; and of the contest at the tomb of Mausolus in which celebrated writers took part.

ARTEMISIA is said to have loved her husband Mausolus with a love surpassing all the tales of passion and beyond one's conception of human affec-

ii, 72, Ribbeck[3].

2 fidem. Mausolus autem fuit, ut M. Tullius ait, rex terrae Cariae, ut quidam Graecarum historiarum scriptores, provinciae[1] praefectus σατράπην Graeci
3 vocant. Is Mausolus, ubi fato perfunctus inter lamenta et manus uxoris funere magnifico sepultus est, Artemisia, luctu atque desiderio mariti flagrans uxor, ossa cineremque eius mixta odoribus contusaque in faciem pulveris aquae indidit ebibitque multaque
4 alia violenti amoris indicia fecisse dicitur. Molita quoque est ingenti impetu operis conservandae mariti memoriae sepulcrum illud memoratissimum dignatumque numerari inter septem omnium terrarum specta-
5 cula. Id monumentum Artemisia cum dis manibus sacrum[2] Mausoli dicaret, "agona," id est certamen laudibus eius dicundis, facit ponitque praemia pecu-
6 niae aliarumque rerum bonarum amplissima. Ad eas laudes decertandas venisse dicuntur viri nobiles ingenio atque lingua praestabili, Theopompus, Theodectes, Naucrates; sunt etiam qui Isocratem ipsum cum his certavisse memoriae mandaverint. Sed eo certamine vicisse Theopompum iudicatum est. Is fuit Isocrates discipulus.

---

[1] provinciae, *Lipsius*; pr. Gr(a)ece, *ω*; pr. Cariae, *Thysius*.
[2] sacrum, *Mommsen*; sacris, *ω*.

---

[1] *Tusc. Disp.* iii. 75.
[2] In 353 B.C.
[3] The famous Mausoleum at Halicarnassus, adorned by Scopas, Bryaxis, Timotheus and Leochares with sculptures, the remains of which are now in the British Museum. It was a square building, 140 feet high, surrounded by Ionic columns. It stood upon a lofty base and was surmounted by a pyramid of steps ending in a platform, on which was a four-horse chariot. The term *mausoleum* was applied by the

tion. Now Mausolus, as Marcus Tullius tells us,[1] was king of the land of Caria; according to some Greek historians he was governor of a province, the official whom the Greeks term a satrap. When this Mausolus had met his end amid the lamentations and in the arms of his wife,[2] and had been buried with a magnificent funeral, Artemisia, inflamed with grief and with longing for her spouse, mingled his bones and ashes with spices, ground them into the form of a powder, put them in water, and drank them; and she is said to have given many other proofs of the violence of her passion. For perpetuating the memory of her husband, she also erected, with great expenditure of labour, that highly celebrated tomb,[3] which has been deemed worthy of being numbered among the seven wonders of the world.[4] When Artemisia dedicated this monument, consecrated to the deified shades of Mausolus, she instituted an *agon,* that is to say, a contest in celebrating his praises, offering magnificent prizes of money and other valuables. Three men distinguished for their eminent talent and eloquence are said to have come to contend in this eulogy, Theopompus, Theodectes [5] and Naucrates; some have even written that Isocrates himself entered the lists with them. But Theopompus was adjudged the victor in that contest. He was a pupil of Isocrates.

Romans to large and magnificent tombs such as the mausoleum of Augustus and that of Hadrian.

[4] The other six "wonders" were: The walls and hanging gardens of Babylon; the temple of Diana at Ephesus; the statue of Olympian Zeus by Phidias; the Pyramids; and the Pharos, or lighthouse, at Alexandria.

[5] The more approved spelling is Theodectas; see *C.I.G.* ii. 977.

7 Extat nunc quoque Theodecti tragoedia, quae inscribitur *Mausolus*; in qua eum magis quam in prosa placuisse Hyginus in *Exemplis* refert.

XIX

Non purgari neque levari peccatum, cum praetenditur peccatorum quae alii quoque peccaverunt similitudo; atque inibi verba ex oratione super ea re Demosthenis.

1 INCESSEBAT quempiam Taurus philosophus severa atque vehementi obiurgatione adulescentem a rhetoribus et a facundiae studio ad disciplinas philosophiae transgressum, quod factum quiddam esse ab eo diceret inhoneste et improbe. At ille non ibat infitias fecisse, sed id solitum esse fieri defendebat turpitudinemque delicti exemplorum usu et consue-

2 tudinis venia deprecabatur. Atque ibi Taurus isto ipso defensionis genere inritatior: "Homo," inquit, "stulte et nihili, si te a malis exemplis auctoritates et rationes philosophiae non abducunt, ne illius quidem Demosthenis vestri sententia tibi in mentem venit, quae, quia lepidis et venustis vocum modis vincta est, quasi quaedam cantilena rhetorica facilius

3 adhaerere memoriae tuae potuit? Nam si me" inquit "non fallit quod quidem in primori pueritia legerim, verba haec sunt Demosthenis adversus eum, qui, ut tu nunc facis, peccatum suum peccatis alienis exemptum purgatumque ibat: Σὺ δὴ μὴ λέγε, ὡς γέγονε τοῦτο πολλάκις, ἀλλ᾽ ὡς οὕτω προσήκει γίγνεσθαι· οὐ γάρ, εἴ τι πώποτε μὴ κατὰ τοὺς νόμους ἐπράχθη, σὺ δὲ

---

[1] Fr. 1, Peter. [2] *Adv. Androt.* 7, p. 595.

The tragedy of Theodectes, entitled *Mausolus*, is still extant to-day; and that in it Theodectes was more pleasing than in his prose writings is the opinion of Hyginus in his *Examples*.[1]

XIX

That a sin is not removed or lessened by citing in excuse similar sins which others have committed ; with a passage from a speech of Demosthenes on that subject.

THE philosopher Taurus once reproved a young man with severe and vigorous censure because he had turned from the rhetoricians and the study of eloquence to the pursuit of philosophy, declaring that he had done something dishonourable and shameful. Now the young man did not deny the allegation, but urged in his defence that it was commonly done and tried to justify the baseness of the fault by citing examples and by the excuse of custom. And then Taurus, being the more irritated by the very nature of his defence, said : "Foolish and worthless fellow, if the authority and rules of philosophy do not deter you from following bad examples, does not even the saying of your own celebrated Demosthenes occur to you ? For since it is couched in a polished and graceful form of words, it might, like a sort of rhetorical catch, the more easily remain fixed in your memory. For," said he, "if I do not forget what as a matter of fact I read in my early youth, these are the words of Demosthenes, spoken against one who, as you now do, tried to justify and excuse his own sin by those of others : [2] 'Say not, Sir, that this has often been done, but that it ought to be so done ; for if anything was ever done contrary to the

τοῦτο ἐμιμήσω, διὰ τοῦτο ἀποφύγοις ἂν δικαίως, ἀλλά
πολλῷ μᾶλλον ἁλίσκοιο· ὥσπερ γάρ, εἴ τις ἑάλω, σὺ
ταῦτα[1] οὐκ ἂν ἔγραψας, οὕτως, ἐὰν σὺ νῦν δίκην δῷς,
4 ἄλλος οὐ γράψει." Sic Taurus, omni suasionum admoni-
tionumque genere utens, sectatores suos ad rationes
bonae inculpataeque indolis ducebat.

XX

Quid sit "rogatio," quid "lex," quid "plebisscitum," quid
"privilegium"; et quantum ista omnia differant.

1 QUAERI audio quid "lex" sit, quid "plebisscitum,"
2 quid "rogatio," quid "privilegium." Ateius Capito,
publici privatique iuris peritissimus, quid "lex"
esset hisce verbis definivit. "Lex," inquit, "est
generale iussum populi aut plebis, rogante magi-
3 stratu." Ea definitio si probe facta est, neque de
imperio Cn. Pompei neque de reditu M. Ciceronis
neque de caede P. Clodi quaestio neque alia id genus
4 populi plebisve iussa "leges" vocari possunt. Non
sunt enim generalia iussa neque de universis civibus,
sed de singulis concepta; quocirca "privilegia"
potius vocari debent, quia veteres "priva" dixerunt
quae nos "singula" dicimus. Quo verbo Lucilius in
primo *Satirarum* libro usus est:

abdomina thynni
Advenientibus priva dabo cephalaeaque acarnae.

---

[1] ἐκείνων προήλω, σὺ τάδ', *Demos.*

---

[1] Fr. 22, Huschke; *Conict.* fr. 13, Bremer.
[2] That is, a *rogatio.*   [3] v. 49, Marx.
[4] The *acarne* was a kind of sea-fish.

laws, and you followed that example, you would not for that reason justly escape punishment, but you would suffer much more severely. For just as, if anyone had suffered a penalty for it, you would not have proposed this, so if you suffer punishment now, no one else will propose it.'" Thus did Taurus, by the use of every kind of persuasion and admonition, incline his disciples to the principles of a virtuous and blameless manner of life.

XX

The meaning of *rogatio, lex, plebisscitum* and *privilegium*, and to what extent all those terms differ.

I HEAR it asked what the meaning is of *lex, plebisscitum, rogatio,* and *privilegium.* Ateius Capito, a man highly skilled in public and private law, defined the meaning of *lex* in these words :[1] " A law," said he, " is a general decree of the people, or of the commons, answering an appeal [2] made to them by a magistrate." If this definition is correct, neither the appeal for Pompey's military command, nor about the recall of Cicero, nor as to the murder or Clodius, nor any similar decrees of the people of commons, can be called laws. For they are not general decrees, and they are framed with regard, not to the whole body of citizens, but to individuals. Hence they ought rather to be called *privilegia,* or " privileges," since the ancients used *priva* where we now use *singula* (private or individual). This word Lucilius used in the first book of his *Satires* :[3]

I'll give them, when they come, each his own (*priva*) piece
Of tunny belly and acarne [4] heads.

5 "Plebem" autem Capito in eadem definitione
seorsum a "populo" divisit, quoniam in "populo"
omnis pars civitatis omnesque eius ordines contine-
antur, "plebes" vero ea dicatur, in qua gentes
6 civium patriciae non insunt. "Plebisscitum" igitur
est secundum eum Capitonem lex, quam plebes, non
populus, accipit.
7 Sed totius huius rei iurisque, sive cum populus
sive cum plebs rogatur, sive quod ad singulos [1] sive
quod ad universos pertinet, caput ipsum et origo et
8 quasi fons [2] "rogatio" est. Ista enim omnia vocabula
censentur continenturque "rogationis" principali
genere et nomine; nam, nisi populus aut plebs
rogetur, nullum plebis aut populi iussum fieri potest.
9 Sed quamquam haec ita sunt, in veteribus tamen
scriptis non magnam vocabulorum istorum differentiam esse animadvertimus. Nam et "plebisscita"
et "privilegia" translaticio nomine "legis" appellaverunt eademque omnia confuso et indistincto voca-
10 bulo "rogationes" dixerunt.
Sallustius quoque, proprietatum in verbis retinen-
tissimus, consuetudini concessit et privilegium, quod
de Cn. Pompei reditu ferebatur, "legem" appellavit. Verba ex secunda eius *Historia* haec sunt : " Nam
Sullam consulem de reditu eius legem ferentem ex
conposito tr. pl. C. Herennius prohibuerat."

[1] sive quod ad singulos, *supplied by J. F. Gronov.*
[2] frons, δ.

---

[1] Fr. 23, Huschke ; **14**, Bremer.
[2] The older form of the nominative *plebs*.
[3] ii. 21, Maur.

Capito, however, in the same definition divided[1] the *plebes*,[2] or "commons," from the *populus*, or "people," since in the term "people" are embraced every part of the state and all its orders, but "commons" is properly applied to that part in which the patrician families of the citizens are not included. Therefore, according to Capito, a *plebisscitum* is a law which the commons, and not the people, adopt.

But the head itself, the origin, and as it were the fount of this whole process of law is the *rogatio*, whether the appeal (*rogatio*) is to the people or to the commons, on a matter relating to all or to individuals. For all the words under discussion are understood and included in the fundamental principle and name of *rogatio*; for unless the people or commons be appealed to (*rogetur*), no decree of the people or commons can be passed.

But although all this is true, yet in the old records we observe that no great distinction is made among the words in question. For the common term *lex* is used both of decrees of the commons and of "privileges," and all are called by the indiscriminate and inexact name *rogatio*.

Even Sallust, who is most observant of propriety in the use of words, has yielded to custom and applied the term "law" to the "privilege" which was passed with reference to the return of Gnaeus Pompeius. The passage, from the second book of his *Histories*, reads as follows:[3] "For when Sulla, as consul, proposed a law (*legem*) touching his return, the tribune of the commons, Gaius Herennius, had vetoed it by previous arrangement."

XXI

Quam ob causam M. Cicero his omnino verbis "novissime"
et "novissimus" observantissime uti vitarit.

1   NON paucis verbis, quorum frequens usus est nunc
et fuit, M. Ciceronem noluisse uti manifestum est,
quod ea non probaret; velut est et "novissimus" et
2 "novissime."   Nam cum et M. Cato et Sallustius et
alii quoque aetatis eiusdem verbo isto promisce usi-
tati sint, multi etiam non indocti viri in libris id suis
scripserint, abstinuisse eo tamen tamquam non Latino
videtur, quoniam qui doctissimus eorum temporum
fuerat, L. Aelius Stilo, ut novo et inprobo verbo uti
vitaverat.
    Propterea, quid M. quoque Varro de ista voce
existimaverit, verbis ipsius Varronis ex libro *De
Lingua Latina ad Ciceronem* sexto demonstrandum
putavi. "Quod 'extremum,'" inquit, "dicebatur,
dici 'novissimum' coeptum vulgo, quod mea memoria ut Aelius, sic senes aliquot,[1] quod nimium
novum verbum esset, vitabant; cuius origo, ut a
'vetere' 'vetustius' ac 'veterrimum,' sic a 'novo'
declinatum 'novius' et[2] 'novissimum.'"

---

[1] aliquot, *Varro ;* alii, ω.
[2] novius et, *omitted by MSS. of Varro (Heraeus).*

---

[1] Fr. inc. 51, Jordan.
[2] *Cat.* xxxiii. 2 ; *Jug.* x. 2 ; xix. 7, etc.

XXI

Why Marcus Cicero very scrupulously avoided any use of the words *novissime* and *novissimus*.

It is clear that Marcus Cicero was unwilling to use many a word which is now in general circulation, and was so in his time, because he did not approve of them; for instance, *novissimus* and *novissime*. For although both Marcus Cato [1] and Sallust,[2] as well as others also of the same period, have used that word generally, and although many men besides who were not without learning wrote it in their books, yet he seems to have abstained from it, on the ground that it was not good Latin, since Lucius Aelius Stilo,[3] who was the most learned man of his time, had avoided its use, as that of a novel and improper word.

Moreover, what Marcus Varro too thought of that word I have deemed it fitting to show from his own words in the sixth book of his *De Lingua Latina*, dedicated to Cicero: [4] "What used to be called *extremum* or 'last,'" says he, "is beginning to be called generally *novissimum*, a word which within my own memory both Aelius and several old men avoided as too new a term; as to its origin, just as from *vetus* we have *vetustior* and *veterrimus*, so from *novus* we get *novior* and *novissimus*." [5]

---

[3] p. 53, 15, Fun.   [4] vii. 59.
[5] *Novissimus* occurs in Caesar and in Cicero, *Rosc. Com.* 30; *novior* is avoided wholly by the classical writers.

XXII

Locus exemptus ex Platonis libro qui inscribitur *Gorgias*,
de falsae philosophiae probris, quibus philosophos temere
incessunt qui emolumenta verae philosophiae ignorant.

1 PLATO, veritatis homo amicissimus eiusque omnibus exhibendae promptissimus, quae omnino dici
possint in desides istos ignavosque, qui obtentu
philosophiae nominis inutile otium et linguae vitae-
que tenebras secuntur, ex persona quidem non gravi
2 neque idonea, vere tamen ingenueque dixit. Nam
etsi Callicles, quem dicere haec facit, verae philosophiae ignarus, inhonesta indignaque in philosophos
confert, proinde tamen accipienda sunt quae dicuntur, ut nos sensim moneri intellegamus, ne ipsi
quoque culpationes huiuscemodi mereamur neve
inerti inanique desidia cultum et studium philosophiae mentiamur.

3 Verba ipsa super hac re Platonis ex libro qui
appellatur *Gorgias* scripsi, quoniam vertere ea consilium non fuit, cum ad proprietates eorum nequaquam possit Latina oratio aspirare ac multo minus
4 etiam mea: φιλοσοφία γάρ τοί ἐστιν, ὦ Σώκρατες,
χαρίεν, ἐάν τις αὐτοῦ μετρίως ἅψηται ἐν τῇ ἡλικίᾳ· ἐὰν
δὲ περαιτέρω τοῦ δέοντος ἐνδιατρίψῃ, διαφθορὰ τῶν ἀν-
5 θρώπων. ἐὰν γὰρ καὶ πάνυ εὐφυὴς ᾖ καὶ πόρρω τῆς
ἡλικίας φιλοσοφῇ, ἀνάγκη πάντων ἄπειρον γεγονέναι
ἐστίν, ὧν χρὴ ἔμπειρον εἶναι τὸν μέλλοντα καλὸν κἀγα-
6 θὸν καὶ εὐδόκιμον ἔσεσθαι ἄνδρα. καὶ γὰρ τῶν νόμων
ἄπειροι γίγνονται τῶν κατὰ τὴν πόλιν καὶ τῶν λόγων, οἷς

---

[1] *Gorgias* 40, p. 484 C–D ; 485 A–E.

XXII

A passage taken from Plato's book entitled *Gorgias*, on the abuses of false philosophy, with which those who are ignorant of the rewards of true philosophy assail philosophers without reason.

PLATO, a man most devoted to the truth and most ready to point it out to all, has said truly and nobly, though not from the mouth of a dignified or suitable character, all that in general may be said against those idle and worthless fellows, who, sheltered under the name of philosophy, follow profitless idleness and darkness of speech and life. For although Callicles, whom he makes his speaker, being ignorant of true philosophy, heaps dishonourable and undeserved abuse upon philosophers, yet what he says is to be taken in such a way that we may gradually come to understand it as a warning to ourselves not to deserve such reproofs, and not by idle and foolish sloth to feign the pursuit and cultivation of philosophy.

I have written down Plato's own words on this subject from the book called *Gorgias*, not attempting to translate them, because no Latinity, much less my own, can emulate their qualities:[1] "Philosophy, Socrates, is indeed a nice thing, if one pursue it in youth with moderation; but if one occupy oneself with it longer than is proper, it is a corrupter of men. For even if a man be well endowed by nature and follow philosophy when past his youth, he must necessarily be ignorant of all those things in which a man ought to be versed if he is to be honourable, good and of high repute. For such men are ignorant both of the laws relating to the city, and of the language which

δεῖ χρώμενον ὁμιλεῖν ἐν τοῖς συμβολίαοις τοῖς ἀνθρώποις,
καὶ ἰδίᾳ καὶ δημοσίᾳ, καὶ τῶν ἡδονῶν τε καὶ ἐπιθυμιῶν
τῶν ἀνθρωπείων, καὶ συλλήβδην τῶν ἠθῶν παντάπασιν
7 ἄπειροι γίγνονται. ἐπειδὰν οὖν ἔλθωσιν εἴς τινα ἰδίαν
ἢ πολιτικὴν πρᾶξιν, καταγέλαστοι γίγνονται ὥσπερ γε,
8 οἶμαι, οἱ πολιτικοί, ἐπειδὰν αὖ εἰς τὰς ὑμετέρας διατριβὰς
9 ἔλθωσι καὶ τοὺς λόγους, καταγέλαστοί εἰσι.
10   Paulo post addit haec : ἀλλ', οἶμαι, τὸ ὀρθότατόν
ἐστιν, ἀμφοτέρων μετασχεῖν. φιλοσοφίας μέν, ὅσον
παιδείας χάριν, καλὸν μετέχειν, καὶ οὐκ αἰσχρὸν μειρακίῳ ὄντι φιλοσοφεῖν· ἐπειδὰν δὲ ἤδη πρεσβύτερος ὢν
ἄνθρωπος ἔτι φιλοσοφῇ, καταγέλαστον, ὦ Σώκρατες, τὸ
11 χρῆμα γίγνεται, καὶ ἔγωγε ὁμοιότατον πάσχω πρὸς τοὺς
φιλοσοφοῦντας, ὥσπερ πρὸς τοὺς ψελλιζομένους καὶ
12 παίζοντας. ὅταν μὲν γὰρ παιδίον ἴδω, ᾧ ἔτι προσήκει
διαλέγεσθαι οὕτω, ψελλιζόμενον καὶ παῖζον, χαίρω τε,
καὶ χαρίεν μοι φαίνεται καὶ ἐλευθέριον καὶ πρέπον τῇ
13 τοῦ παιδίου ἡλικίᾳ. ὅταν δὲ σαφῶς διαλεγομένου παι-
δαρίου ἀκούσω, πικρόν τί μοι δοκεῖ χρῆμα εἶναι καὶ
ἀνιᾷ μου τὰ ὦτα καί μοι δοκεῖ δουλοπρεπές τι εἶναι·
14 ὅταν δὲ ἀνδρὸς ἀκούσῃ τις ψελλιζομένου ἢ παίζοντα
ὁρᾷ, καταγέλαστον φαίνεται καὶ ἄνανδρον καὶ πληγῶν
15 ἄξιον. ταὐτὸν οὖν ἔγωγε τοῦτο πάσχω καὶ πρὸς τοὺς
16 φιλοσοφοῦντας. περὶ νέῳ μὲν γὰρ μειρακίῳ ὁρῶν
φιλοσοφίαν ἄγαμαι καὶ πρέπειν μοι δοκεῖ καὶ ἡγοῦμαι
ἐλεύθερόν τινα εἶναι τοῦτον τὸν ἄνθρωπον, τὸν δὲ μὴ
φιλοσοφοῦντα ἀνελεύθερον καὶ οὐδέποτε οὐδενὸς ἀξιώ-
σοντα ἑαυτὸν οὔτε καλοῦ οὔτε γενναίου πράγματος·
17 ὅταν δὲ δὴ πρεσβύτερον ἴδω ἔτι φιλοσοφοῦντα καὶ μὴ
ἀπαλλαττόμενον, πληγῶν μοι δοκεῖ ἤδη δεῖσθαι, ὦ
18 Σώκρατες, οὗτος ὁ ἀνήρ. ὃ γὰρ νῦν δὴ ἔλεγον, ὑπάρ-

it is necessary to use in the intercourse of human society, both privately and publicly, and of the pleasures and desires of human life ; in brief, they are wholly unacquainted with manners. Accordingly, when they engage in any private or public business, they become a laughing-stock ; just exactly as states-men, I suppose, become ridiculous when they enter into your debates and discussions."

A little later he adds the following : " But I think it best to take part in both. It is good to pursue philosophy merely as a matter of education, and to be a philosopher is not dishonourable when one is young ; but when one who is already older persists in the business, the thing becomes laughable, Socrates, and I for my part feel the same towards those who philosophize as towards those who lisp and play. Whenever I see a little boy, to whom it is fitting to speak thus, lisping and playing, I am pleased, and it seems to me becoming and liberal and suited to the age of childhood ; but when I hear a small boy speaking with precision, it seems to me to be a disagreeable thing ; it wounds my ears and appears to be some-thing befitting a slave. When, however, one hears a man lisping, or sees him playing, it appears ridiculous, unmanly and deserving of stripes. I feel just the same way towards the philosophers. When I see philosophy in a young man, I rejoice ; it seems to me fitting, and I think that the young man in question is ingenuous ; that he who does not study philosophy is not ingenuous and will never himself be worthy of anything noble or generous. But when I see an older man still philosophizing and not giving it up, such a man, Socrates, seems to me to deserve stripes. For, as I have just said, it is possible for such a man, even

χει τούτῳ τῷ ἀνθρώπῳ, κἂν πάνυ εὐφυὴς ᾖ, ἀνάνδρῳ
γενέσθαι, φεύγοντι τὰ μέσα τῆς πόλεως καὶ τὰς ἀγοράς,
ἐν αἷς ἔφη ὁ ποιητὴς τοὺς ἄνδρας " ἀριπρεπεῖς " γίγνεσθαι,
καταδεδυκότι δὲ τὸν λοιπὸν βίον βιῶναι μετὰ μειρακίων, ἐν
γωνίᾳ τριῶν ἢ τεττάρων ψιθυρίζοντα, ἐλεύθερον δὲ καὶ
19-23 μέγα καὶ ἱκανὸν μηδέποτε φθέγξασθαι.

24   Haec Plato sub persona quidem, sicuti dixi, non
proba, set cum sensus tamen intellegentiaeque communis fide et cum quadam indissimulabili veritate
disseruit, non de illa scilicet philosophia, quae virtu-
tum omnium disciplina est quaeque in publicis simul
et privatis officiis excellit civitatesque et rempublicam,
si nihil prohibeat, constanter, fortiter et perite ad-
ministrat, sed de ista futtili atque puerili meditatione
argutiarum, nihil ad vitam neque tuendam neque
ordinandam promovente, in qua id genus homines
consenescunt male feriati, quos philosophos esse et
vulgus putat et is putabat, ex cuius persona haec
dicta sunt.

XXIII

Verba ex oratione M. Catonis de mulierum veterum victu et
moribus : atque inibi, quod fuerit ius marito in adulterio
uxorem deprehensam necare.

1   Qui de victu atque cultu populi Romani scripserunt mulieres Romae atque in Latio "aetatem

---

[1] Homer, *Iliad* ix. 441 f. οὔπω εἰδόθ' ὁμοίου πολέμοιο Οὐδ'
ἀγορέων, ἵνα τ' ἄνδρες ἀριπρεπέες τελέθουσιν.

[2] Cf. Hor. *Odes* iv. 6 15, *Troas male feriatos*. Since Gellius
mentions Horace by name only once, and once by possible

though naturally well endowed, to become unmanly, avoiding the business of the city and the market-place, where, as the poet says,[1] men become "most eminent," and living the rest of his life in hiding with young men, whispering in a corner with three or four of them, but never accomplishing anything liberal, great or satisfactory.

These sentiments, as I have said, Plato put into the mouth of a man of no great worth indeed, yet possessing a reputation for common sense and understanding and a kind of uncompromising frankness. He does not, of course, refer to that philosophy which is the teacher of all the virtues, which excels in the discharge of public and private duties alike, and which, if nothing prevents, governs cities and the State with firmness, courage and wisdom; but rather to that futile and childish attention to trifles which contributes nothing to the conduct and guidance of life, but in which people of that kind grow old in "ill-timed playmaking,"[2] regarded as philosophers by the vulgar, as they were by him from whose lips the words that I have quoted come.[3]

XXIII

A passage from a speech of Marcus Cato on the mode of life and manners of women of the olden time; and also that the husband had the right to kill his wife, if she were taken in adultery.

Those who have written about the life and civilization of the Roman people say that the women of Rome and Latium "lived an abstemious life"; that

implication (see Index), the expression had doubtless become proverbial.

[3] That is, Callicles; see § 2.

abstemias egisse," hoc est vino semper, quod "temetum" prisca lingua appellabatur, abstinuisse dicunt,
institutumque ut cognatis osculum ferrent depre-
hendendi causa, ut odor indicium faceret, si bibissent.
2 Bibere autem solitas ferunt loream, passum, murrinam
et quae id genus sapiant potu dulcia. Atque haec
3 quidem in his quibus dixi libris pervulgata sunt, sed
Marcus Cato non solum existimatas, set et multatas
quoque a iudice mulieres refert, non minus si vinum
in se, quam si probrum et adulterium admisissent.
4 Verba Marci Catonis adscripsi ex oratione quae
inscribitur *De Dote,* in qua id quoque scriptum est,
in adulterio uxores deprehensas ius fuisse maritis
necare: "Vir," inquit, "cum divortium fecit, mulieri
iudex pro censore est, imperium quod videtur habet,
si quid perverse taetreque factum est a muliere;
multitatur,[1] si vinum bibit; si cum alieno viro probri
5 quid fecit, condemnatur." De iure autem occi-
dendi ita scriptum: "In adulterio uxorem tuam
si prehendisses, sine iudicio inpune necares; illa
te, si adulterares sive tu adulterarere, digito non
auderet contingere, neque ius est."

[1] multiatur, *BZ*; mulcititur, *Q*; multatur, *γ*; *corrected
by Hertz.*

---

[1] Flavoured with myrrh.   [2] p. 68. 3, Jordan.

is, that they abstained altogether from wine, which in the early language was called *temetum*; that it was an established custom for them to kiss their kinsfolk for the purpose of detection, so that, if they had been drinking, the odour might betray them. But they say that the women were accustomed to drink the second brewing, raisin wine, spiced wine[1] and other sweet-tasting drinks of that kind. And these things are indeed made known in those books which I have mentioned, but Marcus Cato declares that women were not only censured but also punished by a judge no less severely if they had drunk wine than if they had disgraced themselves by adultery.

I have copied Marcus Cato's words from the oration entitled *On the Dowry*, in which it is also stated that husbands had the right to kill wives taken in adultery:[2] "When a husband puts away his wife," says he, "he judges the woman as a censor would, and has full powers if she has been guilty of any wrong or shameful act; she is severely punished if she has drunk wine; if she has done wrong with another man, she is condemned to death." Further, as to the right to put her to death it was thus written: "If you should take your wife in adultery, you may with impunity put her to death without a trial; but if you should commit adultery or indecency, she must not presume to lay a finger on you, nor does the law allow it."

XXIV

"Die pristini," "die crastini" et "die quarti" et "die quinti" qui elegantius locuti sint dixisse, non ut ea nunc vulgo dicuntur.

1 "Die quarto" et "die quinto," quod Graeci εἰς τετάρτην καὶ εἰς πέμπτην dicunt, ab eruditis nunc quoque dici audio, et qui aliter dicit pro rudi atque indocto despicitur. Sed Marci Tullii aetas ac supra eam non, opinor, ita dixerunt, "diequinte" enim et "diequinti" pro adverbio copulate dictum est, secunda in eo syllaba correpta. 2 Divus etiam Augustus, linguae Latinae non nescius munditiarumque patris sui in sermonibus sectator, in epistulis plurifariam significatione ista dierum non aliter usus est. 3 Satis autem erit perpetuae veterum consuetudinis demonstrandae gratia verba sollemnia praetoris ponere, quibus more maiorum ferias concipere solet quae appellantur Compitalia. Ea verba haec sunt: "Dienoni populo Romano Quiritibus Compitalia erunt; quando concepta fuerint, nefas." "Dienoni" praetor dicit, non "die nono."

4 Neque praetor solum, sed pleraque omnis vetustas
5 sic locuta est. Venit ecce illius versus Pomponiani in mentem, qui est ex Atellania, quae *Mevia* inscribitur:

Díes hic sextus, cúm nihil egi:[1] díequarte
moriár fame.

[1] edi, *Pontanus.*

---

[1] That is, his adoptive father, Julius Caesar.
[2] p. 145, Weichert.
[3] A movable festival, celebrated between Dec. 15 and Jan. 5, at cross-roads, in honour of the *Lares compitales.*

XXIV

That the most elegant speakers used the expressions *die pristini*,
die crastini, *die quarti*, and *die quinti*, not those which are
current now.

I HEAR *die quarto* and *die quinto*, which the Greeks
express by εἰς τετάρτην καὶ εἰς πέμπτην, used nowadays
even by learned men, and one who speaks otherwise
is looked down upon as crude and illiterate. But in
the time of Marcus Tullius, and earlier, they did not,
I think, speak in that way; for they used *diequinte*
and *diequinti* as a compound adverb, with the second
syllable of the word shortened. The deified Augustus,
too, who was well versed in the Latin tongue and an
imitator of his father's [1] elegance in discourse, has
often in his letters [2] used that means of designating
the days. But it will be sufficient to show the
undeviating usage of the men of old, if I quote the
regular formula of the praetor, in which, according to
the usage of our forefathers, he is accustomed to
proclaim the festival known as the Compitalia. [3] His
words are as follows: "On the ninth day the Roman
people, the Quirites, will celebrate the Compitalia;
when they shall have begun, legal business ceases."
The praetor says *dienoni*, not *die nono*.

And not the praetor alone, but almost all antiquity,
spoke in that way. Look you, this passage of the
well-known poet Pomponius comes to my mind, from
the Atellan farce entitled *Mevia*: [4]

For six days now I've done no stroke of work;
The fourth day (*diequarte*) I, poor wretch, shall
    starve to death.

[4] ii, 77, Ribbeck. [3]

6 Suppetit etiam Coelianum illud ex libro *Historiarum* secundo: "Si vis mihi equitatum dare et ipse cum cetero exercitu me sequi, diequinti Romae in Capito-
7 lium curabo tibi cena sit cocta." Et historiam autem et verbum hoc sumpsit Coelius ex *Origine* IV.[1] M. Catonis, in qua ita scriptum est: "Igitur dicta-torem Carthaginiensium magister equitum monuit: 'Mitte mecum Romam equitatum; diequinti in Capitolio tibi cena cocta erit.'"

8 Extremam istius vocis syllabam tum per *e* tum per *i* scriptam legi; nam sane quam consuetum is veteribus fuerit, litteris is plerumque uti indifferenter, sicuti "praefiscine" et "praefiscini," "proclivi" et "proclive" atque alia item multa hoc genus varie dixerunt; "die pristini" quoque eodem modo dice-batur, quod significabat "die pristino," id est priore, quod vulgo "pridie" dicitur, converso compositionis ordine, quasi "pristino die." Atque item simili figura "die crastini" dicebatur, id erat "crastino
9 die." Sacerdotes quoque populi Romani, cum condi-
10 cunt in diem tertium, "die[2] perendini" dicunt. Sed ut plerique "die pristini," ita M. Cato in oratione *Contra Furium* "die proximi" dixit, "die quarto" autem Cn. Matius, homo impense doctus, in *Mimi-ambis* pro eo dicit, quod "nudius quartus" nos dicimus, in his versibus:

Nuper die quarto, ut recordor, et certe
Aquarium urceum unicum domi fregit.

---

[1] IV. *added by Hertz.* [2] die, *Skutsch*; diem, *ω.*

---

[1] Fr. 25, Peter[2].
[2] Said to Hannibal by his officer Maharbal after the battle of Cannae, 216 B.C.
[3] Fr. 86, Peter[2]. [4] xix. 7, Jordan. [5] Fr. 11, Bährens.

There is also the following passage from Coelius in the second book of his *Histories*:[1] "If you are willing to give me the cavalry and follow me yourself with the rest of the army, on the fifth day (*diequinti*) I will have your dinner ready for you in the Capitol at Rome."[2] But Coelius took both the story itself and the word from the fourth book of Marcus Cato's *Origines*, where we find the following:[3] "Then the master of the horse thus advised the Carthaginian dictator: 'Send me to Rome with the cavalry; on the fifth day (*diequinti*) your dinner shall be ready for you in the Capitol.'"

The final syllable of that word I find written sometimes with *e* and sometimes with *i*; for it was usual with those men of olden times very often to use those letters without distinction, saying *praefiscine* and *praefiscini*, *proclivi* and *proclive*, and using many other words of that kind with either ending; in the same way too they said *die pristini*, that is, "the day before," which is commonly expressed by *pridie*, changing the order of the words in the compound, as if it were *pristino die*. Also by a similar usage they said *die crastini*, meaning *crastino die* or "to-morrow." The priests of the Roman people, too, when they make a proclamation for the third day, say *diem perendini*. But just as very many people said *die pristini*, so Marcus Cato in his oration *Against Furius*[4] said *die proximi* or "the next day"; and Gnaeus Matius, an exceedingly learned man, in his *Mimiambi*, instead of our *nudius tertius*, or "four days ago," has *die quarto*, in these lines:[5]

Of late, four days ago (*die quarto*), as I recall,
The only pitcher in the house he broke.

Hoc igitur intererit, ut "die quarto" quidem de praeterito dicamus, "diequarte" autem de futuro.

XXV

Telorum et iaculorum gladiorumque, atque inibi navium quoque vocabula, quae scripta in veterum libris reperiuntur.

1   TELORUM, iaculorum gladiorumque vocabula quae in historiis veteribus scripta sunt, item navigiorum genera et nomina, libitum forte nobis est sedentibus in reda conquirere, ne quid malarum[1] ineptiarum va-
2 cantem stupentemque animum occuparet. Quae tum igitur suppetierant, haec sunt: hasta, pilum, phalarica, semiphalarica, soliferrea, gaesa, lancea, spari, rumices, trifaces, tragulae, frameae, mesanculae, cateiae, rumpiae, scorpii, sibones, siciles, veruta, enses, sicae, macherae, spathae, lingulae, pugiones, clunacula.
3   De "lingula," quoniam est minus frequens, admonendum existimo, lingulam veteres dixisse gladiolum oblongum in speciem linguae factum, cuius meminit Naevius in tragoedia *Hesiona*. Versum Naevi apposui:

Sine mi gerere mórem videar língua, verum língula.

4 Item "rumpia" genus teli est Thraecae nationis, positumque hoc vocabulum in Quinti Enni *Annalium* XIV.

---

[1] malarum, *Skutsch*; aliarum, ω.

---

[1] See McCartney, *Figurative Use of Animal Names*, p. 47.
[2] Fr. 1, Ribbeck[3], who gives the title as *Aesiona*. There is of course a word-play on *lingula*.

Therefore the distinction will be found to be, that we use *die quarto* of the past, but *diequarte* of the future.

XXV

The names of certain weapons, darts and swords, and also of boats and ships, which are found in the books of the early writers.

ONCE upon a time, when I was riding in a carriage, to keep my mind from being dull and unoccupied and a prey to worthless trifles, it chanced to occur to me to try to recall the names of weapons, darts and swords which are found in the early histories, and also the various kinds of boats and their names. Those, then, of the former that came to mind at the time are the following : spear, pike, fire-pike, half-pike, iron bolt, Gallic spear, lance, hunting-darts, javelins, long bolts, barbed-javelins, German spears, thonged-javelin, Gallic bolt, broadswords, poisoned arrows,[1] Illyrian hunting-spears, cimeters, darts, swords, daggers, broadswords, double-edged swords, small-swords, poniards, cleavers.

Of the *lingula,* or "little tongue," since it is less common, I think I ought to say that the ancients applied that term to an oblong small-sword, made in the form of a tongue ; it is mentioned by Naevius in his tragedy *Hesione.* I quote the line :[2]

> Pray let me seem to please you with my tongue,
> But with my little tongue (*lingula*).

The *rumpia* too is a kind of weapon of the Thracian people, and the word occurs in the fourteenth book of the *Annals* of Quintus Ennius.[3]

[3] *Ann.* 390, Vahlen[2] ; cf. Livy xxxi. 39. 11.

5 Navium autem, quas reminisci tunc potuimus, appellationes hae sunt: gauli, corbitae, caudicae, longae, hippagines, cercuri, celoces vel, ut Graeci dicunt, κέλητες, lembi, oriae, lenunculi, actuariae, quas Graeci ἰστιοκώπους vocant vel ἐπακτρίδας, prosumiae vel geseoretae vel oriolae, stlattae, scaphae, pontones, vetutiae moediae, phaseli, parones, myoparones, lintres, caupuli, camarae, placidae, cydarum, ratariae, catascopium.

XXVI

Inscite ab Asinio Pollione reprehensum Sellustium, quod transfretationem "transgressum" dixerit, et "transgressos" qui transfretassent.

1 ASINIO POLLIONI in quadam epistula, quam ad Plancum scripsit, et quibusdam aliis C. Sallusti iniquis, dignum nota visum est, quod in primo *Historiarum* maris transitum transmissumque navibus factum "transgressum" appellavit eosque, qui fretum transmiserant, quos "transfretasse" dici solitum est,
2 "transgressos" dixit. Verba ipsa Sallusti posui: "Itaque Sertorius, levi praesidio relicto in Mauretania, nanctus obscuram noctem, aestu secundo furtim aut celeritate vitare proelium in transgressu
3 conatus est." Ac deinde infra ita scripsit: "Transgressos omnis recipit mons[1] praeceptus a Lusitanis."
4 Hoc igitur et minus proprie et ἀπερισκέπτως et nullo gravi auctore dictum aiunt. "Nam 'transgressus,'" inquit, "a transgrediendo dicitur idque ipsum

[1] mons Balleia, Serv. *Aen.* i. 518.

---

[1] Many of these names, both of weapons and ships, are most uncertain; for some no exact equivalent can be found.

The names of ships which I recalled at the time are these: merchant-ships, cargo-carriers, skiffs, war-ships, cavalry-transports, cutters, fast cruisers, or, as the Greeks call them, κέλητες, barques, smacks, sailing-skiffs, light galleys, which the Greeks call ἱστιοκόποι or ἐπακτρίδες, scouting-boats, galliots, tenders, flat-boats, *vetutiae moediae*, yachts, pinnaces, long-galliots, scullers' boats, caupuls,[1] arks, fair-weather craft, pinks, lighters, spy-boats.

XXVI

That Asinius Pollio showed ignorance in criticizing Sallust because he used *transgressus* (crossing) for *transfretatio* (crossing the sea) and *transgressi* (those who had crossed) for *qui transfretaverant* (those who had crossed the sea).

Asinius Pollio, in a letter which he addressed to Plancus, and certain others who were unfriendly to Gaius Sallustius, thought that Sallust deserved censure because in the first book of his *Histories* he called the crossing of the sea and a passage made in ships *transgressus*, using *transgressi* of those who had crossed the sea, for which the usual term is *transfretare*. I give Sallust's own words:[2] "Accordingly Sertorius, having left a small garrison in Mauretania and taking advantage of a dark night and a favourable tide, tried either by secrecy or speed to avoid a battle while crossing *(in transgressu)*." Then later he wrote:[3] "When they had crossed *(transgressos)*, a mountain which had been seized in advance by the Lusitanians gave them all shelter."

This, they say, is an improper and careless usage, supported by no adequate authority. "For *transgressus*," says Pollio, "comes from *transgredi*, 'to step

[2] *Hist.* i. 104, Maur.   [3] *ib.* i. 105.

5 ab ingressu et a pedum gradu appellatum." Idcirco verbum "transgredi" convenire non putavit neque volantibus neque serpentibus neque navigantibus, sed his solis qui gradiuntur et pedibus iter emetiuntur. Propterea negant aput scriptorem idoneum aut navium "transgressum" reperiri posse aut pro transfretatione "transgressum."

6 Sed quaero ego, cur non, sicuti "cursus" navium recte dici solet,[1] ita "transgressus" etiam navibus factus dici possit. Praesertim cum brevitas tam angusti fretus, qui terram Africam Hispaniamque interfluit, elegantissime "transgressionis" vocabulo,

7 quasi paucorum graduum spatium, definita sit. Qui auctoritatem autem requirunt et negant dictum "ingredi" "transgredi" ve in navigantibus, volo uti respondeant quantum existiment interesse "ingredi"

8 atque "ambulare." Atqui Cato De Re Rustica: "Fundus," inquit, "eo in loco habendus est, ut et[2] oppidum prope[3] amplum sit et mare aut amnis, qua naves ambulant."

9 Appetitas porro huiuscemodi translationes habitasque esse pro honestamentis orationis, Lucretius quoque testimonium in hac eadem voce dicit. In quarto enim libro clamorem per arterias et per fauces "gradientem" dicit, quod est nimio confidentius quam illud de navibus Sallustianum. Versus Lucreti hi sunt :

Praeterea radit vox fauces saepe, facitque
Asperiora foras gradiens arteria clamor.

---

[1] solet, *Skutsch* ; solent, *MSS.*
[2] fundus . . . ut et, *not in Cato.*
[3] validum prope, *Cato.*

---

[1] i. 3.   [2] iv. 526.

across,' and this word itself refers to walking and stepping with the feet." Therefore Pollio thought that the verb *transgredi* did not apply to those who fly or creep or sail, but only to those who walk and measure the way with their feet. Hence they say that in no good writer can *transgressus* be found applied to ships, or as the equivalent of *transfretatio.*

But, since *cursus,* or " running," is often correctly used of ships, I ask why it is that ships may not be said to make a *transgressus,* especially since the small extent of the narrow strait which flows between Spain and the Afric land is most elegantly described by the word *transgressio,* as being a distance of only a few steps. But as to those who ask for authority and assert that *ingredi* or *transgredi* has not been used of sailing, I should like them to tell me how much difference they think there is between *ingredi,* or "march," and *ambulare,* or "walk." Yet Cato in his book *On Farming* says : [1] "A farm should be chosen in a situation where there is a large town near by and the sea, or a river where ships pass (*ambulant*)." Moreover Lucretius, by the use of this same expression, bears testimony that such figures are intentional and are regarded as ornaments of diction. For in his fourth book he speaks of a shout as " marching " (*gradientem*) through the windpipe and jaws, which is much bolder than the Sallustian expression about the ships. The lines of Lucretius are as follows : [2]

The voice besides doth often scrape the throat ;
A shout forth marching (*gradiens*) doth make the
  windpipe rough.

10 Propterea Sallustius in eodem libro non eos solum qui navibus veherentur, sed et scaphas quoque nantes "progressas" dicit. Verba ipsa de scaphis posui : "Earum aliae paululum progressae nimio simul et incerto onere, cum pavor corpora agitaverat, deprimebantur."

XXVII

Historia de populo Romano deque populo Poenico, quod pari propemodum vigore fuerint aemuli.

1 IN litteris veteribus memoria extat quod par quondam fuit vigor et acritudo amplitudoque populi
2 Romani atque Poeni. Neque inmerito aestimatum. Cum aliis quidem populis de uniuscuiusque republica, cum Poenis autem de omnium terrarum imperio decertatum.
3 Eius rei specimen est in illo utriusque populi verbo factoque : Q. Fabius, imperator Romanus, dedit ad Carthaginienses epistulam. Ibi scriptum fuit populum Romanum misisse ad eos hastam et caduceum, signa duo belli[1] aut pacis, ex quis utrum vellent eligerent ; quod elegissent, id unum ut esse missum
4 existimarent. Cathaginienses responderunt neutrum sese eligere, sed posse qui adtulissent utrum mallent relinquere ; quod reliquissent, id sibi pro electo futurum.
5 M. autem Varro non hastam ipsam neque ipsum caduceum missa dicit, sed duas tesserulas, in quarum

---

[1] duelli, *Kronenberg.*

---

[1] *Hist.* i. 98, Maur.

Accordingly, Sallust, in the same book, uses *progressus*, not only of those who sailed in ships, but also of floating skiffs. I have added his own words about the skiffs : [1] " Some of them, after going (*progressae*) but a little way, the load being excessive and unstable, when panic had thrown the passengers into disorder, began to sink."

XXVII

A story of the Roman and the Carthaginian people, showing that they were rivals of nearly equal strength.

It is stated in ancient records that the strength, the spirit and the numbers of the Roman and the Carthaginian people were once equal. And this opinion was not without foundation. With other nations the contest was for the independence of one or the other state, with the Carthaginians it was for the rule of the world.

An indication of this is found in the following word and act of each of the two peoples : Quintus Fabius, a Roman general, delivered a letter to the Carthaginians, in which it was written that the Roman people had sent them a spear and a herald's staff, signs respectively of war and peace ; they might choose whichever they pleased and regard the one which they should choose as sent them by the Roman people. The Carthaginians replied that they chose neither one ; those who had brought them might leave whichever they liked ; that whatever should be left them they would consider that they themselves had chosen.

Marcus Varro, however, says that neither the spear itself nor the staff itself was sent, but two

altera caduceum, in altera hastae simulacra fuerint
incisa.

XXVIII

De aetatum finibus pueritiae, iuventae, senectae, ex Tuberonis
historia sumptum.

1   TUBERO in *Historiarum* primo scripsit Servium
Tullium regem, populi Romani cum illas quinque
classes seniorum et [1] iuniorum census faciendi gratia
institueret, "pueros" esse existimasse qui minores
essent annis septem decem, atque inde ab anno
septimo decimo, quo idoneos iam esse reipublicae
arbitraretur, milites scripsisse, eosque ad annum
quadragesimum sextum "iuniores" supraque eum
annum "seniores" appellasse.
2   Eam rem propterea notavi, ut discrimina, quae
fuerint iudicio moribusque maiorum "pueritiae,"
"iuventae," "senectae," ex ista censione Servi
Tulli, prudentissimi regis, noscerentur.

XXIX.

Quod particula "atque" non complexiva tantum sit, sed vim
habeat plusculam variamque.

1   "ATQUE" particula a grammaticis quidem con-
iunctio esse dicitur conexiva. Et plerumque sane
coniungit verba et conectit; sed interdum alias

---

[1] seniorum et, *added by Thysius*; *Lipsius deleted* iuniorum.

tokens, on one of which was engraved the representation of a staff; on the other that of a spear.

XXVIII

TUBERO, in the first book of his *History*,[1] has written that King Servius Tullius, when he divided the Roman people into those five classes of older and younger men for the purpose of making the enrolment, regarded as *pueri*, or "boys," those who were less than seventeen years old; then, from their seventeenth year, when they were thought to be fit for service, he enrolled them as soldiers, calling them up to the age of forty-six *iuniores*, or "younger men," and beyond that age, *seniores*, or "elders."

I have made a note of this fact, in order that from the rating of Servius Tullius, that most sagacious king, the distinctions between boyhood, manhood, and old age might be known, as they were established by the judgment, and according to the usage, of our forefathers.

XXIX

THE particle *atque* is said by the grammarians to be a copulative conjunction. And as a matter of fact, it very often joins and connects words; but sometimes it has certain other powers, which are

Fr. 4, Peter[2].

quasdam potestates habet non satis notas, nisi in
veterum litterarum tractatione atque cura exercitis.

2 Nam et pro adverbio valet, cum dicimus " aliter ego
feci atque tu," significatur enim " aliter quam tu,"
et si gemina fiat, auget incenditque rem de qua
agitur, ut animadvertimus in Q. Enni *Annalibus,*
nisi memoria in hoc versu labor :

Atque atque accedit muros Romana iuventus ;

3 cui significationi contrarium est quod itidem a veteribus dictum est, " deque."

4   Et praeterea pro alio quoque adverbio dicitur, id
est " statim "[1] factum, quod in his Vergili versibus
existimatur, ubi obscure et insequenter particula ista
posita est :[2]

                              sic omnia fatis
In peius ruere ac retro sublapsa referri ;
Non aliter quam qui adverso vix flumine lembum
Remigiis subigit, si brachia forte remisit,
Atque illum in praeceps prono rapit alveus amni.

    [1] statim, γ B ; factum, QZ.
    [2] statim . . . est, *Hosius, reading both* statim *and* factum
and inserting ubi.

----

    [1] *Ann.* 537, Vahlen.[2]
    [2] Text and meaning are uncertain of this and the following
sentence ; see critical note.

not sufficiently observed, except by those engaged in a diligent examination of the early literature. For it has the force of an adverb when we say " I have acted otherwise than (*atque*) you," for it is equivalent to *aliter quam tu ;* and if it is doubled, it amplifies and emphasizes a statement, as we note in the *Annals* of Quintus Ennius, unless my memory of this verse is at fault : [1]

And quickly (*atque atque*) to the walls the Roman manhood came.

The opposite of this meaning is expressed by *deque,* also found in the early writers.[2]

Atque is said to have been used besides for another adverb also, namely *statim,* as is thought to be the case in these lines of Virgil, where that particle is employed obscurely and irregularly : [3]

Thus, by Fate's law, all speeds towards the worse,
And giving way, falls back ; e'en as if one
Whose oars can barely force his skiff upstream
Should chance to slack his arms and cease to drive ;
Then straightway (*atque*) down the flood he's swept away.

[3] *Georg.* i. 199.

BOOK XI

LIBER UNDECIMUS

I

De origine vocabuli "terrae Italiae"; deque ea multa quae
suprema appellatur deque eius nominis ratione ac de lege
Aternia ; et quibus verbis antiquitus multa minima dici
solita ̄sit.

1   TIMAEUS in *Historiis* quas oratione Graeca de
rebus populi Romani composuit, et M. Varro in *Antiquitatibus Rerum Humanarum,* terram Italiam de
Graeco vocabulo appellatam scripserunt, quoniam
boves Graeca vetere lingua ἰταλοί vocitati sint,[1] quorum in Italia magna copia fuerit, bucetaque[2] in ea
terra gigni pascique solita sint complurima.
2   Coniectare autem possumus ob eandem causam,
quod Italia tunc esset armentosissima multam, quae
appellatur "suprema" institutam in dies singulos
duarum ovium, boum triginta, pro copia scilicet boum
proque ovium penuria. Sed cum eiusmodi multa
pecoris armentique a magistratibus dicta erat, adige-
bantur boves ovesque alias pretii parvi, alias maioris,
eaque res faciebat inaequalem multae poenitionem.
Idcirco postea lege Aternia constituti sunt in oves
3 singulas aeris deni, in boves aeris centeni. "Minima"

---

[1] sint, *Lion* ; sunt, *MSS.* (Z *omits*).
[2] buceta, *MSS.*; bucera, *Paris ed. of 1536.*

---

[1] *F.H.G.* i. 195, Müller.   [2] x. fr. 1, Mirsch.
[3] Passed by the consul, A. Atinius, in 454 B.C.

BOOK XI

I

On the origin of the term *terra Italia*, or "the land of
   Italy"; of that fine which is called "supreme"; concerning the reason for the name and on the Aternian
   law; and in what words the "smallest" fine used to be
   pronounced in ancient days.

TIMAEUS, in the *History*[1] which he composed in
the Greek language about the affairs of the Roman
people, and Marcus Varro in his *Human Antiquities*,[2]
wrote that the land of Italy derived its name from
a Greek word, oxen in the old Greek tongue being
called ἰταλοί; for in Italy there was a great abundance of cattle, and in that land pastures are
numerous and grazing is a frequent employment.

Furthermore, we may infer that it was for the
same reason—namely, since Italy at that time so
abounded in cattle—that the fine was established
which is called "supreme," consisting of two sheep
and thirty oxen each day, obviously proportionate
to the abundance of oxen and the scarcity of sheep.
But when a fine of that sort, consisting of cattle
and sheep, was pronounced by a magistrate, oxen
and sheep were brought, now of small, again of
greater value; and this made the penalty of the fine
unequal. Therefore later, by the Aternian law,[3] the
value of a sheep was fixed at ten pieces of brass, of
the cattle at a hundred apiece. Now the "smallest"

autem multa est ovis unius. "Suprema" multa est eius numeri cuius diximus, ultra quem multam dicere in dies singulos ius non est, et propterea "suprema" appellatur, id est summa et maxima.

4   Quando igitur nunc quoque a magistratibus populi Romani more maiorum multa dicitur vel minima vel suprema, observari solet ut "oves" genere virili appellentur; atque ita M. Varro verba haec legitima, quibus minima multa diceretur, concepit: "M. Terentio, quando citatus neque respondit neque excusatus est, ego ei unum ovem multam dico"; ac nisi eo genere diceretur, negaverunt iustam videri multam.

5   Vocabulum autem ipsum "multae" idem M. Varro in uno vicesimo *Rerum Humanarum* non Latinum, sed Sabinum esse dicit, idque ad suam memoriam mansisse ait in lingua Samnitium, qui sunt a Sabinis orti. Sed turba grammaticorum novicia κατ᾽ ἀντίφρασιν, ut quaedam alia, hoc quoque dici

6 tradiderunt. Cum autem usus et mos sermonum is sit, ut ita et nunc loquamur, ut plerique veterum locuti sunt: "multam dixit" et "multa dicta est," non esse abs re putavi notare quod M. Cato aliter dixit. Nam in quarto *Originum* verba haec sunt: "Imperator noster, si quis extra ordinem depugna-

7 tum ivit, ei multam facit." Potest autem videri consulta elegantia mutasse verbum, cum in castris et

---

[1] That is, for a certain number of animals to be paid on a number of successive days.

[2] xxiii. fr. 2, Mirsch.

[3] xxi. fr. 1, Mirsch.

[4] That is, the "lucus a non lucendo" idea.

[5] Fr. 82, Peter[2].

fine is that of one sheep. The "supreme" fine is
of that number which we have mentioned, beyond
which it is not lawful to impose a fine for a period
of successive days;[1] and for that reason it is called
"supreme," that is, greatest and heaviest.

When therefore even now, according to ancient
usage, either the "smallest" or the "supreme" fine
is pronounced by Roman magistrates, it is regularly
observed that *ores* ("sheep") be given the masculine
gender; and Marcus Varro has thus recorded the
words of the law by which the smallest fine was
pronounced:[2] "Against Marcus Terentius, since,
though summoned, he has neither appeared nor
been excused, I pronounce a fine of one sheep
(*unum ovem*)"; and they declared that the fine did
not appear to be legal unless that gender was used.

Furthermore, Marcus Varro, in the twenty-first
book of his *Human Antiquities,* also says[3] that the
word for fine (*multa*) is itself not Latin, but Sabine,
and he remarks that it endured even to within his
own memory in the speech of the Samnites, who are
sprung from the Sabines. But the upstart herd of
grammarians have asserted that this word, like
some others, is used on the principle of opposites.[4]
Furthermore, since it is a usage and custom in
language for us to say even now, as the greater
number of the early men did, *multam dixit* and
multa dicta est, I have thought it not out of place
to note that Marcus Cato spoke otherwise.[5] For in
the fourth book of his *Origins* are these words:
"Our commander, if anyone has gone to battle out
of order, imposes (*facit*) a fine upon him." But it
may seem that Cato changed the word with an eye
to propriety, since the fine was imposed in camp

in exercitu multa fieret, non in comitio nec ad
populum diceretur.

II

Quod "elegantia" apud antiquiores, non de amoeniore
ingenio, sed de nitidiore cultu atque victu dicebatur, eaque
in vitio ponebatur.

1   "ELEGANS" homo non dicebatur cum laude, set
id fere verbum ad aetatem M. Catonis vitii, non
2 laudis fuit.   Est namque hoc animadvertere, cum in
quibusdam aliis, tum in libro Catonis qui inscriptus
est *Carmen De Moribus*.   Ex quo libro verba haec
sunt : "Avaritiam omnia vitia habere putabant ;
sumptuosus, cupidus, elegans, vitiosus, inritus qui
3 habebatur, is laudabatur " ; [1] ex quibus verbis apparet,
"elegantem" dictum antiquitus non ab ingenii
elegantia, sed qui nimis lecto amoenoque cultu
victuque esset.

4   Postea "elegans" reprehendi quidem desiit, sed
laude nulla dignabatur, nisi cuius elegantia erat
moderatissima.   Sic M. Tullius L. Crasso et Q.
Scaevolae non meram elegantiam, set multa parsimonia mixtam, laudi dedit : "Crassus," inquit, "erat
parcissimus elegantium, Scaevola parcorum elegantissimus."

5   Praeterea ex eodem libro Catonis haec etiam
sparsim et intercise commeminimus : "Vestiri,"

----

¹ <avarus> laudabatur, *L. Müller* ; is audiebat avarus,
Bährens.

----

[1] p. 82, 10, Jordan.
[2] That is, in comparison with the miser.

and in the army, not pronounced in the comitium
or in the presence of the people.

II

That the word *elegantia* in earlier days was not used of a
more refined nature, but of excessive fastidiousness in dress
and mode of life, and was a term of reproach.

IT was not customary to call a man *elegans,* or
"elegant," by way of praise, but up to the time of
Marcus Cato that word as a rule was a reproach,
not a compliment. And this we may observe both
in some other writers, and also in the work of Cato
entitled *Carmen de Moribus.* In this book is the
following passage : [1] " They thought that avarice included all the vices ; whoever was considered extravagant, ambitious, elegant, vicious or good-for-
nothing received praise." [2] It is evident from these
words that in days of old the "elegant" man was
so called, not because of refinement of character,
but because he was excessively particular and extravagant in his attire and mode of life.

Later, the "elegant" man ceased indeed to be
reproached, but he was deemed worthy of no com-
mendation, unless his elegance was very moderate.
Thus Marcus Tullius commended Lucius Crassus and
Quintus Scaevola, not for mere elegance, but for
elegance combined with great frugality. "Crassus,"
he says,[3] "was the most frugal of elegant men ;
Scaevola the most elegant of the frugal."

Besides this, in the same work of Cato, I recall
also these scattered and cursory remarks : [4] " It was

[3] *Brut.* 148.   [4] p. 83, 1, Jordan.

inquit, "in foro honeste mos erat, domi quod satis
erat. Equos carius quam coquos emebant. Poeticae
artis honos non erat. Si quis in ea re studebat aut
sese ad convivia adplicabat, ' crassator' vocabatur."
6 Illa quoque ex eodem libro praeclarae veritatis
sententia est : " Nam vita," inquit, " humana prope
uti ferrum est. Si exerceas, conteritur ; si non
exerceas, tamen robigo interficit. Item homines
exercendo videmus conteri ; si nihil exerceas, in-
ertia atque torpedo plus detrimenti facit quam
exercitio."

III

Qualis quantaque sit "pro" particulae varietas; deque
exemplis eius varietatis.

1   Quando ab arbitriis negotiisque otium est et mo-
tandi corporis gratia aut spatiamur aut vectamur,
quaerere nonnumquam aput memet ipsum soleo res
eiusmodi, parvas quidem minutasque et hominibus
non bene eruditis aspernabiles, sed ad veterum
scripta penitus noscenda et ad scientiam linguae
Latinae cumprimis necessarias ; velut est, quod forte
nuper in Praenestino recessu [1] vespertina ambula-
tione solus ambulans, considerabam qualis quantaque
esset particularum quarundam in oratione Latina
2 varietas. Quod genus est praepositio " pro."
Aliter enim dici videbam " pontifices pro conlegio
decrevisse," aliter " quempiam testem introductum

---

[1] secessu, *Juretus.*

---

[1] Id., p. 83, 5.

the custom," says he, "to dress becomingly in the forum, at home to cover their nakedness. They paid more for horses than for cooks. The poetic art was not esteemed. If anyone devoted himself to it, or frequented banquets, he was called a ' ruffian.' " This sentiment too, of conspicuous truthfulness, is to be found in the same work :[1] " Indeed, human life is very like iron. If you use it, it wears out ; if you do not, it is nevertheless consumed by rust. In the same way we see men worn out by toil ; if you toil not, sluggishness and torpor are more injurious than toil."

III

The nature and degree of the variety of usage in the particle *pro* ; and some examples of the differences.

WHEN I have leisure from legal business, and walk or ride for the sake of bodily exercise, I have the habit sometimes of silently meditating upon questions that are trifling indeed and insignificant, even negligible in the eyes of the uneducated, but are nevertheless highly necessary for a thorough understanding of the early writers and a knowledge of the Latin language. For example, lately in the retirement of Praeneste,[2] as I was taking my evening walk alone, I began to consider the nature and degree of variety in the use of certain particles in the Latin language ; for instance, in the preposition *pro*. For I saw that we had one use in " the priests passed a decree *in the name of* their order," and another in " that a witness who had been called in

[2] From this passage some have inferred that Gellius had a villa at Praeneste.

pro testimonio dixisse," aliter M. Catonem in *Originum* quarto : "Proelium factum depugnatumque pro castris" scripsisse et item in quinto : "Urbes insulasque omnis pro agro Illyrio esse," aliter etiam dici "pro aede Castoris," aliter "pro rostris," aliter "pro tribunali," aliter "pro contione" atque aliter

3 "tribunum plebis pro potestate intercessisse." Sed has omnes dictiones qui aut omnino similes et pares aut usquequaque diversas existimaret, errare arbitrabar ; nam varietatem istam eiusdem quidem fontis et capitis, non eiusdem tamen esse finis putabam.

4 Quod profecto facile intelleget, si quis adhibeat ad meditationem suam intentionem et habeat veteris orationis usum atque notitiam celebriorem.

IV

Quem in modum Q. Ennius versus Euripidi aemulatus sit.

1 EURIPIDIS versus sunt in *Hecuba* verbis, sententia,
2 brevitate insignes inlustresque ; Hecuba est ad Ulixen dicens :

---

[1] Fr. 91, Peter[2].   [2] Fr. 96, Peter[2].

[3] On the origin of such expressions, see Frank, *Riv. di Fil.* liii (1925), p. 105.

[4] The preceding statement is not "easy to understand." Gellius seems to mean that all the different significations of *pro* developed from one or two original meanings. Thus "for" or "before" will give the general meaning in nearly

said *by way of* testimony"; that Marcus Cato used it in still another way in the fourth book of his *Origins*:[1] "The battle was fought and ended *before* the camp," and also in the fifth book:[2] "That all the islands and cities were *in favour of* the Illyrian land." Also "*before* the temple of Castor" is one form of expression, "*on* the rostra" another, "*before*, or *on*, the tribunal"[3] another, "*in presence of* the assembly" another, and "the tribune of the commons interposed a veto *in view of* his authority" still another. Now, I thought that anyone who imagined that all these expressions were wholly alike and equal, or were entirely different, was in error; for I was of the opinion that this variety came from the same origin and source, but yet that its end was not the same. And this surely anyone will easily understand,[4] if he attentively considers the question and has a somewhat extensive use and knowledge of the early language.

IV

How Quintus Ennius rivalled[5] certain verses of Euripides.

In the *Hecuba* of Euripides there are some verses remarkable and brilliant in their diction, their thought and their terseness. Hecuba is speaking to Ulysses:[6]

---

all the examples except "on the rostra" and "on the tribunal," for which see Frank's article, cited in the preceding note.

[5] The principle of rivalry, the ἀγών, was a recognized feature of literary technique.

[6] v. 293; the translation is that of Way, *L.C.L.*

Τὸ δ' ἀξίωμα, κἂν κακῶς λέγῃ, τὸ σὸν
Νικᾷ· λόγος γὰρ ἔκ τ' ἀδοξούντων ἰὼν
Κἀκ τῶν δοκούντων αὐτός, οὐ ταὐτὸν σθένει.

3 Hos versus Q. Ennius, cum eam tragoediam verteret,
non sane incommode aemulatus est. Versus totidem
Enniani hi sunt:

> Haéc tu etsi pervérse dices, fácile Achivos
> fléxeris;
> Nám opulenti cúm locuntur páriter atque ignó-
> biles,
> Éadem dicta eadémque oratio aéqua non aequé
> valet.

4 Bene, sicuti dixi, Ennius; sed "ignobiles" tamen et
"opulenti" ἀντὶ ἀδοξούντων καὶ δοκούντων satisfacere
sententiae non videntur; nam neque omnes ignobiles
ἀδοξοῦσι neque omnes opulenti εὐδοξοῦσιν.

V

De Pyrronis philosophis quaedam deque Academicis strictim
notata; deque inter eos differentia.

1 Quos Pyrronios philosophos vocamus, hi Graeco
2 cognomento σκεπτικοί appellantur; id ferme signifi-
3 cat quasi "quaesitores" et "consideratores." Nihil
enim decernunt, nihil constituunt, sed in quaerendo
semper considerandoque sunt quidnam sit omnium
4 rerum de quo decerni constituique possit. Ac ne
videre quoque plane quicquam neque audire sese pu-

---

[1] v. 165, Ribbeck[3].

Thine high repute, how ill soe'er thou speak'st,
Shall sway them; for the same speech carrieth
not
Like weight from men contemned and men
revered.

These verses Quintus Ennius, when he translated
that tragedy, rivalled with no little success. The
verses of Ennius are the same in number, as
follows:[1]

Though thou speak'st ill, thou wilt the Achivi
sway;
The selfsame words and speech have other weight
When spoken by the great and by the obscure.

Ennius, as I have said, did well; but yet *ignobiles*
and *opulenti* do not seem to express the full force
of ἀδοξούντων and δοκούντων; for not all who are
obscure are contemned, nor are the great all
revered.

V

Some brief notes about the Pyrronian philosophers and the
Academics; and of the difference between them.

THOSE whom we call the Pyrronian philosophers
are designated by the Greek name σκεπτικοί, or
"sceptics," which means about the same as "inquirers" and "investigators." For they decide
nothing and determine nothing, but are always
engaged in inquiring and considering what there
is in all nature concerning which it is possible to
decide and determine. And moreover they believe
that they do not see or hear anything clearly,

tant, sed ita pati adficique quasi videant vel audiant,
eaque ipsa quae adfectiones istas in sese efficiant,
qualia et cuiusmodi sint cunctantur atque insistunt,
omniumque rerum fidem veritatemque mixtis con-
fusisque signis veri atque falsi ita inprensibilem
videri aiunt, ut quisquis homo est non praeceps
neque iudicii sui prodigus his uti verbis debeat
quibus auctorem philosophiae istius Pyrronem esse
usum tradunt : οὐ μᾶλλον οὕτως ἔχει τόδε ἢ ἐκείνως ἢ
οὐθετέρως. Indicia enim rei cuiusque et sinceras
proprietates negant posse nosci et percipi, idque
ipsum docere atque ostendere multis modis conantur.

5 Super qua re Favorinus quoque subtilissime argutis-
simeque decem libros composuit, quos Πυρρωνείων
Τρόπων inscribit.

6 Vetus autem quaestio et a multis scriptoribus
Graecis tractata, an quid et quantum Pyrronios et
Academicos philosophos 'ntersit. Utrique enim
σκεπτικοί, ἐφεκτικοί, ἀπορητικοί dicuntur, quoniam
utrique nihil adfirmant nihilque comprehendi putant.
Sed ex omnibus rebus proinde visa dicunt fieri, quas
φαντασίας appellant, non ut rerum ipsarum natura
est, sed ut adfectio animi corporisve est eorum, ad
7 quos ea visa perveniunt. Itaque omnes omnino res
quae sensus hominum movent, τῶν πρός τι esse dicunt. Id verbum significat nihil esse quicquam quod
ex sese constet nec quod habeat vim propriam et naturam, sed omnia prorsus ad aliquid referri taliaque

---

[1] p. 88, Marres. Apparently a discussion of the arguments
by which the Pyrronian philosophers supported their beliefs.
[2] That is, "things relative to something else."

but that they undergo and experience something like seeing and hearing; but they are in doubt as to the nature and character of those very things which cause them those experiences, and they deliberate about them: and they declare that in everything assurance and absolute truth seem so beyond our grasp, owing to the mingling and confusing of the indications of truth and falsehood, that any man who is not rash and precipitate in his judgment ought to use the language which they say was used by Pyrro, the founder of that philosophy : " Does not this matter stand so, rather than so, or is it neither?" For they deny that proofs of anything and its real qualities can be known and understood, and they try in many ways to point this out and demonstrate it. On this subject Favorinus too with great keenness and subtlety has composed ten books, which he entitled Πυρρωνεῖοι Τρόποι, or *The Pyrronian Principles*.[1]

It is besides a question of long standing, which has been discussed by many Greek writers, whether the Pyrronian and Academic philosophers differ at all, and to what extent. For both are called "sceptics, inquirers and doubters," since both affirm nothing and believe that nothing is understood. But they say that appearances, which they call φαντασίαι, are produced from all objects, not according to the nature of the objects themselves, but according to the condition of mind or body of those to whom those appearances come. Therefore they call absolutely all things that affect men's senses τὰ πρός τι.[2] This expression means that there is nothing at all that is self-dependent or which has its own power and nature, but that absolutely all things have " reference

videri qualis sit eorum species dum videntur, qualia-
que apud sensus nostros, quo pervenerunt, creantur,[1]
8 non apud sese, unde profecta sunt. Cum haec autem
consimiliter tam Pyrronii dicant quam Academici,
differre tamen inter sese et propter alia quaedam et
vel maxime propterea existimati sunt, quod Academici quidem ipsum illud nihil posse comprehendi
quasi comprehendunt, et nihil posse decerni quasi
decernunt, Pyrronii ne id quidem ullo pacto verum
videri dicunt, quod nihil esse verum videtur.

VI

Quod mulieres Romae per Herculem non iuraverint neque
viri per Castorem.

1   In veteribus scriptis neque mulieres Romanae per
2 Herculem deiurant neque viri per Castorem. Sed
cur illae non iuraverint Herculem non obscurum est,
3 nam Herculaneo sacrificio abstinent. Cur autem
viri Castorem iurantes non appellaverint non facile
dictu est. Nusquam igitur scriptum invenire est,
apud idoneos quidem scriptores, aut " me hercle "
4 feminam dicere aut " me castor " virum ; " edepol "
autem, quod iusiurandum per Pollucem est, et viro
5 et feminae commune est. Sed M. Varro adseverat

---

[1] cernantur, *Skutsch.*

---

[1] *Comprehendo* is used in a technical sense ; cf. Cic. *Acad.
Pr.* ii. 47, cum plane compresserat (manum) pugnumque

to something else " and seem to be such as their
appearance is while they are seen, and such as they
are formed by our senses, to which they come, not
by the things themselves, from which they have
proceeded. But although the Pyrronians and the
Academics express themselves very much alike about
these matters, yet they are thought to differ from
each other both in certain other respects and especially
for this reason—because the Academics do, as it were,
" comprehend "[1] the very fact that nothing can be
comprehended, and, as it were, decide that nothing
can be decided, while the Pyrronians assert that not
even that can by any means be regarded as true,
because nothing is regarded as true.

VI

That at Rome women did not swear by Hercules nor men by
Castor.

IN our early writings neither do Roman women
swear by Hercules nor the men by Castor. But
why the women did not swear by Hercules is
evident, since they abstain from sacrificing to
Hercules. On the other hand, why the men did not
name Castor in oaths is not easy to say. Nowhere,
then, is it possible to find an instance, among good
writers, either of a woman saying " by Hercules "
or a man, " by Castor "; but *edepol,* which is an
oath by Pollux, is common to both man and woman.
Marcus Varro, however, asserts[2] that the earliest

fecerat, comprehensionem illam esse dicebat ; also *Acad. Post.*
i. 11, where κατάληπτον is rendered by *comprehensio,* and
κατάληψιν by *rebus quae manu prenderentur.*

  [2] p. 375, Bipont.

antiquissimos viros neque per Castorem neque per
Pollucem deiurare solitos, sed id iusiurandum fuisse
tantum feminarum, ex initiis Eleusinis acceptum;
6 paulatim tamen inscitia antiquitatis viros dicere
"edepol" coepisse factumque esse ita dicendi
morem, sed "me castor" a viro dici in nullo vetere
scripto inveniri.

VII

Verbis antiquissimis relictisque iam et desitis minime
utendum.

1   VERBIS uti aut nimis obsoletis exculcatisque aut
insolentibus novitatisque durae et inlepidae, par esse
delictum videtur.   Sed molestius equidem culpatius-
que esse arbitror verba nova, incognita, inaudita
2 dicere quam involgata et sordentia.   Nova autem
videri dico etiam ea quae sunt inusitata et desita,
3 etsi sunt vetusta.   Est adeo id vitium plerumque
serae eruditionis, quam Graeci ὀψιμαθίαν appellant,
ut quod numquam [1] didiceris, diu ignoraveris, cum id
scire aliquando coeperis, magni facias quo in loco
cumque et quacumque in re dicere.   Veluti Romae,
nobis praesentibus, vetus celebratusque homo in
causis, sed repentina et quasi tumultuaria doctrina
praeditus, cum apud praefectum urbi verba faceret
et dicere vellet inopi quendam miseroque victu
vivere et furfureum panem esitare, vinumque eruc-

---

[1] antequam, *Casaubon.*

---

[1] Cf. Hor. *Ars. Poet.* 46 ff.

men were wont to swear neither by Castor nor by Pollux, but that this oath was used by women alone and was taken from the Eleusinian initiations; that gradually, however, through ignorance of ancient usage, men began to say *edepol,* and thus it became a customary expression; but that the use of "by Castor" by a man appears in no ancient writing.

VII

That very old words which have become antiquated and obsolete ought not to be used.

To use words that are too antiquated and worn out, or those which are unusual and of a harsh and unpleasant novelty, seems to be equally faulty. But for my own part I think it more offensive and censurable to use words that are new, unknown and unheard of, than those that are trite and mean. Furthermore, I maintain that those words also seem new which are out of use and obsolete, even though they are of ancient date.[1] In fact, it is a common fault of lately acquired learning, or ὀψιμαθία as the Greeks call it, to make a great point anywhere and everywhere, and in connection with any subject whatever, to talk about what you have never learned and of which you were long ignorant, when at last you have begun to know something about it. For instance, at Rome in my presence a man of experience and celebrated as a pleader, who had acquired a sudden and, so to speak, haphazard kind of education, was speaking before the prefect of the city and wished to say that a certain man lived upon poor and wretched food, ate bread made from bran,

315

tum et fetidum potare, " Hic," inquit, " eques
4 Romanus apludam edit et flocces bibit." Aspexe-
runt omnes qui aderant alius alium, primo tristiores
turbato et requirente voltu, quidnam illud utriusque
verbi foret ; post deinde, quasi nescio quid Tusce aut
5 Gallice dixisset, universi riserunt. Legerat autem
ille " apludam " veteres rusticos frumenti furfurem
dixisse idque a Plauto in comoedia, si ea Flauti est,
6 quae *Astraba* inscripta est, positum esse. Item
" flocces " audierat prisca voce significare vini faecem
e vinaceis expressam, sicuti fraces ex oleis, idque
aput Caecilium in *Polumenis* legerat, eaque sibi duo
verba ad orationum ornamenta servaverat.
7 Alter quoque a lectionibus id genus paucis apiro-
calus, cum adversarius causam differri postularet:
" Rogo, praetor," inquit, " subveni, succurre ! quonam
usque nos bovinator hic demoratur ? " Atque id
voce magna ter quaterve inclamavit : " bovinator
8 est." Commurmuratio fieri coepta est a plerisque
qui aderant, quasi monstrum verbi admirantibus.
9 At ille iactans et gestiens : " Non enim Lucilium,"
inquit, " legistis, qui tergiversatorem ' bovinatorem '
dicit ? " Est autem in Lucili XI. versus hic :

Si tricosus [1] bovinatorque ore improbus duro.

[1] hic stric(h)osus, ω ; *corrected by Lachmann* ; hic : est
tricosus, *Skutsch.*

---

[1] 14, Götz ; 16, Linds.
[2] The Πωλούμενοι, or " Men offered for sale."

and drank flat and spoiled wine: "This Roman knight," said he, "eats *apluda* and drinks *flocces*." All who were present looked at one another, at first somewhat seriously, with a disturbed and inquiring aspect, wondering what in the world the two words meant; then presently they all burst into a laugh, as if he had said something in Etruscan or Gallic. Now that man had read that the farmers of ancient days called the chaff of grain *apluda*, and that the word was used by Plautus in the comedy entitled *Astraba*,[1] if that play be the work of Plautus. He had also heard that *flocces* in the early language meant the lees of wine pressed from the skins of grapes, corresponding to the dregs of oil from olives. This he had read in the *Polumeni*[2] of Caecilius,[3] and he had saved up those two words as ornaments for his speeches.

Another *Einfaltspinsel* also, after some little reading of that kind, when his opponent requested that a case be postponed, said: "I pray you, praetor, help me, aid me! How long, pray, shall this *bovinator* delay me?" And he bawled it out three or four times in a loud voice: "He is a *bovinator*." A murmur began to arise from many of those who were present, as if in wonder at this monster of a word. But he, waving his arms and gesticulating, cried: "What, haven't you read Lucilius, who calls a shuffler *bovinator*?" And, in fact, this verse occurs in Lucilius' eleventh book:[4]

If trifling shuffler (*bovinator*) with abusive tongue.

[3] 190, Ribbeck[3].
[4] 417, Marx.

VIII

Quid senserit dixeritque M. Cato de Albino, qui homo
Romanus Graeca oratione res Romanas, venia sibi ante eius
imperitiae petita, composuit.

1 Iuste venusteque admodum reprehendisse dicitur
2 Aulum Albinum M. Cato. Albinus, qui cum L.
Lucullo consul fuit, res Romanas oratione Graeca
3 scriptitavit. In eius *Historiae* principio scriptum est
ad hanc sententiam : neminem suscensere sibi convenire, si quid in his libris parum composite aut
minus eleganter tum scriptum foret ; " nam sum,"
inquit, " homo Romanus natus in Latio, Graeca
oratio a nobis alienissima est," ideoque veniam
gratiamque malae existimationis, si quid esset erra-
4 tum, postulavit. Ea cum legisset M. Cato : " Ne
tu," inquit, " Aule, nimium nugator es, cum maluisti
culpam deprecari quam culpa vacare. Nam petere
veniam solemus, aut cum inprudentes erravimus aut
cum compulsi peccavimus. Dic," [1] inquit, " oro te,
quis perpulit ut id committeres, quod, priusquam
5 faceres, peteres ut ignosceretur ? " Scriptum hoc
est in libro Corneli Nepotis *De Inlustribus Viris*
XIII.

IX

Historia de legatis Mileti ac Demosthene rhetore in libris
Critolai reperta.

1 Critolaus scripsit legatos Mileto publicae rei
causa venisse Athenas, fortasse an auxilii petendi

[1] dic, *Hosius*; tibi, *MSS.*

---

[1] In 151 B.C.   [2] Fr. 1, Peter[2].

VIII

What Marcus Cato thought and said of Albinus, who, though
a Roman, wrote a history of Rome in the Greek language,
having first asked indulgence for his lack of skill in that
tongue.

MARCUS CATO is said to have rebuked Aulus
Albinus with great justice and neatness. Albinus,
who had been consul with Lucius Lucullus,[1] composed a *Roman History* in the Greek language. In
the introduction to his work he wrote to this effect:[2]
that no one ought to blame him if he had written
anything then in those books that was incorrect or
inelegant; "for," he continues, "I am a Roman, born
in Latium, and the Greek language is quite foreign
to me"; and accordingly he asked indulgence and
freedom from adverse criticism in case he had made
any errors. When Marcus Cato had read this,
"Surely, Aulus," said he, "you are a great trifler in
preferring to apologize for a fault rather than avoid
it. For we usually ask pardon either when we have
erred through inadvertence or done wrong under
compulsion. But tell me, I pray you," said he,
"who compelled you to do that for which you ask
pardon before doing it." This is told in the thirteenth book of Cornelius Nepos' work *On Famous
Men*.[3]

IX

The story of the Milesian envoys and the orator Demosthenes,
found in the works of Critolaus.

CRITOLAUS has written[4] that envoys came from
Miletus to Athens on public business, perhaps for

[3] Fr. 15, Peter².   [4] *F. H. G.* iv. 373.

gratia.[1] Tum qui pro sese verba facerent quos
visum erat advocavisse, advocatos, uti erat mandatum, verba pro Milesiis ad populum fecisse, Demosthenen Milesiorum postulatis acriter respondisse,
neque Milesios auxilio dignos neque ex republica id
esse contendisse ; rem in posterum diem prolatam.
Legatos ad Demosthenen venisse magnoque opere
orasse uti contra ne diceret ; eum pecuniam petivisse
et quantam petiverat abstulisse. Postridie, cum res
agi denuo coepta esset, Demosthenen, lana multa
collum cervicesque circumvolutum, ad populum
prodisse et dixisse se synanchen pati, eo contra
Milesios loqui non quire. Tum e populo unum
exclamasse, non " synanchen," quod Demosthenes
pateretur, sed " argyranchen " esse.

2   Ipse etiam Demosthenes, ut idem Critolaus refert,
non id postea concelavit, quin gloriae quoque hoc
sibi adsignavit. Nam cum interrogasset Aristo-
demum, actorem fabularum, quantum mercedis, uti
ageret, accepisset, et Aristodemus " talentum"
respondisset, "At ego plus," inquit, " accepi, ut
tacerem."

X

Quod C. Gracchus in oratione sua historiam supra scriptam
   Demadi rhetori, non Demostheni, adtribuit ; verbaque
   ipsius C. Gracchi relata.

1   Quod in capite superiore a Critolao scriptum esse
diximus super Demosthene, id C. Gracchus in ora-

---

[1] fortasse an dixerit, *MSS.* ; dixerit *deleted by Scaliger,*
fortasse . . . gratia, *by Heitz.*

---

[1] Ps.-Plutarch, *Decem Orat. Vitae, Demosth.,* p. 848, B, says
that the actor was Polos. Famous actors made large sums

the purpose of asking aid. Then they engaged
such advocates as they chose, to speak for them,
and the advocates, according to their instructions,
addressed the people in behalf of the Milesians.
Demosthenes vigorously opposed the demands of the
Milesians, maintaining that the Milesians did not
deserve aid, nor was it to the interest of the State to
grant it. The matter was postponed to the next day.
The envoys came to Demosthenes and begged him
earnestly not to speak against them; he asked for
money, and received the amount which he demanded.
On the following day, when the case was taken up
again, Demosthenes, with his neck and shoulders
wrapped in thick wool, came forward before the people
and said that he was suffering from quinsy and hence
could not speak against the Milesians. Then one of
the populace cried out that it was, not quinsy, but
"silverinsy" from which Demosthenes was suffering.

Demosthenes himself too, as Critolaus also relates,
did not afterwards conceal that matter, but actually
made a boast of it. For when he had asked Aristodemus, the player, what sum he had received for
acting, and Aristodemus[1] had replied, "a talent,"
Demosthenes rejoined : "Why, I got more than that
for holding my tongue."

X

That Gaius Gracchus in a speech of his applied the story
related above to the orator Demades, and not to Demosthenes ; and a quotation of Gracchus' words.

THE story which in the preceding chapter we said
was told by Critolaus about Demosthenes, Gaius

of money ; according to Pliny, *N. H.* vii. 129, the celebrated
Roman actor Roscius made 500,000 sesterces yearly.

tione, *Qua legem Aufeiam dissuasit,* in Demaden
2 contulit verbis hisce : " Nam vos, Quirites, si velitis
sapientia atque virtute uti, etsi quaeritis, neminem
nostrum invenietis sine pretio huc prodire. Omnes
nos qui verba facimus aliquid petimus, neque ullius
rei causa quisquam ad vos prodit, nisi ut aliquid
3 auferat. Ego ipse, qui aput vos verba facio uti
vectigalia vestra augeatis, quo facilius vestra com-
moda et rempublicam administrare possitis, non
gratis prodeo ; verum peto a vobis, non pecuniam,
4 sed bonam existimationem atque honorem. Qui
prodeunt dissuasuri ne hanc legem accipiatis, petunt
non honorem a vobis, verum a Nicomede pecuniam ;
qui suadent ut accipiatis, hi quoque petunt non a
vobis bonam existimationem, verum a Mitridate rei
familiari suae pretium et praemium ; qui autem ex
eodem loco atque ordine tacent, hi vel acerrimi
sunt, nam ab omnibus pretium accipiunt et omnis
5 fallunt. Vos, cum putatis eos ab his rebus remotos
6 esse, inpertitis bonam existimationem ; legationes
autem a regibus, cum putant eos sua causa reticere,
sumptus atque pecunias maximas praebent, item uti
in terra Graecia, quo in tempore Graecus tragoedus
gloriae sibi ducebat talentum magnum ob unam
fabulam datum esse, homo eloquentissimus civitatis
suae Demades ei respondisse dicitur : ' Mirum tibi
videtur, si tu loquendo talentum quaesisti ? Ego, ut
tacerem, decem talenta a rege accepi.' Item nunc
isti pretia maxima ob tacendum accipiunt." •

---

[1] *O. R. F.,* p. 242, Meyer[2].

Gracchus, in the speech *Against the Aufeian Law*, applied to Demades in the following words : [1] " For you, fellow citizens, if you wish to be wise and honest, and if you inquire into the matter, will find that none of us comes forward here without pay. All of us who address you are after something, and no one appears before you for any purpose except to carry something away. I myself, who am now recommending you to increase your taxes, in order that you may the more easily serve your own advantage and administer the government, do not come here for nothing ; but I ask of you, not money, but honour and your good opinion. Those who come forward to persuade you not to accept this law, do not seek honour from you, but money from Nicomedes ; those also who advise you to accept it are not seeking a good opinion from you, but from Mithridates a reward and an increase of their possessions ; those, however, of the same rank and order who are silent are your very bitterest enemies, since they take money from all and are false to all. You, thinking that they are innocent of such conduct, give them your esteem ; but the embassies from the kings, thinking it is for their sake that they are silent, give them great gifts and rewards. So in the land of Greece, when a Greek tragic actor boasted that he had received a whole talent for one play, Demades, the most eloquent man of his country, is said to have replied to him : ' Does it seem wonderful to you that you have gained a talent by speaking? I was paid ten talents by the king for holding my tongue.' Just so, these men now receive a very high price for holding their tongues."

XI

Verba P. Nigidii, quibus differre dicit "mentiri" et "mendacium dicere."

1 VERBA sunt ipsa haec P. Nigidii, hominis in studiis
bonarum artium praecellentis, quem M. Cicero
ingenii doctrinarumque nomine summe reveritus
est : " Inter mendacium dicere et mentiri distat.
Qui mentitur ipse non fallitur, alterum fallere
conatur ; qui mendacium dicit, ipse fallitur." Item
2 hoc addidit : " Qui mentitur," inquit, " fallit, quantum in se est ; at qui mendacium dicit, ipse non
3 fallit, quantum in se est." Item hoc quoque super
eadem re dicit : " Vir bonus," inquit, " praestare
debet ne mentiatur, prudens, ne mendacium dicat ;
4 alterum incidit in hominem, alterum non." Varie
me hercule et lepide Nigidius tot sententias in
eandem rem, quasi aliud atque aliud diceret, dis-
paravit.

XII

Quod Chrysippus philosophus omne verbum ambiguum
dubiumque esse dicit, Diodorus contra nullum verbum
ambiguum esse putat.

1 CHRYSIPPUS ait omne verbum ambiguum natura
esse, quoniam ex eodem duo vel plura accipi possunt.
2 Diodorus autem, cui Crono cognomentum fuit,
" Nullum," inquit, " verbum est ambiguum, nec
quisquam ambiguum dicit aut sentit, nec aliud dici

---

[1] Fr. 49, Swoboda.   [2] ii. 152, Arn.

XI

The words of Publius Nigidius, in which he says that there is a difference between "lying" and "telling a falsehood."

THESE are the very words of Publius Nigidius,[1] a man of great eminence in the pursuit of the liberal arts, whom Marcus Cicero highly respected because of his talent and learning: "There is a difference between telling a falsehood and lying. One who lies is not himself deceived, but tries to deceive another; he who tells a falsehood is himself deceived." He also adds this: "One who lies deceives, so far as he is able; but one who tells a falsehood does not himself deceive, any more than he can help." He also had this on the same subject: "A good man," says he, "ought to take pains not to lie, a wise man, not to tell what is false; the former affects the man himself, the latter does not." With variety, by Heaven! and neatness has Nigidius distinguished so many opinions relating to the same thing, as if he were constantly saying something new.

XII

That the philosopher Chrysippus says that every word is ambiguous and of doubtful meaning, while Diodorus, on the contrary, thinks that no word is ambiguous.

CHRYSIPPUS asserts[2] that every word is by nature ambiguous, since two or more things may be understood from the same word. But Diodorus, surnamed Cronus, says: "No word is ambiguous, and no one speaks or receives a word in two senses; and it ought not to seem to be said in any other sense than

videri debet quam quod se dicere sentit is qui dicit.
3 At cum ego," inquit, "aliud sensi, tu aliud accepisti, obscure magis dictum videri potest quam ambigue; ambigui enim verbi natura illa esse debuit, ut qui id diceret duo vel plura diceret. Nemo autem duo vel plura dicit, qui se sensit unum dicere."

XIII

Quid Titus Castricius de verbis deque sententia quadam C. Gracchi existimarit; quodque esse eam sine ullo sensus emolumento docuerit.

1 APUD Titum Castricium, disciplinae rhetoricae doctorem, gravi atque firmo iudicio virum, legebatur
2 oratio C. Gracchi *In P. Popilium*. In eius orationis principio conlocata verba sunt accuratius modulatius-
3 que quam veterum oratorum consuetudo fert. Ea verba, sicuti dixi conposita, haec sunt: "Quae vos cupide per hosce annos adpetistis atque voluistis, ea si temere repudiaritis, abesse non potest quin aut olim cupide adpetisse aut nunc temere repudiasse dicamini."
4 Cursus igitur hic et sonus rotundae volubilisque sententiae eximie nos et unice delectabat, tanto id magis, quod iam tunc C. Graccho, viro inlustri et severo, eiusmodi compositionem fuisse cordi videba-
5 mus. Sed enim, cum eadem ipsa verba saepius

---

[1] *O. R. F.*, p. 238, Meyer.

that which the speaker feels that he is giving to it. But when I," said he, "meant one thing and you have understood another, it may seem that I have spoken obscurely rather than ambiguously; for the nature of an ambiguous word should be such that he who speaks it expresses two or more meanings. But no man expresses two meanings who has felt that he is expressing but one."

XIII

What Titus Castricius thought about the wording of a sentence of Gaius Gracchus; and that he showed that it contributed nothing to the effectiveness of the sentence.

THE speech of Gaius Gracchus *Against Publius Popilius*[1] was read before Titus Castricius, a teacher of the art of rhetoric and a man of sound and solid judgment. At the beginning of that speech the sentences were constructed with more care and regard for rhythm than was customary with the early orators. The words, arranged as I have said, are as follows: "If you now reject rashly the things which all these years you have earnestly sought and longed for, it must be said either that you formerly sought them earnestly, or now have rejected them without consideration."

Well then, the flow and rhythm of this well-rounded and smooth-flowing sentence pleased us to a remarkable and unparalleled degree, and still more the evidence that composition of that kind appealed even in those early days to Gaius Gracchus, a man of distinction and dignity. But when those very same words were read again and again at our request, we

petentibus nobis lectitarentur, admoniti a Castricio
sumus ut consideraremus quae vis quodve emolu-
mentum eius sententiae foret, neque pateremur ut
aures nostrae cadentis apte orationis modis eblandi-
tae animum quoque nobis voluptate inani per-
funderent.

Cumque nos admonitione ista adtentiores fecisset,
"Inspicite," inquit, "penitus quid efficiant verba
haec, dicatque mihi, quaeso, aliqui vestrum, an sit
ulla huiusce sententiae gravitas aut gratia: 'Quae
vos cupide per hosce annos adpetistis atque voluistis,
ea si temere repudiaritis, abesse non potest quin aut
olim cupide adpetisse aut nunc temere repudiasse
6 dicamini.' Cui enim omnium hominum in mentem
non venit id profecto usu venire, ut quod cupide
adpetieris, cupide adpetisse et quod temere repudi-
7 averis, temere repudiasse dicaris? At si, opinor,"
inquit, "ita scriptum esset: 'Quae vos per hosce
annos adpetistis atque voluistis, ea nunc si repudiaritis, abesse non potest quin aut olim cupide adpetisse
8 aut nunc temere repudiasse dicamini'; si ita," inquit,
"diceretur, gravior scilicet solidiorque fieret sententia
et acciperet aliquid iustae in audiendo expectationis;
9 nunc autem verba haec 'cupide' et 'temere,' in
quibus verbis omne momentum rei est, non in con-
cludenda sententia tantum dicuntur, sed supra quoque nondum desiderata ponuntur et quae nasci
oririque ex ipsa rei conceptione debebant, ante
omnino quam res postulat dicuntur. Nam qui ita
dicit: 'si hoc feceris, cupide fecisse diceris,' rem

were admonished by Castricius to consider what the force and value of the thought was, and not to allow our ears to be charmed by the rhythm of a well-turned sentence and through mere pleasure to confuse our judgment as well.

And when by this admonition he had made us more alert, "Look deeply," said he, "into the meaning of these words, and tell me pray, some of you, whether there is any weight or elegance in this sentence : ' If you rashly reject the things which all these years you have earnestly sought and longed for, it must be said either that you formerly sought them earnestly or now reject them without consideration.' For to whom of all men does it not occur, that it is certainly natural that you should be said earnestly to have sought what you earnestly sought, and to have rejected without consideration what you rejected without consideration? But I think," said he, "if it had been written thus : ' If you now reject what you have sought and longed for these many years, it must be said that you formerly sought it earnestly or that you now reject it without consideration '; if," said he, "it were spoken thus, the sentence would be weightier and more solid and would arouse some reasonable expectation in the hearer; but as it is, these words 'earnestly' and 'without consideration,' on which the whole effect of the sentence rests, are not only spoken at the end of the sentence, but are also put earlier where they are not needed, so that what ought to arise and spring from the very conception of the subject is spoken wholly before the subject demands it. For one who says : ' If you do this, you will be said to have done it earnestly,' says something that is composed and

dicit sensus alicuius ratione conlectam et consertam ;
qui vero ita dicit : ' si cupide feceris, cupide fecisse
diceris,' non longe secus dicit atque si diceret : ' si
10 cupide feceris, cupide feceris.'   Haec ego," inquit,
" admonui, non ut C. Graccho vitio darem,—dii
enim mentem meliorem mihi ! nam, si quicquam in
tam fortis facundiae viro vitii vel erroris esse dici
potest, id omne et auctoritas eius exhausit et
vetustas consumpsit,—sed uti caveretis ne vos facile
praestringeret modulatus aliqui currentis facundiae
sonitus atque ut vim ipsam rerum virtutemque verborum prius pensitaretis et, si quidem gravis atque
integra et sincera sententia diceretur, tum, si ita
videretur, gressibus quoque ipsis orationis[1] et gesti-
bus plauderetis ; si vero frigidi et leves et futtiles
sensus in verba apte numeroseque posita includeren·
tur, non esse id secus crederetis quam cum homines
insigni deformitate ac facie deridicula imitantur
histriones et gestiunt."

XIV

Sobria et pulcherrima Romuli regis responsio circa vini
usum.

1   SIMPLICISSIMA suavitate et rei et orationis L. Piso
Frugi usus est in primo *Annali,* cum de Romuli regis
2 vita atque victu scriberet.   Ea verba, quae scripsit,
haec sunt : " Eundem Romulum dicunt, ad cenam

---

[1] oratoris, *Eussner.*

arranged with some regard to sense; but one who says: 'If you do it earnestly, you will be said to have done it earnestly,' speaks in much the same way as if he should say: 'If you do it earnestly, you will do it earnestly.' I have warned you of this," said he, " not with the idea of censuring Gaius Gracchus—may the gods give me a wiser mind! for if any fault or error can be mentioned in a man of such powerful eloquence, it is wholly excused by his authority and overlooked in view of his antiquity—but in order that you might be on your guard lest the rhythmic sound of any flowing eloquence should easily dazzle you, and that you might first balance the actual weight of the substance against the high quality of the diction; so that if any sentence was uttered that was weighty, honest and sound, then, if you thought best, you might praise also the mere flow of the language and the delivery; that if, on the contrary, thoughts that were cold, trifling and futile should be conveyed in words neatly and rhythmically arranged, they might have the same effect upon you as when men conspicuous for their deformity and their ludicrous appearance imitate actors and play the buffoon."

XIV

The discreet and admirable reply of King Romulus as to his use of wine.

Lucius Piso Frugi has shown an elegant simplicity of diction and thought in the first book of his *Annals*, when writing of the life and habits of King Romulus. His words are as follows:[1] "They say also of

---

[1] Fr. 8, Peter.

vocatum, ibi non multum bibisse, quia postridie negotium haberet. Ei dicunt: 'Romule, si istud omnes homines faciant, vinum vilius sit.' His respondit: 'immo vero carum, si quantum quisque volet bibat; nam ego bibi, quantum volui.'"

XV

De "ludibundo" et "errabundo" atque id genus verborum productionibus; et quod Laberius sic "amorabundam" dixit, ut dicitur "ludibunda" et "errabunda"; atque inibi quod Sisenna per huiuscemodi verbum nova figura usus est.

1 LABERIUS in *Lacu Averno* mulierem amantem,
2 verbo inusitatius ficto, "amorabundam" dixit. Id verbum Caesellius Vindex in *Commentario Lectionum Antiquarum* ea figura scriptum dixit, qua "ludibunda" et "ridibunda" et "errabunda" dicitur
3 "ludens" et "ridens" et "errans." Terentius autem Scaurus, divi Hadriani temporibus grammaticus vel nobilissimus, inter alia quae *De Caeselli Erroribus* conposuit, in hoc quoque verbo errasse eum scripsit, quod idem esse putaverit "ludens" et "ludibunda," "ridens" et "ridibunda," "errans" et "errabunda." "Nam 'ludibunda,'" inquit, "et 'ridibunda' et 'errabunda' ea dicitur quae ludentem vel ridentem vel errantem agit aut simulat."
4 Sed qua ratione Scaurus adductus sit ut Caesellium in eo reprehenderet, non hercle reperiebamus. Non est enim dubium quin haec, genere ipso dum-

---

[1] That is, his table companions.

Romulus, that being invited to dinner, he drank but little there, giving the reason that he had business for the following day. They [1] answer: 'If all men were like you, Romulus, wine would be cheaper.' 'Nay, dear,' answered Romulus, 'if each man drank as much as he wished; for I drank as much as I wished.' "

XV

On *ludibundus* and *errabundus* and the suffix in words of that kind; that Laberius used *amorabunda* in the same way as *ludibunda* and *errabunda*; also that Sisenna in the case of a word of that sort made a new form.

LABERIUS in his *Lake Avernus* spoke [2] of a woman in love as *amorabunda,* coining a word in a somewhat unusual manner. Caesellius Vindex in his *Commentary on Archaic Words* said that this word was used on the same principle that *ludibunda, ridibunda* and *errabunda* are used for *ludens, ridens* and *errans.* But Terentius Scaurus, a highly distinguished grammarian of the time of the deified Hadrian, among other things which he wrote *On the Mistakes of Caesellius,* declared [3] that about this word also he was wrong in thinking that *ludens* and *ludibunda, ridens* and *ridibunda, errans* and *errabunda* were identical. " For *ludibunda, ridibunda,* and *errabunda,*" he says, " are applied to one who plays the part of, or imitates, one who plays, laughs or wanders."

But why Scaurus was led to censure Caesellius on this point, I certainly could not understand. For there is no doubt that these words, each after its

---

[2] 57, Ribbeck[3].   [3] Fr. 9, Kummrow.

taxat, idem significent quod ea demonstrant a quibus producuntur. Quid esset autem ludentem agere vel imitari non intellegere videri maluimus quam insimulare eum tamquam ipsum minus intellegentem.

5 Quin magis Scaurum oportuit, commentaria Caeselli criminantem, hoc ab eo praeteritum requirere, quod non dixerit an quid et quantulum differret a " ludibundo " " ludens " et " ridibundo " " ridens " et " errabundo " " errans " ceteraque quae horum sunt similia, an a principalibus verbis paulum aliquid distarent, et quam omnino vim haberet particula
6 haec extrema eiusmodi vocabulis addita. Hoc enim fuit potius requirendum in istiusmodi figurae tractatu, sicuti requiri solet in " vinulento " et " lutulento " et " turbulento," vacuane et inanis sit istaec productio, cuiusmodi sunt quae παραγωγάς Graeci dicunt, an extrema illa particula habeat aliquid suae propriae significationis.

7 Cum reprehensionem autem illam Scauri notaremus, in memoriam nobis rediit quod Sisenna in quarto *Historiarum* eiusdem figurae verbo ita usus est. " Populabundus," inquit, " agros ad oppidum pervenit," quod scilicet significat " cum agros popularetur," non, ut Scaurus in consimilibus verbis ait, " cum populantem ageret " vel " cum imitaretur."

8 Sed inquirentibus nobis quaenam ratio et origo esset huiuscemodi figurae " populabundus " et " errabundus " et " laetabundus " et " ludibundus " multorumque aliorum id genus verborum, εὐεπιβόλως hercle Apollinaris noster videri sibi ait particulam istam postremam in quam verba talia exeunt vim et copiam et quasi abundantiam rei cuius id verbum

---

[1] That is, " an addition to the end of a syllable."
[2] Fr. 55, Peter.

own kind, have the same meaning that is indicated
by the words from which they are derived. But I
should prefer to seem not to understand the meaning
of "act the laugher" or "imitate the laugher"
rather than charge Scaurus himself with lack of
knowledge. But Scaurus ought rather, in censuring
the commentaries of Caesellius, to have taken him
to task for what he left unsaid; namely, whether
ludibundus, ridibundus and *errabundus* differ at all from
ludens, ridens and *errans,* and to what extent, and so
with other words of the same kind; whether they
differ only in some slight degree from their primi-
tives, and what is the general force of the suffix which
is added to words of that kind. For in examining a
phenomenon of that nature that were a more pertinent
inquiry, just as in *vinulentus, lutulentus* and *turbulentus*
it is usual to ask whether that suffix is superfluous
and without meaning, παραγωγή, as the Greeks say,[1]
or whether the suffix has some special force of its own.

However, in noting this criticism of Scaurus it
occurred to me that Sisenna, in the fourth book of
his *Histories,* used a word of the same form. He
says:[2] "He came to the town, laying waste the
fields (*populabundus*)," which of course means "while
he was laying waste the fields," not, as Sisenna says
of similar words, "when he played the part of, or
imitated, one laying waste."

But when I was inquiring about the signification and
origin of such forms as *populabundus, errabundus, laetabundus, ludibundus,* and many other words of that kind,
our friend Apollinaris—very appositely by Heaven!
—remarked that it seemed to him that the final
syllable of such words indicated force and abundance,
and as it were, an excess of the quality belonging to

335

esset demonstrare, ut " laetabundus " is dicatur qui abunde laetus sit, et " errabundus," qui longo atque abundanti errore sit, ceteraque omnia ex ea figura ita dici ostendit, ut productio haec et extremitas largam et fluentem vim et copiam declararet.

XVI

Quod Graecorum verborum quorundam difficillima est in Latinam linguam mutatio, velut quod Graece dicitur πολυ-πραγμοσύνη.

1 ADIECIMUS saepe animum ad vocabula rerum non paucissima quae neque singulis verbis, ut a Graecis, neque, si maxime pluribus eas res verbis dicamus, tam dilucide tamque apte demonstrari Latina oratione

2 possunt quam Graeci ea dicunt privis vocibus. Nuper etiam cum adlatus esset ad nos Plutarchi liber et eius libri indicem legissemus, qui erat Περὶ Πολυ-πραγμοσύνης, percontanti cuipiam qui et litterarum et vocum Graecarum expers fuit cuiusnam liber et qua de re scriptus esset, nomen quidem scriptoris statim diximus, rem de qua scriptum[1] fuit dicturi,

3 haesimus. Ac tum quidem primo, quia non satis commode opinabar interpretaturum me[2] esse, si dicerem librum scriptum " De Negotiositate," aliud institui aput me exquirere, quod, ut dicitur, verbum

4 de verbo expressum esset. Nihil erat prorsus quod

---

[1] scriptus, *J. Gronov.*   [2] me *added by Hertz.*

---

[1] In general these words in-*bundus* have the same force as the pres. participle; the intensive force in a few words

the primitive word. Thus *laetabundus* is used of one who is excessively joyful, and *errabundus* of one who has wandered long and far, and he showed that all other words of that form are so used that this addition and ending indicates a great and overflowing force and abundance.[1]

XVI

That the translation of certain Greek words into the Latin language is very difficult, for example, that which in Greek is called πολυπραγμοσύνη.[2]

WE have frequently observed not a few names of things which we cannot express in Latin by single words, as in Greek; and even if we use very many words, those ideas cannot be expressed in Latin so aptly and so clearly as the Greeks express them by single terms. Lately, when a book of Plutarch had been brought to me, and I had read its title, which was Περὶ Πολυπραγμοσύνης, a man who was unacquainted with Greek letters and words asked who the author was and what the book was about. The name of the writer I gave him at once, but I hesitated when on the point of naming the subject of the work. At first indeed, since it did not seem to me that it would be a very apt interpretation if I said that it was written *De Negotiositate* or "On Busyness," I began to rack my brains for something else which would render the title word for word, as the saying is. But there was absolutely nothing that

comes originally from forms like *versabundus*, formed from intensive verbs. See Stolz, *Hist. Lat. Gr.* i, p. 570.

[2] The word means "being busy about many things," often with the idea of "officiousness" or "meddling."

aut meminissem legere me aut, si etiam vellem
fingere, quod non insigniter asperum absurdumque
esset, si[1] ex multitudine et negotio verbum unum
compingerem, sicuti " multiiuga " dicimus et " mul-
5 ticolora " et " multiformia." Sed non minus inlepide
ita diceretur quam si interpretari voce una velis
6 πολυφιλίαν aut πολυτροπίαν aut πολυσαρκίαν. Quamobrem, cum diutule tacitus in cogitando fuissem,
respondi tandem non videri mihi significari eam rem
posse uno nomine, et idcirco iuncta oratione quid
vellet Graecum id verbum parabam[2] dicere.

" Ad multas igitur res adgressio earumque omnium
rerum actio πολυπραγμοσύνη," inquam, " Graece dicitur, de qua hunc librum conpositum esse, inscriptio
7 ista indicat." Tum ille opicus, verbis meis inchoatis
et inconditis adductus virtutemque esse πολυπραγ-
μοσύνην ratus,[3] " Hortatur," inquit, " nos profecto
nescio quis hic Plutarchus ad negotia capessenda et
ad res obeundas plurimas cum industria et celeritate,
nomenque ipsius virtutis de qua locuturus esset libro
ipsi, sicuti dicis, non incommode praescripsit."
8 " Minime," inquam, " vero ; neque enim ista omnino
virtus est, cuius Graeco nomine argumentum hoc
libri demonstratur, neque id quod tu opinare aut
ego me dicere sentio aut Plutarchus facit. Deterret
enim nos hoc quidem in libro, quam potest maxime,
a varia[4] promiscaque et non necessaria rerum cuius-

---

[1] velut si, *Skutsch.*
[2] parabam, *Skutsch* ; pararam, *MSS.*
[3] ratus, *Bentley* ; iratus, *QZ* ; tratus, *B* ; *omitted by* γ.
[4] a varia, ς ; avaritia (-cia), ω.

I remembered to have read, or even that I could invent, that was not to a degree harsh and absurd, if I fashioned a single word out of *multitudo*, or " multitude," and *negotium*, or " business," in the same way that we say *multiiugus* (" manifold "), *multicolorus* (" multicoloured ") and *multiformius* (" multiform "). But it would be no less uncouth an expression than if you should try to translate by one word πολυφιλία (abundance of friends), πολυτροπία (versatility), or πολυσαρκία (fleshiness). Therefore, after spending a brief time in silent thought, I finally answered that in my opinion the idea could not be expressed by a single word, and accordingly I was preparing to indicate the meaning of that Greek word by a phrase.

" Well then," said I, " undertaking many things and busying oneself with them all is called in Greek πολυπραγμοσύνη, and the title shows that this is the subject of our book." Then that illiterate fellow, misled by my unfinished, rough-and-ready language and believing that πολυπραγμοσύνη was a virtue, said : " Doubtless this Plutarch, whoever he is, urges us to engage in business and to undertake very many enterprises with energy and dispatch, and properly enough he has written as the title of the book itself the name of this virtue about which, as you say, he is intending to speak." " Not at all," said I ; " for that is by no means a virtue which, expressed by a Greek term, serves to indicate the subject of this book ; and neither does Plutarch do what you suppose, nor do I intend to say that he did. For, as a matter of fact, it is in this book that he tries to dissuade us, so far as he can, from the haphazard, promiscuous and unnecessary planning and pursuit

9 cemodi plurimarum et cogitatione et petitione. Sed huius," inquam, "tui erroris culpam esse intellego in mea scilicet infacundia, qui ne pluribus quidem verbis potuerim non obscurissime dicere quod a Graecis perfectissime verbo uno et planissime dicitur."

XVII

Quid significet in veteribus praetorum edictis : " qui flumina retanda publice redempta habent."

1 EDICTA veterum praetorum sedentibus forte nobis in bibliotheca templi Traiani et aliud quid quaerentibus cum in manus incidissent, legere atque co-
2 gnoscere libitum est. Tum in quodam edicto antiquiore ita scriptum invenimus : " Qui flumina retanda publice redempta habent, si quis eorum ad me eductus fuerit, qui dicatur quod eum ex lege loca-
3 tionis facere oportuerit non fecisse." " Retanda " igitur quid esset quaerebatur.

4 Dixit ibi quispiam nobiscum sedens amicus meus in libro se Gavi *De Origine Vocabulorum VII.* legisse, " retas " vocari arbores quae aut ripis fluminum eminerent aut in alveis eorum extarent, appellatasque esse a retibus, quod praetereuntes naves inpedirent et quasi inretirent ; idcircoque sese arbitrari, " retanda "

---

[1] The *Bibliotheca Ulpia* in the temple in Trajan's forum. Other great public libraries at Rome were in Vespasian's temple of Peace (see v. 21. 9 and the note), in Augustus' temple of Apollo on the Palatine hill, and in the *porticus Octariae.* The first public library at Rome was founded by Asinius Pollio.

of such a multitude of things. But," said I, " I realize that this mistake of yours is due to my imperfect command of language, since even in so many words I could not express otherwise than very obscurely what in Greek is expressed with perfect elegance and clearness by a single term."

XVII

The meaning of the expression found in the old praetorian edicts : " those who have undertaken public contracts for clearing the rivers of nets."

As I chanced to be sitting in the library of Trajan's temple,[1] looking for something else, the edicts of the early praetors fell into my hands, and I thought it worth while to read and become acquainted with them. Then I found this, written in one of the earlier edicts : " If anyone of those who have taken public contracts for clearing the rivers of nets shall be brought before me, and shall be accused of not having done that which by the terms of his contract he was bound to do." Thereupon the question arose what "clearing of nets" meant.

Then a friend of mine who was sitting with us said that he had read in the seventh book of Gavius *On the Origin of Words*[2] that those trees which either projected from the banks of rivers, or were found in their beds, were called *retae*, and that they got their name from nets, because they impeded the course of ships and, so to speak, netted them. Therefore he thought that the custom was to farm

[2] Fr. 2, Fun.; *Jur. Civ.* 126, Bremer.

flumina locari solita esse, id est purganda, ne quid
aut morae aut periculi navibus in ea virgulta inciden-
tibus fieret.

XVIII

Qua poena Draco Atheniensis, in legibus quas populo Athe-
niensi scripsit, fures adfecerit ; et qua postea Solon ; et
qua item decemviri nostri, qui *Duodecim Tabulas* scripserunt ; atque inibi adscriptum quod aput Aegyptios furta
licita et permissa sunt, aput Lacedaemonios autem cum
studio quoque adfectata et pro exercitio utili celebrata ;
ac praeterea M. Catonis de poeniendis furtis digna memoria
sententia.

1 DRACO Atheniensis vir bonus multaque esse
prudentia existimatus est iurisque divini et humani
2 peritus fuit. Is Draco leges, quibus Athenienses
3 uterentur, primus omnium tulit. In illis legibus
furem cuiusmodicumque furti supplicio capitis
poeniendum esse et alia pleraque nimis severe
censuit sanxitque.

4 Eius igitur leges, quoniam videbantur impendio
acerbiores, non decreto iussoque, set tacito inlittera-
toque Atheniensium consensu oblitteratae sunt.

5 Postea legibus aliis mitioribus, a Solone compositis,
usi sunt. Is Solon e septem illis inclutis sapientibus
fuit. Is sua lege in fures, non, ut Draco antea,
mortis, sed dupli poena vindicandum existimavit.

6 Decemviri autem nostri, qui post reges exactos
leges, quibus populus Romanus uteretur, in *XII.*
Tabulis scripserunt, neque pari severitate in poeni-

---

[1] See note 2, vol. i. p. 11.

out the rivers to be "cleaned of nets," that is to
say, cleaned out, in order that vessels meeting such
branches might suffer neither delay nor danger.

XVIII

The punishment which Draco the Athenian, in the laws
which he made for his fellow-citizens, inflicted upon
thieves ; that of Solon later ; and that of our own
decemvirs, who compiled the *Twelve Tables* ; to which it is
added, that among the Egyptians thefts were permitted
and lawful, while among the Lacedaemonians they were
even strongly encouraged and commended as a useful
exercise ; also a memorable utterance of Marcus Cato about
the punishment of theft.

Draco the Athenian was considered a good man
and of great wisdom, and he was skilled in law,
human and divine. This Draco was the first of all
to make laws for the use of the Athenians. In those
laws he decreed and enacted that one guilty of any
theft whatsoever should be punished with death, and
added many other statutes that were excessively
severe.

Therefore his laws, since they seemed very much
too harsh, were abolished, not by order and decree,
but by the tacit, unwritten consent of the Athenians.
After that, they made use of other, milder laws,
compiled by Solon. This Solon was one of the
famous seven wise men.[1] He thought proper by
his law to punish thieves, not with death, as Draco
had formerly done, but by a fine of twice the value
of the stolen goods.

But our decemvirs, who after the expulsion of the
kings compiled laws on *Twelve Tables* for the use of
the Romans, did not show equal severity in punish-

343

endis omnium generum furibus neque remissa nimis
7 lenitate usi sunt. Nam furem qui manifesto furto
prensus esset tum demum occidi permiserunt, si aut,
cum faceret furtum, nox esset, aut interdiu telo se,
8 cum prenderetur, defenderet. Ex ceteris autem
manifestis furibus liberos verberari addicique iusserunt ei cui furtum factum esset, si modo id luci
fecissent neque se telo defendissent; servos item
furti manifesti prensos verberibus adfici et e saxo
praecipitari, sed pueros inpuberes praetoris arbitratu
verberari voluerunt noxiamque ab his factam sarciri.
9 Ea quoque furta quae per lancem liciumque concepta essent, proinde ac si manifesta forent, vindicaverunt.
10   Sed nunc a lege illa decemvirali discessum est.
Nam si qui super manifesto furto iure et ordine
11 experiri velit, actio in quadruplum datur. "Manifestum" autem "furtum est," ut ait Masurius, "quod
deprehenditur dum fit. Faciendi finis est, cum
12 perlatum est quo ferri coeperat." Furti concepti,
item oblati, tripli poena est.
    Sed quod sit "oblatum," quod "conceptum," et
pleraque alia ad eam rem ex egregiis veterum
moribus accepta neque inutilia cognitu neque iniu-
cunda qui legere volet, inveniet Sabini librum cui
13 titulus est *De Furtis*. In quo id quoque scriptum

---

1 viii. 13 ff.
2 To be his bondsman, until the debt was paid.
3 That is, the Tarpeian Rock on the Capitoline Hill.
4 See Paul. Festus, pp. 104–5, Lindsay. The searchers
were clad only in a girdle, that they might not be suspected
of bringing anything in with them and saying that it had
been stolen, and they held a perforated plate before their
faces, because of the presence of the women of the household.

ing thieves of every kind, nor yet too lax leniency.
For they permitted[1] a thief who was caught in the
act to be put to death, only if it was night when he
committed the theft, or if in the daytime he defended himself with a weapon when taken. But
other thieves taken in the act, if they were freemen,
the decemvirs ordered to be scourged and handed
over[2] to the one from whom the theft had been made,
provided they had committed the theft in daylight
and had not defended themselves with a weapon.
Slaves taken in the act were to be scourged and
hurled from the rock,[3] but they decided that boys
under age should be flogged at the discretion of the
praetor and the damage which they had done made
good. Those thefts also which were detected by the
girdle and mask,[4] they punished as if the culprit had
been caught in the act.

But to-day we have departed from that law of the
decemvirs; for if anyone wishes to try a case of
manifest theft by process of law, action is brought
for four times the value. But "manifest theft," says
Masurius,[5] "is one which is detected while it is being
committed. The act is completed when the stolen
object is carried to its destination." When stolen
goods are found in possession of the thief (*concepti*)
or in that of another (*oblati*), the penalty is threefold.

But one who wishes to learn what *oblatum* means,
and *conceptum*, and many other particulars of the same
kind taken from the admirable customs of our forefathers, and both useful and agreeable to know, will
consult the book of Sabinus entitled *On Thefts*. In
this book there is also written[6] a thing that is not

[5] Fr. 7, Huschke ; *Jur. Civ.* 126, Bremer (ii, p. 517).
[6] Fr. 7, Huschke ; 3-5, Bremer (ii, p. 383).

est, quod volgo inopinatum est, non hominum
tantum neque rerum moventium, quae auferri occulte
et subripi possunt, sed fundi quoque et aedium fieri
furtum ; condemnatum quoque furti colonum, qui
fundo quem conduxerat vendito, possessione eius

14 dominum intervertisset. Atque id etiam, quod
magis inopinabile est, Sabinus dicit, furem esse
hominis iudicatum, qui cum fugitivus praeter oculos
forte domini iret, obtentu togae, tamquam se
amiciens, ne videretur a domino, obstitisset.

15   Aliis deinde furtis omnibus, quae " nec manifesta "
16 appellantur, poenam imposuerunt dupli. Id etiam
memini legere me in libro Aristonis iureconsulti,
hautquaquam indocti viri, aput veteres Aegyptios,
quod genus hominum constat et in artibus reperien-
dis sollertes extitisse et in cognitione rerum inda-
ganda sagaces, furta omnia fuisse licita et inpunita.

17   Aput Lacedaemonios quoque, sobrios illos et acres
viros, cuius rei non adeo ut Aegyptiis fides longinqua
est, non pauci neque ignobiles scriptores, qui de
moribus legibusque eorum memorias condiderunt,
ius atque usum fuisse furandi dicunt, idque a
iuventute eorum non ad turpia lucra neque ad
sumptum libidini praebendum comparandamve opu-
lentiam, sed pro exercitio disciplinaque rei bellicae
factitatum, quod et furandi sollertia et adsuetudo
acueret firmaretque animos adulescentium et ad
insidiarum astus et ad vigilandi tolerantiam et ad
obrependi celeritatem.

18   Sed enim M. Cato in oratione, quam *De Praeda*

---

1 *XII. Tab.* viii. 16.
2 Fr. 1, Huschke ; ii. 2, p. 393, Bremer.

commonly known, that thefts are committed, not only of men and movable objects which can be purloined and carried off secretly, but also of an estate and of houses; also that a farmer was found guilty of theft, because he had sold the farm which he had rented and deprived the owner of its possession. And Sabinus tells this also, which is still more surprising, that one person was convicted of having stolen a man, who, when a runaway slave chanced to pass within sight of his master, held out his gown as if he were putting it on, and so prevented the slave from being seen by his master.

Then upon all other thefts, which were called "not manifest," they imposed a two-fold penalty.[1] I recall also that I read in the work of the jurist Aristo,[2] a man of no slight learning, that among the ancient Egyptians, a race of men known to have been ingenious in inventions and keen in getting at the bottom of things, thefts of all kinds were lawful and went unpunished.

Among the Lacedaemonians too, those serious and vigorous men (a matter for which the evidence is not so remote as in the case of the Egyptians) many famous writers, who have composed records of their laws and customs, affirm that thieving was lawful and customary, and that it was practised by their young men, not for base gain or to furnish the means for indulgence or amassing wealth, but as an exercise and training in the art of war; for dexterity and practice in thieving made the minds of the youth keen and strong for clever ambuscades, and for endurance in watching, and for the swiftness of surprise.

Marcus Cato, however, in the speech which he

Militibus Dividenda scripsit, vehementibus et inlustribus verbis de inpunitate peculatus atque licentia
conqueritur. Ea verba, quoniam nobis inpense
placuerunt, adscripsimus : " Fures," inquit, " privato-
rum furtorum in nervo atque in compedibus aetatem
agunt, fures publici in auro atque in purpura."

19   Quam caste autem ac religiose a prudentissimis
viris quid esset "furtum" definitum sit, praeter-
eundum non puto, ne quis eum solum esse furem

20 putet, qui occulte tollit aut clam subripit. Verba sunt
Sabini ex libro *Iuris Civilis* secundo : " Qui alienam
rem adtrectavit, cum id se invito domino facere

21 iudicare deberet, furti tenetur." Item alio capite :
" Qui alienum tacens [1] lucri faciendi causa sustulit,
furti obstringitur, sive scit cuius sit, sive nescit."

22   Haec quidem sic, in eo quo nunc dixi, Sabinus

23 scripsit de rebus furti faciendi causa adtrectatis. Sed
meminisse debemus, secundum ea quae supra scripsi,
furtum sine ulla quoque adtrectatione fieri posse, sola

24 mente atque animo ut furtum fiat adnitente. Quocirca ne id quidem Sabinus [2] dubitare se ait, quin
dominus furti sit condemnandus qui servo suo uti
furtum faceret imperavit.

---

[1] alienum quid iacens, *Dig.* xlvii. 2. 43. 4.
[2] *Fr.* 4, *H* ; 127 Br.

---

[1] p. 69, 1, Jordan.
[2] Fr. 2, Huschke ; 113, Bremer (ii, p. 513).
[3] Fr. 3, Huschke ; 119, Bremer (ii, p. 515).
[4] Fr. 4, Huschke ; 127, Bremer.

wrote *On Dividing Spoils among the Soldiers*, complains in strong and choice language about unpunished thievery and lawlessness. I have quoted his words, since they pleased me greatly : [1] "Those who commit private theft pass their lives in confinement and fetters; plunderers of the public, in purple and gold."

But I think I ought not to pass over the highly ethical and strict definition of theft made by the wisest men, lest anyone should consider him only a thief who privately purloins anything or secretly carries it off. The words are those of Sabinus in his second book *On Civil Law* : [2] "He is guilty of theft who has touched anything belonging to another, when he has reason to know that he does so against the owner's will." Also in another chapter : [3] "He who silently carries off another's property for the sake of gain is guilty of theft, whether he knows to whom the object belongs or not."

Thus has Sabinus written, in the book which I just now mentioned, about handling things for the purpose of stealing them. But we ought to remember, according to what I have written above, that a theft may be committed even without touching anything, when the mind alone and the thoughts desire that a theft be committed. Therefore Sabinus says [4] that he has no doubt that a master should be convicted of theft who has ordered a slave of his to steal something.

BOOK XII

LIBER DUODECIMUS

I

Dissertatio Favorini philosophi, qua suasit nobili feminae uti liberos quos peperisset, non nutricum aliarum, sed sibi suo lacte aleret.

1 NUNTIATUM quondam est Favorino philosopho, nobis praesentibus, uxorem auditoris sectatorisque sui paululum ante enixam auctumque eum esse nato 2 filio. "Eamus," inquit, "et puerum visum et patri gratulatum."

3 Is erat loci senatorii, ex familia nobiliore. Imus una qui tum aderamus prosecutique eum sumus ad domum quo pergebat, et cum eo simul introgressi 4 sumus. Tum in primis aedibus complexus hominem congratulatusque adsedit. Atque ubi percontatus est quam diutinum puerperium et quam laboriosi nixus fuissent, puellamque defessam labore ac vigilia somnum capere cognovit, fabulari instituit prolixius et: "Nihil," inquit, "dubito quin filium lacte suo 5 nutritura sit." Sed cum mater puellae parcendum esse ei diceret adhibendasque puero nutrices, ne ad dolores quos in enitendo tulisset munus quoque nutricationis grave ac difficile accederet, "Oro te," inquit, "mulier, sine eam totam integram matrem

---

[1] The addition of a son to his family gave the father certain privileges.

BOOK XII

I

A discourse of the philosopher Favorinus, in which he urged a lady of rank to feed with her own milk, and not with that of other nurses, the children whom she had borne.

WORD was once brought in my presence to the philosopher Favorinus that the wife of an auditor and disciple of his had been brought to bed a short time before, and that his pupil's family had been increased by the birth of a son. "Let us go," said he, "both to see the child and to congratulate the father." [1]

The father was of senatorial rank and of a family of high nobility. We who were present at the time went with Favorinus, attended him to the house to which he was bound, and entered it with him. Then the philosopher, having embraced and congratulated the father immediately upon entering, sat down. And when he had asked how long the labour had been and how difficult, and had learned that the young woman, overcome with fatigue and wakefulness, was sleeping, he began to talk at greater length and said: "I have no doubt she will suckle her son herself!" But when the young woman's mother said to him that she must spare her daughter and provide nurses for the child, in order that to the pains which she had suffered in childbirth there might not be added the wearisome and difficult task of nursing, he said: "I beg you, madam, let her be wholly and

353

6 esse filii sui. Quod est enim hoc contra naturam inperfectum atque dimidiatum matris genus, peperisse ac statim a sese abiecisse ? aluisse in utero sanguine suo nescio quid quod non videret, non alere nunc suo lacte quod videat, iam viventem, iam

7 hominem, iam matris officia inplorantem ? An tu quoque," inquit, " putas naturam feminis mammarum ubera quasi quosdam venustiores naevulos, non liberum alendorum, sed ornandi pectoris causa

8 dedisse ? Sic enim, quod a vobis scilicet abest, pleraeque istae prodigiosae mulieres fontem illum sanctissimum corporis, generis humani educatorem, arefacere et extinguere cum periculo quoque aversi corruptique lactis laborant, tamquam pulcritudinis sibi insignia devenustet, quod quidem faciunt eadem vecordia, qua quibusdam commenticiis fraudibus nituntur ut fetus quoque ipsi, in corpore suo concepti, aboriantur, ne aequor illud ventris inrugetur ac de

9 gravitate oneris et labore partus fatiscat. Quod cum sit publica detestatione communique odio dignum, in ipsis hominem primordiis, dum fingitur, dum animatur, inter ipsas artificis naturae manus interfectum ire, quantulum hinc abest, iam perfectum, iam genitum, iam filium proprii atque consueti atque cogniti sanguinis alimonia privare ?

10 " ' Sed nihil interest,' hoc enim dicitur, ' dum
11 alatur et vivat, cuius id lacte fiat.' Cur igitur iste qui hoc dicit, si in capessendis naturae sensibus tam

entirely the mother of her own child. For what kind
of unnatural, imperfect and half-motherhood is it to
bear a child and at once send it away from her?
to have nourished in her womb with her own blood
something which she could not see, and not to feed
with her own milk what she sees, now alive, now
human, now calling for a mother's care? Or do
you too perhaps think," said he, "that nature gave
women nipples as a kind of beauty-spot, not for the
purpose of nourishing their children, but as an
adornment of their breast? For it is for that
reason (though such a thing is of course far from your
thoughts) that many of those unnatural women try
to dry up and check that sacred fount of the body,
the nourisher of mankind, regardless of the danger
of diverting and spoiling the milk, because they
think it disfigures the charms of their beauty. In
so doing they show the same madness as those who
strive by evil devices to cause abortion of the fetus
itself which they have conceived, in order that their
beauty may not be spoiled by the weight of the
burden they bear and by the labour of parturition.
But since it is an act worthy of public detestation
and general abhorrence to destroy a human being in
its inception, while it is being fashioned and given
life and is still in the hands of Dame Nature, how
far does it differ from this to deprive a child, already
perfect, already brought into the world, already a
son, of the nourishment of its own familiar and
kindred blood?

"'But it makes no difference,' for so they say,
'provided it be nourished and live, by whose milk
that is effected.' Why then does not he who affirms
this, if he is so dull in comprehending natural feel-

obsurduit, non id quoque nihil interesse putat, cuius
in corpore cuiusque ex sanguine concretus homo et
12 coalitus sit? an quia spiritu multo et calore exalbuit,
non idem sanguis est nunc in uberibus, qui in utero
13 fuit? Nonne hac quoque in re sollertia naturae
evidens est, quod, postquam sanguis ille opifex in
penetralibus suis omne corpus hominis finxit, adven-
tante iam partus tempore, in supernas se partis
perfert, ad fovenda vitae atque lucis rudimenta
praesto est et recens natis notum et familiarem
14 victum offert? Quamobrem non frustra creditum
est, sicut valeat ad fingendas corporis atque animi
similitudines vis et natura seminis, non secus ad
eandem rem lactis quoque ingenia et proprietates
15 valere. Neque in hominibus id solum, sed in pecu-
dibus quoque animadversum. Nam si ovium lacte
haedi aut caprarum agni alantur, constat ferme in
his lanam duriorem, in illis capillum gigni teneriorem.
16 In arboribus etiam et frugibus maior plerumque vis
et potestas est ad earum indolem vel detrectandam
vel augendam aquarum atque terrarum quae alunt,
quam ipsius quod iacitur seminis, ac saepe videas
arborem laetam et nitentem, in locum alium transpo-
17 sitam, deterioris terrae suco deperisse. Quae, malum,
igitur ratio est, nobilitatem istam nati modo hominis
corpusque et animum, bene ingeniatis primordiis in-
choatum, insitivo degenerique alimento lactis alieni
corrumpere? praesertim si ista quam ad praebendum
lactem adhibebitis, aut serva aut servilis est et, ut
plerumque solet, externae et barbarae nationis est,[1]
si inproba, si informis, si inpudica, si temulenta est;

---

[1] et si improba, *Damsté.*

ing, think that it also makes no difference in whose
body and from whose blood a human being is formed
and fashioned? Is the blood which is now in the
breasts not the same that it was in the womb, merely
because it has become white from abundant air and
warmth? Is not the wisdom of nature evident also
in this, that as soon as the blood, the artificer, has
fashioned the whole human body within its secret
precincts, when the time for birth comes, it rises into
the upper parts, is ready to cherish the first beginnings
of life and of light, and supplies the newborn children
with the familiar and accustomed food? Therefore
it is believed not without reason that, just as the
power and nature of the seed are able to form like-
nesses of body and mind, so the qualities and
properties of the milk have the same effect. And
this is observed not only in human beings, but in
beasts also; for if kids are fed on the milk of ewes,
or lambs on that of goats, it is a fact that as a rule
the wool is harsher in the former and the hair softer
in the latter. In trees too and grain the power and
strength of the water and earth which nourish them
have more effect in retarding or promoting their
growth than have those of the seed itself which is
sown; and you often see a strong and flourishing
tree, when transplanted to another spot, die from
the effect of an inferior soil. What the mischief, then,
is the reason for corrupting the nobility of body and
mind of a newly born human being, formed from
gifted seeds, by the alien and degenerate nourishment
of another's milk? Especially if she whom you
employ to furnish the milk is either a slave or of
servile origin and, as usually happens, of a foreign
and barbarous nation, if she is dishonest, ugly,

nam plerumque sine discrimine, quaecumque id temporis lactans est adhiberi solet.

18 "Patiemurne igitur infantem hunc nostrum pernicioso contagio infici et spiritum ducere in animum atque in corpus suum ex corpore et animo deterrimo?

19 Id hercle ipsum est quod saepenumero miramur, quosdam pudicarum mulierum liberos parentum suorum neque corporibus neque animis similes

20 existere. Scite igitur et perite noster Maro, quod, cum versus illos Homeri consectaretur :

οὐκ ἄρα σοί γε πατὴρ ἦν ἱππότα Πηλεύς,
Οὐδὲ Θέτις μήτηρ· γλαυκὴ δέ σε τίκτε θάλασσα
Πέτραι τ' ἠλίβατοι, ὅτι τοι νόος ἐστὶν ἀπηνής,[1]

non partionem solam, tamquam ille quem sequebatur, sed alituram quoque feram et saevam criminatus est ; addidit enim hoc de suo :

Hyrcanaeque admorunt ubera tigres,[2]

quoniam videlicet in moribus inolescendis magnam fere partem ingenium altricis et natura lactis tenet, quae iam a principio imbuta paterni seminis concretione, ex matris etiam corpore et animo recentem indolem configurat.

21 "Et praeter haec autem, quis illud etiam neglegere aspernarique possit, quod quae partus suos deserunt ablegantque a sese et aliis nutriendos dedunt, vinculum illud coagulumque animi atque amoris, quo parentes cum filiis natura consociat, interscin-

---

[1] *Iliad* xvi. 33 ff.   [2] *Aen.* iv. 366 f.

unchaste and a wine-bibber; for as a rule anyone
who has milk at the time is employed and no
distinction made.

" Shall we then allow this child of ours to be infected
with some dangerous contagion and to draw a spirit
into its mind and body from a body and mind of the
worst character? This, by Heaven! is the very
reason for what often excites our surprise, that some
children of chaste women turn out to be like their
parents neither in body nor in mind. Wisely then
and skilfully did our Maro make use of these lines
of Homer :[1]

> The horseman Peleus never was thy sire,
> Nor Thetis gave thee birth; but the gray sea
> Begat thee, and the hard and flinty rocks ;
> So savage is thy mind.

For he bases his charge, not upon birth alone, as
did his model, but on fierce and savage nurture,
for his next verse reads :

> And fierce Hyrcanian tigers gave thee suck.[2]

And there is no doubt that in forming character the
disposition of the nurse and the quality of the milk
play a great part; for the milk, although imbued from
the beginning with the material of the father's seed,
forms the infant offspring from the body and mind
of the mother as well.

" And in addition to all this, who can neglect or
despise this consideration also, that those who
desert their offspring, drive them from them, and
give them to others to nurse, do sever, or at any rate
loosen and relax, that bond and cementing of the
mind and of affection with which nature attaches

22 dunt aut certe quidem diluunt deteruntque. Nam ubi infantis aliorsum dati facta ex oculis amolitiost, vigor ille maternae flagrantiae sensim atque paulatim restinguitur omnisque inpatientissimae sollicitudinis strepitus consilescit, neque multo minor amendati ad nutricem aliam filii, quam morte amissi, obliviost.

23 Ipsius quoque infantis adfectio animi, amoris, consuetudinis[1] in ea sola unde alitur occupatur, et proinde, ut in expositis usu venit, matris quae genuit neque sensum ullum neque desiderium capit. Ac propterea, oblitteratis et abolitis nativae pietatis elementis, quicquid ita educati liberi amare patrem atque matrem videntur, magnam fere partem non naturalis ille amor est, sed civilis et opinabilis."

24 Haec Favorinum dicentem audivi Graeca oratione. Cuius sententias communis utilitatis gratia, quantum meminisse potui, rettuli, amoenitates vero et copias ubertatesque verborum Latina omnis facundia vix quaedam indipisci potuerit, mea tenuitas nequaquam.

II

Quod Annaeus Seneca, iudicans de Q. Ennio deque M. Tullio, levi futtilique iudicio fuit.

1 DE Annaeo Seneca partim existimant ut de scriptore minime utili, cuius libros adtingere nullum pretium operae sit, quod oratio eius vulgaria videatur et protrita, res atque sententiae aut inepto inanique

[1] amoris consuetudine, *Eussner*

parents to their children? For when the child is
given to another and removed from its mother's sight,
the strength of maternal ardour is gradually and little
by little extinguished, every call of impatient anxiety
is silenced, and a child which has been given over to
another to nurse is almost as completely forgotten as
if it had been lost by death. Moreover, the child's
own feelings of affection, fondness, and intimacy are
centred wholly in the one by whom it is nursed, and
therefore, just as happens in the case of those who
are exposed at birth, it has no feeling for the mother
who bore it and no regret for her loss. Therefore,
when the foundations of natural affection have been
destroyed and removed, however much children thus
reared may seem to love their father and mother,
that affection is in a great measure not natural but
merely courteous and conventional."

I heard Favorinus make this address in the Greek
language. I have reproduced his sentiments, so far
as I was able, for the sake of their general utility,
but the elegance, copiousness and richness of his
words hardly any power of Latin eloquence could
equal, least of all my humble attainments.

II

That the judgment passed by Annaeus Seneca on Quintus
Ennius and Marcus Cicero was trifling and futile.

Some think of Annaeus Seneca as a writer of little
value, whose works are not worth taking up, since
his style seems commonplace and ordinary, while the
matter and the thought are characterized, now by a
foolish and empty vehemence, now by an empty and

impetu sint aut levi et causidicali argutia, eruditio
autem vernacula et plebeia nihilque ex veterum
scriptis habens neque gratiae neque dignitatis. Alii
vero elegantiae quidem in verbis parum esse non
infitias eunt, sed et rerum quas dicat scientiam
doctrinamque ei non deesse dicunt et in vitiis morum
obiurgandis severitatem gravitatemque non inve-

2 nustam. Mihi de omni eius ingenio deque omni
scripto iudicium censuramque facere non necessum
est ; sed quod de M. Cicerone et Q. Ennio et P.
Vergilio iudicavit, ea res cuiusmodi sit, ad considerandum ponemus.

3 In libro enim vicesimo secundo *Epistularum
Moralium* quas ad Lucilium conposuit, derideculos
versus Q. Ennium de Cetego antiquo viro fecisse hos
dicit :

> is dictust ollis popularibus olim
> Qui tum vivebant homines atque aevum agi-
> tabant,[1]
> Flos delibatus populi, Suadaeque [2] medulla.

4 Ac deinde scripsit de isdem versibus verba haec :
" Admiror eloquentissimos viros et deditos Ennio
pro optimis ridicula laudasse. Cicero certe inter
5 bonos eius versus et hos refert." Atque id etiam
de Cicerone dicit : " Non miror," inquit, " fuisse
qui hos versus scriberet, cum fuerit qui laudaret ;
nisi forte Cicero summus orator agebat causam suam

---

[1] agebant, *codd. Cic.*
[2] suadaque, *Cic.* ; suada, *ω*.

---

[1] Besides Caligula, who called Seneca's essays "mere
declamation exercises" and his style "sand without lime"
(Suet. *Calig.* liii), there were other critics of Seneca in his
own day, as well as in the following Flavian epoch.

affected cleverness; and because his learning is
common and plebeian, gaining neither charm nor
distinction from familiarity with the earlier writers.[1]
Others, on the contrary, while not denying that
his diction lacks elegance, declare that he is not
without learning and a knowledge of the subjects
which he treats, and that he censures the vices of
the times with a seriousness and dignity which are
not wanting in charm. I myself do not feel called
upon to criticize and pass judgment upon his talents
in general, or upon his writings as a whole; but I
shall select for consideration the nature of the
opinions which he has expressed about Marcus
Cicero, Quintus Ennius and Publius Vergilius.

For in the twenty-second book of his *Moral Epistles,*
which he addressed to Lucilius, he says[2] that the
following verses which Quintus Ennius wrote[3] about
Cethegus, a man of the olden time, are absurd:

He by his fellow citizens was called,
By every man who lived and flourished then,
The people's chosen flower, Persuasion's marrow.

He then wrote the following about these lines: " I
am surprised that men of great eloquence, devoted
to Ennius, have praised those absurd verses as his
best. Cicero, at any rate, includes them among
examples of his good verses." [4] He then goes on to
say of Cicero: " I am not surprised that there existed
a man who could write such verses, when there
existed a man who could praise them; unless haply
Cicero, that great orator, was pleading his own cause

[2] pp. 610 f. Hense; except for these fragments, only
twenty books have come down to us.

[3] *Ann.* 306 ff., Vahlen[2]; quoted by Cicero, *Brut.* 58.

[4] *Cic. Brut.* 58.

6 et volebat suos [1] versus videri bonos." Postea hoc
etiam addidit insulsissime : " Aput ipsum quoque,"
inquit, " Ciceronem invenies, etiam in prosa oratione,
quaedam ex quibus intellegas illum non perdidisse
7 operam, quod Ennium legit." Ponit deinde quae
apud Ciceronem reprehendat, quasi Enniana, quod
ita scripserit in libris *De Republica* : " Ut Menelao
Laconi quaedam fuit suaviloquens iucunditas," et
quod alio in loco dixerit: " breviloquentiam in
dicendo colit." Atque ibi homo nugator Ciceronis
errores deprecatur et : " Non fuit," inquit, " Ciceronis hoc vitium, sed temporis ; necesse erat haec dici,
9 cum illa legerentur." Deinde adscribit Ciceronem
haec ipsa interposuisse ad effugiendam infamiam
nimis lascivae orationis et nitidae.
10 De Vergilio quoque eodem in loco verba haec
ponit : " Vergilius quoque noster non ex alia causa
duros quosdam versus et enormes et aliquid supra
mensuram trahentis interposuit quam ut Ennianus
populus adgnosceret in novo carmine aliquid antiquitatis."
11 Sed iam verborum Senecae piget ; haec tamen
inepti et insubidi hominis ioca non praeteribo :
" Quidam sunt," inquit, " tam magni sensus Q.
Ennii, ut, licet scripti sint inter hircosos, possint
tamen inter unguentatos placere " ; et, cum repre-
hendisset versus quos supra de Cetego posuimus :
" Qui huiuscemodi," inquit, " versus amant, liqueat
tibi eosdem admirari et Soterici lectos."

---

[1] suos, *Skutsch*; hos, *MSS.*

---

[1] V. 9, 11.
[2] Lit., "those who smell like a he-goat"; cf. Hor. *Serm.* i.
2. 27, pastillos Rufillus olet, Gargonius hircum ; *Epod.* xii. 5.

and wished his own verse to appear excellent." Later
he adds this very stupid remark : " In Cicero himself too you will find, even in his prose writings, some
things which will show that he did not lose his labour
when he read Ennius." Then he cites passages
from Cicero which he criticizes as taken from Ennius;
for example, when Cicero wrote as follows in his
Republic :[1] " As Menelaus, the Laconian, had a kind
of sweet-speaking charm," and said in another place :
" he cultivates brevity of speech in his oratory."
And then that trifler apologizes for what he considers
Cicero's errors, saying : " This was not the fault of
Cicero, but of the times; it was necessary to say
such things when such verses were read." Then he
adds that Cicero inserted these very things in order
to escape the charge of being too diffuse and orna-
mental in his style.

In the same place Seneca writes the following
about Virgil also : " Our Virgil too admitted some
verses which are harsh, irregular and somewhat
beyond the proper length, with no other motive than
that those who were devoted to Ennius might find a
flavour of antiquity in the new poem."

But I am already weary of quoting Seneca; yet I
shall not pass by these jokes of that foolish and
tasteless man : " There are some thoughts in Quintus
Ennius," says he, " that are of such lofty tone that
though written among the unwashed,[2] they nevertheless can give pleasure among the anointed " ; and,
after censuring the verses about Cethegus which I
have quoted above, he said : " It would be clear to
you that those who love verses of this kind admire
even the couches of Sotericus."[3]

[3] Obviously, an unskilful workman.

12 Dignus[1] sane[2] Seneca videatur lectione ac studio
adulescentium, qui honorem coloremque veteris
orationis Soterici lectis compararit, quasi minimae
13 scilicet gratiae et relictis iam contemptisque.[3] Audias
tamen commemorari ac referri pauca quaedam quae
idem ipse Seneca bene dixerit, quale est illud, quod
in hominem avarum et avidum et pecuniae sitientem
dixit : "Quid enim refert quantum habeas? multo
14 illud plus est quod non habes." Benene hoc? sane
bene ; sed adulescentium indolem non tam iuvant
quae bene dicta sunt quam inficiunt quae pessime,
multoque tanto magis, si et plura sunt quae deteriora
sunt, et quaedam in his non pro enthymemate aliquo
rei parvae ac simplicis, sed in re ancipiti pro consilio
dicuntur.

III

Lictoris vocabulum qua ratione conceptum ortumque sit ; et
super eo diversae sententiae Valgi Rufi et Tulli Tironis.[4]

1 VALGIUS RUFUS in secundo librorum quos inscripsit
De Rebus per Epistulam Quaesitis, "lictorem" dicit a
"ligando" appellatum esse, quod, cum magistratus
populi Romani virgis quempiam verberari iussissent,
crura eius et manus ligari vincirique a viatore
solita sint, et inde is qui[5] ex conlegio viatorum
officium ligandi haberet "lictor" sit appellatus;

---

[1] indignus, *Skutsch.*   [2] iamne or anne, *Damsté.*
[3] *Weiss makes the sentence interrogative.*
[4] Tironis, *Bentley*; Ciceronis, O²X ; Ciceronis versus
accepti, ω (*from lemma of* xii. 4).
[5] et inde is qui, *Mommsen* ; is qui, δ ; isque, γ.

Worthy indeed would Seneca appear [1] of the reading and study of the young, a man who has compared the dignity and beauty of early Latin with the couches of Sotericus, implying forsooth that they possessed no charm and were already obsolete and despised ! Yet listen to the relation and mention of a few things which that same Seneca has well said, for example what he said of a man who was avaricious, covetous and thirsting for money : "Why, what difference does it make how much you have ? There is much more which you do not have." Is not that well put ? Excellently well ; but the character of the young is not so much benefited by what is well said, as it is injured by what is very badly put ; all the more so, if the bad predominates, and if a part of the bad is uttered, not as an argument about some slight and trivial affair, but as advice in a matter requiring decision.

III

The meaning and origin of the word *lictor* and the varying opinions of Valgius Rufus and Tullius Tiro on that subject.

VALGIUS RUFUS, in the second of the books which he entitled *On Matters Investigated by Letter*, says [2] that the *lictor* was so called from *ligando* or "binding," because when the magistrates of the Roman people had given orders that anyone should be beaten with rods, his legs and arms were always fastened and bound by an attendant, and therefore that the member of the college of attendants who had the duty of binding him was called a *lictor*. And he quotes as

---

[1] Ironical, of course.   [2] p. 485, Fun.

utiturque ad eam rem testimonio M. Tulli verbaque eius refert ex oratione quae dicta est *Pro C. Rabirio*:

2 " Lictor," inquit, " conliga manus." Haec ita Valgius.

3 Et nos sane cum illo sentimus ; sed Tiro Tullius M. Ciceronis libertus, " lictorem " vel a " limo " vel a " licio " dictum scripsit : " Licio enim transverso, quod ' limum ' appellatur, qui magistratibus," inquit, " praeministrabant cincti erant."

4 Si quis autem est qui propterea putat probabilius esse quod Tiro dixit, quoniam prima syllaba in " lictore," sicuti in " licio," producta est et in eo verbo quod est " ligo " correpta est, nihil ad rem istud pertinet. Nam sicut a " ligando " " lictor " et a " legendo " " lector " et a " viendo " " vitor " [1] et " tuendo " " tutor " et " struendo " " structor " productis quae corripiebantur vocalibus dicta sunt.

IV

Versus accepti ex Q. Enni septimo *Annalium*, quibus depingitur finiturque ingenium comitasque hominis minoris erga amicum superiorem.

1 DESCRIPTUM definitumque est a Quinto Ennio in *Annali* septimo graphice admodum sciteque sub historia Gemini Servili, viri nobilis, quo ingenio, qua comitate, qua modestia, qua fide, qua linguae parsimonia, qua loquendi opportunitate, quanta rerum antiquarum morumque veterum ac novorum scientia quantaque servandi tuendique secreti religione, qualibus denique ad muniendas vitae molestias fomentis,

---

[1] vivendo victor, ω; *corr. by Lachmann*; vincendo victor, ς.

evidence on this subject Marcus Tullius, citing these words from the speech entitled *In Defence of Gaius Rabirius*:[1] "Lictor, bind his hands." This is what Valgius says.

Now, I for my part agree with him; but Tullius Tiro, the freedman of Marcus Cicero, wrote[2] that the *lictor* got his name from *limus* or *licium*. "For," says he, "those men who were in attendance upon the magistrates were girt across with a kind of girdle called *limus*."

But if there is anyone who thinks that what Tiro said is more probable, because the first syllable[3] in *lictor* is long like that of *licium*, but in the word *ligo* is short, that has nothing to do with the case. For in *lictor* from *ligando*, *lector* from *legendo*, *vitor* from *viendo*, *tutor* from *tuendo*, and *structor* from *struendo*, the vowels, which were originally short, are lengthened.

IV

Lines taken from the seventh book of the *Annals* of Ennius, in which the courteous bearing of an inferior towards a friend of higher rank is described and defined.

QUINTUS ENNIUS in the seventh book of his *Annals* describes and defines very vividly and skilfully in his sketch of Geminus Servilius, a man of rank, the tact, courtesy, modesty, fidelity, restraint and propriety in speech, knowledge of ancient history and of customs old and new, scrupulousness in keeping and guarding a secret; in short, the various remedies and methods of relief and solace for guarding against the annoy-

---

[1] § 13. [2] p. 8, Lion.
[3] The vowel is long, not merely the syllable, as Gellius goes on to say.

levamentis, solacis amicum esse conveniat hominis
2 genere et fortuna superioris. Eos ego versus non
minus frequenti adsiduoque memoratu dignos puto
3 quam philosophorum de officiis decreta. Ad hoc color
quidam vestustatis in his versibus tam reverendus est,
suavitas tam inpromisca tamque a fuco omni remota
est, ut mea quidem sententia pro antiquis sacratisque
amicitiae legibus observandi, tenendi colendique sint.
4 Quapropter adscribendos eos existimavi, si quis iam
statim desideraret:

Haece locutus vocat quocum bene saepe libenter
Mensam sermonesque suos rerumque suarum
Comiter inpertit, magnam cum lassus diei
Partem fuisset, de summis rebus regundis
Consilio indu foro lato sanctoque senatu;
Cui res audacter magnas parvasque iocumque
Eloqueretur sed cura [1] malaque et bona dictu
Evomeret, si qui vellet, tutoque locaret,
Quocum multa volup ac [2] gaudia clamque palam-
    que;
Ingenium cui nulla malum sententia suadet
Ut faceret facinus levis aut malus; doctus, fidelis,
Suavis homo, facundus, suo contentus, beatus,
Scitus, secunda loquens in tempore, commodus,
    verbum
Paucum, multa tenens antiqua sepulta, vetustas
Quem facit et mores veteresque novosque tenen-
    tem,
Multorum veterum leges divumque hominumque;
Prudenter qui dicta loquive tacereve posset;
Hunc inter pugnas conpellat Servilius sic.

---

[1] sed cura, *Hosius* (*sed* = *sine*); et cuncta, γ.
[2] ac, *added in* σ; volup sibi fecit clamque, *Vahlen*[1].

ances of life, which the friend of a man who is his
superior in rank and fortune ought to have. Those
verses in my opinion are no less worthy of frequent,
attentive perusal than the rules of the philosophers
about duties. Besides this, there is such a venerable
flavour of antiquity in these verses, such a sweetness,
so unmixed and so removed from all affectation, that
in my opinion they ought to be observed, remembered and cherished as old and sacred laws of
friendship. Therefore I thought them worthy of
quotation, in case there should be anyone who
desired to see them at once : [1]

So saying, on a friend he called, with whom
He oft times gladly shared both board and speech
And courteously informed of his affairs,
On coming wearied from the sacred House
Or Forum broad, where he all day had toiled,
Directing great affairs with wisdom ; one with whom
He freely spoke of matters great and small,
Confiding to him thoughts approved or not,
If he so wished, and found him trustworthy ;
With whom he took much pleasure openly
Or privily ; a man to whom no thought
Suggested heedlessness or ill intent,
A cultured, loyal and a winsome man,
Contented, happy, learned, eloquent,
Speaking but little and that fittingly,
Obliging, knowing well all ancient lore,
All customs old and new, the laws of man
And of the gods, who with due prudence told
What he had heard, or kept it to himself :
Him 'mid the strife Servilius thus accosts.

[1] *Ann.* 234 ff., Vahlen.[2]

L. Aelium Stilonem dicere solitum ferunt Q. Ennium de semet ipso haec scripsisse picturamque istam morum et ingenii ipsius Q. Ennii factam esse.

V

Sermo Tauri philosophi de modo atque ratione tolerandi doloris secundum Stoicorum decreta.

1 Cum Delphos ad Pythia conventumque totius ferme Graeciae visendum philosophus Taurus iret nosque ei comites essemus inque eo itinere Lebadiam venissemus, quod est oppidum anticum in terra Boeotia, adfertur ibi ad Taurum amicum eius quempiam, nobilem in Stoica disciplina philosophum, aegra vali-
2 tudine oppressum, decumbere. Tunc omisso itinere, quod alioquin maturandum erat, et relictis vehiculis, pergit eum propere videre, nosque de more, quem in locum cumque iret, secuti sumus. Et ubi ad aedes in quis ille aegrotus erat pervenimus, videmus hominem doloribus cruciatibusque alvi, quod Graeci κόλον dicunt, et febri simul rapida adflictari gemitusque ex eo conpressos erumpere spiritusque et anhelitus e pectore eius evadere, non dolorem magis indicantes quam pugnam adversum dolorem.
3 Post deinde, cum Taurus et medicos accersisset conlocutusque de facienda medella esset et eum ipsum ad retinendam patientiam, testimonio tolerantiae

---

[1] p. 51, Fun.

They say that Lucius Aelius Stilo used to declare [1] that Quintus Ennius wrote these words about none other than himself, and that this was a description of Quintus Ennius' own character and disposition.

V

A discourse of the philosopher Taurus on the manner and method of enduring pain, according to the principles of the Stoics.

WHEN the philosopher Taurus was on his way to Delphi, to see the Pythian games and the throng that gathered there from almost all Greece, I was his companion. And when, in the course of the journey, we had come to Lebadia, which is an ancient town in the land of Boeotia, word was brought to Taurus there that a friend of his, an eminent philosopher of the Stoic sect, had been seized with illness and had taken to his bed. Then interrupting our journey, which otherwise would have called for haste, and leaving the carriages, he hastened to visit his friend, and I followed, as I usually did wherever he went. When we came to the house in which the sick man was, we saw that he was suffering anguish from pains in the stomach, such as the Greeks call κόλος, or "colic," and at the same time from a high fever. The stifled groans that burst from him, and the heavy sighs that escaped his panting breast, revealed his suffering, and no less his struggle to overcome it.

Later, when Taurus had sent for physicians and discussed with them the means of cure, and had encouraged the patient to keep up his endurance by commending the fortitude which he was showing,

373

quam videbat perhibito, stabilisset, egressique inde
ad vehicula et ad comites rediremus: "Vidistis,"
inquit Taurus, "non sane iucundum spectaculum,
sed cognitu tamen utile, congredientes conpug-
nantesque philosophum et dolorem. Faciebat vis
illa et natura morbi, quod erat suum, distractionem
cruciatumque membrorum, faciebat contra ratio et
natura animi, quod erat aeque suum: perpetiebatur et
cohibebat coercebatque infra sese violentias effrenati
doloris. Nullos eiulatus, nullas conplorationes, ne
ullas quidem voces indecoras edebat, signa tamen
quaedam, sicut vidistis, existebant virtutis et corporis,
de possessione hominis pugnantium."

4 Tum e sectatoribus Tauri iuvenis, in disciplinis
philosophiae non ignavus, "Si tanta," inquit, "doloris
acerbitas est, ut contra voluntatem contraque iudicium animi nitatur invitumque hominem cogat ad
gemendum confitendumque de malo morbi saevientis,
cur dolor aput Stoicos indifferens esse dicitur, non
malum? Cur deinde aut Stoicus homo cogi aliquid
potest aut dolor cogere, cum et dolorem Stoici nihil
cogere et sapientem nihil cogi posse dicant?"

5 Ad ea Taurus vultu iam propemodum laetiore,
delectatus enim videbatur inlecebra quaestionis, "Si
iam amicus," inquit, "hic noster melius valeret,
gemitus eiusmodi necessarios a calumnia defendisset
et hanc, opinor, tibi quaestionem dissolvisset, me
autem scis cum Stoicis non bene convenire, vel cum
Stoa [1] potius; est enim pleraque et sibi et nobis incon-

---

[1] Stoa, *Thysius*; Stoica, *MSS.*; Stoa potius portica *or*
secta, *suggested by Hosius (but cf. Porph. on Hor. Epist.* i. 1.
16–17).

we left the house. And as we were returning to the carriages, and our companions, Taurus said: "You were witness of no very pleasant sight, it is true, but one which was, nevertheless, a profitable experience, in beholding the encounter and contest of a philosopher with pain. The violent character of the disorder, for its part, produced anguish and torture of body; reason and the spiritual nature, on the other hand, similarly played their part, supporting and restraining within bounds the violence of well-nigh ungovernable pain. He uttered no shrieks, no complaints, not even any unseemly outcries; yet, as you saw, there were obvious signs of a battle between soul and body for the man's possession."

Then one of the disciples of Taurus, a young man not untrained in philosophy, said: "If the bitterness of pain is such that it struggles against the will and judgment, forcing a man to groan involuntarily and confess the evil of his violent disorder, why is it said among the Stoics that pain is a thing indifferent and not an evil? Furthermore, why can a Stoic be compelled to do anything, or how can pain compel him, when the Stoics say that pain exerts no compulsion, and that a wise man cannot be forced to do anything?"[1]

To this Taurus, with a face that was now somewhat more cheerful, for he seemed pleased at being lured into a discussion, replied as follows: "If this friend of ours were now in better health, he would have defended such unavoidable groans against reproach and, I dare say, would have answered your question; but you know that I am no great friend of the Stoics, or rather, of the Stoa; for it is often

[1] iii. 168, Arn.

gruens, sicut libro quem supra illa re composuimus
6 declaratur. Sed ut tibi a me mos geratur, dicam
ego 'indoctius,' ut aiunt, 'et apertius,' quae fuisse
dicturum puto sinuosius atque sollertius, si quis nunc
adesset Stoicorum ; nosti enim, credo, verbum illud
vetus et pervolgatum :

 'Αμαθέστερόν πως εἰπὲ καὶ σαφέστερον λέγε." [1]

Atque hinc exorsus de dolore atque de gemitu
7 Stoici aegrotantis ita disseruit : " Natura," inquit,
" omnium rerum quae nos genuit, induit nobis ino-
levitque in ipsis statim principiis quibus nati sumus,
amorem nostri et caritatem, ita prorsus ut nihil quicquam esset carius pensiusque nobis quam nosmet
ipsi, atque hoc esse fundamentum ratast conservandae hominum perpetuitatis, si unusquisque nostrum,
simul atque editus in lucem foret, harum prius rerum
sensum adfectionemque caperet quae a veteribus
philosophis τὰ πρῶτα κατὰ φύσιν appellata sunt ; ut
omnibus scilicet corporis sui commodis gauderet, ab
incommodis omnibus abhorreret. Postea per incre-
menta aetatis exorta e seminibus suis ratiost et
utendi consilii reputatio et honestatis utilitatisque
verae contemplatio subtiliorque et exploratior com-
modorum incommodorumque [2] dilectus ; atque ita
prae ceteris omnibus enituit et praefulsit decori et
honesti dignitas ac, si ei retinendae obtinendaeve
incommodum extrinsecus aliquod obstaret, contemptum est ; neque aliud esse vere et simpliciter bonum
nisi honestum, aliud quicquam malum nisi quod

---

[1] λέγε *not in MSS. of Arist.*
[2] incommodorum *supplied by Bentley.*

---

[1] Aristophanes, *Frogs*, 1445.

inconsistent with itself and with us, as is shown in
the book which I have written on that subject.
But to oblige you, I will say 'unlearnedly and
clearly,' as the adage has it, what I imagine that any
Stoic now present would have said more intricately
and cleverly. For you know, I suppose, that old and
familiar proverb : [1]

Less eruditely speak and clearer, please."

And with that preamble he discoursed as follows
about the pain and groans of the ailing Stoic:[2]
"Nature," said he, "who produced us, implanted in
us and incorporated in the very elements from
which we sprang a love and affection for ourselves,
to such a degree that nothing whatever is dearer or
of more importance to us than ourselves. And this,
she thought, would be the underlying principle for
assuring the perpetuation of the human race, if each
one of us, as soon as he saw the light, should have
a knowledge and understanding first of all of those
things which the philosophers of old have called τὰ
πρῶτα κατὰ φύσιν, or 'the first principles of nature';
that is, that he might delight in all that was agreeable to his body and shrink from everything disagreeable. Later, with increasing years, reason
developed from its first elements, and reflection in
taking counsel, and the consideration of honour and
true expediency, and a wiser and more careful choice
of advantages as opposed to disadvantages ; and in this
way the dignity of virtue and honour became so pre-
eminent and so superior, that any disadvantage from
without which prevented our holding and retaining
this quality was despised. Nothing was considered
truly and wholly good unless it was honourable, and

[2] iii. 181, Arn.

turpe esset existimatum est. Reliqua omnia, quae
in medio forent ac neque honesta essent neque
turpia, neque bona esse neque mala decretum est.
Productiones tamen et relationes suis quaeque
momentis distinctae divisaeque sunt, quae προηγμένα
et ἀποπροηγμένα ipsi vocant. Propterea voluptas
quoque et dolor, quod ad finem ipsum bene beateque
vivendi pertinet, et in mediis relicta et neque in
8 bonis neque in malis iudicata sunt. Sed enim
quoniam his primis sensibus doloris voluptatisque
ante consilii et rationis exortum recens natus homo
inbutus est et voluptati quidem a natura conciliatus,
a dolore autem, quasi a gravi quodam inimico, ab-
iunctus alienatusque est—idcirco adfectiones istas
primitus penitusque inditas ratio ipsi post addita
convellere ab stirpe atque extinguere vix potest.
Pugnat autem cum his semper et exultantis eas
opprimit obteritque et parere sibi atque oboedire
9 cogit. Itaque vidistis philosophum, ratione decreti
sui nixum, cum petulantia morbi dolorisque exultan-
tia conluctantem, nihil cedentem, nihil confitentem,
neque ut plerique dolentes solent, eiulantem atque
lamentantem ac miserum sese et infelicem appellan-
tem, sed acres tantum anhelitus et robustos gemitus
edentem, signa atque indicia non victi nec obpressi
a dolore, sed vincere eum atque obprimere enitentis.
10 "Sed haut scio," inquit, "an dicat aliquis, ipsum
illud quod pugnat, quod gemit, si malum dolor non
est, cur necesse est gemere et pugnare? Quia enim

---

[1] Cf. i. 2. 9.

nothing evil unless it is dishonourable. All other things which lay between, and were neither honourable nor dishonourable, were decided to be neither good nor evil.[1] But *productiones* and *relationes*, which the philosophers call προηγμένα, or 'things desirable,' and ἀποπροηγμένα, or 'things undesirable,' are distinguished and set apart each by their own qualities. Therefore pleasure also and pain, so far as the end of living well and happily is concerned, are regarded as indifferent and classed neither with good nor with evil. But since the newly-born child is endowed with these first sensations of pain and pleasure before the appearance of judgment and reason, and is attracted to pleasure by nature, but averted and alienated from pain, as if from some bitter enemy—therefore reason, which is given to him later, is hardly able to uproot and destroy those inclinations which were originally and deeply implanted in him. Yet he constantly struggles with them, checks and tramples them under foot when they are excessive, and compels them to obey and submit to him. Hence you saw the philosopher, relying upon the efficacy of his system, wrestling with the insolent violence of disease and pain, yielding nothing, admitting nothing; not, as sufferers commonly do, shrieking, lamenting and calling himself wretched and unhappy, but giving vent only to panting breathing and deep sighs, which are signs and indications, not that he is overcome or subdued by pain, but that he is struggling to overcome and subdue it.

"But very likely," said he, "because of the mere fact that he struggles and groans, someone may ask, if pain is not an evil, why it is necessary to groan and struggle? It is because all things which are not

379

omnia quae non sunt mala molestia quoque omni
non carent, sed sunt pleraque noxa quidem magna
et pernicie privata, quia non sunt turpia, contra
naturae tamen mansuetudinem lenitatemque opposita
sunt et infesta per obscuram quandam et necessariam
ipsius naturae consequentiam. Haec ergo vir sapiens
tolerare et exanclare [1] potest, non admittere omnino
in sensum sui non potest ; ἀναλγησία enim atque
ἀπάθεια non meo tantum," inquit, " sed quorundam
etiam ex eadem porticu prudentiorum hominum,
sicuti iudicio Panaetii, gravis atque docti viri, inpro-
bata abiectaque est.

11 " Sed cur contra voluntatem suam gemitus facere
cogitur philosophus Stoicus, quem nihil cogi posse
dicunt ? Nihil sane potest cogi vir sapiens, cum est
rationi obtinendae locus ; cum vero natura cogit,
ratio quoque a natura data cogitur. Quaere etiam,
si videtur, cur manu alicuius ob oculos suos repente
agitata invitus coniveat, cur fulgente caelo a luminis
iactu non sua sponte et caput et oculos declinet, cur
tonitru vehementius facto [2] sensim pavescat, cur
sternumentis quatiatur, cur aut in ardoribus solis
12 aestuet aut in pruinis inmanibus obrigescat. Haec
enim et pleraque alia non voluntas nec consilium nec
ratio moderatur, set naturae necessitatisque decreta
sunt.

13 " Fortitudo autem non east, quae contra naturam
monstri vicem nititur ultraque modum eius egreditur
aut stupore animi aut inmanitate aut quadam misera

---

[1] *Hosius* ; cun(c)tari, ω ; eluctari, *Madvig.*
[2] facto, *Q* ; facto sensim, γ ; impavescat, *Skutsch.*

---

[1] That is, they do not involve any guilt.
[2] Fr. 14, Fowler.

evil are not also wholly lacking in annoyance, but there are very many things which, though free from any great harm or baneful effect, as not being base,[1] are none the less opposed to the gentleness and mercy of nature through a certain inexplicable and inevitable law of nature herself. These, then, a wise man can endure and put up with, but he cannot exclude them altogether from his consciousness; for ἀναλγησία, or 'insensibility,' and ἀπάθεια, or 'lack of feeling,' not only in my judgment," said he, " but also in that of some of the wise men of that same school (such as Panaetius,[2] a serious and learned man) are disapproved and rejected.

" But why is a Stoic philosopher, upon whom they say no compulsion can be exerted, compelled to utter groans against his will? It is true that no compulsion can be exerted upon a wise man when he has the opportunity of using his reason; but when nature compels, then reason also, the gift of nature, is compelled. Inquire also, if you please, why a man involuntarily winks when someone's hand is suddenly directed against his eyes, why when the sky is lit up by a flash of lightning he involuntarily drops his head and closes his eyes, why as the thunder grows louder he gradually becomes terrified, why he is shaken by sneezing, why he sweats in the heat of the sun or grows cold amid severe frosts. For these and many other things are not under the control of the will, the judgment, or the reason, but are decrees of nature and of necessity.

" Moreover, that is not fortitude which, like a giant, struggles against nature and goes beyond her bounds, either through insensibility of spirit, or

et necessaria in perpetiendis doloribus exercitatione—
qualem fuisse accepimus ferum quendam in ludo Caesaris gladiatorem, qui, cum vulnera eius a medicis
exsecabantur, ridere solitus fuit—sed ea vera et
proba fortitudost, quam maiores nostri scientiam
esse dixerunt rerum tolerandarum et non toleranda-

14 rum. Per quod apparet esse quaedam intolerabilia,
a quibus fortes viri aut obeundis abhorreant aut
sustinendis."

15 Cum haec Taurus dixisset videreturque in eandem
rem plura etiam dicturus, perventum est ad vehicula
et conscendimus.

VI

De aenigmate.

1 Quae Graeci dicunt "aenigmata," hoc genus
quidam ex nostris veteribus "scirpos" appellaverunt.
Quale est quod nuper invenimus per hercle anti-
quum, perquam lepidum, tribus versibus senariis
compositum aenigma, quod reliquimus inenarratum,
ut legentium coniecturas in requirendo acueremus.

2 Versus tres hi sunt:

Semel minusne an bis minus sit, nescio;
An utrumque eorum, ut quondam audivi dicier,
Iovi ipsi regi noluit concedere.

3 Hoc qui nolit diutius aput sese quaerere, inveniet
quid sit in M. Varronis *De Sermone Latino ad Marcellum* libro secundo.

---

¹ Apparently so called from the involved pattern of plaited
rushes.
² The answer is Terminus. Once *minus* and twice *minus* =
thrice (*ter*) *minus*. In the *cella* of Jupiter on the Capitolium,

savage pride, or some unhappy and compulsory
practice in bearing pain—such as we heard of in a
certain savage gladiator of Caesar's school, who used
to laugh when his wounds were probed by the
doctors—but that is true and noble fortitude which
our forefathers called a knowledge of what is endur-
able and unendurable. From this it is evident that
there are some insupportable trials, from the under-
going or endurance of which brave men may
shrink."

When Taurus had said this and seemed to intend
to say even more, we reached our carriages and
entered them.

VI

On the Enigma.

The kind of composition which the Greeks call
"enigmas," some of our early writers called *scirpi*, or
"rushes." [1] An example is the enigma composed of
three iambic trimeters which I recently found—
very old, by Jove! and very neat. I have left it
unanswered, in order to excite the ingenuity of my
readers in seeking for an answer. The three verses
are these:

> I know not if he's minus once or twice,
> Or both of these, who would not give his place,
> As I once heard it said, to Jove himself.

He who does not wish to puzzle himself too long
will find the answer [2] in the second book of Varro's
Latin Language, addressed to Marcellus. [3]

or possibly in the *pronaos*, there was a terminal *cippus*, representing Terminus, who refused to be removed from his
original site.   [3] Fr. 55. G. & S.

VII

Quam ob causam Cn. Dolabella proconsul ream mulierem
veneficii confitentemque ad Ariopagitas reiecerit.

1 AD Cn. Dolabellam, proconsulari imperio provinciam Asiam obtinentem, deducta mulier Smyrnaea est.
2 Eadem mulier virum et filium eodem tempore venenis
clam datis vita interfecerat atque id fecisse se confi-
tebatur dicebatque habuisse se faciendi causam, quoniam idem illi maritus et filius alterum filium
mulieris, ex viro priore genitum, adulescentem optimum et innocentissimum, exceptum insidiis occidis-
sent. Idque ita esse factum, controversia non erat.
3 Dolabella retulit ad consilium. Nemo quisquam ex
4 consilio sententiam ferre in causa tam ancipiti audebat, quod et confessum veneficium, quo maritus et
filius necati forent, non admittendum inpunitum
videbatur et digna tamen poena in homines sceleratos
vindicatum fuisset. Dolabella eam rem Athenas ad
5 Ariopagitas, ut ad iudices graviores exercitatioresque,
6 reiecit. Ariopagitae, cognita causa, accusatorem
mulieris et ipsam quae accusabatur centesimo anno
7 adesse iusserunt. Sic neque absolutum mulieris
veneficium est, quod per leges non licuit, neque
nocens damnata poenitaque quae digna venia fuit.
8 Scripta haec historiast in libro Valerii Maximi
Factorum et Dictorum Memorabilium nono.

---

[1] A very ancient court at Athens, so called because it held
its meetings on the Areopagus, or Hill of Mars.

VII

Why Gnaeus Dolabella, the proconsul, referred to the court of the Areopagus the case of a woman charged with poisoning and admitting the fact.

WHEN Gnaeus Dolabella was governing the province of Asia with proconsular authority, a woman of Smyrna was brought before him. This woman had killed her husband and her son at the same time by secretly giving them poison. She confessed the crime, and said that she had reason for it, since her husband and son had treacherously done to death another son of hers by a former husband, an excellent and blameless youth; and there was no dispute about the truth of this statement. Dolabella referred the matter to his council. No member of the council ventured to render a decision in so difficult a case, since the confession of the poisoning which had resulted in the death of the husband and son seemed to call for punishment, while at the same time a just penalty had thereby been inflicted upon two wicked men. Dolabella referred the question to the Areopagites[1] at Athens, as judges of greater authority and experience. The Areopagites, after having heard the case, summoned the woman and her accuser to appear after a hundred years. Thus the woman's crime was not condoned, for the laws did not permit that, nor, though guilty, was she condemned and punished for a pardonable offence. The story is told in the ninth book of Valerius Maximus' work on *Memorable Occurrences and Sayings*.[2]

[2] viii. 1 amb. 2, Kempf; Gellius' reference is wrong.

VIII

Reditiones in gratiam nobilium virorum memoratu dignae.

1 P. Africanus superior et Tiberius Gracchus, Tiberii et C. Gracchorum pater, rerum gestarum magnitudine et honorum atque vitae dignitate inlustres viri, dissenserunt saepenumero de republica et ea sive qua alia re non amici fuerunt. Ea simultas cum diu 2 mansisset et sollemni die epulum Iovi libaretur atque ob id sacrificium senatus in Capitolio epularetur, fors fuit ut aput eandem mensam duo illi iunctim locarentur. Tum, quasi diis inmortalibus arbitris in 3 convivio Iovis Optimi Maximi dexteras eorum conducentibus, repente amicissimi facti. Neque solum amicitia incepta, sed adfinitas simul instituta ; nam 4 P. Scipio filiam virginem habens iam viro maturam, ibi tunc eodem in loco despondit eam Tiberio Graccho, quem probaverat elegeratque exploratissimo iudicii tempore, dum inimicus esset.

5 Aemilius quoque Lepidus et Fulvius Flaccus, nobili genere amplissimisque honoribus ac summo loco in civitate praediti, odio inter sese gravi et simultate 6 diutina conflictati sunt. Postea populus eos simul censores facit. Atque illi, ubi voce praeconis renuntiati sunt, ibidem in campo statim, nondum dimissa

---

[1] On the 13th of September, which was also the anniversary of the founding of the Capitoline Temple. See Fowler, *Roman Festivals*, pp. 217 f.

VIII

Noteworthy reconciliations between famous men.

PUBLIUS AFRICANUS the elder and Tiberius Gracchus, father of Tiberius and Gaius Gracchus, men illustrious for their great exploits, the high offices which they held, and the uprightness of their lives, often disagreed about public questions, and for that reason, or some other, were not friends. When this hostility had lasted for a long time, the feast was offered to Jupiter on the appointed day,[1] and on the occasion of that ceremony the senate banqueted in the Capitol. It chanced that the two men were placed side by side at the same table, and immediately, as if the immortal gods, acting as arbiters at the feast of Jupiter, Greatest and Best of Gods, had joined their hands, they became the best of friends. And not only did friendship spring up between them, but at the same time their families were united by a marriage; for Publius Scipio, having a daughter that was unwedded and marriageable at the time, thereupon on the spot betrothed her to Tiberius Gracchus, whom he had chosen and approved at a time when judgment is most strict; that is, while he was his personal enemy.

Aemilius Lepidus, too, and Fulvius Flaccus, men of noble birth, who had held the highest offices, and occupied an exalted place in public life, were opposed to each other in a bitter hatred and enmity of long standing. Later, the people chose them censors at the same time. Then they, as soon as their election was proclaimed by the herald, in the Campus Martius itself, before the assembly was dis-

contione, ultro uterque et pari voluntate coniuncti complexique sunt, exque eo die et in ipsa censura et postea iugi concordia fidissime amicissimeque vixerunt.

IX

Quae dicantur vocabula ancipitia; et quod honoris quoque vocabulum ancipiti sententia fuerit.

1 Est plurifariam videre atque animadvertere in veteribus scriptis pleraque vocabula, quae nunc in sermonibus vulgi unam certamque rem demonstrent, ita fuisse media et communia ut significare et capere possent duas inter se res contrarias. Ex quibus quaedam satis nota sunt, ut "tempestas," "valitudo," "facinus," "dolus," "gratia," "industria." Haec
2 enim fere iam vulgatum est ancipitia esse et utroqueversus dici posse.

"Periculum" etiam et "venenum" et "contagium" non, uti nunc dicuntur, pro malis tantum dicta esse, multum exemplorum huiusmodi reperias.
3 Sed "honorem" quoque mediam vocem fuisse et ita appellatum, ut etiam "malus honos" diceretur et significaret iniuriam, id profecto rarissimum. Quintus
4 autem Metellus Numidicus, in oratione quam *De Triumpho Suo* dixit, his verbis usus est: "Qua in re quanto universi me unum antistatis, tanto vobis quam mihi maiorem iniuriam atque contumeliam facit, Quirites, et quanto probi iniuriam facilius accipiunt

---

¹ *Tempestas* means good or bad weather; *valitudo*, good or ill health, etc.
² *O. R. F.*, p. 275, Meyer.²

persed, both voluntarily and with equal joy, immediately joined hands and embraced each other, and from that day, both during their censorship and afterwards, they lived in continual harmony as loyal and devoted friends.

IX

What is meant by "ambiguous" words; and that even
honos was such a word.

ONE may very often see and notice in the early writings many words which at present in ordinary conversation have one fixed meaning, but which then were so indifferent and general, that they could signify and include two opposite things. Some of these are well known, such as *tempestas* (weather), *valitudo* (health), *facinus* (act), *dolus* (device), *gratia* (favour), *industria* (activity).[1] For it is well-nigh a matter of general knowledge that these are ambiguous and can be used either in a good or in a bad sense.

That *periculum* (trial), too, and *venenum* (drug) and *contagium* (contagion) were not used, as they now are, only in a bad sense, you may learn from many examples of that usage. But the use of *honor* as an indifferent word, so that people even spoke of "bad honour," signifying "wrong" or "injury," is indeed very rare. However, Quintus Metellus Numidicus, in a speech which he delivered *On his Triumph*, used these words:[2] "In this affair, by as much as the whole of you are more important than my single self, by so much he inflicts upon you greater insult and injury than on me; and by as much as honest men are more willing to suffer wrong than to

quam alteri tradunt, tanto ille vobis quam mihi
peiorem honorem habuit; nam me iniuriam ferre,
vos facere vult, Quirites, ut hic conquestio, istic
vituperatio relinquatur." "Honorem," inquit,
5 "peiorem vobis habuit quam[1] mihi"; cuius verbi
sententia est quam ipse quoque supra dicit: "maiore
vos adfecit iniuria et contumelia quam me."
6 Praeter huius autem verbi notionem adscribendam
esse hanc sententiam ex oratione Quinti Metelli
existimavi, ut definiremus Socratis esse decretum:
κάκιον εἶναι τὸ ἀδικεῖν ἢ τὸ ἀδικεῖσθαι.

X

Quod "aeditumus" verbum Latinum sit.

1 "AEDITIMUS" verbum Latinum est et vetus, ea
2 forma dictum qua "finitimus" et "legitimus." Pro
eo a plerisque nunc "aedituus" dicitur nova et
3 commenticia usurpatione, quasi a tuendis aedibus
appellatus. Satis hoc esse potuit admonendi gratia
dixisse *** propter agrestes quosdam et indomitos
certatores, qui nisi auctoritatibus adhibitis non com-
primuntur.
4 M. Varro in libro secundo *Ad Marcellum De Latino
Sermone* "aeditumum" dici oportere censet magis
quam "aedituum," quod alterum sit recenti novitate
fictum, alterum antiqua origine incorruptum. Laevius

---

[1] quam gratiam, ω; gratiam *deleted by Carrio.*

---

[1] Plato, *Gorgias*, p. 473 A ; 489 A ; 508 B.
[2] So the MSS. ; *aeditumus* is a variant spelling.

do wrong to another, by so much has he shown worse honour (*peiorem honorem*) to you than to me; for he wishes me to suffer injustice, Romans, and you to inflict it, so that I may be left with cause for complaint, and you may be open to reproach." He says, "he has shown worse honour to you than to me," and the meaning of the expression is the same as when he himself says, just before that, "he has inflicted a greater injury and insult on you than on me."

In addition to the citation of this word, I thought I ought to quote the following saying from the speech of Quintus Metellus, in order to point out that it is a precept of Socrates; the saying in question is: "It is worse to be unjust than to suffer injustice."[1]

X

That *aeditumus* is a Latin word.

Aeditimus[2] is a Latin word and an old one at that, formed in the same way as *finitimus* and *legitimus*. In place of it many to-day say *aedituus* by a new and false usage, as if it were derived from guarding the temples.[3] This ought to be enough to say as a warning[4] . . . because of certain rude and persistent disputants, who are not to be restrained except by the citation of authorities.

Marcus Varro, in the second book of his *Latin Language addressed to Marcellus*, thinks[5] that we ought to use *aeditumus* rather than *aedituus*, because the latter is made up by a late invention, while the former is pure and of ancient origin. Laevius too,

---

[3] That is, from *aedes* and *tueor*.
[4] There is a lacuna in the text.
[5] Fr. 56, G. & S.

5 quoque, ut opinor in *Protesilaodamia*, "claustritumum" dixit qui claustris ianuae praeesset, eadem scilicet figura qua "aeditumum" dici videbat qui aedibus 6 praeest. In *IV in* [1] *Verrem* M. Tullii in exemplaribus fidelissimis ita inveni scriptum : " Aeditumi custo-desque mature sentiunt," in libris autem hoc vulgariis 7 "aeditui" scriptum est. Pomponi fabula Atellania est quae ita scripta est : *Aeditumus.* In qua hic versus est :

Quí postquam tibi appáreo atque aedítumor in templó tuo.

8 Titus autem Lucretius in carmine suo pro " aedituis " "aeдituentes" appellat.

XI

Errare istos qui spe et fiducia latendi peccent, cum latebra peccati perpetua nulla sit; et super ea re Peregrini philosophi sermo et Sophocli poetae sententia.

1 PHILOSOPHUM nomine Peregrinum, cui postea cognomentum Proteus factum est, virum gravem atque constantem, vidimus, cum Athenis essemus, deversantem in quodam tugurio extra urbem. Cumque ad eum frequenter ventitaremus, multa hercle dicere eum utiliter et honeste audivimus. In quibus id fuit, quod praecipuum auditu meminimus :
2 Virum quidem sapientem non peccaturum esse dicebat, etiamsi peccasse eum dii atque homines

---

[1] IV in, *added by Vogel.*

---

[1] Fr. 16, Bährens.   [2] ii. 4. 96.
[3] v. 2, Ribbeck.[3]   [4] vi. 1273

in the *Protesilaodamia* I think, used *claustritumum* [1] of one who had charge of the fastenings of a door, evidently using the same formation by which he saw that *aeditumus,* or "one who guards the temples," is made. In the most reliable copies of Marcus Tullius' *Fourth Oration against Verres* I find it written: [2] "The custodians (*aeditumi*) and guards quickly perceive it," but in the ordinary copies *aeditui* is read. There is an Atellan farce of Pomponius' entitled *Aeditumus.* In it is this line: [3]

As soon as I attend you and keep your temple-door (*aeditumor*).

Titus Lucretius too in his poem [4] speaks of *aedituentes,* instead of *aeditui.* [5]

XI

That those are deceived who sin in the confident hope of being undetected, since there is no permanent concealment of wrongdoing; and on that subject a discourse of the philosopher Peregrinus and a saying of the poet Sophocles.

When I was at Athens, I met a philosopher named Peregrinus, who was later surnamed Proteus, a man of dignity and fortitude, living in a hut outside the city. And visiting him frequently, I heard him say many things that were in truth helpful and noble. Among these I particularly recall the following:

He used to say that a wise man would not commit a sin, even if he knew that neither gods nor men

[5] Both *aeditumus* and *aedituus* are good Latin words. The former is made like *finitumus* and originally meant "belonging to a temple"; it derived its meaning "guardian of a temple" from *aedituus* (*aedes* and *tueor*).

3 ignoraturi forènt. Non enim poenae aut infamiae
metu non esse peccandum censebat, sed iusti honesti-
4 que studio et officio. Si qui tamen non essent tali
vel ingenio vel disciplina praediti, uti se vi sua ac
sua sponte facile a peccando tenerent, eos omnis tunc
peccare proclivius existimabat, cum latere posse id
peccatum putarent inpunitatemque ex ea latebra
5 sperarent. " At si sciant," inquit, "homines nihil
omnium rerum diutius posse celari, repressius pu-
6 dentiusque peccabitur." Propterea versus istos
Sophocli, prudentissimi poetarum, in ore esse habendos dicebat :

Πρὸς ταῦτα κρύπτε μηδέν, ὡς ἅπανθ' ὁρῶν
Καὶ πάντ' ἀκούων πάντ' ἀναπτύσσει χρόνος.

7 Alius quidam veterum poetarum, cuius nomen
mihi nunc memoriae non est, Veritatem Temporis
filiam esse dixit.

XII

Faceta responsio M. Ciceronis, amolientis a se crimen manifesti mendacii.

1 HAEC quoque disciplina rhetorica[1] est, callide et
cum astu res criminosas citra periculum confiteri, ut
si obiectum sit turpe aliquid quod negari non queat,
responsione ioculari eludas et rem facias risu magis
dignam quam crimine, sicut fecisse Ciceronem scriptum est, cum id quod infitiari non poterat urbano

[1] Hoc . . . disciplinae rhetoricae, *Nettleship.*

would know it; for he thought that one ought to
refrain from sin, not through fear of punishment or
disgrace, but from love of justice and honesty and
from a sense of duty. If, however, there were any
who were neither so endowed by nature nor so well
disciplined that they could easily keep themselves
from sinning by their own will power, he thought
that such men would all be more inclined to sin
whenever they thought that their guilt could be
concealed and when they had hope of impunity because of such concealment. " But," said he, " if men
know that nothing at all can be hidden for very long,
they will sin more reluctantly and more secretly."
Therefore he said that one should have on his lips
these verses of Sophocles, the wisest of poets : [1]

> See to it lest you try aught to conceal ;
> Time sees and hears all, and will all reveal.

Another one of the old poets, whose name has
escaped my memory at present, called Truth the
daughter of Time.

XII

A witty reply of Marcus Cicero, in which he strives to refute
the charge of a direct falsehood.

This also is part of a rhetorical training, cunningly
and cleverly to admit charges not attended with
danger, so that if something base is thrown up to
you which cannot be denied, you may turn it off by
a jocular reply, making the thing seem deserving of
laughter rather than censure. This we read that
Cicero did, when by a witty and clever remark he

[1] Fr. 280 N[2].

2 facetoque dicto diluit. Nam cum emere vellet in
Palatio domum et pecuniam in praesens non haberet,
a P. Sulla, qui tum reus erat, mutua sestertium
3 viciens tacita accepit. Ea res tamen, priusquam
emeret, prodita est et in vulgus exivit, obiectumque
ei est quod pecuniam domus emendae causa a reo
4 accepisset. Tum Cicero, inopinata obprobratione
permotus, accepisse se negavit ac domum quoque se
empturum negavit atque "Adeo," inquit, "verum
sit accepisse me pecuniam, si domum emero." Sed
cum postea emisset et hoc mendacium in senatu ei ab
amicis obiceretur, risit satis atque inter ridendum :
"'Ακοινονόητοι," inquit, "homines estis, cum ignoratis
prudentis et cauti patrisfamilias esse, quod emere
velit empturum sese negare propter competitores
emptionis."

XIII

' Intra Kalendas " cum dicitur, quid significet, utrum "ante
Kalendas " an "Kalendis " an utrumque ; atque inibi.
quid sit in oratione M. Tulli "intra oceanum " et "intra
montem Taurum " et in quadam epistula "intra modum."

1 CUM Romae a consulibus iudex extra ordinem datus
pronuntiare "intra Kalendas " iussus essem, Sulpicium

---

1 About $100,000 or £20,000.
2 He was charged with participation in the conspiracy of
Catiline.
3 From early times the examination of the evidence in
cases at law was turned over by the magistrates to private
persons, who acted under instruction from the magistrate.
Lawsuits consisted of two parts : a preliminary hearing
before the magistrate (in iure) and the proceedings in iudicio

put aside what could not be denied. For when he wished to buy a house on the Palatine, and did not have the ready money, he received a loan of 2,000,000 sesterces[1] privately from Publius Sulla, who was at the time under accusation.[2] But before he bought the house, the transaction became known and reached the ears of the people, and he was charged with having received money from an accused man for the purpose of buying a house. Then Cicero, disturbed by the unexpected reproach, said that he had not received the money and also declared that he had no intention of buying a house, adding: "Therefore, if I buy the house, let it be considered that I did receive the money." But when later he had bought the house and was twitted in the senate with this falsehood by friends, he laughed heartily, saying as he did so: "You are men devoid of common sense, if you do not know that it is the part of a prudent and careful head of a family to get rid of rival purchasers by declaring that he does not intend to buy something that he wishes to purchase."

XIII

What is meant by the expression "within the Kalends," whether it signifies "before the Kalends" or "on the Kalends," or both: also the meaning of "within the Ocean" and "within Mount Taurus" in a speech of Marcus Tullius, and of "within the limit" in one of his letters.

WHEN I had been named by the consuls a judge extraordinary at Rome,[3] and ordered to give judgment "within the Kalends," I asked Sulpicius Apollinaris,

before the private judge. Gellius mentions a similar appointment by the praetors in xiv. 2. 1.

Apollinarem, doctum hominem, percontatus sum an his verbis " intra Kalendas" ipsae quoque Kalendae tenerentur, dixique ei me [1] videlicet datum Kalendas que mihi prodictas, ut intra eum diem pronuntiarem.

2 " Cur," inquit, " hoc me potius rogas quam ex istis aliquem peritis studiosisque iuris, quos adhibere in consilium iudicaturi soletis?" Tum illi ego ita 3 respondi : " Si aut de vetere," inquam, "iure et [2] recepto aut controverso et ambiguo aut novo et constituto discendum esset, issem plane sciscitatum ad 4 istos quos dicis ; sed cum verborum Latinorum sententia, usus, ratio exploranda sit, scaevus profecto et caecus animi forem, si, cum haberem tui copiam, 5 issem magis ad alium quam ad te." " Audi igitur," inquit, " de ratione verbi quid existimem, sed eo tamen pacto ut id facias, non quod ego de proprietate vocis disseruero, sed quod in ea re omnium pluriumve consensu observari cognoveris ; non enim verborum tantum communium verae atque propriae significationes longiore usu mutantur, sed legum quoque ipsarum iussa consensu tacito oblitterantur."

6 Tum deinde disseruit, me et plerisque aliis audientibus, in hunc ferme modum : " Cum dies," inquit, " ita praefinita est, ut iudex ' intra Kalendas ' pronuntiet, occupavit iam haec omnes opinio, non esse dubium quin ante Kalendas iure pronuntietur, et id tantum

---

[1] me iudicem, *Hertz* (N[2]) ; me *omitted by Q*.
[2] et, *Hosius* ; aut, ω.

---

[1] That is, *intra*.

a learned man, whether the phrase "within the Kalends" included the Kalends themselves; and I told him that I had been duly appointed, that the Kalends had been set as the limit, and that I was to give judgment "within" that day. "Why," said he, "do you make this inquiry of me rather than of some one of those who are students of the law and learned in it, whom you are accustomed to take into your counsel when about to act as judge?" Then I answered him as follows: "If I needed information about some ancient point of law that had been established, one that was contested and ambiguous, or one that was newly ratified, I should naturally have gone to inquire of those whom you mention. But when the meaning, use and nature of Latin words is to be investigated, I should indeed be stupid and mentally blind, if, having the opportunity of consulting you, I had gone to another rather than to you." "Hear then," said he, "my opinion about the meaning of the word,[1] but be it understood that you will not act according to what I shall say about its nature, but according to what you shall learn to be the interpretation agreed upon by all, or by very many, men; for not only are the true and proper significations of common words changed by long usage, but even the provisions of the laws themselves become a dead letter by tacit consent."

Then he proceeded to discourse, in my hearing and that of several others, in about this fashion: "When the time," said he, "is so defined that the judge is to render a decision 'within the Kalends,' everyone at once jumps to the conclusion that there is no doubt that the verdict may lawfully be rendered before the Kalends, and I observe that the only

ambigi video quod tu quaeris, an Kalendis quoque
7 iure pronuntietur. Ipsum autem verbum sic procul
dubio natum est atque ita sese habet, ut, cum dicitur
'intra Kalendas,' non alius accipi dies debeat quam
solae Kalendae. Nam tres istae voces 'intra, citra,
ultra,' quibus certi locorum fines demonstrantur, singu-
laribus apud veteres syllabis appellabantur 'in, cis,
8 uls.' Haec deinde particulae quoniam parvo exiguo-
que sonitu obscurius promebantur, addita est tribus
omnibus eadem syllaba, et quod dicebatur 'cis Tiberim' et 'uls Tiberim' dici coeptum est 'citra Tiberim' et 'ultra Tiberim'; item quod erat 'in,' acce-
9 dente eadem syllaba, 'intra' factum est. Sunt ergo
haec omnia quasi contermina iunctis inter se finibus
cohaerentia: 'intra oppidum,' 'ultra oppidum,'
'citra oppidum,' ex quibus 'intra,' sicuti dixi, 'in'
10 significat; nam qui dicit 'intra oppidum,' 'intra
cubiculum,' 'intra ferias,' non dicit aliud quam 'in
oppido,' 'in cubiculo,' 'in feriis.'
11 "'Intra Kalendas' igitur non 'ante Kalendas' est,
sed 'in Kalendis'; id est, eo ipso die quo Kalendae
12 sunt. Itaque secundum verbi ipsius rationem qui
iussus est 'intra Kalendas' pronuntiare, nisi Kalendis
13 pronuntiet, contra iussum vocis facit; nam, si ante id
14 fiat, non 'intra' pronuntiat, sed 'citra.' Nescio quo
autem pacto recepta vulgo interpretatio est absur-

question is the one which you raise, namely, whether the decision may lawfully be rendered also on the Kalends. But undoubtedly the word itself is of such origin and such a nature that when the expression 'within the Kalends' is used, no other day ought to be meant than the Kalends alone. For those three words *intra, citra, ultra* (within, this side, beyond), by which definite boundaries of places are indicated, among the early writers were expressed by monosyllables, *in, cis, uls*. Then, since these particles had a somewhat obscure utterance because of their brief and slight sound, the same syllable was added to all three words, and what was formerly *cis Tiberim* (on this side of the Tiber) and *uls Tiberim* (beyond the Tiber) began to be called *citra Tiberim* and *ultra Tiberim*; and *in* also became *intra* by the addition of the same syllable. Therefore all these expressions are, so to speak, related, being united by common terminations: *intra oppidum, ultra oppidum, citra oppidum*, of which *intra*, as I have said, is equivalent to *in*; for one who says *intra oppidum, intra cubiculum, intra ferias* means nothing else than *in oppido* (in the town), *in cubiculo* (in the room), *in feriis* (during the festival).

" 'Within the Kalends,' then, is not 'before the Kalends,' but 'on the Kalends'; that is, on the very day on which the Kalends fall. Therefore, according to the meaning of the word itself, one who is ordered to give judgment 'within the Kalends,' unless he do so on the Kalends, acts contrary to the order contained in the phrase; for if he does so earlier, he renders a decision not 'within' but 'before the Kalends.' But somehow or other the utterly absurd interpretation has been generally adopted,

dissima, ut ' intra Kalendas ' significare videatur etiam
' citra Kalendas' vel 'ante Kalendas,' nihil enim

15 ferme interest. Atque insuper dubitatur an Kalendis
quoque pronuntiari possit, quando neque ultra
neque citra, set, quod inter haec medium est, 'intra

16 Kalendas,' id est Kalendis,[1] pronuntiandum sit. Sed
nimirum consuetudo vicit, quae cum omnium domina
rerum, tum maxime verborum est."

17   Ea omnia cum Apollinaris scite perquam atque
enucleate disputavisset, tum ego haec dixi : " Cordi,"
inquam, "mihi fuit, priusquam ad te irem, quaerere
explorareque quonam modo veteres nostri particula
ista qua de agitur usi sint, atque ita invenimus
Tullium in *Tertia in Verrem* scripsisse istoc modo :
' Locus intra oceanum iam nullus est, neque tam
longincus neque tam reconditus, quo non per haec
tempora nostrorum hominum libido iniquitasque

18 pervaserit.' ' Intra oceanum ' dicit contra rationem
tuam ; non enim vult, opinor, dicere ' in oceano ' ;
terras enim demonstrat omnis quae oceano ambiun-
tur, ad quas a nostris hominibus adiri potest, quae
sunt ' citra oceanum,' non ' in oceano ' ; neque enim
videri potest insulas significare nescio quas, quae
penitus esse intra aequora ipsa oceáni dicuntur."

19   Tunc Sulpicius Apollinaris renidens : " Non me
hercule inargute," inquit, " nec incallide opposuisti
hoc Tullianum ; sed Cicero ' intra oceanum,' non, ut

20 tu interpretare, ' citra oceanum ' dixit. Quid enim
potest dici ' citra oceanum ' esse, cum undique

---

[1] id est Kalendis, *deleted by Hertz.*

---

[1] ii. 3. 207.

that 'within the Kalends' evidently means also 'on this side of the Kalends' or 'before the Kalends'; for these are nearly the same thing. And, besides, it is doubted whether a decision may be rendered on the Kalends also, since it must be rendered neither beyond nor before that date, but 'within the Kalends,' a time which lies between these; that is to say, 'on the Kalends.' But no doubt usage has gained the victory, the mistress not only of all things, but particularly of language."

After this very learned and clear discussion of the subject by Apollinaris, I then spoke as follows: "It occurred to me," said I, "before coming to you, to inquire and investigate how our ancestors used the particle in question. Accordingly, I found that Tullius in his *Third Oration against Verres* wrote thus:[1] 'There is no place within the ocean (*intra oceanum*) either so distant or so hidden, that the licentiousness and injustice of our countrymen has not penetrated it.' He uses 'within the ocean' contrary to your reasoning; for he does not, I think, wish to say 'in the ocean,' but he indicates all the lands which are surrounded by the ocean and to which our countrymen have access; and these are 'this side the ocean,' not 'in the ocean.' For he cannot be supposed to mean some islands or other, which are spoken of as far within the waters of the ocean itself."

Then with a smile Sulpicius Apollinaris replied: "Keenly and cleverly, by Heaven! have you confronted me with this Ciceronian passage; but Cicero said 'within the ocean,' not, as you interpret it, 'this side ocean.' What pray can be said to be 'on this side of the ocean,' when the ocean surrounds and

oceanus circumscribat omnis terras et ambiat? Nam
'citra' quod est, id extra est; qui autem potest
'intra' esse dici, quod extra est? Sed si ex una
tantum parte orbis oceanus foret, tum quae terra ad
eam partem foret, 'citra oceanum' esse dici posset
vel 'ante oceanum'; cum vero omnis terras omni-
fariam et undiqueversum circumfluat, nihil citra eum
est, sed, undarum illius ambitu terris omnibus con-
vallatis, in medio eius sunt omnia, quae intra oras
eius inclusa sunt, sicuti hercle sol non citra caelum
vertitur, sed in caelo et intra caelum."

Haec tunc Apollinaris scite acuteque dicere visus
21 est. Set postea in libro M. Tullii *Epistularum ad
Servium Sulpicium* sic dictum esse invenimus " intra
modum," ut "intra Kalendas" dicunt qui dicere
22 " citra Kalendas" volunt. Verba haec Ciceronis
sunt, quae adposui: " Sed tamen, quoniam effugi
eius offensionem,[1] qui fortasse arbitraretur me hanc
rem publicam [2] non putare, si perpetuo tacerem,
modice hoc faciam aut etiam intra modum, ut et
23 illius voluntati et meis studiis serviam." " Modice "
dixerat " hoc faciam," [3] id est cum modo aequo et
24 pari; deinde, quasi hoc displiceret et corrigere id
vellet, addit: " aut etiam intra modum," per quod
ostendit minus sese id facturum esse quam quod
fieri modice videretur; id est, non ad ipsum modum,
sed retro paululum et citra modum.

---

[1] offensionem, *Cic.*; occasionem, ω.
[2] rem publicam, *Cic.*; rem imperite, ω (impertire, Q).
[3] faciam *omitted by* ω.

---

[1] The Greeks of early times regarded the ocean as a great
river encircling the earth.

encircles all lands on every side?[1] For that which is 'on this side' of a thing, is outside of that thing; but how can that be said to be 'within' which is without? But if the ocean were only on one side of the world, then the land in that part might be said to be 'this side the ocean,' or 'before the ocean.' But since the ocean surrounds all lands completely and everywhere, nothing is on this side of it, but, all lands being walled in by the embrace of its waters, everything which is included within its shore is in its midst, just as in truth the sun moves, not on this side of the heavens, but within and in them."

At the time, what Sulpicius Apollinaris said seemed to be learned and acute. But later, in a volume of *Letters to Servius Sulpicius* by Marcus Tullius, I found "within moderation" (*intra modum*) used in the same sense that those give to "within the Kalends" who mean to say "this side of the Kalends." These are the words of Cicero, which I quote:[2] "But yet since I have avoided the displeasure of Caesar, who would perhaps think that I did not regard the present government as constitutional if I kept silence altogether, I shall do this[3] moderately, or even less than moderately (*intra modum*), so as to consult both his wishes and my own desires." He first said "I shall do this moderately," that is, to a fair and temperate degree; then, as if this expression did not please him and he wished to correct it, he added "or even within moderation," thus indicating that he would do it to a less extent than might be considered moderate; that is, not up to the very limit, but somewhat short of, or "on this side of" the limit.

---

[2] *Ad Fam.* IV. 4. 4.
[3] *i.e.*, take part in politics.

25 In oratione etiam, quam *Pro P. Sestio* scripsit,
"intra montem Taurum" sic dicit, ut non significet
"in monte Tauro," sed "usque ad montem cum ipso
26 monte." Verba sunt haec ipsius M. Tullii ex ea qua
dixi oratione : "Antiochum Magnum illum maiores
nostri magna belli contentione terra marique supera-
tum intra montem Taurum regnare iusserunt ; Asiam,
qua illum multarunt, Attalo, ut is in ea regnaret,
27 condonarunt." "Intra montem," inquit, "Taurum
regnare iusserunt," quod non proinde est, ut "intra
cubiculum" dicimus, nisi videri potest id esse
"intra montem" quod est intra regiones quae Tauri
28 montis obiectu separantur. Nam sicuti qui "intra
cubiculum" est, is non in cubiculi parietibus, sed
intra parietes est quibus cubiculum includitur, qui
tamen ipsi quoque parietes in cubiculo sunt, ita, qui
regnat "intra montem Taurum," non solum in monte
Tauro regnat, sed in his etiam regionibus quae Tauro
monte clauduntur.

29 Num igitur secundum istam verborum M. Tullii
similitudinem, qui iubetur "intra Kalendas" pronuntiare, is et ante Kalendas et ipsis Kalendis iure
pronuntiare potest ? Neque id fit quasi privilegio
quodam inscitae consuetudinis, sed certa rationis
observatione, quoniam omne tempus, quod Kalenda-
rum die includitur, "intra Kalendas" esse recte
dicitur.

---

[1] § 58.

Also in the speech which he wrote *In Defence of Publius Sestius* Cicero says "within Mount Taurus" in such a way as to mean, not "on Mount Taurus," but "as far as the mountain and including the mountain itself." These are Cicero's own words in the speech which I have mentioned:[1] "Our forbears, having overcome Antiochus the Great after a mighty struggle on land and sea, ordered him to confine his realm 'within Mount Taurus.' Asia, which they had taken from him, they gave to Attalus, to be his kingdom." Cicero says: "They ordered him to confine his realm within Mount Taurus," which is not the same as when we say "within the room," unless "within the mountain" may appear to mean what is within the regions which are separated by the interposition of Mount Taurus.[2] For just as one who is "within a room" is not in the walls of the room, but is within the walls by which the room is enclosed, which walls themselves are yet equally in the room, just so one who rules "within Mount Taurus," not only rules on Mount Taurus but also in those regions which are bounded by Mount Taurus.

According therefore to the analogy of the words of Marcus Tullius may not one who is bidden to make a decision "within the Kalends" lawfully make it before the Kalends and on the Kalends themselves? And this results, not from a sort of privilege conceded to ignorant usage, but from an accurate regard for reason, since all time which is embraced by the day of the Kalends is correctly said to be "within the Kalends."

[2] This is the usage of the Greek geographers, such as Strabo, who uses ἔσω τοῦ ἰσθμοῦ and ἔσω τοῦ Ταύρου in the sense of "south of the isthmus" and "south of Taurus."

XIV

"Saltem" particula quam vim habeat et quam originem.

1   " SALTEM " particula quam haberet principem significationem, quaeque vocis istius origo esset, quaere-
2 bamus.   Ita enim primitus factam esse apparet, ut
non videatur, sicuti quaedam subplementa orationis,
3 temere et incondite adsumpta.   Atque erat qui
diceret legisse se in *Grammaticis Commentariis* P.
Nigidii, "saltem" ex eo dictum quod esset "si
aliter," idque ipsum dici solitum per defectionem,
nam plenam esse sententiam, " si aliter non potest."
4 Sed id nos in isdem commentariis P. Nigidii, cum
eos non, opinor, incuriose legissemus, nusquam invenimus.
5   Videntur autem verba ista " si aliter non potest"
a significatione quidem voculae huius de qua quaeri-
mus non abhorrere.   Set tot verba tamen in paucis-
simas litteras cludere, inprobae cuiusdam subtilitatis
6 est.   Fuit etiam qui diceret, homo in libris atque in
litteris adsiduus, "saltem " sibi dictum videri *u* littera
media extrita ; " salutem " enim ante dictum, quod
nos "saltem " diceremus.   " Nam cum alia quaedam
petita et non impetrata sunt, tum solemus," inquit,
" quasi extremum aliquid petituri quod negari minime
debeat, dicere ' hoc saltem fieri aut dari oportere,'
tamquam salutem postremo petentes, quam impe-
7 trari certe et obtineri sit aequissimum."   Sed hoc

XIV

The meaning and origin of the particle *saltem*.

WE were inquiring what the original meaning of the particle *saltem* (at least) was, and what was the derivation of the word; for it seems to have been so formed from the first that it does not appear, like some aids to expression, to have been adopted inconsiderately and irregularly. And there was one man who said that he had read in the *Grammatical Notes* of Publius Nigidius[1] that *saltem* was derived from *si aliter*, and that this itself was an elliptical expression, since the complete sentence was *si aliter non potest*, "if otherwise, it cannot be." But I myself have nowhere come upon that statement in those *Notes* of Publius Nigidius, although I have read them, I think, with some care.

However, that phrase *si aliter non potest* does not seem at variance with the meaning of the word under discussion. But yet to condense so many words into a very few letters shows a kind of misplaced subtlety. There was also another man, devoted to books and letters, who said that *saltem* seemed to him to be formed by the syncope of a medial *u*, saying that what we call *saltem* was originally *salutem*. "For when some other things have been requested and refused, then," said he, "we are accustomed, as if about to make a final request which ought by no means to be denied, to say 'this at least (*saltem*) ought to be done or given,' as if at last seeking safety (*salutem*), which it is surely most just to grant and to obtain." But this also,

[1] p. 19, 66, Swoboda.

itidem non inlepide quidem fictum, nimis tamen esse
videtur commenticium. Censuimus igitur amplius
quaerendum.

XV

Quod Sisenna in libris *Historiarum* adverbis huiuscemodi
saepenumero usus est: "celatim," "vellicatim," "saltuatim."

1   Cum lectitaremus *Historiam* Sisennae adsidue,
huiuscemodi figurae adverbia in oratione eius animadvertimus cuimodi sunt haec: "cursim," "properatim," "celatim," "vellicatim," "saltuatim."
2   Ex quibus duo prima, quia sunt notiora, exemplis
non indigebant, reliqua in *Historiarum* sexto sic
scripta sunt: "Quam maxime celatim poterat, in
insidiis suos disponit." Item alio in loco: "Nos
una aestate in Asia et Graecia gesta litteris idcirco
continentia mandavimus, ne vellicatim aut saltuatim scribendo lectorum animos impediremus."

---

¹ *Saltem* or *saltim* is the accusative of a noun (cf. *partim*,
etc.) derived by some from the root of *sal-vus* and *sal-us*; by
others from that of *sal-io*; Walde, *Lat. Etym. Wörterb. s.v.*
accepts Warren's derivation from *si alitem* (formed from *item*),
meaning "if otherwise."

though ingeniously contrived, seems too far-fetched. I thought therefore that further investigation was necessary.[1]

XV

That Sisenna in his Histories *has frequently used adverbs of the type of* celatim, vellicatim *and* saltuatim.

WHILE diligently reading the *History* of Sisenna, I observed that he used adverbs of this form: *cursim* (rapidly), *properatim* (hastily), *celatim*, *vellicatim*, *saltuatim*. Of these the first two, since they are more common, do not require illustration. The rest are to be found in the sixth book of the *Histories* in these passages: "He arranged his men in ambush as secretly (*celatim*) as he could."[2] Also in another place:[3] "I have written of the events of one summer in Asia and Greece in a consecutive form, that I might not by writing piecemeal or in disconnected fashion (*vellicatim aut saltuatim*) confuse the minds of my readers."[4]

[2] Fr. 126, Peter[2].   [3] Fr. 127, Peter[2].
[4] These adverbs too are accusatives; see note 1 on chapter xiv.

BOOK XIII

LIBER TERTIUS DECIMUS

I

Inquisitio verborum istorum M. Tulli curiosior quae sunt [1] in primo *Antonianarum* libro, "multa autem inpendere videntur praeter naturam etiam praeterque fatum"; tractatumque an idem duo ista significent, "fatum" atque "natura," an diversum.

1 MARCUS CICERO in primo *Antonianarum* ita scriptum reliquit: "Hunc igitur ut sequerer properavi quem praesentes non sunt secuti; non ut proficerem aliquid, neque enim sperabam id nec praestare poteram, sed ut, si quid mihi humanitus accidisset, multa autem inpendere videntur praeter naturam etiam [2] praeterque fatum, huius diei vocem testem reipublicae relinquerem meae perpetuae erga se

2 voluntatis." "Praeter naturam," inquit, "praeterque fatum." An utrumque idem valere voluerit "fatum" atque "naturam" et duas res καθ᾽ ἑνὸς ὑποκειμένου posuerit, an vero diviserit separaritque, ut alios casus natura ferre videatur, alios fatum, considerandum equidem puto, atque id maxime requirendum, qua ratione dixerit accidere multa humanitus posse praeter fatum, quando sic ratio et ordo et insuperabilis quaedam necessitas fati

---

[1] sunt, *Damsté*; fuit, ω.
[2] *Many MSS. of Cic. omit* etiam.

---

[1] *Phil.* i. 10.
[2] This is the recognized figure of speech known as hendiadys.

BOOK XIII

I

A somewhat careful inquiry into these words of Marcus
Tullius in his first *Oration against Antony* : "But many
things seem to threaten contrary even to nature and to
fate"; and a discussion ⸱f the question whether the words
"fate" and "nature" mean the same thing or something
different.

MARCUS CICERO, in his first *Oration against Antony,*[1]
has left us these words : "I hastened then to follow
him whom those present did not follow; not that I
might be of any service, for I had no hope of that
nor could I promise it, but in order that if anything
to which human nature is liable should happen to me
(and many things seem to threaten contrary even to
nature and contrary to fate) I might leave what I
have said to-day as a witness to my country of my
constant devotion to its interests." Cicero says
"contrary to nature and contrary to fate." Whether
he intended both words, "fate" and "nature," to
have the same meaning and has used two words to
designate one thing,[2] or whether he so divided and
separated them that nature seems to bring some
casualties and fate others, I think ought to be
investigated; and this question ought especially to
be asked—how it is that he has said that many things
to which humanity is liable can happen contrary to
fate, when the plan and order and a kind of un-
conquerable necessity of fate are so ordained that

constituitur, ut omnia intra fatum claudenda sint, nisi illud sane Homeri secutus est:

Μὴ καὶ ὑπὲρ μοῖραν δόμον ''Αιδος εἰσαφίκηαι.

3 Nihil autem dubium est quin violentam et inopinatam mortem significaverit, quae quidem potest recte videri accidere praeter naturam.

4 Sed cur id quoque genus mortis extra fatum posuerit, neque operis huius est explorare neque

5 temporis. Illud tamen non praetermittendum est, quod Vergilius quoque id ipsum quod Cicero de fato opinatus est, cum hoc in quarto libro dixit de Elissa, quae mortem per vim potita est:

Nam quia nec fato, merita nec morte peribat,

tamquam in faciendo fine vitae quae violenta sunt

6 non videantur e fato venire. Demosthenis autem, viri prudentia pari atque facundia praediti, verba idem fere significantia de natura atque fato M. Cicero secutus videtur. Ita enim scriptum est in oratione illa egregia, cui titulus est Ὑπὲρ Στεφάνου: Ὁ μὲν τοῖς γονεῦσι νομίζων μόνον γεγενῆσθαι, τὸν τῆς εἱμαρμένης καὶ τὸν αὐτόματον θάνατον περιμένει· ὁ δὲ καὶ τῇ πατρίδι, ὑπὲρ τοῦ μὴ ταύτην ἐπιδεῖν δουλεύουσαν

7 ἀποθνῄσκειν βουλεύσεται. Quod Cicero "fatum" atque "naturam" videtur dixisse, id multo ante Demosthenes τὴν πεπρωμένην et τὸν αὐτόματον θάνατον

8 appellavit. Αὐτόματος enim θάνατος, quasi naturalis et fatalis, nulla extrinsecus vi coactus venit.

---

[1] *Iliad*, xx. 336.   [2] *Aen*. iv. 696.
[3] 205, p. 296.

all things must be included within the decrees of fate ; unless perhaps he has followed Homer's saying :

Lest, spite of fate, you enter Hades' home.[1]

But there is no doubt that Cicero referred to a violent and sudden death, which may properly seem to happen contrary to nature.

But why he has put just that kind of death outside the decrees of fate it is not the part of this work to investigate, nor is this the time. The point, however, must not be passed by, that Virgil too had that same opinion about fate which Cicero had, when in his fourth book he said of Elissa, who inflicted a violent death upon herself :[2]

For since she perished not by fate's decree,
Nor earned her death ;

just as if, in making an end of life, those deaths which are violent do not seem to come by fate's decree. Cicero, however, seems to have followed the words of Demosthenes, a man gifted with equal wisdom and eloquence, which express about the same idea concerning nature and fate. For Demosthenes in that splendid oration entitled *On the Crown* wrote as follows[3] : " He who thinks that he was born only for his parents, awaits the death appointed by fate, the natural death ; but he who thinks that he was born also for his country, will be ready to die that he may not see his country enslaved." What Cicero seems to have called "fate" and "nature," Demosthenes long before termed "fate" and "the natural death." For "a natural death" is one which comes in the course of fate and nature, as it were, and is caused by no force from without.

II

Super poetarum Pacuvii et Accii conloquio familiari in oppido
Tarentino.

1   Quibus otium et studium fuit vitas atque aetates
doctorum hominum quaerere ac memoriae tradere,
de M. Pacuvio et L. Accio tragicis poetis historiam
2 scripserunt huiuscemodi : " Cum Pacuvius," inquiunt,
" grandi iam aetate et morbo corporis diutino
adfectus, Tarentum ex urbe Roma concessisset,
Accius tunc, haut parvo iunior, proficiscens in
Asiam, cum in oppidum venisset, devertit ad Pacuvium comiterque invitatus plusculisque ab eo diebus
retentus, tragoediam suam cui Atreus nomen est desi-
3 deranti legit." Tum Pacuvium dixisse aiunt sonora
quidem esse quae scripsisset et grandia, sed videri
4 tamen ea sibi duriora paulum et acerbiora. " Ita
est," inquit Accius, " uti dicis, neque id me sane
paenitet ; meliora enim fore spero, quae deinceps
5 scribam. Nam quod in pomis, itidem," inquit, " esse
aiunt in ingeniis ; quae dura et acerba nascuntur,
post fiunt mitia et iucunda ; sed quae gignuntur
statim vieta et mollia atque in principio sunt uvida,
6 non matura mox fiunt, sed putria. Relinquendum
igitur visum est in ingenio quod dies atque aetas
mitificet."

II

About an intimate talk of the poets Pacuvius and Accius in
the town of Tarentum.

THOSE who have had leisure and inclination to
inquire into the life and times of learned men and
hand them down to memory, have related the
following anecdote of the tragic poets Marcus
Pacuvius and Lucius Accius : " Pacuvius," they say,
" when already enfeebled by advanced age and constant bodily illness, had withdrawn from Rome to
Tarentum. Then Accius, who was a much younger
man, coming to Tarentum on ·his way to Asia,
visited Pacuvius, and being hospitably received and
detained by him for several days, at his request read
him his tragedy entitled *Atreus.*" Then they say
that Pacuvius remarked that what he had written
seemed sonorous and full of dignity, but that
nevertheless it appeared to him somewhat harsh and
rugged. "What you say is true," replied Accius,
"and I do not greatly regret it ; for it gives me hope
that what I write hereafter will be better. For they
say it is with the mind as it is with fruits ; those
which are at first harsh and bitter, later become mild
and sweet ; but those which at once grow mellow
and soft, and are juicy in the beginning, presently
become, not ripe, but decayed. Accordingly, it
has seemed to me that something should be left in
the products of the intellect for time and age to
mellow."

III

An vocabula haec, " necessitudo " et " necessitas," differenti significatione sint.

1 Rɪsu prorsus atque ludo res digna est, cum plerique grammaticorum adseverant, " necessitudinem " et " necessitatem " mutare differreque, ideo quod " necessitas " sit vis quaepiam premens et cogens, " necessitudo " autem dicatur ius quoddam et vinculum religiosae coniunctionis, idque unum solitarium 2 significet. Sicut autem nihil quicquam interest, " suavitudo " dicas an " suavitas," " sanctitudo " an " sanctitas," " acerbitudo " an " acerbitas," " acritudo " an, quod Accius in *Neoptolemo* scripsit, " acritas," ita nihil rationis dici potest qui " neces- 3 situdo " et " necessitas " separentur. Itaque in libris veterum vulgo reperias, " necessitudinem " 4 dici pro eo quod necessum est. Sed " necessitas " sane pro iure officioque observantiae adfinitatisve infrequens est, quamquam qui ob hoc ipsum ius adfinitatis familiaritatisque coniuncti sunt " neces- 5 sarii " dicuntur. Repperi tamen in oratione C. Caesaris, *Qua Plautiam Rogationem Suasit,* " necessitatem " dictam pro " necessitudine," id est iure adfinitatis. Verba haec sunt : " Equidem mihi videor pro nostra necessitate non labore, non opera, non industria defuisse."

6 Hoc ego scripsi de utriusque vocabuli indifferentia,

III

Whether the words *necessitudo* and *necessitas* differ from each
other in meaning.

It is a circumstance decidedly calling for laughter
and ridicule, when many grammarians assert that
necessitudo and *necessitas* are unlike and different, in
that *necessitas* is an urgent and compelling force, but
necessitudo is a certain right and binding claim of
consecrated intimacy, and that this is its only meaning. But just as it makes no difference at all whether
you say *suavitudo* or *suavitas* (sweetness), *acerbitudo*
or *acerbitas* (bitterness), *acritudo* or *acritas* (sharp-
ness), as Accius wrote in his *Neoptolemus*,[1] in the
same way no reason can be assigned for separating
necessitudo and *necessitas*. Accordingly, in the books
of the early writers you may often find *necessitudo*
used of that which is necessary; but *necessitas* certainly
is seldom applied to the law and duty of respect and
relationship, in spite of the fact that those who are
united by that very law and duty of relationship and intimacy are called *necessarii* (kinsfolk).
However, in a speech of Gaius Caesar,[2] *In Support
of the Plautian Law,* I found *necessitas* used for
necessitudo, that is for the bond of relationship.
His words are as follows:[3] "To me indeed it
seems that, as our kinship (*necessitas*) demanded,
I have failed neither in labour, in pains, nor in
industry."

I have written this with regard to the lack of dis-

---

[1] 467, Ribbeck[3].
[2] *i.e.* Gaius Iulius Caesar.
[3] ii., p. 121, Dinter; *O. R. F.*[2], p. 412.

admonitus forte verbi istius, cum legerem Sempronii Asellionis, veteris scriptoris, quartum ex *Historia* librum, in quo de P. Africano, Pauli filio, ita scriptum est: " Nam se patrem suum audisse dicere L. Aemilium Paulum, nimis[1] bonum imperatorem signis conlatis non decertare, nisi summa necessitudo aut summa occasio data esset."

IV

Descripta Alexandri ad matrem Olympiadem epistula; et quid Olympias festive ei rescripserit.[2]

1 IN plerisque monimentis rerum ab Alexandro gestarum, et paulo ante in libro M. Varronis qui inscriptus est *Orestes vel De Insania,* Olympiadem, Philippi uxorem, festivissime rescripsisse legimus 2 Alexandro filio. Nam cum is ad matrem ita scripsisset: " Rex Alexander, Iovis Hammonis filius, Olympiadi matri salutem dicit," Olympias ei rescripsit ad hanc sententiam: " Amabo," inquit, " mi fili, quiescas neque deferas me neque criminere adversum Iunonem ; malum mihi prorsus illa magnum dabit, cum tu me litteris tuis paelicem esse illi 3 confiteris." Ea mulieris scitae atque prudentis erga ferocem filium comitas sensim et comiter admonuisse eum visa est deponendam esse opinionem vanam quam ille ingentibus victoriis et adulantium blandimentis et rebus supra fidem prosperis inbiberat, genitum esse sese de Iove.

---

[1] minime, *Hosius, omitting* non ; *he regards* L. Aemilius Paulus *as a gloss.*

[2] ad matrem . . . rescripserit, *supplied by Hertz.*

tinction between these two words as the result of reading the fourth book of the *History* of Sempronius Asellio, an early writer, in which he wrote as follows about Publius Africanus, the son of Paulus:[1] "For he had heard his father, Lucius Aemilius Paulus, say that a really able general never engaged in a pitched battle, unless the utmost necessity (*necessitudo*) demanded, or the most favourable opportunity offered."

IV

Copy of a letter of Alexander to his mother Olympias; and Olympias' witty reply.

In many of the records of Alexander's deeds, and not long ago in the book of Marcus Varro entitled *Orestes or On Madness*, I have read[2] that Olympias, the wife of Philip, wrote a very witty reply to her son Alexander. For he had addressed his mother as follows: "King Alexander, son of Jupiter Hammon, greets his mother Olympias." Olympias replied to this effect: "Pray, my son," said she, "be silent, and do not slander me or accuse me before Juno; undoubtedly she will take cruel vengeance on me, if you admit in your letters that I am her husband's paramour." This courteous reply of a wise and prudent woman to her arrogant son seemed to warn him in a mild and polite fashion to give up the foolish idea which he had formed from his great victories, from the flattery of his courtiers, and from his incredible success—that he was the son of Jupiter.

[1] Fr. 5, Peter.
[2] p. 255, Riese.

V

De Aristotele et Theophrasto et Eudemo philosophis ; deque eleganti verecundia Aristotelis successorem diatribae suae eligentis.

1 ARISTOTELES philosophus, annos iam fere natus duo et sexaginta, corpore aegro adfectoque ac spe vitae
2 tenui fuit. Tunc omnis eius sectatorum cohors ad eum accedit, orantes obsecrantesque ut ipse deligeret loci sui et magisterii successorem, quo post summum eius diem proinde ut ipso uterentur ad studia doctrinarum conplenda excolendaque quibus ab eo
3 inbuti fuissent. Erant tunc in eius ludo boni multi, sed praecipui duo, Theophrastus et Eudemus. Ingenio hi atque doctrinis ceteros praestabant ; alter
4 ex insula Lesbo fuit, Eudemus autem Rodo. Aristoteles respondit facturum esse quod vellent, cum id sibi foret tempestivum.
5 Postea brevi tempore, cum idem illi qui de magistro destinando petierant praesentes essent, vinum ait quod tum biberet non esse id ex valitudine sua, sed insalubre esse atque asperum ac propterea quaeri debere exoticum, vel Rodium aliquod vel
6 Lesbium. Id sibi utrumque ut curarent petivit,
7 usurumque eo dixit quod sese magis iuvisset. Eunt,
8 quaerunt, inveniunt, adferunt. Tum Aristoteles Rodium petit, degustat : " Firmum," inquit, " hercle
9 vinum et iucundum." Petit mox Lesbium. Quo item degustato : " Utrumque," inquit, " oppido
10 bonum, sed ἡδίων ὁ Λέσβιος." Id ubi dixit, nemini fuit dubium quin lepide simul et verecunde succes-

424

V

On the philosophers Aristotle, Theophrastus and Eudemus; and of the graceful tact of Aristotle in selecting a successor as head of his school.

THE philosopher Aristotle, being already nearly sixty-two years of age, was sickly and weak of body and had slender hope of life. Then the whole band of his disciples came to him, begging and entreating that he should himself choose a successor to his position and his office, to whom, as to himself, they might apply after his last day, to complete and perfect their knowledge of the studies into which he had initiated them. There were at the time in his school many good men, but two were conspicuous, Theophrastus and Eudemus, who excelled the rest in talent and learning. The former was from the island of Lesbos, but Eudemus from Rhodes. Aristotle replied that he would do what they asked, so soon as the opportunity came.

A little later, in the presence of the same men who had asked him to appoint a master, he said that the wine he was then drinking did not suit his health, but was unwholesome and harsh; that therefore they ought to look for a foreign wine, something either from Rhodes or from Lesbos. He asked them to procure both kinds for him, and said that he would use the one which he liked the better. They went, sought, found, brought. Then Aristotle asked for the Rhodian and tasting it said: "This is truly a sound and pleasant wine." Then he called for the Lesbian. Tasting that also, he remarked: "Both are very good indeed, but the Lesbian is the sweeter." When he said this, no one doubted that gracefully, and at the same time tactfully, he had

11 sorem illa voce sibi, non vinum delegisset. Is erat
e Lesbo Theophrastus, suavitate homo insigni
12 linguae pariter atque vitae. Itaque non diu post
Aristotele vita defuncto, ad Theophrastum omnes
concesserunt.

VI

Quid veteres Latini dixerint quas Graeci προσῳδίας appellant ;
item quod vocabulum "barbarismi" non usurpaverint
neque Romani antiquiores neque Attici.

1 QUAS Graeci προσῳδίας dicunt, eas veteres docti
tum "notas vocum," tum "moderamenta," tum
2 "accentiunculas," tum "voculationes" appellabant ;
quod nunc autem "barbare" quem loqui dicimus, id
vitium sermonis non "barbarum" esse, sed "rusti-
cum," et cum eo vitio loquentes "rustice" loqui
3 dictitabant. P. Nigidius in *Commentariis Grammaticis* :
"Rusticus fit sermo," inquit, "si adspires perperam."
4 Itaque id vocabulum, quod dicitur vulgo "barbarismus," qui ante divi Augusti aetatem pure atque
integre locuti sunt an dixerint, nondum equidem
inveni.

VII

Diversum de natura leonum dixisse Homerum in carminibus
et Herodotum in historiis.

1 LEAENAS inter omnem vitam semel parere eoque
uno partu numquam edere plures quam unum, Hero-

---

¹ In 322 B.C.
² The Greeks had a pitch accent, pronouncing the accented
syllable with a higher tone.
³ Fr. 39, Swoboda.   ⁴ Cf. Catull. lxxxiv.

by those words chosen his successor, not his wine.
This was Theophrastus, from Lesbos, a man equally
noted for the fineness of his eloquence and of his life.
And when, not long after this, Aristotle died,[1] they
accordingly all became followers of Theophrastus.

VI

The term which the early Latins used for the Greek word
προσῳδίαι ; also that the term *barbarismus* was used neither
by the early Romans nor by the people of Attica.

WHAT the Greeks call προσῳδίαι, or " tones," [2] our
early scholars called now *notae vocum,* or " marks of
tone," now *moderamenta,* or " guides," now *accenti-
culae,* or " accents," and now *voculationes,* or " intona-
tions." But the fault which we designate when we
say now that anyone speaks *barbare,* or " outlandishly,"
they did not call " outlandish" but " rustic," and
they said that those speaking with that fault spoke
" in a countrified manner" (*rustice*). Publius Nigidius, in his *Grammatical Notes,*[3] says : " Speech
becomes rustic, if you misplace the aspirates." [4]
Whether therefore those who before the time of
the deified Augustus expressed themselves purely
and properly used the word *barbarismus* (outlandishness), which is now common, I for my part have not
yet been able to discover.

VII

That Homer in his poems and Herodotus in his *Histories*
spoke differently of the nature of the lion

HERODOTUS, in the third book of his *Histories,* has
left the statement that lionesses give birth but once
during their whole life, and at that one birth that

2 dotus in tertia *Historia* scriptum reliquit. Verba
ex eo libro haec sunt : Ἡ δὲ δὴ λέαινα, ἐὸν ἰσχυρὸν [1]
καὶ θρασύτατον, ἅπαξ ἐν τῷ βίῳ τίκτει ἕν· τίκτουσα γὰρ
συνεκβάλλει τῷ τέκνῳ τὰς μήτρας. Homerus autem
3 leones, sic enim feminas quoque virili genere appellat, quod grammatici ἐπίκοινον vocant, pluris gig-
nere atque educare catulos dicit. Versus, quibus
4 hoc aperte demonstrat, hi sunt :

Εἱστήκει, ὥς τίς τε λέων περὶ οἷσι τέκεσσιν,
Ὧι ῥά τε νήπι᾽ ἄγοντι συι αντήσωνται ἐν ὕλῃ
Ἄνδρες ἐπακτῆρες.

5 Item alio in loco idem significat :

Πυκνὰ μάλα στενάχων· ὥς τε λὶς ἠυγένειος,
Ὧι ῥά θ᾽ ὑπὸ σκύμνους ἐλαφηβόλος ἁρπάσῃ ἀνήρ
Ὕλης ἐκ πυκινῆς.

6   Ea nos dissensio atque diversitas cum agitaret inclu-
tissimi poetarum et historicorum nobilissimi, placuit
libros Aristotelis philosophi inspici quos *De Animalibus*
exquisitissime composuit. In quibus quod super
ista re scriptum invenerimus, cum ipsius Aristotelis
verbis in his commentariis scribemus.[2]

---

[1] ἰσχυρότατον, *Hdt.*
[2] *Aristotle's words in Hist. Anim.* vi. *31, p. 579, are added
in σ ; omitted by* ω.

---

[1] iii. 108.   [2] *Iliad,* xvii. 133.
[3] *Iliad.* xviii. 318.
[4] The passage is not quoted ; see critical note. Aristotle
tells us that the lioness gives birth to young every year,

they never produce more than one cub. His words
in that book are as follows : [1] " But the lioness,
although a strong and most courageous animal, gives
birth once only in her lifetime to one cub; for in
giving birth she discharges her womb with the whelp."
Homer, however, says that lions (for so he calls the
females also, using the masculine or " common "
(epicene) gender, as the grammarians call it) produce
and rear many whelps. The verses in which he
plainly says this are these : [2]

> He stood, like to a lion before its young,
> Beset by hunters in a gloomy wood
> And leading them away.

In another passage also he indicates the same
thing : [3]

> With many a groan, like lion of strong beard,
> From which a hunter stole away its young
> Amid dense woods.

Since this disagreement and difference between
the most famous of poets and the most eminent of
historians troubled me, I thought best to consult
that very thorough treatise which the philosopher
Aristotle wrote *On Animals*. And what I find that
he has written there upon this subject I shall include
in these notes, in Aristotle's own language.[4]

usually two, at most six, sometimes only one. The current
idea that the womb is discharged with the young is absurd ;
it arose from the fact that lions are rare and that the inventor
of the story did not know the real reason, which is that their
habitat is of limited extent. The lionesses in Syria give birth
five times, producing at first five cubs, then one less at each
successive birth.

VIII

Quod Afranius poeta prudenter et lepide Sapientiam filiam
esse Usus et Memoriae dixit.

1 EXIMIE hoc atque verissime Afranius poeta de
gignenda conparandaque Sapientia opinatus est,
2 quod eam filiam esse Usus et Memoriae dixit. Eo
namque argumento demonstrat, qui sapiens rerum
esse humanarum velit, non libris solis neque disciplinis rhetoricis dialecticisque opus esse, sed
oportere eum versari quoque exercerique in rebus
comminus noscendis periclitandisque eaque omnia
acta et eventa firmiter meminisse et proinde sapere
atque consulere ex his quae pericula ipsa rerum
docuerint, non quae libri tantum aut magistri per
quasdam inanitates verborum et imaginum tamquam
3 in mimo aut in somnio deliraverint.[1] Versus Afrani
sunt in togata, cui *Sellae* nomen est:

Usús me genuit, máter peperit Mémoria,
Sophiám vocant me Grái, vos Sapiéntiam.

4 Item versus est in eandem ferme sententiam Pacuvii,
quem Macedo philosophus, vir bonus, familiaris
meus, scribi debere censebat **pro** foribus omnium
templorum:

Ego odi[2] homines ígnava opera et phílosopha
senténtia.

5 Nihil enim fieri posse indignius neque intolerantius
dicebat quam quod homines ignavi ac desides, operti
barba et pallio, mores et emolumenta philosophiae

[1] delectaverint, ω; *corrected by Ott*; delineaverint, *Kronenberg (cf. Cic. N.D* i. 75).
[2] ergo *or* odi ego, *Bothe.*

VIII

That the poet Afranius wisely and prettily called Wisdom
the daughter of Experience and Memory.

THAT was a fine and true thought of the poet
Afranius about the birth of Wisdom and the means
of acquiring it, when he said that she was the
daughter of Experience and Memory. For in that
way he shows that one who wishes to be wise in
human affairs does not need books alone or instruction in rhetoric and dialectics, but ought also to
occupy and train himself in becoming intimately
acquainted with and testing real life, and in firmly
fixing in his memory all such acts and events; and
accordingly he must learn wisdom and judgment
from the teaching of actual experience, not from
what books only, or masters, through vain words and
fantasies, have foolishly represented as though in a
farce or a dream. The verses of Afranius are in a
Roman comedy called *The Chair* :[1]

My sire Experience was, me Memory bore,
In Greece called Sophia, Wisdom in Rome.

There is also a line of Pacuvius to about the same
purport, which the philosopher Macedo, a good man
and my intimate friend, thought ought to be written
over the doors of all temples :[2]

I hate base men who preach philosophy.

For he said that nothing could be more shameful or
insufferable than that idle, lazy folk, disguised with
beard and cloak, should change the character and

---

[1] 298, Ribbeck[3].   [2] 348, Ribbeck[3].

in linguae verborumque artes converterent et vitia
facundissime accusarent, intercutibus ipsi vitiis
madentes.

IX

Quid Tullius Tiro in commentariis scripserit de " Suculis " et
" Hyadibus," quae sunt stellarum vocabula.

1 TULLIUS TIRO M. Ciceronis alumnus et libertus
2 adiutorque in litteris studiorum eius fuit. Is libros
compluris de usu atque ratione linguae Latinae,
item de variis atque promiscis quaestionibus com-
3 posuit. In his esse praecipui videntur quos Graeco
titulo Πανδέκτας inscripsit, tamquam omne rerum
4 atque doctrinarum genus continentis. Ibi de his
stellis quae appellantur " suculae " hoc scriptum
est : " Adeo," inquit, " veteres Romani litteras
Graecas nesciverunt et rudes Graecae linguae fuerunt, ut stellas quae in capite tauri sunt propterea
' suculas' appellarint, quod eas Graeci ὑάδας vocant,
tamquam id verbum Latinum Graeci verbi interpretamentum sit, quia quae[1] Graece ὕες, ' sues '
Latine dicantur. Sed ὑάδες," inquit, " οὐκ ἀπὸ τῶν
ὑῶν (id est, non a subus), ita ut nostri opici putaverunt, sed ab eo quod est ὕειν, appellantur ; nam
et cum oriuntur et cum occidunt, tempestates pluvias
largosque imbres cient. Pluere autem Graeca lingua
ὕειν dicitur."
5 Haec quidem Tiro in *Pandectis*. Sed enim veteres
nostri non usque eo rupices et agrestes fuerunt, ut

[1] quae *added by Skutsch.*

---

[1] Literally, all-embracing.　　　　[2] pp. 7 ff. Lion.

advantages of philosophy into tricks of the tongue and of words, and, themselves saturated with vices, should eloquently assail vice.

IX

What Tullius Tiro wrote in his commentaries about the *Suculae*, or "Little Pigs," and the *Hyades*, which are the names of constellations.

TULLIUS TIRO was the pupil and freedman of Marcus Cicero and an assistant in his literary work. He wrote several books on the usage and theory of the Latin language and on miscellaneous questions of various kinds. Pre-eminent among these appear to be those to which he gave the Greek title Πανδέκται,[1] implying that they included every kind of science and fact. In these he wrote the following about the stars which are called the *Suculae*, or "Little Pigs":[2] "The early Romans," says he, "were so ignorant of Grecian literature and so unfamiliar with the Greek language, that they called those stars which are in the head of the Bull *Suculae*, or 'The Little Pigs,' because the Greeks call them ὑάδες; for they supposed that Latin word to be a translation of the Greek name because ὕες in Greek is *sues* in Latin. But the ὑάδες," says he, "are so called, οὐκ ἀπὸ τῶν ὑῶν (that is, not from pigs), as our rude forefathers believed, but from the word ὕειν; for both when they rise and when they set they cause rainstorms and heavy showers. And *pluere*, (to rain) is expressed in the Greek tongue by ὕειν."

So, indeed, Tiro in his *Pandects*. But, as a matter of fact, our early writers were not such boors and

stellas hyadas idcirco "suculas" nominarent, quod
ὕες Latine "sues" dicantur; sed ut quod Graeci
ὑπέρ, nos "super" dicimus, quod illi ὕπτιος, nos
"supinus," quod illi ὑφορβός, nos "subulcus," quod
item illi ὕπνος, nos primo "sypnus," deinde per y
Graecae Latinaeque o [1] litterae cognationem "somnus": sic quod ab illis ὑάδες, a nobis primo "syades,"
deinde "suculae." appellatae.

6   Stellae autem istae non in capite tauri sunt, ut
Tiro dicit, nullum enim videtur praeter eas stellas
tauri caput, set hae ita circulo qui "zodiacus"
dicitur sitae locataeque sunt, ut ex earum positu
species quaedam et simulacrum esse videatur tauri
capitis, sicuti ceterae partes et reliqua imago tauri
conformata et quasi depicta est locis regionibusque
earum stellarum quas Graeci Πλειάδας, nos "Ver-
gilias" vocamus.

X

Quid "sororis" ἔτυμον esse dixerit Labeo Antistius, et quid
"fratris" P. Nigidius.

1   LABEO ANTISTIUS iuris quidem civilis disciplinam
principali studio exercuit et consulentibus de iure
publice responsitavit; ceterarum quoque bonarum
artium non expers fuit et in grammaticam sese atque
dialecticam litterasque antiquiores altioresque pene-
traverat Latinarumque vocum origines rationesque
percalluerat, eaque praecipue scientia ad enodandos
2 plerosque iuris laqueos utebatur. Sunt adeo libri

---

[1] o *added in* σ; litterae cum o littera, *Hertz.*

clowns as to give to the stars called *hyades* the name of *suculae*, or "little pigs," because ὕες are called *sues* in Latin; but just as what the Greeks call ὑπέρ we call *super*, what they call ὕπτιος we call *supinus*, what they call ὑφορβός we call *subulcus*, and finally, what they call ὕπνος we call first *sypnus*, and then, because of the kinship of the Greek letter *y* and the Latin *o*, *somnus*—just so, what they call ὑάδες were called by us, first *syades*, and then *suculae*.

But the stars in question are not in the head of the Bull, as Tiro says, for except for those stars the Bull has no head; but they are so situated and arranged in the circle that is called the "zodiac," that from their position they seem to present the appearance and semblance of a bull's head, just as the other parts, and the rest of the figure of the Bull, are formed and, as it were, pictured by the place and location of those stars which the Greeks call Πλειάδες and we, *Vergiliae*.

X

The derivation of *soror*, according to Antistius Labeo, and that of *frater*, according to Publius Nigidius.

ANTISTIUS LABEO cultivated the study of civil law with special interest, and gave advice publicly to those who consulted him on legal questions; he was also not unacquainted with the other liberal arts, and he had delved deep into grammar and dialectics, as well as into the earlier and more recondite literature. He had also become versed in the origin and formation of Latin words, and applied that knowledge in particular to solving many knotty points of law. In fact, after his death works of his were published,

post mortem eius editi, qui *Posteriores* inscribuntur, quorum librorum tres continui, tricesimus octavus et tricesimus nonus et quadragesimus, pleni sunt id genus rerum ad enarrandam et inlustrandam linguam 3 Latinam conducentium. Praeterea in libris quos *Ad Praetoris Edictum* scripsit multa posuit, partim lepide atque argute reperta. Sicuti hoc est quod in quarto *Ad Edictum* libro scriptum legimus: "' Soror,' " inquit, " appellata est, quod quasi seorsum nascitur separaturque ab ea domo in qua nata est et in aliam familiam transgreditur."

4   " Fratris " autem vocabulum P. Nigidius, homo inpense doctus, non minus arguto subtilique ἐτύμῳ interpretatur : "' Frater,' " inquit, " est dictus quasi ' fere alter.' "

XI

Quem M. Varro aptum iustumque esse numerum convivarum existimarit ; ac de mensis secundis et de bellariis.

1   LEPIDISSIMUS liber est M. Varronis ex *Satiris Menippeis*, qui inscribitur *Nescis Quid Vesper Serus Vehat,* in quo disserit de apto convivarum numero 2 deque ipsius convivii habitu cultuque. Dicit autem, convivarum numerum incipere oportere a Gratiarum numero et progredi ad Musarum, id est proficisci a

---

[1] Fr. 26, Huschke ; 2, Bremer (ii, p. 85).
[2] That is to say, by marriage.   [3] Fr. 50, Swoboda.
[4] These derivations are, of course, purely fanciful ; *soror* and *frater* are cognate with "sister" and "brother," and are not of Latin derivation.

which are entitled *Posteriores*, of which three successive books, the thirty-eighth, thirty-ninth and fortieth, are full of information of that kind, tending to explain and illustrate the Latin language. Moreover, in the books which he wrote *On the Praetor's Edict* he has included many observations, some of which are graceful and clever. Of such a kind is this, which we find written in the fourth book *On the Edict :* [1] " *A soror*, or ' sister,' " he says, " is so called because she is, as it were, born *seorsum*, or ' outside,' and is separated from that home in which she was born, and transferred to another family." [2]

Moreover, Publius Nigidius, a man of prodigious learning, explains the word *frater*, or " brother," by a no less clever and ingenious derivation : [3] " A *frater*," he says, " is so called because he is, as it were, *fere alter*, that is, ' almost another self.' " [4]

XI

Marcus Varro's opinion of the just and proper number of banqueters ; his views about the dessert and about sweetmeats.

THAT is a very charming book of Marcus Varro's, one of his *Menippean Satires*, entitled *You know not what the Late Evening may Bring*,[5] in which he descants upon the proper number of guests at a dinner, and about the order and arrangement of the entertainment itself. Now he says [6] that the number of the guests ought to begin with that of the Graces and end with that of the Muses ; that is,

---

[5] Apparently a proverbial expression ; cf. Virg. *Georg.* i. 461, *Denique, quid vesper serus vehat . . . sol tibi signa dabit.*
[6] Fr. 333, Bücheler.

tribus et consistere in novem, ut, cum paucissimi
convivae sunt, non pauciores sint quam tres, cum
3 plurimi, non plures quam novem. " Nam multos,"
inquit, " esse non convenit, quod turba plerumque
est turbulenta et Romae quidem stat,[1] sedet Athenis,
nusquam autem cubat. Ipsum deinde convivium
constat," inquit, " ex rebus quattuor et tum denique
omnibus suis numeris absolutum est, si belli homun-
culi conlecti sunt, si electus locus, si tempus lectum,
si apparatus non neglectus. Nec loquaces autem,"
inquit, " convivas nec mutos legere oportet, quia
.eloquentia in foro et aput subsellia, silentium vero
4 non in convivio, set in cubiculo esse debet." Ser-
mones igitur id temporis habendos censet non super
rebus anxiis aut tortuosis, sed iucundos atque in-
vitabiles et cum quadam inlecebra et voluptate
utiles, ex quibus ingenium nostrum venustius fiat et
5 amoenius. " Quod profecto," inquit, " eveniet, si
de id genus rebus ad communem vitae usum perti-
nentibus confabulemur, de quibus in foro atque in
negotiis agendi non est otium. Dominum autem,"
inquit, " convivii esse oportet non tam lautum, quam
sine sordibus," et: " In convivio legi nec[2] omnia
debent, sed[3] ea potissimum, quae simul sint
βιωφελῆ et delectent."

---

[1] stat, *Hertz*; constat, *MSS.*; concio stat, *Boot.*
[2] nec, *Gell.* i. 22. 5; non, *MSS.*
[3] et, *Gell.* i. 22. 5.

---

[1] There is a word-play on *turba* and *turbulenta*, which it
seems difficult to reproduce. Cf. Ausonius, p. 12, 146,
Peiper; i., p. 22, *L. C. L.*:

> Quinque advocavi; sex enim convivium
> Cum rege iustum; si super, convicium est.

it should begin with three and stop at nine, so that when the guests are fewest, they should not be less than three, when they are most numerous, not more than nine. "For it is disagreeable to have a great number, since a crowd is generally disorderly,[1] and at Rome it stands,[2] at Athens it sits, but nowhere does it recline. Now, the banquet itself," he continues, "has four features, and then only is it complete in all its parts: if a nice little group has been got together, if the place is well chosen, the time fit, and due preparation not neglected. Moreover, one should not," he says, "invite either too talkative or too silent guests, since eloquence is appropriate to the Forum and the courts, but silence to the bedchamber and not to a dinner." He thinks, then, that the conversation at such a time ought not to be about anxious and perplexing affairs, but diverting and cheerful, combining profit with a certain interest and pleasure, such conversation as tends to make our character more refined and agreeable. "This will surely follow," he says, "if we talk about matters which relate to the common experience of life, which we have no leisure to discuss in the Forum and amid the press of business. Furthermore, the host," he says, "ought rather to be free from meanness than over-elegant," and, he adds: "At a banquet not everything should be read,[3] but such things as are at once edifying and enjoyable."

[2] Referring to *turba* as the throng of citizens in public assembly.

[3] Readings or music were common forms of entertainment at a Roman dinner (cf. *e.g.* Pliny, *Epist.* iii. 1. 9). *Legi*, however, may have the meaning of *legere* in § 3 (end), in which case the reference would be to the viands and βιωφελῆ would mean "wholesome."

6   Neque non de secundis quoque mensis, cuiusmodi esse eas oporteat, praecipit. His enim verbis utitur: "Bellaria," inquit, "ea maxime sunt mellita, quae mellita non sunt; πέμμασιν enim cum πέψει societas infida."

7   Quod Varro hoc in loco dixit "bellaria," ne quis forte in ista voce haereat, significat id vocabulum omne mensae secundae genus. Nam quae πέμματα Graeci aut τραγήματα dixerunt, ea veteres nostri "bellaria" appellaverunt. Vina quoque dulciora est invenire in comoediis antiquioribus hoc nomine appellata dictaque esse ea "Liberi bellaria."

XII

Tribunos plebis prensionem habere, vocationem non habere.

1   In quadam epistula Atei Capitonis scriptum legimus, Labeonem Antistium legum atque morum populi Romani iurisque civilis doctum adprime fuisse.

2   "Sed agitabat," inquit, "hominem libertas quaedam nimia atque vecors usque eo ut, divo Augusto iam principe et rempublicam obtinente, ratum tamen pensumque nihil haberet, nisi quod iussum sanctum-

3 que esse in Romanis antiquitatibus legisset," ac deinde narrat, quid idem Labeo per viatorem a

4 tribunis plebi vocatus responderit: "Cum a muliere," inquit, "quadam tribuni plebis adversum eum aditi,

---

[1] An example of Varro's fondness for word-plays; "sweetest" is used in the double sense of sweetest to the taste and pleasantest in their after-effects.

[2] *mensa secunda bellariorum* occurs in the *Transactions of the Arval Brethren* for May 27, A.D. 218.

And he does not omit to tell what the nature of the dessert ought to be. For he uses these words: "Those sweetmeats (*bellaria*) are sweetest which are not sweet;[1] for harmony between delicacies and digestion is not to be counted upon."

That no one may be puzzled by the word *bellaria* which Varro uses in this passage, let me say that it means all kinds of dessert. For what the Greeks called πέμματα or τραγήματα, our forefathers called *bellaria*.[2] In the earlier comedies [3] one may find this term applied also to the sweeter wines, which are called *Liberi bellaria,* or "sweetmeats of Bacchus."

XII

That the tribunes of the commons have the right to arrest, but not to summon.

In one of the letters of Ateius Capito we read [4] that Antistius Labeo was exceedingly learned in the laws and customs of the Roman people and in the civil law. "But," he adds, "an excessive and mad love of freedom possessed the man, to such a degree that, although the deified Augustus was then emperor and was ruling the State, Labeo looked upon nothing as lawful and accepted nothing, unless he had found it ordered and sanctioned by the old Roman law." He then goes on to relate the reply of this same Labeo, when he was summoned by the messenger of a tribune of the commons. He says: "When the tribunes of the commons had been appealed to by a woman against Labeo and had sent to him at

[3] p. 144, 65, Ribbeck [3].
[4] Fr. 19, Huschke: ii. p. 287, Bremer.

in Gallianum ad eum misissent, ut veniret et mulieri
responderet, iussit eum qui missus erat redire et
tribunis dicere ius eos non habere neque se neque
alium quemquam vocandi, quoniam moribus maiorum
tribuni plebis prensionem haberent, vocationem non
haberent; posse igitur eos venire et prendi se iubere,
sed vocandi absentem ius non habere."

5   Cum hoc in ea Capitonis epistula legissemus, id
ipsum postea in M. Varronis *Rerum Humanarum* uno
et vicesimo libro enarratius scriptum invenimus,
verbaque ipsa super ea re Varronis adscripsimus:

6   " In magistratu," inquit, " habent alii vocationem,
alii prensionem, alii neutrum; vocationem, ut consules et ceteri qui habent imperium; prensionem,
ut tribuni plebis et alii qui habent viatorem; neque
vocationem neque prensionem, ut quaestores et
ceteri qui neque lictorem habent neque viatorem.
Qui vocationem habent, idem prendere, tenere,
abducere possunt, et haec omnia sive adsunt quos
vocant sive acciri iusserunt. Tribuni plebis vocationem habent nullam, neque minus multi imperiti,
proinde atque haberent, ea sunt usi; nam quidam
non modo privatum, sed etiam consulem, in rostra
vocari iusserunt. Ego triumvirum, vocatus a Porcio,
tribuno plebis, non ivi, auctoribus principibus, et
vetus ius tenui. Item tribunus cum essem, vocari

---

¹ Probably Labeo's country place. He spent half the year in
retirement (*Dig.* i. 2. 2. 47), and *praedia Galliana* are mentioned
in *C.I.L.* iii. 536, and ix. 1455, col. iii, lines 62—64.
² Fr. 2, Mirsch.   ³ The right of commanding an army
conferred by the *Lex Curiata de imperio* on the dictator, consuls,

the Gallianum[1] bidding him come and answer the woman's charge, he ordered the messenger to return and say to the tribunes that they had the right to summon neither him nor anyone else, since according to the usage of our forefathers the tribunes of the commons had the power of arrest, but not of summons; that they might therefore come and order his arrest, but they did not have the right to summon him when absent."

Having read this in that letter of Capito's, I later found the same statement made more fully in the twenty-first book of Varro's *Human Antiquities,* and I have added Varro's own words on the subject:[2] " In a magistracy" says he, "some have the power of summons, others of arrest, others neither; summoning, for example, belongs to the consuls and others possessing the *imperium*[3]; arrest, to the tribunes of the commons and the rest who are attended by a messenger; neither summoning nor arrest to the quaestors and others who have neither a lictor nor a messenger. Those who have the power of summons may also arrest, detail, and lead off to prison, all this whether those whom they summon are present or are sent for by their order. The tribunes of the commons have no power of summons, nevertheless many of them in ignorance have used that power, as if they were entitled to it; for some of them have ordered, not only private persons, but even a consul to be summoned before the rostra. I myself, when a triumvir,[4] on being summoned by Porcius, tribune of the commons, did not appear, following the authority of our leading men, but I held to the old law. Similarly, when I was a tribune, I ordered

magister equitum and praetors.

[4] That is, one of the *triumviri capitales,* a minor office.

neminem iussi, nec vocatum a conlega parere in-
vitum."

7   Huius ego iuris quod M. Varro tradit Labeonem
arbitror vana tunc fiducia, cum privatus esset, voca-
8 tum a tribunis non isse. Quae, malum, autem ratio
fuit vocantibus nolle obsequi quos confiteare ius
habere prendendi? Nam qui iure prendi potest et
9 in vincula duci potest. Sed quaerentibus nobis
quam ob causam tribuni, qui haberent summam
coercendi potestatem, ius vocandi non habuerint . . .,
quod tribuni plebis antiquitus creati videntur non
iuri dicundo nec causis querelisque de absentibus
noscendis, sed intercessionibus faciendis quibus usus
praesens fuisset, ut iniuria quae coram fieret arce-
retur; ac propterea ius abnoctandi ademptum,
quoniam, ut vim fieri vetarent, adsiduitate eorum et
praesentium oculis opus erat.

XIII

Quod in libris *Humanarum* [1] M. Varronis scriptum est aediles
et quaestores populi Romani in ius a privato ad praetorem
vocari posse.

1   Cum ex angulis secretisque librorum [2] ac magistro-
rum in medium iam hominum et in lucem fori prod-

[1] Humanarum Rerum, *Damsté.*
[2] ludorum, *Eussner.*

---

[1] That is, he had not yet held a magisterial office.

no one to be summoned, and required no one who was summoned by one of my colleagues to obey, unless he wished."

I think that Labeo, being a private citizen at the time,[1] showed unjustified confidence in that law of which Marcus Varro has written, in not appearing when summoned by the tribunes. For how the mischief was it reasonable to refuse to obey those whom you admit to have the power of arrest? For one who can lawfully be arrested may also be taken to prison. But since we are inquiring why the tribunes, who had full power of coercion, did not have the right to summon . . .[2] because the tribunes of the commons seem to have been elected in early times, not for administering justice, nor for taking cognizance of suits and complaints when the parties were absent, but for using their veto-power when there was immediate need, in order to prevent injustice from being done before their eyes; and for that reason the right of leaving the city at night was denied them, since their constant presence and personal oversight were needed to prevent acts of violence.

XIII

That it is stated in Marcus Varro's books on *Human Antiquities* that the aediles and quaestors of the Roman people might be cited before a praetor by a private citizen.

WHEN from the secluded retreat of books and masters I had come forth among men and into the light of the forum, I remember that it was the

[2] There seems to be a lacuna in the text. Supply "we may assume that it was," or something similar.

issem, quaesitum esse memini in plerisque Romae stationibus ius publice docentium aut respondentium, an quaestor populi Romani a praetore in ius vocari

2 posset. Id autem non ex otiosa quaestione agitabatur, sed usus forte natae rei ita erat, ut vocandus

3 esset in ius quaestor. Non pauci igitur existimabant ius vocationis in eum praetori non esse, quoniam magistratus populi Romani procul dubio esset et neque vocari neque, si venire nollet, capi atque prendi, salva ipsius magistratus maiestate, posset.

4 Sed ego, qui tum adsiduus in libris M. Varronis fui, cum hoc quaeri dubitarique animadvertissem, protuli unum et vicesimum *Rerum Humanarum,* in quo ita scriptum fuit: "Qui potestatem neque vocationis populi viritim habent neque prensionis, eos magistratus a privato in ius quoque vocari est potestas. M. Laevinus, aedilis curulis, a privato ad praetorem in ius est eductus; nunc stipati servis publicis non modo prendi non possunt, sed etiam ultro submovent populum."

5 Hoc Varro in ea libri parte de aedilibus, supra autem in eodem libro quaestores neque vocationem

6 habere neque prensionem dicit. Utraque igitur libri parte recitata, in Varronis omnes sententiam concesserunt, quaestorque in ius ad praetorem vocatus est.

---

[1] From his bookcase.
[2] Fr. 3, Mirsch.

subject of inquiry in many of the quarters frequented by those who gave public instruction in law, or offered counsel, whether a quaestor of the Roman people could be cited by a praetor. Moreover, this was not discussed merely as an academic question, but an actual instance of the kind had chanced to arise, in which a quaestor was to be called into court. Now, not a few men thought that the praetor did not have the right to summon him, since he was beyond question a magistrate of the Roman people and could neither be summoned, nor if he refused to appear could he be taken and arrested without impairing the dignity of the office itself which he held. But since at that time I was immersed in the books of Marcus Varro, as soon as I found that this matter was the subject of doubt and inquiry, I took down [1] the twenty-first book of his *Human Antiquities,* in which the following is written : [2] " It is lawful for those magistrates who have the power neither of summoning the people as individuals nor of arrest, even to be called into court by a private citizen. Marcus Laevinus, a curule aedile, was cited before a praetor by a private citizen ; to-day, surrounded as they are by public servants, aediles not only may not be arrested, but even presume to disperse the people."

This is what Varro says in the part of his work which concerns the aediles, but in an earlier part of the same book he says [3] that quaestors have the right neither to summon nor to arrest. Accordingly, when both parts of the book had been read, all came over to Varro's opinion, and the quaestor was summoned before the praetor.

[3] See xiii. 12. 6, above.

XIV

Quid sit "pomerium."

1 "POMERIUM" quid esset augures populi Romani qui libros *De Auspiciis* scripserunt istiusmodi sententia definierunt : "Pomerium est locus intra agrum effatum per totius urbis circuitum pone muros regionibus certeis determinatus, qui facit finem

2 urbani auspicii." Antiquissimum autem pomerium, quod a Romulo institutum est, Palatini montis radicibus terminabatur. Sed id pomerium pro incrementis reipublicae aliquotiens prolatum est et multos

3 editosque collis circumplexum est. Habebat autem ius proferendi pomerii qui populum Romanum agro de hostibus capto auxerat.

4 Propterea quaesitum est, ac nunc etiam in quaestione est, quam ob causam ex septem urbis montibus, cum ceteri sex intra pomerium sint, Aventinus solum, quae pars non longinqua nec infrequens est, extra pomerium sit, neque id Servius Tullius rex neque Sulla, qui proferendi pomerii titulum quaesivit, neque postea divus Iulius, cum pomerium proferret, intra effatos urbi fines incluserint.

5 Huius rei Messala aliquot causas videri scripsit ; sed praeter eas omnis ipse unam probat, quod in eo monte Remus urbis condendae gratia auspicaverit avesque inritas habuerit superatusque in auspicio a

---

[1] That is to say, the *pomerium* separated the *ager Romanus*, or country district, from the city. The auspices could be taken only within the *pomerium*. When a furrow was drawn and the earth turned inward to mark the line of the city walls, the furrow represented the *pomerium*. On the derivation of the word see *T.A.P.A.* xliv. 19 ff.

XIV

The meaning of pomerium.

THE augurs of the Roman people who wrote books *On the Auspices* have defined the meaning of pomerium in the following terms : "The pomerium is the space within the rural district designated by the augurs along the whole circuit of the city without the walls, marked off by fixed bounds and forming the limit of the city auspices."[1] Now, the most ancient pomerium, which was established by Romulus, was bounded by the foot of the Palatine hill. But that pomerium, as the republic grew, was extended several times and included many lofty hills. Moreover, whoever had increased the domain of the Roman people by land taken from an enemy had the right to enlarge the pomerium.

Therefore it has been, and even now continues to be, inquired why it is that when the other six of the seven hills of the city are within the pomerium, the Aventine alone, which is neither a remote nor an unfrequented district, should be outside the pomerium ; and why neither king Servius Tullius nor Sulla, who demanded the honour of extending the pomerium, nor later the deified Julius, when he enlarged the pomerium, included this within the designated limits of the city.

Messala wrote[2] that there seemed to be several reasons for this, but above them all he himself approved one, namely, because on that hill Remus took the auspices with regard to founding the city, but found the birds unpropitious and was less

[2] Fr. 3, Huschke; id., Bremer (ii, p. 265).

6 Romulo sit : " Idcirco," inquit, " omnes qui pomerium
protulerunt montem istum excluserunt, quasi avibus
obscenis ominosum."

7 Sed de Aventino monte praetermittendum non
putavi quod non pridem ego in Elydis,[1] grammatici veteris, *Commentario* offendi, in quo scriptum
erat Aventinum antea, sicuti diximus, extra pomerium
exclusum, post auctore divo Claudio receptum et intra
pomerii fines observatum.

XV

Verba ex libro Messalae auguris, quibus docet qui sint minores
magistratus, et consulem praetoremque conlegas esse ; et
quaedam alia de auspiciis.

1 IN edicto consulum, quo edicunt quis dies comitiis
centuriatis futurus sit, scribitur ex vetere forma perpetua : "Ne quis magistratus minor de caelo servasse
2 velit." Quaeri igitur solet qui sint magistratus mi-
3 nores. Super hac re meis verbis nil opus fuit, quoniam liber M. Messalae auguris *De Auspiciis*
4 primus, cum hoc scriberemus, forte adfuit. Propterea ex eo libro verba ipsius Messalae subscripsimus :
" Patriciorum auspicia in duas sunt divisa potes-

[1] Felicis, *Mercklin* ; Heraclidis, *Hertz* ; Epelydis, *Bergk* ;
some one of the Aelii, *Hosius.*

---

[1] The name is obviously corrupt ; see critical note.
[2] That is, for omens.

successful in his augury than Romulus. "Therefore," says he, "all those who extended the pomerium excluded that hill, on the ground that it was made ill-omened by inauspicious birds."

But speaking of the Aventine hill, I thought I ought not to omit something which I ran across recently in the *Commentary* of Elys,[1] an early grammarian. In this it was written that in earlier times the Aventine was, as we have said, excluded from the pomerium, but afterwards by the authority of the deified Claudius it was admitted and honoured with a place within the limits of the pomerium.

XV

A passage from the book of the augur Messala, in which he shows who the minor magistrates are and that the consul and the praetor are colleagues ; and certain observations besides on the auspices.

In the edict of the consuls by which they appoint the day for the centuriate assembly it is written in accordance with an old established form : "Let no minor magistrate presume to watch the skies."[2] Accordingly, the question is often asked who the minor magistrates are. On this subject there is[3] no need for words of mine, since by good fortune the first book of the augur Messala *On Auspices* is at hand, when I am writing this. Therefore I quote from that book Messala's own words :[4] "The auspices of the patricians are divided into two classes. The

---

[3] This and the following verbs seem to be in epistolary past tenses ; that is, Gellius uses the tenses which would represent the time from the standpoint of his future readers.

[4] Fr. 1, Huschke ; 1ᵃ, Bremer (i, p. 263).

tates. Maxima sunt consulum, praetorum, censorum. Neque tamen eorum omnium inter se eadem aut eiusdem potestatis, ideo quod conlegae non sunt censores consulum aut praetorum, praetores consulum sunt. Ideo neque consules aut praetores censoribus neque censores consulibus aut praetoribus turbant aut retinent auspicia ; at censores inter se, rursus praetores consulesque inter se, et vitiant et obtinent. Praetor, etsi conlega consulis est, neque praetorem neque consulem iure rogare potest, ut quidem nos a superioribus accepimus aut ante haec tempora serva- tum est et ut in *Commentario* tertio decimo C. Tuditani patet, quia imperium minus praetor, maius habet consul, et a minore imperio maius aut maior a minore [1] conlega rogari iure non potest. Nos his temporibus, praetore praetores creante, veterum auctoritatem sumus secuti neque his comitiis in auspicio fuimus. Censores aeque non eodem rogan- tur auspicio atque consules et praetores. Reliquorum magistratuum minora sunt auspicia. Ideo illi ' minores,' hi ' maiores ' magistratus appellantur. Minoribus creatis magistratibus, tributis comitiis magistratus, sed iustus curiata datur lege ; maiores centuriatis comitiis fiunt."

5 Ex his omnibus verbis Messalae manifestum fit, et qui sint magistratus minores et quamobrem " mino-
6 res " appellentur. Sed et conlegam esse praetorem

[1] a minore, *added by Hertz.*

---

[1] Explained in § 6, below.
[2] Fr. 8, Peter[2]; 2, Huschke ; id., Bremer (i, p. 35).
[3] On these *comitia* see xv. 27, below.

greatest are those of the consuls, praetors and
censors. Yet the auspices of all these are not the
same or of equal rank, for the reason that the
censors are not colleagues of the consuls or praetors,[1]
while the praetors are colleagues of the consuls.
Therefore neither do the consuls or the praetors
interrupt or hinder the auspices of the censors, nor
the censors those of the praetors and consuls ; but
the censors may vitiate and hinder each other's
auspices and again the praetors and consuls those of
one another.   The praetor, although he is a colleague of the consul, cannot lawfully elect either
a praetor or a consul, as indeed we have learned
from our forefathers, or from what has been observed in the past, and as is shown in the thirteenth
book of the *Commentaries* of Gaius Tuditanus ;[2] for
the praetor has inferior authority and the consul
superior, and a higher authority cannot be elected
by a lower, or a superior colleague by an inferior.
At the present time, when a praetor elects the
praetors, I have followed the authority of the men
of old and have not taken part in the auspices at
such elections.   Also the censors are not chosen
under the same auspices as the consuls and praetors.
The lesser auspices belong to the other magistrates.
Therefore these are called ' lesser ' and the others
' greater ' magistrates.   When the lesser magistrates
are elected, their office is conferred upon them by
the assembly of the tribes, but full powers by a law
of the assembly of the *curiae* ; the higher magistrates are chosen by the assembly of the centuries."[3]

From this whole passage of Messala it becomes clear
both who the lesser magistrates are and why they
are so called.   But he also shows that the praetor

7 consuli docet, quod eodem auspicio creantur. Maiora
autem dicuntur auspicia habere, quia eorum auspicia
magis rata sunt quam aliorum.

XVI

Item verba eiusdem Messalae, disserentis aliud esse ad populum loqui, aliud cum populo agere; et qui magistratus a
quibus avocent comitiatum.

1 IDEM Messala in eodem libro de minoribus magistratibus ita scripsit: " Consul ab omnibus magistratibus et comitiatum et contionem avocare
potest. Praetor et comitiatum et contionem usquequaque avocare potest, nisi a consule. Minores
magistratus nusquam nec comitiatum nec contionem
avocare possunt. Ea re, qui eorum primus vocat
ad comitiatum, is recte agit, quia bifariam cum
populo agi non potest nec avocare alius alii potest.[1]
Set, si contionem habere volunt uti ne cum populo
agant, quamvis multi magistratus simul contionem
2 habere possunt." Ex his verbis Messalae manifestum
est, aliud esse " cum populo agere," aliud " con-
3 tionem habere." Nam " cum populo agere " est

[1] potest, *Madvig;* posset ω (-ent, Π).

---

[1] Fr. 2, Huschke: id., Bremer (i, p. 263).

is a colleague of the consul, because they are chosen under the same auspices. Moreover, they are said to possess the greater auspices, because their auspices are esteemed more highly than those of the others.

XVI

Another passage from the same Messala, in which he argues that to address the people and to treat with the people are two different things ; and what magistrates may call away the people when in assembly, and from whom.

THE same Messala in the same book has written as follows about the lesser magistrates : [1] " A consul may call away the people from all magistrates, when they are assembled for the elections or for another purpose. A praetor may at any time call away the people when assembled for the elections or for another purpose, except from a consul. Lesser magistrates may never call away the people when assembled for the elections or another purpose. Hence, whoever of them first summons the people to an election has the law on his side, because it is unlawful to take the same action twice with the people (*bifariam cum populo agi*), nor can one minor magistrate call away an assembly from another. But if they wish to address the people (*contionem habere*) without laying any measure before them, it is lawful for any number of magistrates to hold a meeting (*contionem habere*) at the same time." From these words of Messala it is clear that *cum populo agere*, " to treat with the people," differs from *contionem habere*, " to address the people." For the former means to ask something of the people

455

rogare quid populum, quod suffragiis suis aut
iubeat aut vetet; "contionem" autem "habere" est
verba facere ad populum sine ulla rogatione.

XVII

"Humanitatem" non significare id quod vulgus putat, sed eo
vocabulo qui sinceriter locuti sunt magis proprie esse usos.

1 Qui verba Latina fecerunt quique his probe usi
sunt "humanitatem" non id esse voluerunt quod
vulgus existimat quodque a Graecis φιλανθρωπία
dicitur et significat dexteritatem quandam beni-
volentiamque erga omnis homines promiscam; sed
"humanitatem" appellaverunt id propemodum quod
Graeci παιδείαν vocant, nos "eruditionem institutionemque in bonas artes" dicimus. Quas qui sinceriter
percupiunt adpetuntque, hi sunt vel maxime
humanissimi. Huius enim scientiae cura et disciplina
ex universis animantibus uni homini data est idcircoque "humanitas" appellata est.

2 Sic igitur eo verbo veteres esse usos, et cumprimis
M. Varronem Marcumque Tullium, omnes ferme
libri declarant. Quamobrem satis habui unum
3 interim exemplum promere. Itaque verba posui
Varronis e libro *Rerum Humanarum* primo, cuius
principium hoc est: "Praxiteles, qui propter artifi-
cium egregium nemini est paulum modo humaniori
4 ignotus." "Humaniori" inquit non ita ut vulgo

---

[1] *De Orat.* i. 71; ii. 72, etc.
[2] Fr. 1, Mirsch.

which they by their votes are to order or forbid;
the latter, to speak to the people without laying any
measure before them.

XVII

That *humanitas* does not mean what the common people
think, but those who have spoken pure Latin have given
the word a more restricted meaning.

THOSE who have spoken Latin and have used the
language correctly do not give to the word *humanitas*
the meaning which it is commonly thought to have,
namely, what the Greeks call φιλανθρωπία, signifying
a kind of friendly spirit and good-feeling towards
all men without distinction; but they gave to
humanitas about the force of the Greek παιδεία;
that is, what we call *eruditionem institutionemque in
bonas artes,* or "education and training in the liberal
arts." Those who earnestly desire and seek after
these are most highly humanized. For the pursuit
of that kind of knowledge, and the training given
by it, have been granted to man alone of all the
animals, and for that reason it is termed *humanitas,*
or "humanity."

That it is in this sense that our earlier writers
have used the word, and in particular Marcus Varro
and Marcus Tullius,[1] almost all the literature shows.
Therefore I have thought it sufficient for the present
to give one single example. I have accordingly
quoted the words of Varro from the first book of
his *Human Antiquities,* beginning as follows:[2]
"Praxiteles, who, because of his surpassing art, is
unknown to no one of any liberal culture (*humaniori*)."
He does not use *humanior* in its usual sense of

dicitur, "facili et tractabili et benivolo," tametsi rudis litterarum sit, hoc enim cum sententia nequaquam convenit, sed " eruditiori doctiorique," qui Praxitelem, quid fuerit, et ex libris [1] et ex historia cognoverit.

XVIII

Quid aput M. Catonem significent verba haec "inter os atque offam."

1   ORATIO est M. Catonis Censorii *De Aedilibus Vitio Creatis.* Ex ea oratione verba haec sunt : " Nunc ita aiunt, in segetibus, in herbis bona frumenta esse. Nolite ibi nimiam spem habere. Saepe audivi inter os atque offam multa intervenire posse ; verumvero inter offam atque herbam, ibi vero longum 2 intervallum est." Erucius Clarus, qui praefectus urbi et bis consul fuit, vir morum et litterarum veterum studiosissimus, ad Sulpicium Apollinarem scripsit, hominem memoriae nostrae doctissimum, quaerere sese et petere, uti sibi rescriberet quaenam 3 esset eorum verborum sententia. Tum Apollinaris, nobis praesentibus, nam id temporis ego adulescens Romae sectabar eum discendi gratia, rescripsit Claro ut viro erudito brevissime, vetus esse proverbium [2] "inter os et offam," idem significans quod Graecus ille παροιμιώδης versus :

Πολλὰ μεταξὺ πέλει κύλικος καὶ χείλεος ἄκρου.

---

[1] litteris, *Eussner* ; hiis libris, *Z.*
[2] proverbium *omitted by Q, perhaps rightly.*

"good-natured, amiable, and kindly," although without knowledge of letters, for this meaning does not at all suit his thought; but in that of a man of "some cultivation and education," who knew about Praxiteles both from books and from story.

XVIII

The meaning of Marcus Cato's phrase " betwixt mouth and morsel."

THERE is a speech by Marcus Cato Censorius *On the Improper Election of Aediles.* In that oration is this passage :[1] " Nowadays they say that the standing-grain, still in the blade, is a good harvest. Do not count too much upon it. I have often heard that many things may come *inter os atque offam,* or ' between the mouth and the morsel'; but there certainly is a long distance between a morsel and the blade." Erucius Clarus, who was prefect of the city and twice consul, a man deeply interested in the customs and literature of early days, wrote to Sulpicius Apollinaris, the most learned man within my memory, begging and entreating that he would write him the meaning of those words. Then, in my presence, for at that time I was a young man in Rome and was in attendance upon him for purposes of instruction, Apollinaris replied to Clarus very briefly, as was natural when writing to a man of learning, that " between mouth and morsel " was an old proverb, meaning the same as the poetic Greek adage :

'Twixt cup and lip there's many a slip.

[1] lxv. 1, Jordan.

XIX

Platonem tribuere Euripidi Sophocli versum ; et similia quaedam alia.[1]

1 VERSUS est notae vetustatis senarius :

Σοφοὶ τύραννοι τῶν σοφῶν ξυνουσίᾳ.

2 Eum versum Plato in *Theaeteto* Euripidi esse dicit. Quod quidem nos admodum miramur ; nam scriptum eum legimus in tragoedia Sophocli quae inscripta est Αἴας Λοκρός, prior autem natus fuit Sophocles quam Euripides.

3 Sed etiam ille versus non minus notus :

Γέρων γέροντα παιδαγωγήσω σ᾽ ἐγώ,

et in tragoedia Sophocli scriptus est, cui titulus est Φθιώτιδες, et in *Bacchis* Euripidi.

4 Id quoque animadvertimus, aput Aeschylum ἐν τῷ Πυρφόρῳ Προμηθεῖ et aput Euripidem in tragoedia quae inscripta est Ἰνώ, eundem esse versum absque paucis syllabis. Aeschylus sic :

Σιγῶν θ᾽ ὅπου δεῖ καὶ λέγων τὰ καίρια,

Euripides ita :

Σιγᾶν θ᾽ ὅπου δεῖ καὶ λέγειν ἵν᾽ ἀσφαλές.

Fuit autem Aeschylus non brevi antiquior.

---

[1] *Lemma omitted by* ω.

---

[1] Really *Theages* 6, p. 125 B.   [2] Fr. 13, Nauck[2].
[3] Id. 633.   [4] 193.
[5] Fr. 208, Nauck[2] (*Coeph.* 576).   [6] Id. 413.
[7] According to tradition Euripides was born on the day of the battle of Salamis (480 B.C.), Aeschylus took part in the

XIX

That Plato attributes a line of Sophocles to Euripides; and
some other matters of the same kind.

THERE is an iambic trimeter verse of notorious
antiquity:

> By converse with the wise wax tyrants wise.

This verse Plato in his *Theaetetus*[1] attributes to
Euripides. I am very much surprised at this; for I
have met it in the tragedy of Sophocles entitled
Ajax the Locrian,[2] and Sophocles was born before
Euripides.

But the following line is equally well known:

> I who am old shall lead you, also old.

And this is found both in a tragedy of Sophocles, of
which the title is *Phthiotides*,[3] and in the *Bacchae* of
Euripides.[4]

I have further observed that in the *Fire-bringing
Prometheus* of Aeschylus and in the tragedy of
Euripides entitled *Ino* an identical verse occurs,
except for a few syllables. In Aeschylus it runs
thus:[5]

> When proper, keeping silent, and saying what
> is fit.

In Euripides thus:[6]

> When proper, keeping silent, speaking when
> 'tis safe.

But Aeschylus was considerably the earlier writer.[7]

fight, and Sophocles, then about sixteen years old, figured in
the celebration of the victory. Christ, *Griech. Lit.*, assigns
Euripides' birth to 484.

XX

De genere atque nominibus familiae Porciae.

1 CUM in domus Tiberianae bibliotheca sederemus
ego et Apollinaris Sulpicius et quidam alii mihi aut
illi familiares, prolatus forte liber est ita inscriptus:
2 M. Catonis Nepotis. Tum quaeri coeptum est
3 quisnam is fuisset M. Cato Nepos. Atque ibi adulescens quispiam, quod ex eius sermonibus coniectare
potui, non abhorrens a litteris, "Hic," inquit, "est
M. Cato, non cognomento Nepos, sed M. Catonis
Censorii ex filio nepos, qui pater fuit M. Catonis,
praetorii viri, qui bello civili Uticae necem sibi gladio
manu sua conscivit, de cuius vita liber est M.
Ciceronis, qui inscribitur *Laus Catonis*, quem in
eodem libro idem Cicero pronepotem fuisse dicit
4 M. Catonis Censorii. Eius igitur quem Cicero laudavit pater hic fuit M. Cato, cuius orationes feruntur
inscriptae M. Catonis Nepotis."
5 Tum Apollinaris, ut mos eius in reprehendendo
fuit, placide admodum leniterque: "Laudo," inquit,
"te, mi fili, quod in tantula aetate, etiamsi hunc
M. Catonem, de quo nunc quaeritur, quis fuerit igno-
ras, auditiuncula tamen quadam de Catonis familia
6 aspersus es. Non unus autem, sed conplures M.
illius Catonis Censorii nepotes fuerunt, geniti non
7 eodem patre; duos enim M. ille Cato, qui et orator

---

[1] Fr. 1, p. 987, Orelli[2].

XX

Of the lineage and names of the Porcian family.

When Sulpicius Apollinaris and I, with some others who were friends of his or mine, were sitting in the library of the Palace of Tiberius, it chanced that a book was brought to us bearing the name of Marcus Cato Nepos. We at once began to inquire who this Marcus Cato Nepos was. And thereupon a young man, not unacquainted with letters, so far as I could judge from his language, said : " This Marcus Cato is called Nepos, not as a surname, but because he was the grandson of Marcus Cato Censorius through his son, and father of Marcus Cato the ex-praetor, who slew himself with his own sword at Utica during the civil war. There is a book of Marcus Cicero's about the life of the last-named, entitled *Laus Catonis*, or *A Eulogy of Cato*, in which Cicero says[1] that he was the great-grandson of Marcus Cato Censorius. Therefore the father of the man whom Cicero eulogized was this Marcus Cato, whose orations are circulated under the name of Marcus Cato Nepos."

Then Apollinaris, very quietly and mildly, as was his custom when passing criticism, said : " I congratulate you, my son, that at your age you have been able to favour us with a little lecture on the family of Cato, even though you do not know who this Marcus Cato was, about whom we are now inquiring. For the famous Marcus Cato Censorius had not one, but several grandsons, although not all were sprung from the same father. For the famous Marcus Cato, who was both an orator and

et censor fuit, filios habuit, et matribus diversos et
8 aetatibus longe dispares. Nam iam adulescente
altero, matre eius amissa, ipse quoque iam multum
senex, Saloni clientis sui filiam virginem duxit in
matrimonium, ex qua natus est ei M. Cato Salonianus; hoc enim illi cognomentum fuit a Salonio,
9 patre matris, datum. Ex maiore autem Catonis filio,
qui praetor designatus patre vivo mortuus est, et
egregios *De Iuris Disciplina* libros reliquit, nascitur
hic de quo quaeritur, M. Cato, M. filius, M. nepos.
10 Is satis vehemens orator fuit multasque orationes ad
exemplum avi scriptas reliquit et consul cum Q.
Marcio Rege fuit, inque eo consulatu in Africam
11 profectus, in ea provincia mortem obiit. Sed is
non, ita ut dixisti, M. Catonis, praetorii viri, qui se
Uticae occidit et quem Cicero laudavit, pater fuit;
nec, quia hic nepos Catonis Censorii, ille autem
pronepos fuit, propterea necessum est patrem hunc
12 ei fuisse. Hic enim nepos, cuius haec modo prolata
oratio est, filium quidem M. Catonem habuit; sed
non eum qui Uticae periit, sed qui, cum aedilis
curulis et praetor fuisset, in Galliam Narbonensem
13 profectus, ibi vita functus est. Ex altero autem illo
Censorii filio, longe natu minore, quem Salonianum
esse appellatum dixi, duo nati sunt L. Cato et M.
14 Cato. Is M. Cato tribunus plebis fuit et praeturam
petens mortem obiit ex eoque natus est M. Cato
praetorius, qui se bello civili Uticae interemit, de

a censor, had two sons, born of different mothers
and of very different ages; since, when one of them
was a young man, his mother died and his father,
who was already well on in years, married the
maiden daughter of his client Salonius, from whom
was born to him Marcus Cato Salonianus, a surname
which he derived from Salonius, his mother's father.
But from Cato's elder son, who died when praetor-
elect, while his father was still living, and left some
admirable works on *The Science of Law*, there was
born the man about whom we are inquiring, Marcus
Cato, son of Marcus, and grandson of Marcus. He
was an orator of some power and left many speeches
written in the manner of his grandfather; he was
consul with Quintus Marcius Rex, and during his
consulship went to Africa and died in that province.
But he was not, as you said he was, the father of
Marcus Cato the ex-praetor, who killed himself at
Utica and whom Cicero eulogized; nor because he
was the grandson of Cato the censor and Cato of Utica
was the censor's great-grandson does it necessarily
follow that the former was the father of the latter.
For this grandson whose speech was just brought to
us did, it is true, have a son called Marcus Cato, but
he was not the Cato who died at Utica, but the one
who, after being curule aedile and praetor, went to
Gallia Narbonensis and there ended his life. But
by that other son of Censorius, a far younger man,
who, as I said, was surnamed Salonianus, two sons
were begotten: Lucius and Marcus Cato. That
Marcus Cato was tribune of the commons and died
when a candidate for the praetorship; he begot
Marcus Cato the ex-praetor, who committed suicide
at Utica during the civil war, and when Marcus

cuius vita laudibusque cum M. Tullius scriberet,
pronepotem eum Catonis Censorii dixit fuisse.
15 Videtis igitur hanc partem familiae, quae ex minore
Catonis filio progenita est, non solum generis ipsius
tramitibus, sed temporum quoque spatio differre ;
nam quia ille Salonianus in extrema patris aetate,
sicuti dixi, natus fuit, prognati quoque ab eo ali-
quanto posteriores fuerunt quam qui a maiore fratre
16 eius geniti erant. Hanc temporum differentiam
facile animadvertetis ex hac ipsa oratione, cum
eam legetis."
17 Haec Sulpicius Apollinaris audientibus nobis dixit.
Quae postea ita esse, uti dixerat, cognovimus, cum
et *Laudationes Funebres* et *Librum Commentarium De
Familia Porcia* legeremus.

XXI

Quod a scriptoribus elegantissimis maior ratio habita sit
sonitus vocum atque verborum iucundioris, quae a Graecis
εὐφωνία dicitur, quam regulae disciplinaeque quae a
grammaticis reperta est.

1 INTERROGATUS est Probus Valerius, quod ex familiari eius quodam conperi, " hasne urbis" an
" has urbes" et " hanc turrem" an " hanc turrim"
dici oporteret. " Si aut versum," inquit, " pangis
aut orationem solutam struis atque ea tibi verba
dicenda sunt, non finitiones illas praerancidas neque
fetutinas grammaticas spectaveris, sed aurem tuam
interroga quo quid loco conveniat dicere ; quod illa
2 suaserit, id profecto erit rectissimum." Tum is qui
quaesierat, " Quonam modo," inquit, " vis aurem
3 meam interrogem ? " Et Probum ait respondisse :
" Quo suam Vergilius percontatus est, qui diversis in

Tullius wrote the latter's life and panegyric he said that he was the great-grandson of Cato the censor. You see therefore that the branch of the family which is descended from Cato's younger son differs not only in its pedigree, but in its dates as well; for because that Salonianus was born near the end of his father's life, as I said, his descendants also were considerably later than those of his elder brother. This difference in dates you will readily perceive from that speech itself, when you read it."

Thus spoke Sulpicius Apollinaris in my hearing. Later we found that what he had said was so, when we read the *Funeral Eulogies* and the *Genealogy of the Porcian Family.*

XXI

That the most elegant writers pay more attention to the pleasing sound of words and phrases (what the Greeks call εὐφωνία, or "euphony") than to the rules and precepts devised by the grammarians.

VALERIUS PROBUS was once asked, as I learned from one of his friends, whether one ought to say *has urbis* or *has urbes* and *hanc turrem* or *hanc turrim.* "If," he replied, "you are either composing verse or writing prose and have to use those words, pay no attention to the musty, fusty rules of the grammarians, but consult your own ear as to what is to be said in any given place. What it favours will surely be the best." Then the one who had asked the question said : "What do you mean by 'consult my ear'?" and he told me that Probus answered : "Just as Vergil did his, when in different passages

locis 'urbis' et 'urbes' dixit arbitrio consilioque
4 usus auris. Nam in primo *Georgicon*, quem ego,"
inquit, "librum manu ipsius correctum legi, 'urbis,'
per i litteram scripsit. Verba e versibus eius haec
sunt:

> urbisne invisere, Caesar,
> Terrarumque velis curam.

Verte enim et muta, ut 'urbes' dicas, insubidius
5 nescio quid facies et pinguius. Contra in tertio
Aeneidis 'urbes' dixit per e litteram:

> Centum urbes habitant magnas.

Hic item muta, ut 'urbis' dicas, nimis exilis vox erit
et exanguis, tanta quippe iuncturae differentia est in
6 consonantia vocum proximarum. Praeterea idem
Vergilius 'turrim' dixit, non 'turrem,' et 'securim,'
non 'securem':

> Turrim in praecipiti stantem

et:

> incertam excussit cervice securim.

Quae sunt, opinor, iucundioris gracilitatis quam si
7 suo utrumque loco per e litteram dicas." At ille qui
interrogaverat, rudis profecto et aure agresti homo,
"Cur," inquit, "aliud alio in loco potius rectiusque
8 esse dicas, non sane intellego." Tum Probus iam
commotior, "Noli," inquit, "igitur laborare, utrum
istorum debeas dicere, 'urbis' an 'urbes.' Nam

---

[1] *Georg.* i. 25.   [2] *Aen.* iii. 106.
[3] *Aen.* ii. 460.   [4] *Aen.* ii. 224,

he has used *urbis* and *urbes*, following the taste and judgment of his ear.   For in the first *Georgic*, which," said he, " I have read in a copy corrected by the poet's own hand, he wrote *urbis* with an *i*.   These are the words of the verses : [1]

> O'er cities (*urbis*) if you choose to watch, and rule
> Our lands, O Caesar great.

But turn and change it so as to read *urbes*, and somehow you will make it duller and heavier.   On the other hand, in the third *Aeneid* he wrote *urbes* with an *e* : [2]

> An hundred mighty cities (*urbes*) they inhabit.

Change this too so as to read *urbis* and the word will be too slender and colourless, so great indeed is the different effect of combination in the harmony of neighbouring sounds.   Moreover, Vergil also said *turrim*, not *turrem*, and *securim*, not *securem* :

> A turret (*turrim*) on sheer edge standing,[3]

and

> Has shaken from his neck the ill-aimed axe (*securim*).[4]

These words have, I think, a more agreeable lightness than if you should use the form in *e* in both places."   But the one who had asked the question, a boorish fellow surely and with untrained ear, said : " I don't just understand why you say that one form is better and more correct in one place and the other in the other."   Then Probus, now somewhat impatient, retorted : " Don't trouble then to inquire whether you ought to say *urbis* or *urbes*.   For since

cum id genus sis quod video, ut sine iactura tua pecces, nihil perdes, utrum dixeris."

9 His tum verbis Probus et hac fini hominem dimisit, ut mos eius fuit erga indociles, prope inclementer.

10 Nos autem aliud quoque postea consimiliter a Vergilio duplici modo scriptum invenimus. Nam et tres et tris posuit eodem in loco ea iudicii subtilitate, ut si aliter dixeris mutaverisque et aliquid tamen auris

11 habeas, sentias suavitatem sonitus claudere. Versus ex decimo hi sunt:

> Tres quoque Threicios Boreae de gente suprema
> Et tris quos Idas pater et patria Ismara mittit.

Tres illic, tris hic; pensicula utrumque modulareque,

12 reperies suo quidque in loco sonare aptissime. Sed in illo quoque itidem Vergilii versu:

> Haec finis Priami fatorum,

si mutes "haec" et "hic finis" dicas, durum atque absonum erit respuentque aures quod mutaveris. Sicut illud contra eiusdem Vergilii insuavius facias, si mutes:

> quem das finem, rex magne, laborum?

Nam si ita dicas: "quam das finem," iniucundum nescio quo pacto et laxiorem vocis sonum feceris.

---

[1] *Aen.* x. 350.   [2] *Aen.* ii. 554.
[3] *Aen.* i. 241.

you are the kind of man that I see you are and err without detriment to yourself, you will lose nothing whichever you say."

With these words then and this conclusion Probus dismissed the man, somewhat rudely, as was his way with stupid folk. But I afterwards found another similar instance of double spelling by Vergil. For he has used *tres* and *tris* in the same passage with such fineness of taste, that if you should read differently and change one for the other, and have any ear at all, you would perceive that the sweetness of the sound is spoiled. These are the lines, from the tenth book of the *Aeneid*[1]:

> Three (*tres*) Thracians too from Boreas' distant race,
> And three (*tris*) whom Idas sent from Ismarus' land.

In one place he has *tres*, in the other *tris*; weigh and ponder both, and you will find that each sounds most suitable in its own place. But also in this line of Vergil,[2]

> This end (*haec finis*) to Priam's fortunes then,

if you change *haec* and say *hic finis*, it will be hard and unrhythmical and your ears will shrink from the change. Just as, on the contrary, you would make the following verse of Vergil less sweet, if you were to change it:[3]

> What end (*quem finem*) of labours, great king, dost thou grant?

For if you should say *quam das finem*, you would somehow make the sound of the words harsh and somewhat weak.

13 Ennius item rectos cupressos dixit contra receptum
vocabuli genus hoc versu :

Cautibus [1] nutantis pinos rectosque cupressos.

Firmior ei, credo, et viridior sonus esse vocis visus
14 est, "rectos" dicere "cupressos" quam "rectas."
Contra vero idem Ennius in *Annali* duodevicesimo
"aere fulva" dixit, non "fulvo," non ob id solum,
quod Homerus ἠέρα βαθεῖαν dicit, sed quod hic sonus,
opinor, vocabilior visus et amoenior.

15 Sicuti Marco etiam Ciceroni mollius teretiusque
visum, in *Quinta in Verrem* "fretu" scribere quam
"freto" : "Perangusto," inquit, "fretu divisa."
Erat enim crassius iam vetustiusque, "perangusto
16 freto" dicere. Itidem in *Secunda,* simili usus modu-
lamine, "manifesto peccatu," inquit, non "peccato" ;
hoc enim scriptum in uno atque in altero antiquissi-
17 mae fidei libro Tironiano repperi. Verba sunt Ciceronis haec : "Nemo ita vivebat ut nulla eius vitae pars
summae turpitudinis esset expers, nemo ita in manifesto peccatu tenebatur ut cum inpudens fuisset
in facto, tum inpudentior videretur, si negaret."

18 Huius autem vocis cum elegantior hoc in loco
19 sonus est, tum ratio certa et probata est. "Hic"
enim "peccatus," quasi "peccatio," recte Latineque
dicitur, sicut "hic incestus," non qui admisit, sed quod
admissum est, et "hic tributus," quod "tributum"

---

[1] cautibus, *Stowasser*; capitibus, ω; vertice, *Onions*; comp-
tibus, *Damsté* (*cf. Lucr.* i. 87).

---

[1] *Ann.* 490, Vahlen.[2] Ennius also has *longi cupressi* in *Ann.*
262.

[2] *Ann.* 454, Vahlen[2], cf. ii. 26. 4.

[3] *Iliad* xx. 446 ; xxi. 6.

Ennius too spoke of *rectos cupressos,* or " straight cypresses," contrary to the accepted gender of that word, in the following verse:

On cliffs the nodding pine and cypress straight.[1]

The sound of the word, I think, seemed to him stronger and more vigorous, if he said *rectos cupressos* rather than *rectas.* But, on the other hand, this same Ennius in the eighteenth book of his *Annals*[2] said *aere fulva* instead of *fulvo,* not merely because Homer said ἠέρα βαθεῖα,[3] but because this sound, I think, seemed more sonorous and agreeable.

In the same way Marcus Cicero also thought it smoother and more polished to write, in his fifth *Oration against Verres,*[4] *fretu* rather than *freto.* He says " divided by a narrow strait (*fretu*)"; for it would have been heavier and more archaic to say *perangusto freto.* Also in his second *Oration against Verres,* making use of a like rhythm, he said [5] " by an evident sin," using *peccatu* instead of *peccato;* for I find this written in one or two of Tiro's copies, of very trustworthy antiquity. These are Cicero's words: " No one lived in such a way that no part of his life was free from extreme disgrace, no one was detected in such manifest sin (*peccatu*) that while he had been shameless in committing it, he would seem even more shameless if he denied it."

Not only is the sound of this word more elegant in this passage, but the reason for using the word is definite and sound. For *hic peccatus,* equivalent to *peccatio,* is correct and good Latin, just as many of the early writers used *incestus* (criminal), not of the one who committed the crime, but of the crime

[4] ii. 5. 169.   [5] ii. 2. 191.

nos dicimus, a plerisque veterum dicta sunt. " Hic"
quoque "adlegatus "et " hic arbitratus " pro " adlega-
tione " proque "arbitratione " dicuntur, qua ratione
servata " arbitratu " et " adlegatu meo " dicimus.

20 Sic igitur " in manifesto peccatu " dixit, ut " in
manifesto incestu " veteres dixerunt, non quin
Latinum esset " peccato " dicere, sed quia in loco isto
positum subtilius ad aurem molliusque est.

21 Lucretius aeque auribus inserviens "funem " femi-
nino genere appellavit in hisce versibus :

Haut, ut opinor, enim mortalia saecla superne
Aurea de caelo demisit funis in arva,

cum dicere usitatius manente numero posset :

Aureus e caelo demisit funis in arva.

22 Sacerdotes quoque feminas M. Cicero "antistitas"
dicit, non secundum grammaticam legem "antistites."
Nam cum insolentias verborum a veteribus dictorum
plerumque respueret, huius tamen verbi in ea parte
sonitu delectatus : " Sacerdotes," inquit, " Cereris

23 atque illius fani antistitae." Usque adeo in quibusdam neque rationem verbi neque consuetudinem, sed
solam aurem secuti sunt, suis verba modulis pensi-

24 tantem. " Quod qui non sentiunt," inquit idem ipse
M. Cicero, cum de numerosa et apta oratione
dissereret, "quas auris habeant aut quid in his hominis
simile sit, nescio."

---

[1] ii. 1153. [2] *In Verr*. iv. 99.
[3] cf. Hor. *Epist*. i. 7. 98. [4] *Orat*. 168.

itself, and *tributus,* where we say *tributum* (tribute). *Adlegatus* (instigation) too and *arbitratus* (judgment) are used for *adlegatio* and *arbitratio,* and preserving these forms we say *arbitratu* and *adlegatu meo.* So then Cicero said *in manifesto peccatu,* as the early writers said *in manifesto incestu,* not that it was not good Latin to say *peccato,* but because in that context the use of *peccatu* was finer and smoother to the ear.

With equal regard for our ears Lucretius made *funis* feminine in these verses: [1]

> No golden rope (*aurea funis*), methinks, let down from heaven
> The race of mortals to this earth of ours,

although with equally good rhythm he might have used the more common *aureus funis* and written:

> Aureus e caelo demisit funis in arva.

Marcus Cicero calls [2] even priests by a feminine term, *antistitae,* instead of *antistites,* which is demanded by the grammarians' rule. For while he usually avoided the obsolete words used by the earlier writers, yet in this passage, pleased with the sound of the word, he said: "The priests of Ceres and the guardians (*antistitae*) of her shrine." To such a degree have writers in some cases followed neither reason nor usage in choosing a word, but only the ear, which weighs words according to its own standards. [3] "And as for those who do not feel this," says Marcus Cicero himself, [4] when speaking about appropriate and rhythmical language, "I know not what ears they have, or what there is in them resembling a man."

25 Illud vero cumprimis apud Homerum veteres gramʌatici adnotaverunt, quod, cum dixisset quodam in loco κολοιούς τε ψῆράς τε, alio in loco, non ψηρῶν τε, set ψαρῶν dixit:

Τῶν δ' ὥς τε ψαρῶν νέφος ἔρχεται ἠὲ κολοιῶν,

secutus non communem, sed propriam in quoque vocis situ iucunditatem; nam si alterum in alterius loco ponas, utrumque feceris sonitu insuave.

XXII

Verba Titi Castricii rhetoris ad discipulos adulescentes de vestitu atque calciatu non decoro.

1 T. Castricius, rhetoricae disciplinae doctor, qui habuit Romae locum principem declamandi ac docendi, summa vir auctoritate gravitateque et a divo Hadriano in mores atque litteras spectatus, cum me forte praesente, usus enim sum eo magistro, discipulos quosdam suos senatores vidisset die feriato tunicis et lacernis indutos et gallicis calciatos, " Equidem," inquit, " maluissem vos togatos esse; si [1] pigitum est, cinctos saltem esse et paenulatos. Sed si hic vester huiusmodi vestitus de multo iam usu ignoscibilis est, soleatos tamen vos, populi Romani senatores, per urbis vias ingredi nequaquam decorum

---

[1] si *added by Dziatzko.*

---

[1] *Iliad* xvi. 583.   [2] *Iliad* xvii. 755.
[3] Instead of the senatorial shoe; this was red or black and was fastened on by four black thongs which passed

But the early grammarians have noted this feature in Homer above all, that when he had said in one place[1] κολοιούς τε ψῆράς τε, "both crows and starlings," in another place[2] he did not use ψηρῶν τε, but ψαρῶν:

As lights a cloud of starlings (ψαρῶν) or of daws,

not conforming to general usage, but seeking the pleasing effect peculiar to the word in each of the two positions; for if you change one of these for the other, you will give both a harsh sound.

XXII

The words of Titus Castricius to his young pupils on unbecoming clothes and shoes.

Titus Castricius, a teacher of the art of rhetoric, who held the first rank at Rome as a declaimer and an instructor, a man of the greatest influence and dignity, was highly regarded also by the deified Hadrian for his character and his learning. Once when I happened to be with him (for I attended him as my master) and he had seen some pupils of his who were senators wearing tunics and cloaks on a holiday, and with sandals on their feet,[3] he said: "For my part, I should have preferred to see you in your togas, or if that was too much trouble, at least with girdles and mantles. But if this present attire of yours is now pardonable from long custom, yet it is not at all seemly for you, who are senators of the Roman people, to go through the streets of the city

crosswise around the ankle and the calf of the leg; cf. Hor. *Sat.* i. 6. 27.

est, non hercle vobis minus quam illi tum fuit, cui hoc M. Tullius pro turpi crimine obiectavit."

2 Haec, me audiente, Castricius et quaedam alia ad eam rem conducentia Romane et severe dixit.
3 Plerique autem ex his qui audierant requirebant cur "soleatos" dixisset, qui gallicas, non soleas, haberent.
4 Sed Castricius profecto scite atque incorrupte locu-
5 tus est; omnia enim ferme id genus, quibus plantarum calces tantum infimae teguntur, cetera prope nuda et teretibus habenis vincta sunt, "soleas" dixerunt,
6 nonnumquam voce Graeca "crepidulas." "Gallicas" autem verbum esse opinor novum, non diu ante aetatem M. Ciceronis usurpari coeptum, itaque ab eo ipso positum est in secunda *Antonianarum:* "Cum
7 gallicis,"[1] inquit, " et lacerna cucurristi." Neque in ea significatione id apud quemquam alium scriptum lego gravioris dumtaxat auctoritatis scriptorem ; sed, ut dixi, "crepidas" et "crepidulas," prima syllaba correpta, id genus calciamentum appellaverunt, quod Graeci κρηπῖδας vocant, eiusque calciamenti sutores
8 "crepidarios" dixerunt. Sempronius Asellio in libro *Rerum Gestarum* XIV: "Crepidarium," inquit, "cultellum rogavit a crepidario sutore."

XXIII (XXII)

De Neriene Martis in antiquis conprecationibus.[2]

1 CONPRECATIONES deum inmortalium, quae ritu Romano fiunt, expositae sunt in libris sacerdotum

---

[1] caligis. *most MSS. of Cic.*
[2] lemma omitted by ω, *supplied by Hertz.*

in sandals, nor by Jove! is this less criminal in you than it was in one whom Marcus Tullius once reproved for such attire."

This, and some other things to the same purport, Castricius said in my hearing with true Roman austerity. But several of those who had heard him asked why he had said *soleatos,* or "in sandals," of those who wore *gallicae,* or "Gallic slippers," and not *soleae.* But Castricius certainly spoke purely and properly; for in general all kinds of foot-gear which cover only the bottom of the soles, leaving the rest almost bare, and are bound on by slender thongs, are called *soleae,* or sometimes by the Greek word *crepidulae.* But *gallicae,* I think, is a new word, which came into use not long before the time of Marcus Cicero. In fact, he himself uses it in his second *Oration against Antony*:[1] "You ran about," says he, "in slippers (*gallicis*) and cloak." Nor do I find this word with that meaning in any other writer—a writer of high authority, that is; but, as I have said, they called that kind of shoe *crepidae* and *crepidulae,* shortening the first syllable of the Greek word κρηπῖδες, and the makers of such shoes they termed *crepidarii.* Sempronius Asellio in the fourteenth book of his *Histories* says:[2] "He asked for a cobbler's knife from a maker of slippers (*crepidarius sutor*)."

XXIII

Of the Nerio of Mars in ancient prayers.

Prayers to the immortal gods, which are offered according to the Roman ritual, are set forth in the

[1] *Phil.* ii. 76.   [2] Fr. 11, Peter[2].

populi Romani et in plerisque antiquis orationibus.
2 In his scriptum est: "Luam Saturni, Salaciam
Neptuni, Horam Quirini, Virites Quirini, Maiam
Volcani, Heriem Iunonis, Moles Martis Nerienemque
3 Martis." Ex quibus id quod postremum posui sic
plerosque dicere audio, ut primam in eo syllabam
producant, quo Graeci modo dicunt Νηρείδας. Sed
qui proprie locuti sunt primam correptam dixerunt,
4 tertiam produxerunt. Est enim rectus casus
vocabuli, sicut in libris veterum scriptum est,
"Nerio," quamquam M. Varro in *Satura Menippea*,
quae inscribitur Σκιομαχία,[1] non "Nerio," sed
"Nerienes" vocative dicit in his versibus:

Te Anna ác Peranna, Pánda Cela, té Pales,
Neriénes et Minérva, Fortuna ác Ceres.

5 Ex quo nominandi quoque casum eundem fieri
6 necessum est. Sed "Nerio" a veteribus sic declina-
batur, quasi "Anio"; nam perinde ut "Anienem,"
7 sic "Nerienem" dixerunt, tertia syllaba producta.
Id autem, sive "Nerio" sive "Nerienes" est,
8 Sabinum verbum est, eoque significatur virtus et
fortitudo. Itaque ex Claudiis, quos a Sabinis oriun-
dos accepimus, qui[2] erat egregia atque praestanti
9 fortitudine "Nero" appellatus est. Sed id Sabini

---

[1] panda te lato, ω; Panda Celato, ς, *corr. by Mommsen;*
panda te lito, *Hertz.*
[2] quis, Q; quisquis, *C. F. W. Müller.*

---

[1] These names apparently represented characteristics of
the deities with which they are coupled, which in some
cases later became separate goddesses; see Fowler, *Roman
Festivals*, pp. 60 ff. Gellius is apparently right in his explanation of Nerio in §§ 7-10, while later myths made her
the wife of Mars. Lua (cf. *luo*, "purify"), according to
Livy xlv. 33. 2, was a goddess to whom, in company with

books of the priests of the Roman people, as well as in many early books of prayers. In these we find: "Lua,[1] of Saturn; Salacia, of Neptune; Hora, of Quirinus; the Virites of Quirinus; Maia of Vulcan; Heries of Juno; Moles of Mars, and Nerio of Mars." Of these I hear most people pronounce the one which I have put last with a long initial syllable, as the Greeks pronounce Νηρεΐδες ("Nereids"). But those who have spoken correctly made the first syllable short and lengthened the third. For the nominative case of the word, as it is written in the books of early writers, is *Nerio*, although Marcus Varro, in his *Menippean Satire* entitled Σκιομαχία, or "Battle of the Shadows," uses in the vocative *Nerienes*, not *Nerio*, in the following verses :[2]

Thee, Anna and Peranna, Panda Cela, Pales,
Nerienes and Minerva, Fortune and likewise Ceres.

From which it necessarily follows that the nominative case is the same. But *Nerio* was declined by our forefathers like *Anio ;* for, as they said *Aniēnem* with the third syllable long, so they did *Neriēnem*. Furthermore, that word, whether it be *Nerio* or *Nerienes*, is Sabine and signifies valour and courage. Hence among the Claudii, who we are told sprang from the Sabines, whoever was of eminent and surpassing courage was called *Nero*.[3] But the Sabines

Mars and Minerva, the captured arms of an enemy were devoted when they were burned by the victors. Salacia (cf. *sal*, "salt one") was a sea-goddess. Hora, according to Nonius, p. 120, was a goddess of youth. Ovid, *Met.* xiv. 830–851, says that it was the name given to Hersilia, the wife of Romulus, after her deification. For the other names see the Index.

[2] Frag. 506, Bücheler.   [3] See Suet. *Tib.* i. 2.

accepisse·a Graecis videntur, qui vincula et firma-
menta membrorum νεῦρα dicunt, unde nos quoque
10 Latine "nervos" appellamus. "Nerio" igitur Martis vis et potentia et maiestas quaedam esse Martis
demonstratur.

11 Plautus autem in *Truculento* coniugem esse Nerienem Martis dicit, atque id sub persona militis, in hoc
versu :

Márs peregre adveniéns salutat Nérienem uxorém
suam.

12 Super ea re audivi non incelebrem hominem dicere, nimis comice Plautum inperito et incondito
militi falsam novamque opinionem tribuisse, ut
13 Nerienem coniugem esse Martis putaret. Sed id
perite magis quam comice dictum intelleget, qui
leget Cn. Gellii *Annalem* tertium, in quo scriptum
est Hersiliam, cum apud T. Tatium verba faceret
pacemque oraret, ita precatam esse : "Neria Martis
te obsecro, pacem da, te, uti liceat nuptiis propriis
et prosperis uti, quod de tui coniugis consilio contigit uti nos itidem integras raperent, unde liberos
14 sibi et suis, posteros patriae pararent." "De tui," inquit, "coniugis consilio," Martem scilicet significans ;
per quod apparet, non esse id poetice a Plauto
dictum, sed eam quoque traditionem fuisse, ut Nerio
15 a quibusdam uxor esse Martis diceretur. Inibi
autem animadvertendum est quod Gellius "Neria"
16 dicit per a litteram, non "Nerio," neque "Nerienes."
Praeter Plautum etiam praeterque Gellium Licinius

---

[1] 515. [2] Fr. 15, Peter[2].
[3] Referring to the rape of the Sabine women. *Itidem* shows
that Cn. Gellius had in mind the later myth (see note 1,
p. 480) that Mars finally carried off Nerio as his bride.

seem to have derived this word from the Greeks,
who call the sinews and ligaments of the limbs
νεῦρα, whence we also in Latin call them *nervi*.   Therefore *Nerio* designates the strength and power of
Mars and a certain majesty of the War-god.

Plautus, however, in the *Truculentus* says[1] that
Nerio is the wife of Mars, and puts the statement into the mouth of a soldier, in the following
line :

Mars, coming home, greets his wife Nerio.

About this line I once heard a man of some
repute say that Plautus, with too great an eye to
comic effect, attributed this strange and false idea,
of thinking that Nerio was the wife of Mars, to an
ignorant and rude soldier.   But whoever will read
the third book of the *Annals* of Gnaeus Gellius will
find that this passage shows learning, rather than a
comic spirit; for there it is written that Hersilia,
when she pleaded before Titus Tatius and begged for
peace, prayed in these words :[2] " Neria of Mars, I
beseech thee, give us peace ; I beseech thee that it
be permitted us to enjoy lasting and happy marriages,
since it was by thy lord's advice that in like manner
they carried off us maidens,[3] that from us they might
raise up children for themselves and their people, and
descendants for their country."   She says " by thy
lord's advice," of course meaning her husband, Mars ;
and from this it is plain that Plautus made use of no
poetic fiction, but that there was also a tradition
according to which Nerio was said by some to be the
wife of Mars.   But it must be noticed besides that
Gellius writes *Neria* with an *a*, not *Nerio* nor *Nerienes*.
In addition to Plautus too, and Gellius, Licinius

Imbrex, vetus comoediarum scriptor, in fabula quae *Neaera* scripta est, ita scripsit :

> Nolo égo Neaeram té vocent, set Nérienem,
> Cum quidém Mavorti [1] es ín conubiúm data.

17 Ita autem se numerus huiusce versus habet, ut tertia in eo nomine syllaba, contra quam supra dictum est, corripienda sit ; cuius sonitus quanta aput veteres indifferentia sit, notius est quam ut plura in id verba 18 sumenda sint. Ennius autem in primo *Annali* in hoc versu :

> Nerienem Mavortis et Herem,[2]

si, quod minime solet, numerum servavit, primam syllabam intendit, tertiam corripuit.

19 Ac ne id quidem praetermittendum puto, cuius-modi est, quod in *Commentario* Servii Claudii scrip-tum invenimus, " Nerio " dictum quasi " Neirio," hoc est sine ira et cum placiditate, ut eo nomine mitem tranquillumque fieri Martem precemur ; " ne " enim particula, ut apud Graecos, ita plerumque in Latina quoque lingua privativa est.

XXIV

Verba M. Catonis, egere se multis rebus et nihil tamen cu-pere dicentis.

1 M. CATO, consularis et censorius, publicis iam privatisque opulentis rebus, villas suas inexcultas et

---

[1] Mavorti, *Ribbeck* ; Marti, ω.
[2] Herem, *Meursius ;* erdem, X ; Herclem, ω.

---

[1] p. 39, Ribbeck[3].
[2] That is, Nĕrĭĕnem, instead of Nērĭēnem.
[3] *Ann.* 104, Vahlen[2].

Imbrex, an early writer of comedies, in the play entitled *Neaera*, wrote as follows : [1]

Neaera I'd not wish to have thee called ;
Neriene rather, since thou art wife to Mars.

Moreover, the metre of this verse is such that the third syllable in that name must be made short,[2] contrary to what was said above. But how greatly the quantity of this syllable varied among the early writers is so well known that I need not waste many words on the subject. Ennius also, in this verse from the first book of his *Annals*,[3]

Neriene of Mars and Here,[4]

if, as is not always the case, he has preserved the metre, has lengthened the first syllable and shortened the third.

And I do not think that I ought to pass by this either, whatever it amounts to, which I find written in the *Commentary* of Servius Claudius,[5] that *Nerio* is equivalent to *Neirio*, meaning without anger (*ne ira*) and with calmness, so that in using that name we pray that Mars may become mild and calm ; for the particle *ne*, as it is among the Greeks, is frequently privative in the Latin language also.

XXIV

Remarks of Marcus Cato, who declared that he lacked many things, yet desired nothing.

MARCUS CATO, ex-consul and ex-censor, says that when the State and private individuals were abounding in wealth, his country-seats were plain and

---

[4] See Paul. Fest., p. 89, 4, Lindsay: Herem Marteam antiqui accepta hereditate colebant, quae a nomine appellabatur heredum, et esse una ex Martis comitibus putabatur.

[5] Fr. 4, Fun.

rudes, ne tectorio quidem praelitas fuisse dicit ad
annum usque aetatis suae septuagesimum. Atque
ibi postea his verbis utitur : " Neque mihi," inquit,
" aedificatio neque vasum neque vestimentum ullum
est manupretiosum neque pretiosus servus neque an-
cilla. Si quid est," inquit, " quod utar, utor ; si non
est, egeo. Suum cuique per me uti atque frui licet."
2 Tum deinde addit : " Vitio vertunt, quia multa
egeo ; at ego illis, quia nequeunt egere." Haec
mera veritas Tusculani hominis, egere se multis
rebus et nihil tamen cupere dicentis, plus hercle
promovet ad exhortandam parsimoniam sustinen-
damque inopiam quam Graecae[1] istorum praestigiae,
philosophari sese dicentium umbrasque verborum
inanes fingentium, qui se nihil habere et nihil tamen
egere ac nihil cupere dicunt, cum et habendo et
egendo et cupiendo ardeant.

XXV

Quaesitum tractatumque, quid sint "manubiae"; atque
inibi dicta quaedam de ratione utendi verbis pluribus idem
significantibus.

1 In fastigiis fori Traiani simulacra sunt sita circum-
undique inaurata equorum atque signorum militari-
2 um, subscriptumque est : " Ex manubiis." Quaerebat Favorinus, cum in area fori ambularet et amicum

---

[1] Graecorum, *Hertz* ; Graeculorum praestigiae, *Boot.*

unadorned, and not even whitewashed, up to the
seventieth year of his age. And later he uses these
words on the subject:[1] "I have no building, utensil
or garment bought with a great price, no costly slave
or maidservant. If I have anything to use," he says,
"I use it; if not, I do without. So far as I am concerned, everyone may use and enjoy what he has."
Then he goes on to say: "They find fault with me,
because I lack many things; but I with them, because they cannot do without them." This simple
frankness of the man of Tusculum, who says that
he lacks many things, yet desires nothing, truly has
more effect in inducing thrift and contentment with
small means than the Greek sophistries of those who
profess to be philosophers and invent vain shadows
of words, declaring that they have nothing and
yet lack nothing and desire nothing, while all the
time they are fevered with having, with lacking,
and with desiring.

XXV

The meaning of *manubiae* is asked and discussed; with some
observations as to the propriety of using several words of
the same meaning.

ALL along the roof of the colonnades of Trajan's
forum [2] there are placed gilded statues of horses and
representations of military standards, and underneath
is written *Ex manubiis*. Favorinus inquired, when he
was walking in the court of the forum, waiting for

[1] *O.R.F.*, p. 146, Meyer².
[2] The largest and grandest of the imperial fora, including
the basilica Ulpia, the column of Trajan, and the library.

suum consulem opperiretur causas pro tribunali cog-
noscentem nosque tunc eum sectaremur—quaerebat,
inquam, quid nobis videretur significare proprie
"manubiarum" illa inscriptio. Tum quispiam qui
3 cum eo erat, homo in studiis doctrinae multi atque
celebrati nominis: "'Ex manubiis,'" inquit, "significat 'ex praeda'; 'manubiae' enim dicuntur praeda
quae manu capta est." "Etiamsi," inquit Favorinus,
4 "opera mihi princeps et prope omnis in litteris dis-
ciplinisque Graecis sumpta est, non usque eo tamen
infrequens sum vocum Latinarum, quas subsicivo aut
tumultuario studio colo, ut hanc ignorem manubiarum interpretationem vulgariam, quod esse dicantur
'manubiae' praeda. Sed quaero an M Tullius, verborum homo diligentissimus, in oratione quam dixit
De Lege Agraria Kalendis Ianuariis contra Rullum,
inani et inlepida geminatione iunxerit 'manubias' et
'praedam,' si duo haec verba idem significant neque
ulla re aliqua dissident." Atque, ut erat Favorinus
5 egregia vel divina quadam memoria, verba ipsa M.
6 Tulli statim dixit. Ea nos hic adscripsimus: "Praedam, manubias, sectionem, castra denique Cn.
Pompei, sedente imperatore, decemviri vendent"; et
infra itidem duo haec simul iunctim posita dixit: "Ex
7 praeda, ex manubiis, ex auro coronario." Ac deinde
ad eum convertit qui manubias esse praedam dixerat,
et: "Videturne tibi," inquit, "utroque in loco M.

---

[1] *De Leg. Agr.* i., p. 601, Orelli[2].

[2] Id. ii. 59.

[3] It was customary for cities in the provinces to send
golden crowns to a victorious general, which were carried
before him in his triumph. By the time of Cicero the
presents took the form of money, called *aurum coronarium*.
Later, it was a present to the emperor on stated occasions.

his friend the consul, who was hearing cases from
the tribunal—and I at the time was in attendance
on him—he asked, I say, what that inscription
manubiae seemed to us really to mean. Then one
of those who were with him, a man of a great and
wide-spread reputation for his devotion to learned
pursuits, said : "*Ex manubiis* is the same as *ex praeda*;
for *manubiae* is the term for booty which is taken
manu, that is 'by hand.'" Then Favorinus rejoined :
"Although my principal and almost my entire attention has been given to the literature and arts of
Greece, I am nevertheless not so inattentive to the
Latin language, to which I devote occasional or
desultory study, as to be unaware of this common
interpretation of *manubiae*, which makes it a synonym
of *praeda*. But I raise the question, whether Marcus
Tullius, a man most careful in his diction, in the
speech which he delivered against Rullus on the
first of January *On the Agrarian Law*, joined *manubiae*
and *praeda* by an idle and inelegant repetition, if it
be true that these two words have the same meaning
and do not differ in any respect at all." And then,
such was Favorinus' marvellous and almost miraculous
memory, he at once added Cicero's own words.
These I have appended : [1] "The decemvirs will sell
the booty (*praedam*), the proceeds of the spoils
(*manubias*), the goods reserved for public auction, in
fact Gnaeus Pompeius' camp, while the general sits
looking on" ; and just below he again used these
two words in conjunction : [2] "From the booty (*ex
praeda*), from the proceeds of the spoils (*ex manubiis*),
from the crown-money." [3] Then, turning to the man
who had said that *manubiae* was the same as *praeda*,
Favorinus said, "Does it seem to you that in both

Cicero duobus verbis idem, sicuti tu putas, significantibus inepte et frigide esse usus ac tali ioco
dignus quali apud Aristophanen, facetissimum comi-
corum, Euripides Aeschylum insectatus est, cum ait:

Δὶς ταὐτὸν ἡμῖν εἶπεν ὁ σοφὸς Αἰσχύλος.
"Ηκω γὰρ εἰς γῆν, φησί, καὶ κατέρχομαι·
"Ηκω[1] δὲ ταὐτόν ἐστι τῷ κατέρχομαι.
Νὴ τὸν Δί᾽, ὥσπερ γ᾽ εἴ τις εἴποι γείτονι,
Χρῆσον σὺ μάκτραν, εἰ δὲ βούλει, κάρδοπον?

8 "Nequaquam vero," inquit ille, "talia videntur,
quale est μάκτρα et κάρδοπος, qua vel a poetis vel
oratoribus Graecis nostrisque venerandae et ornan-
dae rei gratia duobus eadem pluribusve nominibus
frequentantur."

9 "Quid igitur," inquit Favorinus, "valet haec repetitio instauratioque eiusdem rei sub alio nomine in
'manubiis' et in 'praeda'? Num ornat, ut alioqui
solet, orationem? Num eam modulatiorem aptior-
emque reddit? Num onerandi vel exprobrandi
criminis causa exaggerationem aliquam speciosam
facit? Sicut in libro eiusdem M. Tulli, qui *De Con-
stituendo Accusatore* est, una eademque res pluribus
verbis vehementer atque atrociter dicitur: 'Sicilia
tota, si una voce loqueretur, hoc diceret: "Quod
auri, quod argenti, quod ornamentorum in meis
urbibus, sedibus, delubris fuit."' Nam cum urbes
semel totas dixisset, sedes delubraque addidit, quae

[1] ἥκειν, *Aristoph.*

---

[1] *Frogs* 1154, 1156 ff.   [2] *Div. in Caec.* 19.

these passages Marcus Cicero weakly and frigidly used two words which, as you think, mean the same thing, thus showing himself deserving of the ridicule with which in Aristophanes, the wittiest of comic writers, Euripides assailed Aeschylus, saying :[1]

> Wise Aeschylus has said the same thing twice ;
> ' I come into the land,' says he, ' and enter it.'
> But ' enter ' and ' come into ' are the same.
> By Heaven, yes! It's just as if one said
> To a neighbour : ' Use the pot, or else the pan ' ?

" But by no means," said he, " do Cicero's words seem like such repetitions as μάκτρα, pot, and κάρδοπος, pan, which are used either by our own poets or orators and those of the Greeks, for the purpose of giving weight or adornment to their subject by the use of two or more words of the same meaning."

" Pray," said Favorinus, " what force has this repetition and recapitulation of the same thing under another name in *manubiae* and *praeda*? It does not adorn the sentence, does it, as is sometimes the case? It does not make it more exact or more melodious, does it? Does it make an effective cumulation of words designed to strengthen the accusation or brand the crime? As, for example, in the speech of the same Marcus Tullius *On the Appointment of an Accuser* one and the same thing is expressed in several words with force and severity :[2] ' All Sicily, if it could speak with one voice, would say this : " Whatever gold, whatever silver, whatever jewels I had in my cities, abodes and shrines." ' For having once mentioned the cities as a whole, he added ' abodes ' and ' shrines,' which are themselves a

sunt ipsa quoque in urbibus. Item in eodem libro
10 simili modo : ' Siciliam,' inquit, ' provinciam C.
Verres per triennium depopulatus esse, Siculorum
11 civitates vastasse, domos exinanisse, fana spoliasse
dicitur.' Ecquid videtur, cum Siciliam provinciam
dixerit atque insuper etiam civitates addiderit,
domos etiam et fana, quae infra posuit, conprehend-
isse ? Verba haec item multa atque varia : ' depopulatus esse, vastasse, exinanisse, spoliasse,' nonne
unam et eandem vim in sese habent ? Sane. Sed
quia cum dignitate orationis et cum gravi verborum
copia dicuntur, quamquam eadem fere sint et ex una
sententia cooriantur, plura tamen esse existimantur,
quoniam et aures et animum saepius feriunt.

12   " Hoc ornatus genus in crimine uno vocibus multis
atque saevis extruendo ille iam tunc M. Cato anti-
quissimus in orationibus suis celebravit, sicuti in illa,
quae inscripta est *De Decem Hominibus,* cum Ther-
mum accusavit quod decem liberos homines eodem
tempore interfecisset, hisce verbis eandem omnibus
rem significantibus usus est, quae quoniam sunt
eloquentiae Latinae tunc primum exorientis lumina
quaedam sublustria, libitum est ea mihi ἀπομνημο-
νεύειν : 'Tuum nefarium facinus peiore facinore
operire postulas, succidias humanas facis, tantam
trucidationem facis, decem funera facis, decem cap-
ita libera interficis, decem hominibus vitam eripis,
13 indicta causa, iniudicatis, incondemnatis.' Item M.
Cato in orationis principio, quam dixit in senatu *Pro*

---

part of the cities. Also in the same oration he says in a similar manner:[1] 'During three years Gaius Verres is said to have plundered the province of Sicily, devastated the cities of the Sicilians, emptied their homes, pillaged their shrines.' Does he not seem to you, when he had mentioned the province of Sicily and had besides added the cities as well, to have included the houses also and the shrines, which he later mentioned? So too do not those many and varied words, 'plundered, devastated, emptied, pillaged,' have one and the same force? They surely do. But since the mention of them all adds to the dignity of the speech and the impressive copiousness of its diction, although they are nearly the same and spring from a single idea, yet they appear to contain more meaning because they strike the ears and mind more frequently.

"This kind of adornment, by heaping up in a single charge a great number of severe terms, was frequently used even in early days by our most ancient orator, the famous Marcus Cato, in his speeches; for example in the one entitled *On the Ten,* when he accused Thermus because he had put to death ten freeborn men at the same time, he used the following words of the same meaning, which, as they are brilliant flashes of Latin eloquence, which was just then coming into being, I have thought fit to call to mind:[2] 'You seek to cover up your abominable crime with a still worse crime, you slaughter men like swine, you commit frightful bloodshed, you cause ten deaths, slay ten freemen, take life from ten men, untried, unjudged, uncondemned.' So too Marcus Cato, at the beginning of the speech which he delivered in the senate, *In Defence*

Rodiensibus, cum vellet res nimis prosperas dicere,
14 tribus vocabulis idem sentientibus dixit. Verba eius
haec sunt : ' Scio solere plerisque hominibus in rebus secundis atque prolixis atque prosperis animum
excellere atque superbiam atque ferociam augescere.'
15 Itidem Cato ex *Originum* VII., in oratione quam *Contra Servium Galbam* dixit, conpluribus vocabulis super
eadem re usus est : ' Multa me dehortata sunt huc
prodire, anni, aetas, vox, vires, senectus ; verum en-
imvero cum tantam rem peragier arbitrarer . . .'
16 " Sed ante omnis apud Homerum eiusdem rei atque
sententiae luculenta exaggeratio est :

Ἕκτορα δ' ἐκ βελέων ὕπαγε Ζεὺς ἔκ τε κονίης
Ἐκ τ' ἀνδροκτασίης ἔκ θ' αἵματος ἔκ τε κυδοιμοῦ.

Item alio in versu :

Ὑσμῖναί τε μαχαί τε φόνοι τ' ἀνδροκτασίαι τε.

17 Nam cum omnia ista utrubique multa et cognominata [1] nihil plus demonstrent quam ' proelium,' huius
tamen rei varia facies delectabiliter ac decore multis
18 variisque verbis depicta est. Neque non illa quoque
aput eundem poetam una in duobus verbis sententia
cum egregia ratione repetita est ; Idaeus enim, cum
inter Aiacem et Hectorem decertantes armis inter-
cederet, his ad eos verbis [2] usus est :

Μηκέτι, παῖδε φίλω, πολεμίζετε μηδὲ μάχεσθε,

[1] cognominata, *suggested by Hertz, approved by Heraeus* ;
continua nomina, γ.
[2] *Omitted by Hosius ; but cf.* i. 3. 20.

---

[1] *Orig.* v. 1, p. 21, 8, Jordan.

of the Rhodians, wishing to describe too great prosperity, used three words which mean the same thing.[1]
His language is as follows : ' I know that most men
in favourable, happy and prosperous circumstances
are wont to be puffed up in spirit and to increase in
arrogance and haughtiness.' In the seventh book
of his *Origins* too,[2] in the speech which he spoke
Against Servius Galba, Cato used several words to
express the same thing :[3] 'Many things have dis-
suaded me from appearing here, my years, my time
of life, my voice, my strength, my old age ; but
nevertheless, when I reflected that so important a
matter was being discussed. . . .'

"But above all in Homer there is a brilliant
heaping up of the same idea and thought, in these
lines :[4]

Zeus from the weapons, from the dust and blood,
From carnage, from the tumult Hector bore.

Also in another verse :[5]

Engagements, battles, carnage, deaths of men.

For although all those numerous synonymous terms
mean nothing more than 'battle,' yet the varied
aspects of this concept are elegantly and charmingly
depicted by the use of several different words. And
in the same poet this one thought is repeated with
admirable effect by the use of two words ; for Idaeus,
when he interrupted the armed contest of Hector
and Ajax, addressed them thus :[6]

No longer fight, dear youths, nor still contend,

---

[2] Frag. 108, Peter².   [3] *O.R.F.*, p. 123, Meyer².
[4] *Iliad* xi. 163.   [5] *Odyss.* xi. 612.
[6] *Iliad* vii. 279.

19 in quo versu non oportet videri alterum verbum,
idem quod superius significans, supplendi numeri
causa extrinsecus additum et consarcinatum. Est
enim hoc inane admodum et futtile. Sed cum in
iuvenibus gloriae studio flagrantibus pervicaciam
ferociamque et cupidinem pugnae leniter tamen ac
placide obiurgaret, atrocitatem rei et culpam per-
severandi bis idem dicendo alio atque alio verbo
auxit inculcavitque, duplexque eadem conpellatio
20 admonitionem facit instantiorem. Ne illa quidem
significationis eiusdem repetitio ignava et frigida
videri debet :

Μνηστῆρες δ' ἄρα Τηλεμάχῳ θάνατόν τε μόρον τε
Ἤρτυον,

quod bis idem, θάνατον et μόρον, dixerit ; indignitas
enim moliendae tam acerbae tamque iniustae necis
21 miranda mortis iteratione defleta est. Ceterum quis
tam obtunso ingeniost, quin intellegat :

Βάσκ' ἴθι, οὐλε Ὄνειρε,

et :

Βάσκ' ἴθι, Ἶρι ταχεῖα,

verba idem duo significantia non frustra posita esse
ἐκ παραλλήλων, ut quidam putant, sed hortamentum
esse acre imperatae celeritatis ?
22 " Verba quoque illa M. Ciceronis *In L. Pisonem* tri-
gemina, etiamsi durae auris hominibus non placent,
non venustatem modo numeris quaesiverunt, sed

---

[1] *Odyss.* xx. 241. [2] *Iliad* ii. 8.
[3] *Iliad* viii. 399.

and in this verse it ought not to be supposed that
the second word, meaning the same as the first, was
added and lugged in without reason, merely to fill
out the metre; for that is utterly silly and false.
But while he gently and calmly chided the obstinate
fierceness and love of battle in two youths burning
with a desire for glory, he emphasized and impressed
upon them the atrocity of the act and the sin of
their insistence by adding one word to another; and
that double form of address made his admonition
more impressive. Nor ought the following repetition
of the same thought to seem any more weak and
cold :[1]

> With death the suitors threatened, and with fate,
>   Telemachus,

because he said the same thing twice in θάνατον
(death) and μόρον (fate); for the heinousness of
attempting so cruel and unjust a murder is deplored
by the admirable repetition of the word meaning
'death.' Who too is of so dull a mind as not to
understand that in[2]

> Away, begone, dire dream,

and[3]

> Away, begone, swift Iris,

two words of the same meaning are not used to no
purpose, ἐκ παραλλήλων, 'as the repetition of two
similar words,' as some think, but are a vigorous
exhortation to the swiftness which is enjoined?

" Also those thrice repeated words in the speech of
Marcus Cicero *Against Lucius Piso*, although displeas-
ing to men of less sensitive ears, did not merely aim
at elegance, but buffeted Piso's assumed expression

figuram simulationemque oris pluribus simul vocibus
23 everberaverunt: 'Vultus denique,' inquit, 'totus,
qui sermo quidam tacitus mentis est, hic in frau-
dem homines impulit, hic eos quibus erat ignotus
24 decepit, fefellit, induxit.' Quid igitur? Simile est,"
inquit, "apud eundem in 'praeda' et 'manubiis'?
25 Nihil profecto istiusmodi est. Nam neque ornatius
fit additis 'manubiis' neque exaggeratius modulat-
iusve; sed aliud omnino 'praeda' est, ut in libris
26 rerum verborumque veterum scriptum est, aliud
'manubiae.' Nam 'praeda' dicitur corpora ipsa
rerum quae capta sunt, 'manubiae' vero appellatae
27 sunt pecunia a quaestore ex venditione praedae red-
acta. Utrumque ergo dixit M. Tullius cumulandae
invidiae gratia decemviros ablaturos persecuturos-
que: et praedam quae nondum esset venundata,
et pecuniam quae ex venditione praedae percepta
esset.

28   "Itaque haec inscriptio quam videtis: 'Ex manubiis,' non res corporaque ipsa praedae demonstrat,
nihil enim captum est horum a Traiano ex hostibus,
sed facta esse haec conparataque 'ex manubiis,' id
29 est ex pecunia praedaticia, declarat. 'Manubiae'
enim sunt, sicuti iam dixi, non praeda, sed pecunia
30 per quaestorem populi Romani ex praeda vendita
contracta. Quod 'per quaestorem' autem dixi, intellegi nunc oportet praefectum aerario significari.
31 Nam cura aerarii a quaestoribus ad praefectos trans-
lata est. Est tamen nonnusquam invenire ita

---

[1] *In Pis.* 1.   [2] See Suet. *Claud.* xxiv.

of countenance by the rhythmical accumulation of several words. Cicero says:[1] 'Finally, your whole countenance, which is, so to speak, the silent voice of the mind, this it was that incited men to crime, this deceived, tricked, cheated those to whom it was not familiar.' Well then," continued Favorinus, "is the use of *praeda* and *manubiae* in the same writer similar to this? Truly, not at all! For by the addition of *manubiae* the sentence does not become more ornate, more forcible, or more euphonius; but *manubiae* means one thing, as we learn from the books on antiquities and on the early Latin, *praeda* quite another. For *praeda* is used of the actual objects making up the booty, but *manubiae* designates the money collected by the quaestor from the sale of the booty. Therefore Marcus Tullius, in order to rouse greater hatred of the decemvirs, said that they would carry off and appropriate the two: both the booty which had not yet been sold and the money which had been received from the sale of the booty.

"Therefore this inscription which you see, *ex manubiis*, does not designate the objects and the mass of booty itself, for none of these was taken from the enemy by Trajan, but it declares that these statues were made and procured 'from the *manubiae*,' that is, with the money derived from the sale of the booty. For *manubiae* means, as I have already said, not booty, but money collected from the sale of the booty by a quaestor of the Roman people. But when I said 'by the quaestor,' one ought now to understand that the praefect of the treasury is meant. For the charge of the treasury has been transferred from the quaestors to praefects.[2] However, it is possible to find instances in which

scripsisse quosdam non ignobiles scriptores, ut aut
temere aut incuriose 'praedam' pro 'manubiis' et
'manubias' pro 'praeda' posuerint, aut tropica
quadam figura mutationem vocabuli fecerint, quod
facere concessum est scite id periteque facientibus.
32 Sed enim, qui proprie atque signate locuti sunt, sicut
hoc in loco M. Tullius, 'manubias' pecuniam dixerunt."

XXVI

Verba P. Nigidii quibus dicit in nomine Valeri in casu vocandi primam syllabam acuendam esse; et item alia ex eiusdem verbis ad rectam scripturam pertinentia.

1   P. Nigidii verba sunt ex *Commentariorum Grammaticorum* vicesimo quarto, hominis in disciplinis doctrinarum omnium praecellentis: "Deinde," inquit,
"voculatio qui poterit servari, si non sciemus in
nominibus, ut 'Valeri,' utrum interrogandi an
vocandi sint? Nam interrogandi secunda syllaba
superiore tonost quam prima, deinde novissima
deicitur; at in casu vocandi summo tonost prima,
2 deinde gradatim descendunt." Sic quidem Nigidius
dici praecipit. Sed si quis nunc, Valerium appellans,
in casu vocandi secundum id praeceptum Nigidii
acuerit primam, non aberit quin rideatur. "Sum-
3 mum" autem "tonum" προσῳδίαν acutam dicit et
quem "accentum" nos dicimus "voculationem" appellat et "casum interrogandi" eum dicit, quem
nunc nos "genetivum" dicimus.

---

[1] Fr. 35, Swoboda.
[2] On *casus interrogandi* for the genitive see Fay, *A.J.P.*
xxxvi (1916), p. 78.
[3] See note 2, p. 426.   Many believe this to be true also of
the Latin *sermo urbanus*; see *Class. Phil.* ii. 444 ff.

writers of no little fame have written in such a way as to use *praeda* for *manubiae* or *manubiae* for *praeda*, either from carelessness or indifference; or by some metaphorical figure they have interchanged the words, which is allowable when done with judgment and skill. But those who have spoken properly and accurately, as did Marcus Tullius in that passage, have used *manubiae* of money."

XXVI

A passage of Publius Nigidius in which he says that in *Valeri*, the vocative case of the name *Valerius*, the first syllable should have an acute accent; with other remarks of the same writer on correct writing.

THESE are the words of Publius Nigidius, a man pre-eminent for his knowledge of all the sciences, from the twenty-fourth book of his *Grammatical Notes*:[1] "How then can the accent be correctly used, if in names like *Valeri* we do not know whether they are genitive[2] or vocative? For the second syllable of the genitive has a higher pitch than the first, and on the last syllable the pitch falls again; but in the vocative case the first syllable has the highest pitch, and then there is a gradual descent."[3] Thus indeed Nigidius bids us speak. But if anyone nowadays, calling to a Valerius, accents the first syllable of the vocative according to the direction of Nigidius, he will not escape being laughed at. Furthermore, Nigidius calls the acute accent "the highest pitch," and what we call *accentus*, or "accent," he calls *voculatio*, or "tone," and the case which we now call *genetivus*, or "genitive," he calls *casus interrogandi*, "the case of asking."

4   Id quoque in eodem libro Nigidiano animadvertimus: "Si 'huius,'" inquit, "'amici' vel 'huius
magni' scribas, unum i facito extremum, sin vero
'hei magnei,'[1] 'hei amicei,' casu multitudinis recto,
tum ante i scribendum erit e, atque id ipsum facies
in similibus. Item si 'huius terrai' scribas, i littera
fit extrema, si 'huic terrae,' per e scribendum est.
Item 'mei' qui scribit in casu interrogandi, velut
cum dicimus 'mei studiosus,' per i unum scribat, non
per e; at cum 'mehei,' tum per e et i scribendum
5 est, quia dandi casus est." Haec nos auctoritate
doctissimi hominis adducti, propter eos qui harum
quoque rerum scientiam quaerunt, non praetermit-
tenda existimavimus.

XXVII

De versibus, quos Vergilius sectatus videtur, Homeri ac
Partheni.

1   PARTHENI poetae versus est:

Γλαύκῳ καὶ Νηρεῖ καὶ εἰναλίῳ Μελικέρτῃ.

2 Eum versum Vergilius aemulatus est, itaque fecit
duobus vocabulis venuste inmutatis parem:

Glauco et Panopeae et Inoo Melicertae.

---

[1] In this passage I have followed the revision of the text
made by Kent, *A.J.P.* xxxii (1911), p. 290.

---

[1] 36 Swoboda.   [2] Id. 37.
[3] Really *terrāi.*   [4] Id. 38.

This too I notice in the same book of Nigidius:[1] "If you write the genitive case of *amicus*," he says, "or of *magnus*, end the word with a single *i*; but if you write the nominative plural, you must write *magnei* and *amicei*, with an *e* followed by *i*, and so with similar words. Also[2] if you write *terra* in the genitive, let it end with the letter *i*, as *terrai*;[3] but in the dative with *e*, as *terrae*. Also[4] one who writes *mei* in the genitive case, as when we say *mei studiosus*, or 'devoted to me,' let him write it with *i* only (*mei*), not with *e* (*meei*)[5]; but when he writes *mehei*, it must be written with *e* and *i*, since it is the dative case." Led by the authority of a most learned man, I thought that I ought not to pass by these statements, for the sake of those who desire a knowledge of such matters.

XXVII

Of verses of Homer and Parthenius, which Virgil seems to have followed.

THERE is a verse of the poet Parthenius:[6]

To Glaucus, Nereus and sea-dwelling Melicertes.

This verse Virgil has emulated, and has made it equal to the original by a graceful change of two words:[7]

To Glaucus, Panopea, and Ino's son Melicertes.

---

[5] Gellius refers only to the *ending*, which is *i* alone, and not *i* preceded by *e*.

[6] *Anal. Alex.*, p. 285, fr. 33, Meineke.

[7] *Georg.* i. 437.

3 Sed illi Homerico non sane re parem neque similem fecit; esse enim videtur Homeri simplicior et sincerior, Vergilii autem νεωτερικώτερος et quodam quasi ferumine inmisso fucatior:

Ταῦρον δ' 'Αλφειῷ, ταῦρον δὲ Ποσειδάωνι.
Taurum Neptuno, taurum tibi, pulcher Apollo.

XXVIII

De sententia Panaetii philosophi, quam scripsit in libro *De Officiis* secundo, qua hortatur ut homines ad cavendas iniurias in omni loco intenti paratique sint.

1 LEGEBATUR Panaetii philosophi liber *De Officiis* secundus ex tribus illis inclitis libris, quos M. Tullius magno cum studio maximoque opere aemulatus 2 est. Ibi scriptum est, cum multa alia ad bonam frugem ducentia, tum vel maxime quod esse hae- 3 rereque in animo debet. Id autem est ad hanc fere sententiam: "Vita," inquit, "hominum qui aetatem in medio rerum agunt ac sibi suisque esse usui volunt, negotia periculaque ex improviso adsidua et prope cotidiana fert. Ad ea cavenda atque declinanda perinde esse oportet animo prompto semper atque intento, ut sunt athletarum, qui 4 'pancratiastae' vocantur. Nam sicut illi ad certandum vocati proiectis alte brachiis consistunt caputque et os suum manibus oppositis quasi vallo praemuniunt, membraque eorum omnia, priusquam pugna mota est, aut ad vitandos ictus cauta sunt

---

[1] *Iliad* xi. 728.   [2] *Aen.* iii. 119.
[3] Referring to the otiose epithet *pulcher*, which is "gilding the lily."

But the following verse of Homer he has not indeed equalled, nor approached. For that of Homer [1] seems to be simpler and more natural, that of Virgil [2] more modern and daubed over with a kind of stucco,[3] as it were:

Homer: A bull to Alpheus, to Poseidon one.
Virgil: A bull to Neptune, and to you, Apollo fair.

XXVIII

Of an opinion of the philosopher Panaetius, which he expressed in his second book *On Duties*, where he urges men to be alert and prepared to guard against injuries on all occasions.

THE second book of the philosopher Panaetius *On Duties* was being read to us, being one of those three celebrated books which Marcus Tullius emulated with great care and very great labour. In it there was written, in addition to many other incentives to virtue, one especially which ought to be kept fixed in the mind. And it is to this general purport:[4] " The life of men," he says, " who pass their time in the midst of affairs, and who wish to be helpful to themselves and to others, is exposed to constant and almost daily troubles and sudden dangers. To guard against and avoid these one needs a mind that is always ready and alert, such as the athletes have who are called ' pancratists.' For just as they, when called to the contest, stand with their arms raised and stretched out, and protect their head and face by opposing their hands as a rampart; and as all their limbs, before the battle

⁴ Fr. 8, Fowler.

aut ad faciendos parata—ita animus atque mens
viri prudentis, adversus vim et petulantias iniuri-
arum omni in loco atque in tempore prospiciens,
esse debet erecta, ardua, saepta solide, expedita in
sollicitis, numquam conivens, nusquam aciem suam
flectens, consilia cogitationesque contra fortunae
verbera contraque insidias iniquorum, quasi brachia
et manus, protendens, ne qua in re adversa et
repentina incursio inparatis inprotectisque nobis
oboriatur."

XXIX

Quod Quadrigarius "cum multis mortalibus" dixit; an
quid et quantum differret, si dixisset "cum multis
hominibus."

1 VERBA sunt Claudi Quadrigarii ex *Annalium* eius
XIII : "Contione dimissa, Metellus in Capitolium
venit cum mortalibus multis; inde domum profi-
2 ciscitur, tota civitas eum reduxit." Cum is liber
eaque verba M. Frontoni, nobis ei ac plerisque aliis
adsidentibus, legerentur et cuidam haut sane viro
indocto videretur "mortalibus multis" pro "hominibus multis" inepte frigideque in historia nimisque
id poetice dixisse, tum Fronto illi cui hoc videbatur : "Ain tu," inquit, "aliarum homo rerum
iudicii elegantissimi, 'mortalibus multis' ineptum
tibi videri et frigidum, nil autem arbitrare causae
fuisse quod vir modesti atque puri ac prope

---

[1] Fr. 76, Peter.[2]

has begun, are ready to avoid or to deal blows—so
the spirit and mind of the wise man, on the watch
everywhere and at all times against violence and
wanton injuries, ought to be alert, ready, strongly
protected, prepared in time of trouble, never flag-
ging in attention, never relaxing its watchfulness,
opposing judgment and forethought like arms and
hands to the strokes of fortune and the snares of the
wicked, lest in any way a hostile and sudden on-
slaught be made upon us when we are unprepared
and unprotected."

XXIX

That Quadrigarius used the expression *cum multis mortalibus;* whether it would have made any difference if he had
said *cum multis hominibus,* and how great a difference.

THE following is a passage of Claudius Quadrigarius from the thirteenth book of his *Annals :* [1]
" When the assembly had been dismissed, Metellus
came to the Capitol with many mortals (*cum mortalibus multis*) ; from there he went home attended by
the entire city." When this book and this passage
were read to Marcus Fronto, as I was sitting with
him in company with some others, it seemed to one
of those present, a man not without learning, that
the use of *mortalibus multis* for *hominibus multis* in
a work of history was foolish and frigid, and savoured
too much of poetry. Then Fronto said to the man
who expressed this opinion : " Do you, a man of
most refined taste in other matters, say that *mortalibus multis* seems to you foolish and frigid, and do
you think there is no reason why a man whose
language is chaste, pure and almost conversational,

cotidiani sermonis 'mortalibus' maluit quam 'hominibus' dicere, eandemque credis futuram fuisse
multitudinis demonstrationem, si 'cum multis hominibus,' ac non 'cum multis mortalibus' diceret?
3 Ego quidem," inquit, "sic existimo, nisi si me
scriptoris istius omnisque antiquae orationis amor
atque veneratio caeco esse iudicio facit, longe
longeque esse amplius, prolixius, fusius, in signi-
ficanda totius prope civitatis multitudine 'mortales'
4 quam 'homines' dixisse. Namque 'multorum
hominum' appellatio intra modicum quoque numerum cohiberi atque includi potest, 'multi' autem
'mortales' nescio quo pacto et quodam sensu
inenarrabili omne fere genus quod in civitate est
et ordinum et aetatum et sexus conprehendunt;
quod scilicet Quadrigarius, ita ut res erat, ingentem
atque promiscam multitudinem volens ostendere,
'cum multis mortalibus' Metellum in Capitolium
venisse dixit ἐμφατικώτερον quam si 'cum multis
hominibus' dixisset.
5 Ea nos omnia quae Fronto dixit, cum ita ut par
erat, non adprobantes tantum, sed admirantes
quoque audiremus, "Videte tamen," inquit, "ne
existimetis, semper atque in omni loco 'mortales
multos' pro 'multis hominibus' dicendum, ne plane
fiat Graecum illud de Varronis *Satura* proverbium
6 τὸ ἐπὶ τῇ φακῇ μύρον." Hoc iudicium Frontonis,
etiam in parvis minutisque vocabulis, non praetermittendum putavi, ne nos forte fugeret lateretque
subtilior huiuscemodi verborum consideratio.

preferred to say *mortalibus* rather than *hominibus?*
And do you think that he would have described a
multitude in the same way if he said *cum multis
hominibus* and not *cum multis mortalibus?* For my
part," continued Fronto, "unless my regard and
veneration for this writer, and for all early Latin,
blinds my judgment, I think that it is far, far
fuller, richer and more comprehensive in describing
almost the whole population of the city to have said
mortales rather than *homines.* For the expression
'many men' may be confined and limited to even a
moderate number, but 'many mortals' somehow in
some indefinable manner includes almost all the
people in the city, of every rank, age and sex; so
you see Quadrigarius, wishing to describe the crowd
as vast and mixed, as in fact it was, said that
Metellus came into the Capitol 'with many mortals,
speaking with more force than if he had said 'with
many men.'"

When we, as was fitting, had expressed, not only
approval, but admiration of all this that we had
heard from Fronto, he said: "Take care, however,
not to think that *mortales multi* is to be used always
and everywhere in place of *multi homines*, lest that
Greek proverb, τὸ ἐπὶ τῇ φακῇ μύρον, or 'myrrh on
lentils,'[1] which is found in one of Varro's *Satires*,[2]
be applied to you." This judgment of Fronto's,
though relating to trifling and unimportant words,
I thought I ought not to pass by, lest the somewhat subtle distinction between words of this kind
should escape and elude us.

[1] That is, to use a costly perfumed oil to dress a dish of
lentils; proverbial for a showy entertainment with little
to eat. [2] p. 219, Bücheler.

XXX

Non hactenus esse "faciem" qua vulgo dicitur.

1 ANIMADVERTERE est pleraque verborum Latinorum ex ea significatione de qua nata sunt decessisse vel in aliam longe vel in proximam, eamque decessionem factam esse consuetudine et inscitia temere
2 dicentium quae cuimodi sint non didicerint. Sicuti quidam "faciem" esse hominis putant os tantum et oculos et genas, quod Graeci πρόσωπον dicunt, quando "facies" sit forma omnis et modus et factura quaedam corporis totius, a "faciendo" dicta, ut
3 ab "aspectu" "species" et a "fingendo" "figura."[1] Itaque Pacuvius in tragoedia, quae *Niptra* inscribitur, "faciem" dixit hominis pro corporis longitudine :

aetate (inquit) íntegra,
Feróci ingenio, fácie procerá virum.

4 Non solum autem in hominum corporibus, sed etiam in rerum cuiusquemodi aliarum "facies" dicitur. Nam montis et caeli et maris "facies,"[2]
5 si tempestive dicatur, probe dicitur. Sallustii verba sunt ex *Historia* secunda : "Sardinia in Africo mari facie vestigii humani in orientem quam occidentem
6 latior prominet."[3] Ecce autem id quoque in mentem venit, quod etiam Plautus in *Poenulo* "faciem" pro

---

[1] 253, Ribbeck[3].
[2] Just so we speak of the face of nature, the face of the waters, and the like.
[3] ii. 2, Maur.

XXX

That *facies* has a wider application than is commonly supposed.

WE may observe that many Latin words have departed from their original signification and passed into one that is either far different or near akin, and that such a departure is due to the usage of those ignorant people who carelessly use words of which they have not learned the meaning. As, for example, some think that *facies*, applied to a man, means only the face, eyes and cheeks, that which the Greeks call πρόσωπον; whereas *facies* really designates the whole form, dimensions and, as it were, the make-up of the entire body, being formed from *facio* as *species* is from *aspectus* and *figura* from *fingere*. Accordingly Pacuvius, in the tragedy entitled *Niptra*, used *facies* for the height of a man's body in these lines:[1]

> A man in prime of life, of spirit bold,
> Of stature (*facie*) tall.

But *facies* is applied, not only to the bodies of men, but also to the appearance of other things of every kind. For *facies* may be said properly, if the application be seasonable, of a mountain, the heavens and the sea.[2] The words of Sallust in the second book of his *Histories* are:[3] "Sardinia, in the African Sea, having the appearance (*facies*) of a human foot,[4] projects farther on the eastern than on the western side." And, by the way, it has also occurred to me that Plautus too, in the *Poenulus*, said *facies*, mean-

[4] That is, the sole of the foot.

totius corporis colorisque habitu dixit. Verba Plauti
haec sunt:

Set eárum nutrix quá sit facie mi éxpedi.—
Statúra non[1] magna córpore aquilost.[2]—
          Ipsa east.—
Specié venusta, óre atque oculis pérnigris.—
Formám quidem hercle vérbis depinxtí[3] probe!

7 Praeterea memini Quadrigarium in undevicesimo
"faciem" pro statura totiusque corporis figura
dixisse.

XXXI

Quid sit in satura M. Varronis "caninum prandium."

1 LAUDABAT venditabatque se nuper quispiam in
libraria sedens homo inepte gloriosus, tamquam unus
esset in omni caelo *Saturarum* M. Varronis enarrator,
quas partim *Cynicas*, alii *Menippeas* appellant. Et
iaciebat inde quaedam non admodum difficilia, ad
quae conicienda adspirare posse neminem dicebat.
2 Tum forte ego eum librum ex isdem saturis ferebam,
qui Ὑδροκύων inscriptus est. Propius igitur accessi
3 et: "Nosti," inquam, "magister, verbum illud scilicet
e Graecia vetus, musicam quae sit abscondita, eam
esse nulli rei? Oro ergo te, legas hos versus pauculos
et proverbii istius quod in his versibus est sententiam

---

[1] hau, *Plaut.*   [2] aquilo, *codd. Plaut.*
        [3] depinxit, *ω.*

---

[1] 1111.
[2] This, with the Ἱπποκύων, or *Dog-Knight*, and the Κυνο-
ρήτωρ, or *Dog-Rhetorician*, justifies the term *Cynicae* as
applied to Varro's *Saturae.*

ing the appearance of the whole body and complexion. These are his words:[1]

But tell me, pray, how looks (*qua sit facie*) that
  nurse of yours?—
Not very tall, complexion dark.—'Tis she!—
A comely wench, with pretty mouth, black eyes—
By Jove! a picture of her limned in words!

Besides, I remember that Quadrigarius in his nineteenth book used *facies* for stature and the form of the whole body.

XXXI

The meaning of caninum prandium *in Marcus Varro's satire.*

LATELY a foolish, boastful fellow, sitting in a bookseller's shop, was praising and advertising himself, asserting that he was the only one under all heaven who could interpret the *Satires* of Marcus Varro, which by some are called *Cynical*, by others *Menippean*. And then he displayed some passages of no great difficulty, which he said no one could presume to explain. At the time I chanced to have with me a book of those *Satires*, entitled Ὑδροκύων, or *The Water Dog*.[2] I therefore went up to him and said: "Master, of course you know that old Greek saying, that music, if it be hidden, is of no account.[3] I beg you therefore to read these few lines and tell me the meaning of the proverb con-

---

[3] The same proverb is put into the mouth of Nero by Suetonius (*Nero*, xx. 1), where the meaning is, that it is of no use for one to know how to sing, unless he proves that he knows how by singing in public.

4 dicas mihi." "Lege," inquit, "tu mihi potius quae
5 non intellegis, ut ea tibi ego enarrem." "Quonam,"
inquam, "pacto legere ego possum quae non adsequor?
Indistincta namque et confusa fient quae legero, et
tuam quoque impedient intentionem."
6 Tunc aliis etiam qui ibi aderant compluribus idem
comprobantibus desiderantibusque, accipit a me
librum veterem fidei spectatae, luculente scriptum.
7 Accipit autem inconstantissimo vultu et maestissimo.
8 Sed quid deinde dicam? Non audeo hercle postu-
9 lare ut id credatur mihi. Pueri in ludo rudes, si
eum librum accepissent, non hi magis in legendo deri-
diculi fuissent, ita et sententias intercidebat et verba
10 corrupte pronuntiabat. Reddit igitur mihi librum,
multis iam ridentibus, et "Vides," inquit, "oculos
meos aegros adsiduisque lucubrationibus prope iam
perditos; vix ipsos litterarum apices¹ potui conpre-
hendere; cum valebo ab oculis, revise ad me et
11 librum istum tibi totum legam." "Recte," inquam,
12 "sit oculis, magister, tuis; sed, in quo illis nihil
opus est, id, rogo te, dicas mihi: 'caninum prandium'²
13 in hoc loco quem legisti quid significat?" Atque
ille egregius nebulo, quasi difficili quaestione proter-
ritus, exurgit statim et abiens, "Non," inquit, "parvam rem quaeris; talia ego gratis non doceo."
14 Eius autem loci, in quo id proverbium est, verba
haec sunt: "Non vides apud Mnesitheum³ scribi tria
genera esse vini, nigrum, album, medium, quod

---

¹ *Apices* here seems to refer to the strokes of which the
letters were made up; cf. Cassiodorus vii. 184. 6 K., digamma
nominatur quia duos apices ex gamma littera habere videtur, and Gell. xvii. 9. 12.
² Fr. 575, Bücheler.
³ A celebrated Athenian physician of the fourth century
before our era.

tained in them." "Do you rather," he replied, "read me what you do not understand, in order that I may interpret it for you." "How on earth can I read," I replied, "what I cannot understand? Surely my reading will be indistinct and confused, and will even distract your attention."

Then, as many others who were there present agreed with me and made the same request, I handed him an ancient copy of the satire, of tested correctness and clearly written. But he took it with a most disturbed and worried expression. But what shall I say followed? I really do not dare to ask you to believe me. Ignorant schoolboys, if they had taken up that book, could not have read more laughably, so wretchedly did he pronounce the words and murder the thought. Then, since many were beginning to laugh, he returned the book to me, saying, "You see that my eyes are weak and almost ruined by constant night work; I could barely make out even the forms[1] of the letters. When my eyes have recovered, come to me and I will read the whole of that book to you." "Master," said I, "I hope your eyes may improve; but I pray you, tell me this, for which you will have no need of your eyes; what does *caninum prandium* mean in the passage which you read?" And that egregious blockhead, as if alarmed by the difficulty of the question, at once got up and made off, saying: "You ask no small matter; I do not give such instruction for nothing."

The words of the passage in which that proverb is found are as follows:[2] "Do you not know that Mnesitheus[3] writes that there are three kinds of wine, dark, light and medium, which the Greeks call

vocant κιρρόν,[1] et novum, vetus, medium? Et efficere nigrum virus, album urinam, medium πέψιν? Novum refrigerare, vetus calefacere, medium esse prandium
15 caninum?" Quid significet prandium caninum, rem
16 leviculam, diu et anxie quaesivimus. Prandium autem abstemium, in quo nihil potatur, "caninum"
17 dicitur, quoniam canis vino caret. Cum igitur "medium vinum" appellasset, quod neque novum esset neque vetus—et plerumque homines ita loquantur, ut omne vinum aut novum esse dicant aut vetus —nullam vim habere significavit neque novi neque veteris quod medium esset, et idcirco pro vino non habendum, quia neque refrigeraret neque calefaceret. "Refrigerare" id dicit quod Graece 'ψύχειν' dicitur.

---

[1] viris, δ.

κιρρός or 'tawny'; and new, old and medium? And that the dark gives virility, the light increases the urine, and the medium helps digestion? That the new cools, the old heats, and the medium is a dinner for a dog (*caninum prandium*)?" The meaning of "a dinner for a dog," though a slight matter, I have investigated long and anxiously. Now an abstemious meal, at which there is no drinking, is called "a dog's meal," since the dog has no need of wine. Therefore when Mnesitheus named a medium wine, which was neither new nor old—and many men speak as if all wine was either new or old—he meant that the medium wine had the power neither of the old nor of the new, and was therefore not to be considered wine at all, because it neither cooled nor heated. By *refrigerare* (to cool), he means the same as the Greek ψύχειν.

INDEX *

ACADEMICI PHILOSOPHI, the followers of Plato, so called from the Academia, the grove near Athens in which Plato taught. As subst., Academici, *sc.* philosophi.

Acca, *see* Larentia.

Achaicum bellum, the war which resulted in the destruction of Corinth by the Romans in 146 B.C.

Achivi, the Greeks.

Acilius, C., a Roman senator.

Aeacides, descendant of Aeacus, a term applied to Pyrrhus, king of Epirus, who claimed descent from Achilles, the grandson of Aeacus.

Aedilibus vitio creatis, De, an oration of M. Porcius Cato the censor.

Aedilicia, a play of Quinctius Atta.

Aeditumus, a play of Pomponius.

Aelii, members of the Aelian clan; *see* note 1, p. 132.

Aemilius Lepidus, M., censor with M. Fulvius Flaccus in 179 B.C.

Aeschylus, the famous Greek writer of tragedies (525–456 B.C.); *see* note 7, p. 460.

Afranius, a writer of *fabulae togatae* at Rome, who lived in the latter part of the second century B.C.

Afri homines, the people of Africa.

Africanus, *see* Cornelius Scipio.

Africum mare, a term applied by Sallust to the sea about Sardinia.

Agamemnoniae Mycenae, the famous city of Argolis, ruled by Agamemnon at the time of the Trojan war.

Ajax, son of Telamon, one of the Greek heroes at Troy.

Albania, an unknown and remote land.

Albinus, *see* Postumius.

Alcides, descendant of Alceus, a term applied to his grandson Hercules.

Alexander, the name of a tragedy of Ennius.

Alexandrinum bellum, the war carried on by Julius Caesar against Alexandria and the Egyptians, 48–47 B.C.

Alfenus Varus,[4] a Roman jurist of uncertain date.

Ambracia, a city of Acarnania in the western part of Greece, later included in Epirus.

Amyntas, father of Philip II of Macedon and grandfather of Alexander the Great.

Animalibus, De, works of Aristotle and of Nigidius Figulus.

Anio, a river flowing into the Tiber a short distance north of Rome.

Anna (ac) Peranţa, or Anna Perenna, an early Roman deity of whom many legends were current. She somehow represented the circle or ring of the year (Fowler, *Rom. Fest.* p. 52).

Annaeus Seneca (L.), the well-known Roman philosopher and writer, who lived from about 3 B.C. to A.D. 65.

Annianus, a Roman poet of the early part of the second century A.D.; *see* note 1, p. 38.

Annius, C., the father of Cn. Flavius, a Roman aedile.

Antiquae lectiones, a work of Caesellius Vindex.

---

* See note 1, p. 449 of volume i. Words included in the Index of volume i are not repeated. The numbers below 40 refer to the works cited in vol. i, Index.

INDEX

Antoninianae orationes, Cicero's orations against Mark Antony, also called *Philippics.*

Apolloniu (Rho lius), an epic poet of Alexandria, born about 260 B.C., author of the epic poem called *Argonaut ca,* and one of the librarians of the great library at Alexandria.

Archytas, a celebrated philosopher of Tarentum, noted for his inventions; he died about 394 B.C.

Argei, *see* note 2, p. 252.

Argivum bellum, another name for the Achaicum bellum.

Argos, also Argi, the famous city of Argolis.

Arimaspi, a mythical people of Scythia; *see* note 3, p. 162.

Aristeas, an early epic poet of Proconnesus on the Propontis, put by Hdt. (iv. 15,) 340 years before his time.

Aristo, T.,[4] a Roman jurist of the time of Trajan.

Aristodemus, an actor; a contemporary of Demosthenes.

Aristogiton, one of the tyrannicides; *see* note 1, p. 168.

Artemisia, a queen of Caria, wife of Mausolus.

Arvales fratres, a very ancient priesthood, connected with agriculture and the fertility of the fields. The order was revived and given prominence by Augustus.

Asellio, *see* Sempronius.

Asinaria, a play of Plautus.

Astraba, a play of Plautus.

Atellania (*sc.* fabula), a farce, probably of Oscan origin, with stock characters; it derived its name, which is more commonly *Atellana,* from the town of Atella in Campania.

Aeternia lex, the *lex Aeternia Tarpeia,* passed in 455 B.C. It standardized the value of cattle and sheep; *see* Festus, p. 270, 3, Lindsay.

Atilius Regulus, M., consul in 267 and 256 B.C.[*]

Atreus, the name of a tragedy of Accius.

Atta, *see* Quinctius.

Attalus, Attalus I, king of Pergamum in north-western Asia Minor. He reigned from 241 to 197 B.C.

Aufeia lex, a law proposed in 123 B.C. and advocated by C. Gracchus, but apparently not passed.

Augurii Privati libri, a work of Nigidius Figulus.

Augurinus, *see* Minucius.

Aulularia, a play of Plautus.

Aulus, referring to A. Postumius Albinus.

Aventinus, *sc.* mons, the southernmost of the hills of Rome.

Avernus, *see* Lacus Avernus.

Axius, Q., a friend of Cicero, to whom Tullius Tiro addressed a letter criticizing Cato's speech in defence of the Rhodians.

Bacchae, the name of a tragedy of Euripides.

Bagradas, a river of northern Africa.

Bello Carthaginiensi, De, a speech of M. Porcius Cato Censorinus.

Boeotia, a district of central Greece, north-west of Attica.

Borysthenes, a river of Sarmatia, the modern Dnieper.

Brundisium, a seaport in south-eastern Italy, the regular port of departure for Greece and the Orient.

Bruttiani, the inhabitants of the south-western part of the Italian peninsula; *see* note 2, p. 226.

Bruttii, the same as Bruttiani.

Bucolica, the name of works of Theocritus and of Vergilius.

CAECILIUS METELLUS PIUS, Q., son of Metellus Numidicus and consul with Sulla in 80 B.C.

Caecina, A., Pro, an oration of M. Tullius Cicero.

Coeneus, originally a girl named Caenis, but afterwards changed into a boy

---

[*] The M. Atilius Regulus named in the Index to vol. i was the son of this Regulus, and was consul in 227 B.C.

INDEX

by Neptune. According to Virgil,
he again became female.

Caenis, *see* Caeneus.

Ca slli Erroribus, De, a work of
Terentius Scaurus.

Caleni, the people of Cales, a town of
Campania.

Callicles, a speaker in Plato's *Gorgias.*

(Calpurnius) Piso Frugi, L.,[7] a Roman
writer of annals, consul in 133 B.C.
and an opponent of the Gracchi.

Calvus, *see* Licinius.

Capua, the principal town of ancient
Campania.

Caria, a country in the south-western
part of Asia Minor.

Carmen de Moribus, a work of M.
Porcius Cato Censorinus.

Carneades, a philosopher of Cyrene in
northern Africa, founder of the
New Academy; sent as an envoy
to Rome in 155 B.C.

Carthago, the famous city of northern
Africa. Also applied (vii. 8. 3) to
Carthago Nova, or New Carthage,
on the south-eastern coast of Spain;
modern Cartagena.

Casinum, a town of south-western
Latium, near the border of Samn-
ium.

Cassius Longinus, C., consul in 171 B.C.

Castor, one of the Dioscuri, or sons of
Zeus, and brother of Pollux. *Aedes
Castoris,* the temple of Castor and
Pollux in the Roman Forum.

Catilina, a work of Sallustius Crispus
on the conspiracy of Catiline,
usually called *Bellum Catilinae.*

Cato, *see* Porcius.

Catularius, the name of a mime of
D. Laberius.

Catullus, *see* Valerius.

Cela, *see* Panda.

Cetegus, *see* Cornelius.

Chalcedonius, -a, -um, adj. from
Chalcedon, a city on the Bosphorus,
opposite Byzantium (Constanti-
nople).

Chalcidica arx, a name applied to
Cumae, a town of Campania, a
colony of Chalcis in Euboea.

Chalcidicensis, another form of Chalci-
dicus; *see* Chalcidica arx.

Chrysium, the name of a comedy by
Caecilius Statius.

Cilices, adj. from Cilicia, a country in
south-eastern Asia Minor.

Cincii, a Roman family; *see* note 1,
p. 132.

Cinna, *see* Helvius.

Cistellaria, the name of a comedy by
Plautus.

Clarus, *see* Erucius.

Claudii, the name of a prominent
Roman family.

Claudius, Divus, emperor of Rome
from A.D. 41 to 54.

Claudius, Servius,[13] also Clodius, son-
in-law of L. Aelius Stilo: he was a
grammatical writer and a keen
critic of Plautine language (Cic. *ad
Fam.* ix. 16. 4).

Claudius Caecus, Ap., censor in 312
B.C.; with his colleague he built the
first Roman aqueduct and the via
Appia.

Claudius (Crassus), Ap., consul in
349 B.C.

Claudius Pulcher, C., a colleague of C.
Gracchus in the tribuneship of the
commons.

Claudius Pulcher, P., son of Claudius
Caecus, and consul in 241 B.C.

Coelius Antipater,[7] a Roman historian
of the time of the Gracchi; his
Annals in seven books gave an
account of the second Punic war.

Colorator, the name of a mime of D.
Laberius.

Compitalia, *sc.* sacra; *see* note 3, p. 280.

Conciliatrix, the name of a comedy by
Quinctius Atta.

Coniectanea, a work of Alfenus Varus.

Cornelius Cetegus, M., a famous
Roman orator, consul in 204 B.C.

Cornelius Nepos,[7] a Roman writer of
history and biography, who lived
from about 99 to 24 B.C. Author of
Exempla, De Viris Illustribus, and
other works.

Corvinus, *see* Valerius Maximus (M).

Cossitius, L., a citizen of Thysdrus in
Africa.

Crassus, *see* Licinius and Otacilius.

Cresphontes, the name of a tragedy of
Ennius; *cf.* Polyphontes.

Critolaus, a peripatetic philosopher, a
contemporary of Crates and a
member of the embassy sent to
Rome in 155 B.C.

INDEX

Ctesias, a Greek historian born in Cnidos in Caria, a contemporary of Xenophon, author of a History of Persia and a History of India.

Cynthus, a mountain on the island of Delos in the Cyclades, the birthplace of Apollo.

Cyrus, Cyrus the Great, founder of the Persian monarchy, which he ruled from 559 to 529 B.C.

DAEDALUS, a mythical Greek craftsman, famed for his inventions and his advances in the technique of sculpture.

Darius (Codomannus), the last of the Persian kings (336 to 330 B.C.), overthrown by Alexander the Great.

Decem Hominibus, De, a speech delivered by M. Porcius Cato Censorinus.

Delphi, the famous city of Phocis at the foot of Mt. Parnassus; the seat of the Delphic oracle.

Demades, an Athenian orator, a contemporary and opponent of Demosthenes.

Diodorus (Cronus, also Chronus), a logician of Caria, who owed his surname to the fact that he once asked for time (χρόνος), in order to reply to a question put to him in the presence of Ptolemy Soter (323–285).

Dionysia, *sc.* sacra, the six-day festival of Dionysus at Athens, at which three days were devoted to dramatic performances.

Disciplinae, a work of M. Terentius Varro.

Dote, De, a speech of M. Porcius Cato Censorinus.

Draco, the celebrated Athenian lawgiver, who brought out his code of laws during his archonship, in 624 B.C.

Duodecim Tabulae, the Twelve Tables, a code of laws made by the decemvirs at Rome in 451–449 B.C.

Duodecim Tabulas, Ad, a work of Antistius Labeo.

ELECTRA, the daughter of Agamemnon and sister of Orestes.

Eleusinus, -a, -um, adj. from Eleusis, an ancient city of Attica, about twelve miles north-west of Athens, the seat of the Eleu-inian Mysteries.

Elissa, another name for Dido, queen of Carthage in the time of Aeneas.

Elydis (?), a grammarian; *see* note 1, p. 450.

Ennianus, -a, -um, adj. from Ennius, the "Father of Roman poetry" (239–169 B.C.).

Epirus, a country north of western Greece and west of Thessaly and Macedonia.

Epistolicae Quaestiones, a work of M. Porcius Cato Censorinus.

Epistulae Morales, a work of L. Annaeus Seneca.

Erechtheus, the name of a tragedy by Ennius.

Erucius Clarus, prefect of the city of Roma about A.D. 146, twice consul, perhaps in 117 and 146.

Euclides, a Socratic philosopher, a native of Megara, where he established a school of philosophy after the death of Socrates.

Eudemus, a Rhodian philosopher, a contemporary of Ari-totle, some of whose works he edited and wrote commentaries upon them.

Eurotas, the principal river of Laconia, on which Sparta was situated.

Exempla, a work of Cornelius Nepos in at least five books, apparently of an encyclopaedic character.

FABIUS LICINUS (M.), consul in 246 B.C.

Facta et Dicta Memorabilia, a work of Valerius Maximus.

Falernum vinum, a wine of fine quality and considerable strength, produced in the ager Falernus in northern Campania.

Fato, De, a work of M. Tullius Cicero.

Ferentinum, a town of Latium on the via Latina in the country of the Hernici, modern Ferentino.

Figuris Sententiarum, De, a work of Annaeus Cornutus.

Flavius, Cn., *see* note 2, p. 116.

Floria, De Re, a speech of Cato the Censor.

INDEX

Fortuna, Fortune, personified as a goddess.

Frugi, *see* Calpurnius.

Fufetia, another name of Gaia Taracia.

Fundanius, C., plebeian aedile in 246 B.C.

Furium, Contra, a speech of Cato the Censor.

Furius (Camillus), L., consul in 349 B.C.

Furtis, De, a work of Masurius Sabinus.

GAIA TARACIA, *see* Taracia.

Galatea, a character in Virgil's *Bucolics*.

Galli, the name of a mime by D. Laberius.

Gallus, *see* Sulpicius.

Gellius, Cn.,[7] *see* Introd. p. xii.

Geminus, *see* Servilius.

Georgica, the *Georgics* of Vergil.

Glaucus, a sea-god.

Gorgian, Commentarii in Platonis, a work of Calvisius Taurus.

Gorgias, the name of one of Plato's Dialogues.

Gracchus, *see* Sempronius.

Grai, a name for the Greeks.

Grammatici Commentarii, a work of Nigidius Figulus.

Gratiae, the Graces, three in number.

HAMMON, *see* Iuppiter.

Harmodius, one of the tyrannicides at Athens; *see* note 1, p. 158.

Harpalus, one of the generals of Cyrus the Great, probably an error for Harpagus.

Hector, the Trojan hero, slain by Achilles.

Hecuba, the name of tragedies of Euripides and of Ennius.

Hecuba, wife of Priam, king of Troy.

Hegesias, perhaps the Greek orator of the early part of the third century B.C. who founded the Asianic style of oratory; *see* Cicero, *Orat.* 226.

Helvius Cinna, a Roman poet, a friend of Caesar's. After Caesar's assassination he was mistaken for Cinna the conspirator and torn to pieces by the mob.

Heraclides Ponticus, a philosopher from Heracleia in Pontus, a pupil of Plato and of Aristotle.

Herculaneus, -a, um, adj. from Hercules.

Here, *see* note 4, p. 485.

Herennius, C., tribune of the commons in 80 B.C.

Herie, an attribute of Juno.

Hersilia, the wife of Romulus.

Hesiona, the name of a tragedy of Naevius; *see* note 1, p. 284.

Hibericus, -a, -um, adj. from Hiberia (Spain).

Hiempsal, a king of Numidia, deposed by the Marian party, but restored to his throne by Pompey in 81 B.C.

Hierocles, a Stoic philosopher.

Hippias, son and successor of Pisistratus; *see* note 1, p. 158.

Hispanicus, -a, -um, adj. from Hispania.

Hister or **Histros,** the Danube, also called Danuvius.

Homericus, -a, -um, adj. from Homerus.

Hora Quirini, *see* note 1, p. 480.

Horatia lex, a privilegium of unknown date.

(Hostilius) Mancinus, C., consul in 137 B.C.; tribune of the commons with Ti. Sempronius Gracchus, the father of Gaius and Tiberius Gracchus.

Hyrcanus, -a, -um, adj. to Hyrcania, a Persian province on the southeastern shore of the Caspian Sea.

IDAEUS, a Trojan herald.

Idas, son of Aphareus of Messenia; with his brother Lynceus he was slain in a combat with Castor and Pollux.

Illustribus, De Viris, a work of Cornelius Nepos.

Illyrii, the people of Illyria or Illyricum, a country on the eastern shore of the Adriatic Sea, north of Epirus.

Imbrex, *see* Licinius.

Inous, son of Ino, Melicertes.

Insania, De, a work of M. Terentius Varro.

Isigonus, a native of Nicaea, composer of a book of marvels (*Paradoxa*).

Ismarus, -a, -um. adj. to Ismarus, a town of the Cicones in northern Thrace, according to Homer.

Isocrates, a famous Athenian orator, who lived from 436 to 338 B.C. He is said to have died on hearing of the overthrow of the Athenians at Chaeronea by Philip of Macedon.

(Iunius) Brutus (M.),[4] a juristic writer.

Iure Civili, De, a work of Q. Mucius Scaevola.

Iuris Disciplinis, De, a work of M. Porcius Cato Licinianus.

Ius Civile, a work of Masurius Sabinus.

Lacus Avernus, the name of a mime by D. Laberius.

Laevinus, *see* Valerius.

Larentia, Acca, wife of the shepherd Faustulus and foster-mother of Romulus and Remus.

Latona, the Latin name for Leto, the mother of Apollo and Artemis (Diana).

Laudationes Funebres, eulogies spoken at the funerals of eminent men.

Laurens,adj. to Laurentum, an ancient town of Latium near the sea, the capital of the mythical Latinus.

Laurentinus, -a, -um, adj. to Laurentum; *see* Laurens.

Laus Catonis, a work of M. Tullius Cicero.

Lavinium, an ancient town of Latium near Laurentium, said to have been founded by Aeneas, and named from his wife Lavinia, the daughter of Latinus.

Lavinus, -a, -um, also Lavinius, adj. to Lavinium.

Lebadia, a town of north-western Boeotia, near Chaeronea.

Lege Agraria, De, a speech of M. Tullius Cicero.

Legibus Promulgatis, De, a speech of C. Sempronius Gracchus.

Lepidus, *see* Aemilius.

Lesbia, the name given by Catullus to his love, who was really Clodia, the sister of P. Clodius Pulcher.

Lesbius, -a, -um, adj. from Lesbos; as subst. (*sc.* vinum), Lesbian wine.

Lesbos, an island off the western coast of Asia Minor, west of Pergamum.

Liber, the Italic wine-god, identified by the Romans with Dionysus or Bacchus.

Libra, the constellation of the Balance, one of the signs of the Zodiac.

Librum Commentarium de Familia Porcia, the family record of the Porcian family; *cf.* Suet. *Aug.* lxiv. 2.

Licinius, a tribune of the commons.

(Licinius) Calvus, C.,[3] a celebrated lyric poet and orator, contemporary with Catullus.

Licinius (Calvus) Stolo (C), tribune of the commons from 376 to 367 B.C. He brought the contest between the patricians and plebeians to an end, and was elected consul in 364 and 361.

Licinius Crassus, L., the celebrated orator, consul in 95, censor in 92 B.C.

Licinius Imbrex, a writer of *palliatae*, or comedies based on Greek originals, contemporary with Caecilius Statius and Terence; perhaps the same as P. Licinius Tegula who wrote a hymn in the year 200 B.C. (Livy, xxxi. 12. 9).

Licinius Lucullus, L., consul in 151 B.C.

Licinius Mucianus, consul in A.D. 52, 70, and 75, author of a geographical work which is cited several times by Pliny in his *Natural History*.

Longinus, *see* Cassius.

Lua Saturni, *see* note 1, p. 480.

Lucanus, -a, -um, adj. to Lucania, a district of Italy south-east of Campania.

Lucilius, the friend to whom Seneca addressed his *Epistulae Morales*.

Lucullus, *see* Licinius.

Lusitani, the inhabitants of Lusitania in western Spain, modern Portugal.

Lycium, the Lyceum, a sacred precinct at Athens, in which Aristotle walked with his pupils as he gave them instruction.

MACEDO, a philosopher.

Macedones, the Macedonians.

Macedonia, a country north of Thessaly and east of Epirus and Illyricum.

Macetae, another name for the Macedonians.

Maia Volcani, perhaps originally equivalent to *maiestas*; later re-

INDEX

garded as the wife of Vulcan; *cf.*
Macrobius, *Saturn.* i. 12. 18, Cinginus
mensem (Maiam) nominatum putat
a Maia, quam Vulcani dicit uxorem.

Manlius Torquatus, T., twice dictator
and three times consul (in 347, 344
and 340 B.C.).

Marcius, M., a praetor of uncertain
date.

Marcius Rex, Q., consul in 118 B.C.

Marcus, fore-name of M. Antonius, the
triumvir.

Marius, C., the famous conqueror of
Jugurtha and of the Cimbri and
Teutones, seven times consul (for
the last time in 86 B.C.).

Marius, quaestor at Teanum
Sidicinum in northern Campania.

Martius, campus, the part of Rome
enclosed by the great bend of the
Tiber towards the west.

Massilia, a Greek city in southern
Gaul, modern Marseilles.

Matius, Cn., a writer of *Mimiambi* and
translator into Latin of the *Iliad*;
he lived in the first century B.C.

Mauretania, a country in the north-
eastern part of Africa, modern
Morocco.

Mausolus, a tragedy by Theodectas;
see note 5, p. 263.

Mausolus, king of Caria and husband
of Artemisia.

Mavors, another name for Mars.

Maximus, *see* Valerius.

Megara (-orum), the chief city of
Megaris, the district between Attica
and the territory of Corinth.

Megarenses, the people of Megara.

Melicertes, in mythology, son of
Athamas and Ino, who after his
death by drowning became a sea-
god, Palaemon; really a Phoenician
deity.

Melicus, a dialectic form of *Medicus*,
Median or Medic.

Memoralia, a work of Masurius
Sabinus.

Memoria, Memory, personified.

Menelaus, king of Sparta at the time
of the Trojan war, brother of
Agamemnon and husband of Helen.

Meropa, wife of Chresphontes and
daughter of Cypselus, an Arcadian
king.

Messala, *see* Valerius.

Messana, a city in the north-eastern
part of Sicily, modern Messina.

Mevia, the name of an Atellan farce of
Pomponius.

Milesius, -a, -um, adj. to Miletus.

Miletus, a city in the north-western
part of Caria in Asia Minor.

Mimiambi, realistic scenes from daily
life, described in iambic verse; *see*
Matius.

Minoïus, -a, -um, adj. from Minos, a
mythical king of Crete; probably a
word meaning " king," like Ptolemy.

Minucius Augurinus, C., tribune of the
commons in 187 B.C.

Minucius Thermus, Q., tribune of the
commons in 201 B.C., consul in 193.

Mitridates (also Mithridates and
Mithradates), Mithridates VI, or the
Great, king of Pontus.

Mnesitheus, a celebrated Athenian
physician of the fourth century B.C.

Moles Martis, probably some characteristic of Mars, the toil of War;
later personified as his daughter.

Mummius, L., consul in 146 B.C.,
surnamed Achaicus because of his
victory in the Achaean war; he
destroyed Corinth.

Mycenae, *see* Agamemnoniae Mycenae.

NARBONENSIS, adj. from Narbo, a
town of southern Gaul, whence the
district called Gallia Narbonensis.

Naucrates, a Greek rhetorician, a
pupil of Isocrates.

Naupactus, a town of the Locri
Ozolae on the northern shore of the
Corinthian Gulf.

Nausicaa, daughter of Alcinous, king
of the Phaeaceans.

Neaera, a comedy of Licinius Imbrex.

Neaera, a name associated with Nerio.

Neapolis, a Greek city in Campania,
modern Naples.

Nepos, *see* Cornelius.

Neria, Nerio, Neriones Martis, *see*
note 1, p. 480.

Nero, a name of Sabine origin, meaning strong and valiant.

Nestor, the oldest of the Greeks before
Troy.

Nicaeensis, a native of Nicaea, a city

INDEX

of Bithynia in northern Asia Minor;
see Isigonus.

Nicanor, *see* Seleucus.

Niptra, the name of a tragedy of
Pacuvius.

Nola, a town of Campania.

Nolani, the people of Nola.

OLYMPIAS, the mother of Alexander
the Great.

Onesicritus, a Greek historian who
accompanied Alexander the Great
on his campaigns and wrote an
account of them.

Oppium, ad C., a work of Aelius
Tubero.

Oppius, C., a friend of Julius Caesar.

Orestes, a work of M. Terentius Varro
with the sub-title *De Insania*.

Oriades (also Oreades), mountain
nymphs.

Origine Vocabulorum, De, a work of
Gavius Bassus.

Origines, a work of M. Porcius Cato.

Otacilius Crassus (M.), consul in 246
B.C.

PALATIUM, a name applied to the
Palatine Hill at Rome and also to
the Palace of the emperors on that
hill.

Pales, an Italic goddess of shepherds
and of pastoral life.

Palinurus, the pilot of Aeneas.

Panaetius, a celebrated Greek philosopher of Rhodes, born about 180
B.C.

Panda Cela, a goddess, called by
Festus, *s.v.* Empanda (p. 70, Linds.)
dea paganorum; her temple at the
porta Pandana (Fest. p. 246, L.)
was an asylum which was always
open (cf. *pandere*).

Panopea (also Panope), a sea-nymph,
daughter of Nereus.

Parmenides, the name of a dialogue of
Plato.

Parthenius, a Greek grammarian and
poet of Nicaea in Bithynia, who
is said by Strabo to have lived in
Rome from the time of the Mithri-
datic war to that of Tiberius.

Patroclus, one of the Greeks at Troy.
He was a friend of Achilles and was
slain by Hector.

Peranna, *see* Anna.

Peregrinus Proteus, a Cynic philosopher of Parium in the Troad, who
flourished during the second century A.D. He burned himself to
death publicly at the Olympic
Games in A.D. 165.

Persa, *see* Perses.

Perses (also Perseus), king of Macedonia
from 178 to 168 B.C.

Persicae clades, the capture of Athens
by the Persians in 480 B.C.

Pessinuntius, -a, -um, adj. from
Pessinus, a town in the western part
of Galatia, in Asia Minor.

Philippus, Philip V of Macedon, father
of Perses.

Philostephanus, a pupil of Callimachus, who wrote Περὶ Τῶν Παρα-
δόξων Ποταμῶν, miscalled Polystephanus by Gellius.

Phoenix, the name of a tragedy of
Ennius.

Phrygius, -a, -um, adj. to Phrygia, a
country of Asia Minor west of
Mysia, Lydia, and the northern part
of Caria.

Pisistratus, tyrant of Athens from
560 to 527 B.C.

Piso, *see* Calpurnius.

Pisonem, In, an oration of M. Tullius
Cicero.

Plancio, Pro Cn., an oration of M.
Tullius Cicero.

Platonicus, -a, -um, adj. from Plato,
the great Athenian philosopher
(428–347 B.C.).

Poenulus, a comedy of T. Maccius
Plautus.

Pollux, one of the Dioscuri, or sons of
Zeus; he was immortal, but his
brother Castor was mortal.

Polumeni, a comedy of Caecilius
Statius; *see* note 2, p. 316.

Polus, a Greek tragic actor; *see* note
2, p. 34.

Polybius, a Greek historian, born in
Megalopolis in Arcadia about 204
B.C. He was sent as a hostage to
Rome in 166 and remained there for
seventeen years. He wrote a
History in forty books, covering
the period from 220 to 146 B.C.

Polyphontes, a descendant of Heracles.
He slew Chresphontes, king of

INDEX

Messenia, and took possession of his kingdom and his wife Meropa.

Polystephanus, *see* Philostephanus.

Pomponianus, -a, -um, adj. from Pomponius.

Pomponius, L,.[10] a writer of *fabulae Atellanae*, who flourished about 90 B.C. He was a native of Bononia (Bologna).

Pomponius, M., praetor in 161 B.C.

Pomptinus ager, the region of the Pomptine, or Pontine, Marshes in Latium.

Porcius, -a, -um, adj. to Porcius, the gentile name of the Cato family.

Porcius, a tribune of the commons.

Porcius Cato (Licinianus), M., a son of Cato the Censor.

Porcius Cato Nepos, M., grandson of Cato the Censor.

Porcius Cato Salonianus, M., a son of Cato the Censor.

Porcius Cato, M., son of Salonianus and father of Cato Uticensis.

Posteriores, the name of a work of Antistius Labeo.

Postumia, *see* note 1, p. 84.

Postumius Albinus, A.,[7] a writer of history, consul in 151 B.C. His *History* was dedicated to Ennius and was therefore probably published before 169 B.C.

Praeda Militibus Dividenda, De, a speech of Cato the Censor.

Praenestinus, -a, -um, adj. to Praeneste, a hill town about twenty miles east of Rome, modern Palestrina.

Praxiteles, a famous Greek sculptor, born in Athens about 390 B.C., represented by many beautiful works of art, original and copies.

Priamus, king of Troy at the time of the Trojan war.

Proconnesius, -a, -um, adj. from Proconnesus, an island in the Propontis, or Sea of Marmora. It was celebrated for its marble and is now called Marmora.

Protesilaodamia, a play of Laevius.

Proteus, *see* Peregrinus.

Psyllus, *see* note 7, p. 190.

Ptolemai, the name applied to a series of kings of Egypt, beginning in 323 B.C.

Pugnis Falsis, De, a speech of Cato the Censor.

Puteolanum mare, the sea about Puteoli, a seaport of Campania, modern Pozzuoli.

Pygmaei, a fabulous people (*Iliad*, iii. 5), variously located by different writers in India, Africa, and elsewhere.

Pyrro, also Pyrrho, a native of Elis in the Peloponnesus, founder of the Pyrronian, or Sceptical, school of Philosophy.

Pyrronius, -a, -um, adj. from Pyrro.

Pythia, *sc.* certamina, the Pythian Games, held on the Crissaean plain below Delphi every fourth year.

Qua Legem Aufeiam Dissuasit, a speech of C. Sempronius Gracchus.

Quinctius Atta,[10] a Roman writer of *fabulae togatae,* who died in 77 B.C.

Quirinus, a Sabine god, identified with Romulus after his death and deification.

Re Floria, De, a speech of Cato the Censor.

Re Militari, De, a speech of Cato the Censor.

Re Publica, De, a work of M. Tullius Cicero.

Rebus per Epistulam Quaesitis, De, a work of Valgius Rufus.

Rerum Divinarum libri, a work of M. Terentius Varro, one division of his *Antiquitates* (see Index to vol. i).

Rerum Humanarum libri, a work of M. Terentius Varro, a part of his *Antiquitates* (see Index to vol. i).

Rex, *see* Marcius.

Rodanus (also Rhodanus), the river Rhone.

Rodienses (also Rhodienses), the people of Rhodes.

Rodiensibus (also Rhodiensibus), *Pro,* a speech of Cato the Censor.

Rodiensis (also Rhodiensis), adj. from Rhodus, Rhodes, a large island in the Mediterranean Sea south-west of Asia Minor.

Rodius, -a, -um, adj. from Rodus (Rhodus).

Rodus (also Rhodus), Rhodes.

Romane, adv. from Romanus.

Roscius, **Sex.**, a native of Ameria in southern Etruria, defended by Cicero in one of his early orations.

Rubra, *see* Saxa Rubra.

Rudens, the name of a comedy of Plautus.

Rufus, *see* Valgius.

Rullus, cognomen of P. Servilius Rullus, tribune of the commons in 63 B.C.

Rutilius (Rufus), P., consul in 105 B.C. and *legatus* of Metellus in the war with Jugurtha. He wrote historical works and an autobiography.

SABINI, an Italic people, dwelling in the mountainous district to the north-east of Rome.

Sacrificio Commisso, De, a speech of Cato the censor.

Salacia, *see* note 1, p. 480.

Salonianus, *see* Porcius Cato.

Salonius, a client of Cato the Censor.

Samos, an island off the western coast of Asia Minor, near Ephesus.

Santra, a Roman grammarian; *see* note 1, p. 132.

Sapientia, Wisdom personified **as a** goddess.

Sardinia, a large island in the Mediterranean Sea, between Italy and Spain.

Saturae, the name of works by Ennius, Lucilius, and Varro.

Saturnus, a mythical Italic king, identified by the Romans with the Greek Cronos.

Sauromatae, also called Saramatae, a people of Asia, living north-east of the Palus Maeotis (Sea of Azov).

Saxa Rubra, a place between Rome and Veii, near the river Cremera, modern Grotta Rossa.

Scaurus, *see* Terentius.

Scythae, a barbarian people, living north and north-east of the Euxine (Black) Sea.

Seleucus Nicancr, founder of the Syrian monarchy; he reigned from 312 to 280 B.C.

Sella, the name of a comedy of Afranius.

Sempronius, -a, -um, adj. to Sempronius, the gentile name of the Gracchi. The *leges Semproniae* of Gaius Gracchus made it unlawful to put a Roman citizen to death.

Sempronius, Ti., plebeian aedile in 246 B.C.

Sempronius Asellio, a Roman writer of history, military tribune in 134 B.C.

Sempronius Gracchus, Ti., father of Gaius and Tiberius Gracchus.

Sempronius Tuditanus, C., an orator and historian, consul in 129 B.C.

Seneca, *see* Annaeus.

Servilius Geminus, a character **in the** *Annals* of Ennius.

Servius, *see* Tullius.

Sestio, Pro, an oration of M. Tullius Cicero.

Siculi, early inhabitants of Sicily; the term is also used of the Sicilians of later times.

Sidicinus, -a, -um, adj. to (Teanum) Sidicinum; *see* Teanum.

Smyrna, a city on the coast **of** Lydia in western Asia Minor; **see** Zmyrna.

Sophia, the Greek word for Sapientia, Wisdom.

Sotadica, the name of a work by Accius, so called from the **metre in** which it was written.

Sotericus, *see* note 3, p. 365.

Stichus, the name of **a** comedy of Plautus.

Stoa, a colonnade in the market-place at Athens, in which Zeno, the Stoic, taught, and from which the Stoic philosophers derived their name.

Stoica, *sc.* disciplina, the Stoic doctrine.

Stolo, *see* Licinius.

Studiosi, a work of O. Plinius Secundus.

Suculae, the constellation **of the** Hyades; *see* Ὑάδες.

Suetonius Tranquillus, C.,[41] the famous biographer and encyclopaedic writer of the time of Hadrian.

Sulpicium, Ad Servium, letters of M. Tullius Cicero.

---

[41] For the fragments see A. Reifferscheid, *C. Suetoni . . . Reliquiae,* Leipzig, 1860, and for *De Grammaticis et Rhetoribus,* R. Robinson, Paris, 1925.

INDEX

Sulpicius Gallus, P., a contemporary of P. Scipio Africanus.

TARACIA, Gaia, a Vestal virgin of the early days of Rome.

Tarentum, an important Greek city in south-eastern Italy, on the Gulf of Tarentum, modern Taranto.

Tartesius, -a, -um, adj. to Tartessus, an ancient city of south-western Spain. The name Tartessus was latter applied to the district west of the Straits of Gibraltar.

Tatius, T., a king of the Sabines, who later shared the rule of Rome with Romulus.

Taurus, a mountain range in south-eastern Asia Minor.

Taurus, the constellation of the Bull.

Teanum Sidicinum, a town of Campania.

Terentius, M., used as a typical name.

Terentius Scaurus (Q.), a celebrated grammarian of Hadrian's time, author of an *Ars Grammatica*, and of commentaries on Plautus, Vergil, and Horace's *Ars Poetica*.

Thasius, -a, -um, adj. to Thasos, an island in the northern part of the Aegean Sea, near the coast of Thrace.

Theaetetus, the name of a dialogue of Plato.

Theocritus, the most famous of the Greek bucolic poets, belonging to the early part of the third century B.C.

Theodectes, a Greek rhetorician and tragic poet of Phaselis in Lycia.

Theopompus, a Greek historian born in Chios about 378 B.C. He wrote a work called *Hellenica* in twelve books, a continuation of the *History of Thucydides*, covering the period from 411 to 394 B.C., and *Philippica* in fifty-eight books, dealing with the times of Philip of Macedon.

Thermus, *see* Minucius.

Theseus, a mythological character, the national hero of Athens.

Thraecus, -a, -um, adj. to Thracia.

Threicii, another form for Thraces, Thracians.

Thysdritanus, -a, -um, adj. to

Thysdrus, a city near the coast of northern Africa, south-east of Carthage.

Tiberianus, -a, -um, adj. from Tiberius, the second emperor of Rome. *Tiberiana domus*, the palace of Tiberius on the Palatine hill.

Tiberinus, -a, -um, adj. to Tiberis, the Tiber. *Campus Tiberinus*, another name for the Campus Martius.

Tibur, a town of Latium about sixteen miles north-east of Rome, modern Tivoli.

Timaeus, an historian of Tauromenium in eastern Sicily. He lived from about 352 to 256 B.C. and spent fifty years of his life in Athens. His great work was a *History of Sicily* from the earliest times to 246 B.C., in sixty-eight books.

Titulus, the name of a play of Afranius.

Torquatus, *see* Manlius.

Traianus, Trajan, emperor of Rome from A.D. 98 to 117.

Trigemini, the name of a comedy of Plautus.

Trinummus, the name of a comedy of Plautus.

Triphallus, the name of a comedy of Cn. Naevius.

Triumpho suo, De, a speech of Q. Caecilius Metellus Numidicus.

Triumphus, the name of a play of Caecilius Statius.

Troia, the famous city in north-western Asia Minor.

Truculentus, the name of a comedy of Plautus.

Tuditanus, *see* Sempronius.

Tullianus, -a, um, adj. from Tullius, the gentile name of Cicero.

Tullius, Servius, the sixth king of Rome.

Tyrius, -a, -um, adj. from Tyrus, Tyre; used also of Carthage.

USUS, Experience, personified.

Utica, a Phoenician city in northern Africa on the river Bagradas, about twenty-five miles north-west of Carthage.

VALERIUS, used as an example of a personal name in -ius.

INDEX

Valerius Catullus, the famous lyric poet, born at Verona about 84 B.C. and died in 54.

(Valerius) Laevinus, R., a curule aedile.

Valerius Maximus, a Roman writer of the time of Tiberius.

Valerius Maximus Corvinus (M.), military tribune in 349 B.C.

Valerius Messala, M., consul in 53 B.C. He was noted for his knowledge of augury and wrote a work called *De Auspiciis.*

Valgius Rufus, C.,[42] a poet of the Augustan age, consul in 12 B.C., who also wrote some learned works.

Velia, a seacoast town of Lucania.

Velinus, adj. from Velia.

Venusinus, -a, -um, adj. to Venusia, a town on the borders of Lucania and Apulia, the birthplace of Horace.

Verres, C., the notorious propraetor of Sicily, prosecuted by Cicero.

Vesevus, Mount Vesuvius, the well-known volcano near Naples.

(*Vi et Natura Chamaeliontis, De*), a work of Democritus, mentioned by Pliny the elder.

Victoria, Victory, personified as a deity.

Viris Illustribus, De, a work of Cornelius Nepos.

Virites, deities, or qualities, associated with Quirinus.

Voconiam legem qua suasit, an oration of Cato the Censor.

Voconius, -a, -um, adj. to Voconius. The *lex Voconia,* proposed by Q. Voconius, tribune of the commons, in 169 B.C. and supported by Cato the Censor, regulated bequests, especially to women.

XERXES, king of Persia from 485 to 465 B.C.

ZMYRNA, another form of Smyrna.

---

[42] See no. 5.

GREEK INDEX

Αἴας Λοκρός, *The Locrian Ajax*, a play
of Sophocles.
Ἀΐς, archaic form for Ἀΐδης, Hades,
the god of the Lower World.
Ἀλφειός, Alpheus, the river of Elis in
the Peloponnesus, and the god of
the river.
Ἄρτεμις, Artemis, daughter of Zeus
and Leto, and sister of Apollo.
Identified by the Romans with
Diana.
Ἀρχύτας, *see* Archytas.
Ἀφροδίτη, Aphrodite, the Greek god-
dess of love. Identified by the
Romans with Venus.

Γλαῦκος, *see* Glaucus.

Δημήτηρ, Demeter, the Greek goddess
of agriculture. Identified by the
Romans with Ceres.
Δικαιαρχία, the Greek name of Puteoli,
a seaport of Campania, modern
Pozzuoli.

Ἐδεσμάτων, Περί, a work of M. Teren-
tius Varro, part of his *Saturae
Menippeae*.
Ἕκτωρ, *see* Hector.
Ἐρύμανθος, Erymanthus, a mountain
range of north-western Arcadia.

Θέτις, Thetis, a daughter of Nereus;
mother of Achilles.

Ἰνώ, Ino, a tragedy of Euripides.
Ἶρις, Iris, the personification of the
rainbow, and messenger of the gods.
Ἰταλία, Italia.

Κλεαρίστα, the name of a shepherdess
in the *Idyls* of Theocritus.

Λέσβιος, *see* Lesbius and Lesbos
Λητώ, Leto, the Greek name of Latona,
the mother of Artemis (Diana) and
Apollo.
Λιβυκός, Libyan, of Libya, in northern
Africa.

Μελικέρτης, *see* Melicertes.
Μνήμης, Περί, *On Memory*; *see* note 1,
p. 37.

Νηρείδες, the Nereids, sea-nymphs,
daughters of Nereus.
Νηρεύς, Nereus, an aged sea-god, son
of Pontus and Gaia.

Ὀδύσσεια, the *Odyssey* of Livius
Andronicus.
Ὄνειρος, a Dream, personified.

Πανδέκται, *Pandects*, encyclopaedic
works.
Πηλεύς, *see* Peleus (Index to vol. i).
Πλειάδες, the Pleiades, a constella-
tion, called by the Romans Ver-
giliae.
Πολυπραγμοσύνης, Περί, a work of
Plutarch.
Ποσειδάων, Poseidon, the Greek god
of the sea. Identified by the
Romans with Neptune.
Πυθαγορεῖοι, the followers of Pytha-
goras.
Πυρρωνεῖοι Τρόποι, a work of Favori-
nus.
Πυρφόρος Προμηθεύς, Ὁ, *The Fire-
bearing Prometheus*, a work of
Aeschylus.

Ῥώμη, Rome.

GREEK INDEX

Σκιομαχία, one of the Menippean Satires of M. Terentius Varro.

Σωκράτης, *see* Socrates.

Ταραντῖνος, a native of Tarentum.

Τηλέμαχος, Telemachus, the son of Odysseus (Ulysses).

Τηΰγετος, Taÿgetus, a mountain range between Laconia and Messenia.

Τίτυρος, Tityrus, one of the shepherds in the *Idyls* of Theocritus.

Ὑάδες, the Hyades, a constellation. Also called Suculae.

Ὑάκινθος, Hyacinthus, the name of a boy.

Ὑδροκύων, one of the Menippean Satires of M. Terentius Varro; *see* note 2, p. 512.

Φθιώτιδες, the name of a tragedy of Sophocles.